LIBRARY
PLANO SENIOR HIGH SCHOOL LIB & IMC
PLANO TX

AF412640

ALAINE LANE

ABNORMAL PSYCHOLOGY:

The Problems of Disordered Emotional and Behavioral Development

Special Learning Corporation

42 Boston Post Rd. Guilford, Connecticut 06437

Special Learning Corporation

Publisher's Message:

The Special Education Series is the first comprehensive series designed for special education courses of study. It is also the first series to offer such a wide variety of high quality books. In addition, the series will be expanded and up-dated each year. No other publications in the area of special education can equal this. We stress high quality content, a superb advisory and consulting group, and special features that help in understanding the course of study. In addition we believe we must also publish in very small enrollment areas in order to establish the credibility and strength of our series. We realize the enrollments in courses of study such as Autism, Visually Handicapped Education, or Diagnosis and Placement are not large. Nevertheless, we believe there is a need for course books in these areas and books that are kept up-to-date on an annual basis! Special Learning Corporation's goal is to publish the highest quality materials for the college and university courses of study. With your comments and support we will continue to do so.

John P. Quirk

©1980 by Special Learning Corporation, Guilford, Connecticut 06437

All rights reserved. No part of this book may be reproduced, stored, or communicated by any means--without written permission from Special Learning Corporation.

First Edition

2 3 4 5

ISBN No. 0-89568-109-9

SPECIAL EDUCATION SERIES

* ● Abnormal Psychology: The Problems of
    Disordered Emotional and Behavioral
    Development
  ● Administration of Special Education
  ● Autism
* ● Behavior Modification
    Biological Bases of Learning Disabilities
    Brain Impairments
  ● Career and Vocational Education for the
    Handicapped
  ● Child Abuse
* ● Child Psychology
  ● Classroom Teacher and the Special Child
* ● Counseling Parents of Exceptional Children
    Creative Arts
  ● Curriculum Development for the Gifted
    Curriculum and Materials
* ● Deaf Education
    Developmental Disabilities
* ● Developmental Psychology: The Problems of
    Disordered Mental Development
* ● Diagnosis and Placement
  ● Down's Syndrome
  ● Dyslexia
* ● Early Childhood Education
  ● Educable Mentally Handicapped
* ● Emotional and Behavioral Disorders
    Exceptional Parents
  ● Foundations of Gifted Education
* ● Gifted Education
* ● Human Growth and Development of the
    Exceptional Individual

  ● Hyperactivity
* ● Individualized Education Programs
  ● Instructional Media and Special Education
  ● Language and Writing Disorders
  ● Law and the Exceptional Child: Due Process
* ● Learning Disabilities
  ● Learning Theory
* ● Mainstreaming
* ● Mental Retardation
  ● Motor Disorders
    Multiple Handicapped Education
    Occupational Therapy
  ● Perception and Memory Disorders
* ● Physically Handicapped Education
* ● Pre-School Education for the Handicapped
* ● Psychology of Exceptional Children
  ● Reading Disorders
    Reading Skill Development
    Research and Development
* ● Severely and Profoundly Handicapped
    Social Learning
* ● Special Education
  ● Special Olympics
* ● Speech and Hearing
    Testing and Diagnosis
  ● Three Models of Learning Disabilities
  ● Trainable Mentally Handicapped
  ● Visually Handicapped Education
  ● Vocational Training for the Mentally Retarded

  ●   Published Titles   *Major Course Areas

CONTENTS

4. Cognitive Development in Childhood (5-12 Years)

5. Parenting

GLOSSARY OF TERMS

abreaction The reexperiencing of a past traumatic event by means of conscious recall and the display of the accompanying affect.

aggression Physical or verbal behavior with the intent to injure or destroy.

autism Childhood schizophrenia; inability on the part of the child to relate to other people or to his/her environment.

biochemical The chemistry of living matter.

catatonic schizophrenia A psychosis characterized by bizarre motor behavior including stuporous inactivity, waxy flexibility, or sudden impulsive excitement.

defense (defence) mechanism The methods that an individual develops to cope with conflict or anxiety, operate unconsciously, and are often closely related to the general style of an individual's adjustment.

delusion A strong belief opposed to reality and maintained in spite of logical persuasion and evidence to the contrary.

denial A defense mechanism that enables the individual to report that a previous source of distress no longer exists.

depression A disorder characterized by deep gloom and a slowing down of physical and mental processes.

displacement The unconscious process whereby an impulse is shifted from one object to another.

dissociation A state in which behavior suggestive of 2 or more different personalities are alternatively emitted by the same person.

ego The individual's concept of self; in psychoanalytic theory, the rational aspect of the self.

encopresis A condition in which there is lack of control over the bowels and the passage of feces.

enuresis A condition in which there is lack of control over the bladder and the passage of urine.

hallucination Sensory impression of external objects in the absence of any appropriate stimulus in the environment.

hostile aggression Aggression which is oriented to another person, as a person, following some sort of ego threat, or a perception that another person has behaved intentionally.

hyperactivity Disorganized, disruptive and unpredictable behavior; over-reaction to stimuli.

hypochondria Neurotic preoccupation with the body's activities and state of one's health.

instrumental aggression Aggression which is aimed at the retrieval of an object, territory, or privilege.

intermittent reinforcement A reinforcement schedule on which the response is not always followed by a reinforcer.

intrapsychic That which originates or takes place within the psyche or mind, particularly that which is unconscious.

mania Wild or violent behavior disorder, characterized by abnormal excitability, exaggerated feelings of well-being, flight of ideas, excessive activity, etc.

minimal brain dysfunction (MBD) A mild or minimal neurological abnormality which causes learning difficulties in the child with near average intelligence.

neurosis Emotional disorder characterized by loss of joy in living and overuse of defense mechanisms against anxiety.

obsessive-compulsive neurosis An abnormal reaction characterized by the presence of anxiety, with persisting unwanted thoughts and/or the compulsion to repeat acts over and over.

opiates The family of drugs including opium and its derivatives.

paranoia Psychosis characterized by systematized, intricate delusions.

pathological Pertaining to a physical or mental disease, disorder or abnormality.

pharmacological treatment The treatment or therapy using drugs, also known as **chemotherapy.**

phobic Pathological fear of an object or situation.

positive reinforcement An operant conditioning procedure in which the stimulus increases the frequency of the response that it follows.

projection The defense mechanism by which an individual attributes to others those ideas, impulses, feelings and/or actions that are undesirable or unacceptable in him/herself.

psychoanalytic A method of psychotherapy which seeks to bring unconscious desires into consciousness and make it possible to resolve conflicts which usually date back to early childhood experiences.

psychodynamic theory A group of theories that view behavior as the product of the interplay of active mental forces.

psychopathic An obsolete label, essentially describing the antisocial personality.

psychosis Severe mental disorder characterized by personality disintegration and loss of contact with reality.

psychosocial stages States of ego development as formulated by Erickson, incorporating both sexual and social aspects.

psychosomatic disorder Physical symptoms, often including actual tissue damage, that may result from the continued mobilization of the body during sustained stress.

rationalization (rationalisation) A defense mechanism by which an individual "logically" justifies his/her impulsive, irrational, or otherwise unacceptable feelings, thoughts, or behavior.

reaction formation Defense mechanism in which the individual's conscious attitudes and overt behavior patterns are the opposite of his/her unconscious wishes, which have been repressed.

regression A maladaptive response to stress in which earlier modes of behavior are resumed.

schizophrenia Psychosis characterized by the breakdown of integrated personality functioning, withdrawal from reality, emotional blunting and distortion, and disturbed thought processes.

sensory deprivation Minimal sensory stimulation, may lead to hallucinations and delusions.

somatic Pertaining to the body.

sublimation A defense mechanism by which the energy of a socially unacceptable impulse, desire, or activity is directed into a socially acceptable substitute.

superego In psychoanalytic theory, that part of the personality which guards the ideas of right and wrong learned as a child; the "conscious."

supression A defense mechanism by which an individual intentionally excludes from consciousness those thoughts, desires, or memories that are unacceptable or anxiety-provoking.

thanatology The study of death.

withdrawal Extreme decrease of intellectual and emotional interest in the environment.

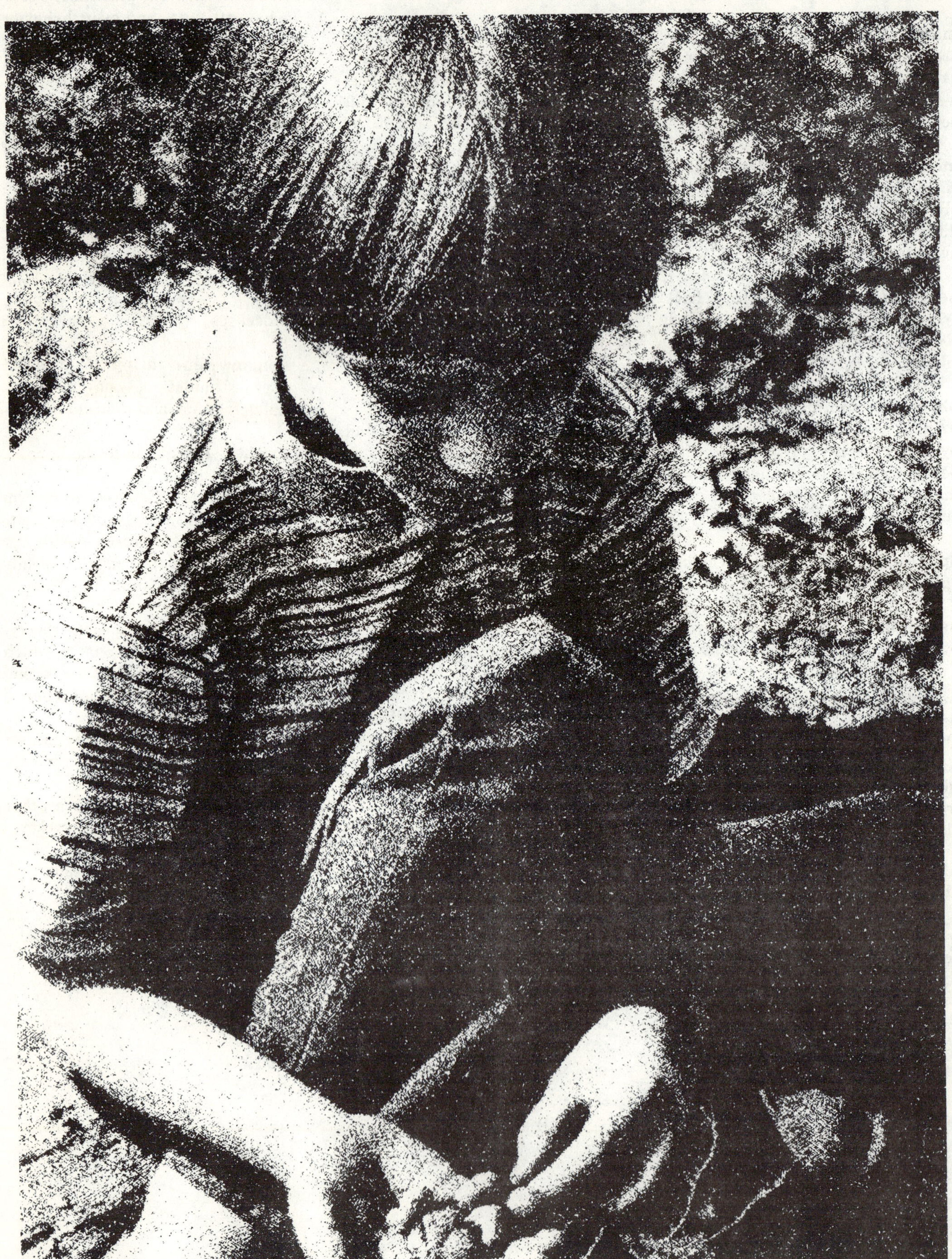

PREFACE

A study of abnormal development is a study of all human behavior. Individuals who are emotionally or behaviorally disordered are identified in all intelligence groups and in all cultural and socio-economic groups. The disability varies from age to age.

Identifying emotionally deviant behavior in the 0 to 2 year old, is the most difficult area for research. Most behavior disorders are believed to be environmentally induced, and, therefore would not appear until the child was four or five.

Studies indicate that various disorders are transient, as "situational" hyperactivity, or school phobia; other disorders are permanent and totally debilitating; e.g. autism. Suicide and alcoholism are deviant coping behaviors that are being identified in younger and younger individuals. The elderly are now being successfully treated for depression and "senility" with proper medical treatment and psychotherapy.

The goal of this reader is to provide an interesting and up-to-date introduction to *Abnormal Psychology: The Problems of Disordered Emotional and Behavioral Development.* We have tried to appeal to all disciplines in the field, by using a balance of popular and trade journals,by choosing salient, non-technical articles from nursing, medical, hospital, educational and psychological publications.

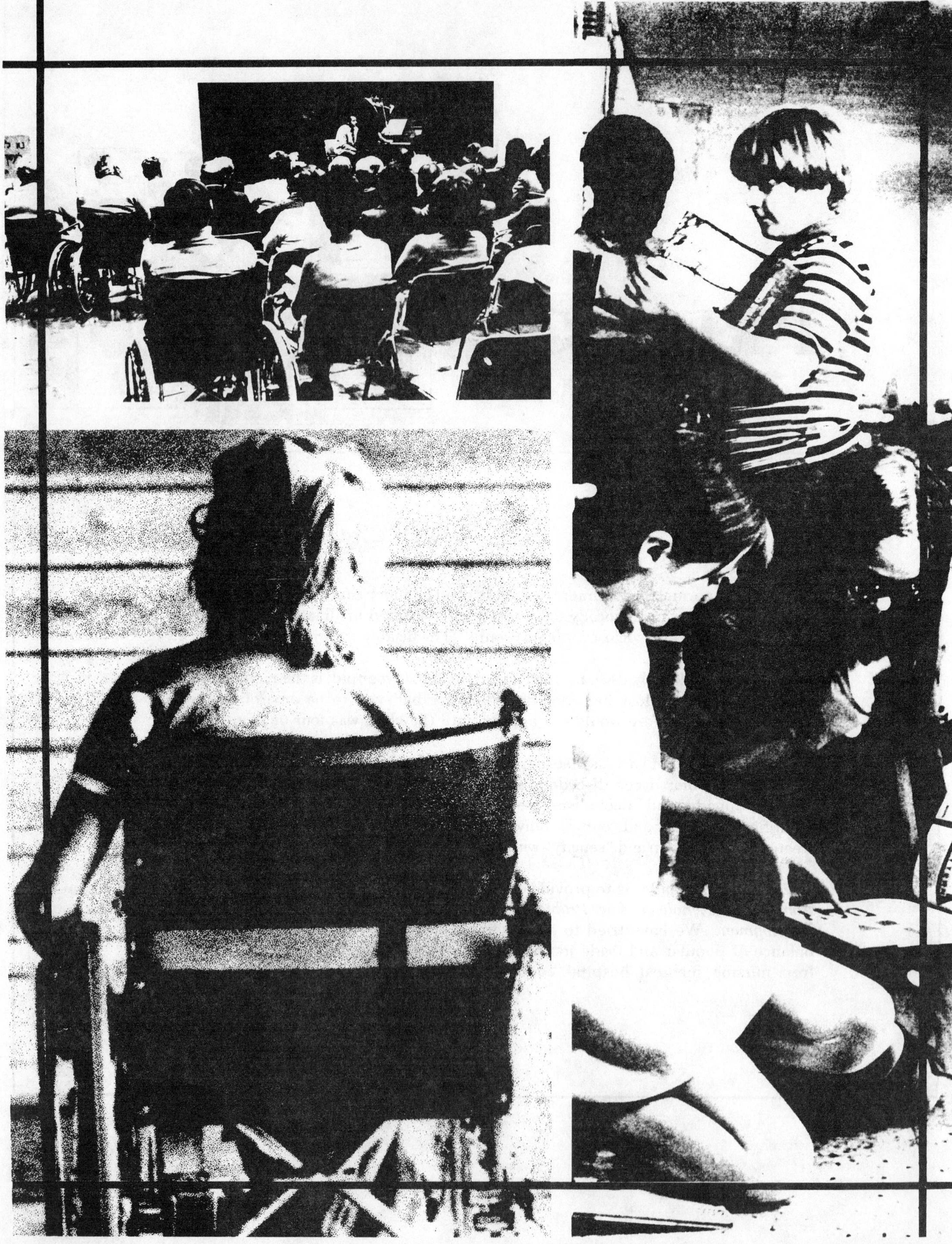

Perspectives

Mental illness, or deviant behavior, can have many etiologies. Some forms of hyperactivity, for example, are biochemical in origin, other forms are environmentally produced and reinforced. A child growing up in a home where one parent behaves in a deviant manner, is being provided with an abnormal role model to either follow, or to react against.

The "cures" for behavior disorders are almost as multitudinous as the types of disorders. Though they fall simply into three categories: psychodynamic, behavioral, drug/medical.

In the psychodynamic approach the patient is helped to explore his/her environment, past and present, and "discover" the underlying cause for the present neuroses or psychoses.

In the behavioral approach a patient identifies for a therapist a behavior that he/she wishes to eliminate and the therapist maps out a behavioral plan to extinguish the undesirable behavior. This therapy requires no examination into the patient's past.

In drug or medicinal therapy, the deviant behavior is caused by a physical problem. A biochemical imbalance can cause behavior disorders, and can be corrected with drugs. A food allergy can cause varying degrees of incorrect behavior, and can be corrected by omitting certain foods.

The different therapies are successful with different personalities and different deviances. The articles in this section delineate various disorders and treatments.

Is Our Diet Driving Us Crazy?

Jeanne Schinto

Drastic changes in our eating patterns since the turn of the century have played havoc with our physical well-being. Diabetes, hypertension, heart disease, and cancer are among the major health problems identified as nutrition-related. Less certain is how a diet that includes more than 126 pounds of sugar and nine pounds of additives each year has affected our mental well-being. A growing number of scientists and physicians are convinced that many of the 6.4 million Americans now under some form of mental health care — as well as the estimated 13.6 million in need of such care — could be cured by better nutrition.

When Benjamin F. Feingold, chief emeritus of the Department of Allergy at the Kaiser-Permanente Medical Center in San Francisco, eliminated artificially dyed and flavored foods from the diets of his hyperactive patients, 40 to 50 per cent showed improvement. Dr. Feingold's hypothesis, first advanced in 1973, is that many of the one million to five million American schoolchildren diagnosed as hyperkinetic are actually displaying a syndrome of behavioral toxicity, due to excessive ingestion of these substances. There are now 100 "Feingold Associations" in twenty-five states, and they claim great success in applying his findings.

When therapists eliminated sugar from the diets of children diagnosed as "hyperactive" and "learning disabled," many improved. The New York Institute of Child Development reports an improvement rate of up to 73 per cent.

Abram Hoffer, a biochemist and physician in Saskatchewan, suggests that 70 per cent of the inmates imprisoned there for serious crimes have vitamin deficiencies which were the primary cause of their aggressive behavior. His research also indicates that about 90 per cent of convicted murderers diagnosed as paranoid schizophrenic suffer from vitamin deficiencies or low-blood sugar (hypoglycemia).

Historically, mental illness attributable to nutrient deficiencies has been extensively demonstrated. Michael Lesser, a Berkeley psychiatrist, cites the example of pellagra: "Less than forty years ago, upwards of 10 per cent of the population of some Southern mental hospitals were suffering from pellagra, a B-vitamin deficiency caused by eating a high-corn, low-protein diet, inadequate in niacin. Until it was discovered that these persons were suffering from malnutrition, they were considered schizophrenic. When they were placed on a corrective diet, their sanity returned."

That poor nutrition causes some mental health problems was also the conclusion of the Senate Select Committee on Nutrition and Human Needs after hearings on Mental Health and Mental Development were held last June. Committee Chairman George McGovern noted, however, that "achieving recognition of the relationship between nutrition and mental health is still very much a struggle. Established scientific thinking remains weighted against those few scientists and practitioners who are striving to understand the complex links between the foods we consume and how we think and behave as individuals."

Frederick J. Stare, a founder and chairman of the Department of Nutrition at Harvard University's School of Public Health, remains one of the country's leading defenders of sugar in our diet. He thinks the substance has been "unduly maligned." He applauds it as "the least expensive important source of calories" and "an important nutrient and food." Dr. Stare also believes as much as 30 per cent of our total calories can be sugar. Yet the McGovern Committee's controversial "Dietary Goals for the United States," released in February 1977, suggests a sugar intake of no more than 15 per cent to protect health.

The American Medical Association and the American Academy of Pediatrics, skeptical of the Feingold hypothesis, are closely allied with the drug industry, which obviously believes hyperactivity is best treated with amphetamines. General Foods Corporation, the second-largest user of sugar in the country, paid for the Nutrition Research labs at Harvard's School of Public Health. Other contributors to Harvard's Department of Nutrition — Amstar, Domino Sugar, Coca-Cola, Kellogg, the International Sugar Research Association, and the Sugar Association — are no more eager for the true sugar story to emerge. (See "Professors on the Take," by Benjamin Rosenthal, Michael Jacobson, and Marcy Bohm, in the November 1976 issue of *The Progressive*.)

In the face of such self-interested opposition, it is

Reprinted by permission from *The Progressive*, 408 West Gorham Street, Madison, Wisconsin 53703. ©1978, The Progressive, Inc.

difficult to locate pockets of real scientific inquiry into the matter, but they do exist. Some scientists can show that severe malnutrition will cause brain damage. But Michael C. Latham, a professor at Cornell's Graduate School of Nutrition, claims that iron-deficient children, one subgroup, score poorly on intelligence tests not because the deficiency directly affects the brain, but because of low energy.

K.E. Moyers, a professor of psychology at Carnegie-Mellon University, says food allergies, not excesses, will "lead to beating, biting, and battle." In his book, *The Psychobiology of Aggression,* Dr. Moyers includes this letter from a mother whose son, he believes, has a food allergy: "You wouldn't believe bananas. Within twenty minutes of eating a banana the child would be in the worst temper tantrum — no, seizures — you have ever seen. I tried this five times because I couldn't believe my eyes. He reacted with behavior to all sugars except maple sugar."

Since all aspects of the relationship between diet and mentality are still highly speculative, many years of research will be needed to unravel the tapestry of cause-and-effect. However, the mental health link is the least funded area of nutrition research, according to the McGovern Committee. The National Institute of Mental Health is currently funding only one project in the field: a $118,000 study of the Feingold hypothesis.

Government, in its own estimation, has been bungling the job of nutrition research in general. According to a report by the Office of Science and Technology Policy (OSTP), "There is little formal coordination of research planning or joint conduct of nutrition research" among various Federal agencies concerned.

Some steps have been taken to achieve coordination, but they seem only to have caused more confusion. The OSTP report, for example, while a good and useful project, was almost identical to reports on the same subject — the state of Government nutrition research — made by the General Accounting Office and the Department of Health, Education, and Welfare. In another instance, while the National Institutes of Health have long been mandated to conduct research on the role of nutrients in major diseases (and, doing so, spent almost 70 per cent of the total $116.6 million budgeted in fiscal year 1977 for all nutrition research), the Food and Agriculture Act of 1977 just recently designated the Department of Agriculture as the lead agency in nutrition research.

Government administrators would have us believe that the bungling and neglect of the mental health link are the inevitable result of the interdisciplinary nature of nutrition. But space exploration encompasses as many sciences as nutrition, and no similar interdisciplinary problems seem to hamper the National Aeronautics and Space Administration. Whatever the reality — honest bureaucratic mismanagement or a calculated shell game — the fact that the research gap exists raises other political questions.

For example, how much adverse scientific information about a product does the Government need before it proposes restrictions? In the case of saccharin, not very much; in the case of sugar, evidently more than we have right now. And how political are these decisions to ban a product, warn against it, or leave it alone? If they are largely political, how can we defend the process and the damage it inflicts?

And what should the Government's policy be in the meantime? The New York City Board of Education announced last December that it would soon introduce such fast foods as tacos, pizza, french fries, cheeseburgers, and milk shakes into three of its large high schools in an effort to appeal to "student tastes" and thus avoid waste. The Las Vegas School Board has already put such a plan into action for the same reasons. These items, it is said, will be "enriched" and will meet current nutrition requirements, but the idea that their less nutritious counterparts are healthful will be unavoidable.

Because the Government is in the formidable position of legislating diet through its Federal food assistance programs — some 44.8 million children are eligible for the National School Lunch Program — that diet should reflect our most recent nutrition information, rather than the questionable products pushed by an industry whose top concern has never been the nation's health.

In addition to enforcing a much sounder nutritional policy for its food assistance programs, the Government should allocate more funds to effective research into the mental health link. Dr. Michael Lesser of Berkeley proposes that we develop community health care systems where we could also do research: "I think it is wrong to do our research in the lab," he told the McGovern Committee. "We are talking about human reactions. When you are studying humans, the research needs to be done in the field. . . . And when you're using nutrients and nutrition, you're using safe substances so it is not dangerous to do clinical research in this area."

Finally, what is the role of the medical community in all this — not researchers, but practicing physicians? Historically, nutrition was a physician's first line of defense against both physical and mental ills. Now, according to a survey of 114 medical schools by the AMA's Department of Foods and Nutrition, only 63 per cent of the responding schools *offered* nutrition courses, and only 23 per cent *required* a nutrition course.

"The students in medical schools are taught to use drugs, not vitamins," laments Dr. Lesser. He views using drugs to treat mental illness as highly destructive. While tranquilizers may gold-plate the drug industry, they are "a chemical strait jacket" for the mentally ill. Nutrients, on the other hand, come closer to treating the mental disease where it starts, according to Dr. Lesser, who adds, "Nobody has ever claimed that mental illness is due to a deficiency of thorazine or valium."

If we are ever going to find the nutritional keys to mental health, a sound Governmental structure that will not be swayed by the special interests of the food or drug industries is needed. We must also demand of the medical community a greater emphasis upon nutritional couseling. If these steps sound basic, it is because good food and health are such basic human rights. That we have let them slip away from us is tragic, but we can get them back.

Understanding anxiety

by Graeme C. Rouhani, BA, SRN, Dip Soc, FRAS, Clinical Instructor,
Sir Charles Gairdner Hospital, Perth, Western Australia

IN THIS ARTICLE, anxiety is seen as a form of energy – a generally little understood source of human energy of enormous potential for good or bad. Properly understood, and constructively used, it lies behind all true advancement in human endeavour. Ventilated or discharged without understanding it can manifest itself in prejudice, disharmony, and destructive behaviour.

For nurses, a clear understanding of the nature and manifestations of anxiety is essential. It has been suggested that nurses and doctors are motivated by high levels of anxiety. If this is so it is of fundamental importance that nurses understand and put into practice positive methods of utilising this tremendous potential in their professional lives, particularly in the field of interpersonal relationships which, at the risk of being accused of heresy, is not one of nursing's stronger areas because of the dysfunctionally high levels of unresolved anxiety endemic in the profession.

Theories

Freud realised that anxiety arose from unconscious mental processes. He saw anxiety arising from inner mental conflicts between the ego (the individuals concept of his "self"), and the id (instinctual primitive urges). Later, he described "super-ego" anxiety (or moral anxiety) in which he saw sexuality broadly as the cause of anxiety arising out of guilt or fear of social disapproval.

Klein saw unconscious aggression as the main conflict causing anxiety; Goldstein saw anxiety being produced when the demands upon an individual exceed

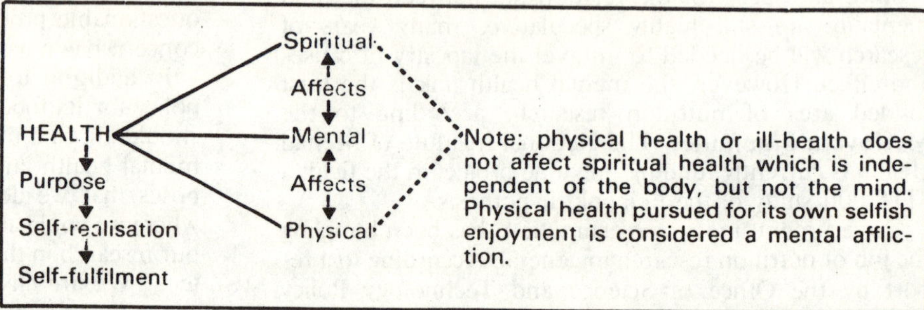

The three aspects of health – body, mind, spirit.

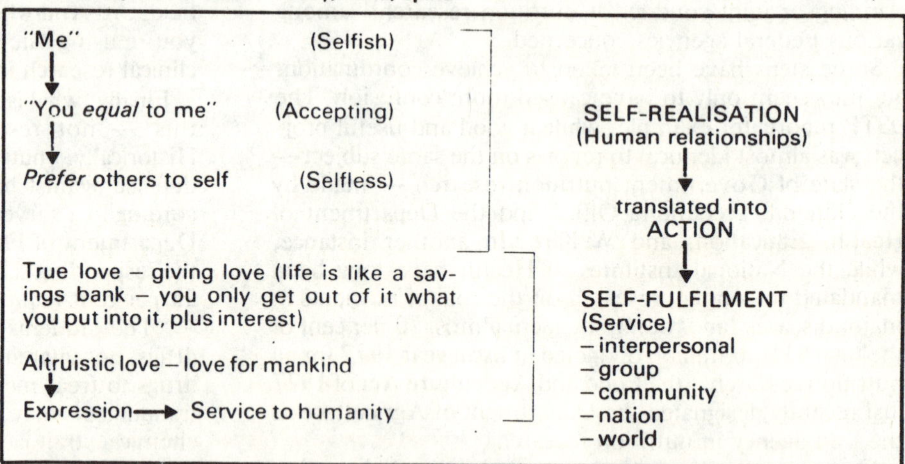

Steps to self-fulfilment

his capacity; Canon viewed anxiety as an expression of a threat to the equilibrium or homeostasis of the organism; Sullivan pointed out that human beings are an integral part of culture, and anxiety arises from a threat to an individual's security in interpersonal relations.

The theologian, Kierkegaard, regarded anxiety as resulting in separation from God when man attempts to emancipate himself from God; as man can never emancipate himself from God with complete self-sufficiency, then anxiety is the inevitable outcome. Religion, with its sense of trust in a "higher power", is a stabilising force in times of stress and anxiety.

Fear and anxiety

Understanding Anxiety, Graeme C. Rouhani, *Nursing Mirror*, Vol. 146, No. 10, Mar. 9, 1978. ©1978 by Business Press Ltd.

The two terms are not synonymous, and an important distinction must be made between them. *Fear,* generally, has a specific identifiable source. Conversely, *anxiety* has a vague, generalised, less easily identifiable source. There is an overall feeling of apprehension without knowledge of the precise origin which may give rise to tensions which may seem, at first glance, to be totally unrelated. Fear is produced when the object or situation is a known and external one; the individual is able to act to resolve the situation.

Fight or flight

Fear is associated with the primordial instinct to run, to escape, and anger or aggression with the instinct to attack. The physiological responses are designed to prepare the organism for emergency action – "fight or flight" – at the expense of digestion and other visceral functions.

However, the parasympathetic nervous system is also involved explaining such effects as increased frequency of urination, slowing of the heart rate, and lowered blood pressure, which may also be part of the anxiety picture. Clinically, the body's response to anxiety and to fear is almost identical – palpitation, tachycardia, sweating, pallor, increased urinary frequency, vertigo, headache, chest pain, syncope, anorexia, nausea, abdominal cramps, tremors, weakness, and sleeplessness. States of chronic anxiety have a number of effects on the body.

Psychosomatic disorders

"Psychosomatic" (from the Greek "psyche" which originally meant "soul" now used to mean "mind", and "soma" meaning "body") refers to the effect of the mind on the body, and of the body on the mind. These disorders account for an enormous range of illnesses – in fact there is a psychosomatic element in all illnesses. Social and cultural factors are also important and these diseases are sometimes called "psychosocial illnesses".

We have seen how in animals and man there is a primitive "fight or flight" mechanism. When confronted with sudden danger the body's defence mechanism prepares to fight the danger or flee from it – adrenalin is poured into the bloodstream, the heart beats faster, blood pressure rises, breathing is more rapid, muscles tense, pupils dilate, and changes take place in the gastrointes-

tinal system.

In nature, the animal's body quickly returns to a state of normal equilibrium (homeostasis) once the danger has passed. In man, however, vague anxieties, especially those occasioned by modern living, confront us with fears which cannot be so easily defined, causing the body to remain in a state of continual preparedness for "fight or flight". Since this vague apprehension of impending danger continues without being resolved, so the physiological and psychological effects continue. Eventually this leads to structural damage to organs and systems. A vicious circle is set up where anxiety causes physical problems, which in turn cause more anxiety.

A few examples include skin disorders (psoriasis, rashes, dandruff, loss of hair); muscular-skeletal system (fibrositis, backache, cramps, poor posture); gastrointestinal (gastric ulcers, colitis, diarrhoea, constipation); respiratory system (asthma, tightness in chest, high, harsh, or unpleasant voice); hypertension, heart disease, kidney disease, sexual problems, gynaecological problems, violence, anti-social behaviour, drug addiction, poor memory, over-tiredness, inefficiency, difficulty in thinking, etc.

Anxiety and behaviour

However we choose to view it, anxiety is one of the main motivating forces in much of human behaviour and provides a tremendous impetus to learning and adjustment throughout life. A degree of anxiety is necessary for healthy growth and mental development and acts as a necessary spur to motivation. Many of our actions are seen to be determined by the avoidance of anxiety.

It has been suggested that order of birth has a bearing on anxiety orientation in later life. In general, first born and only children have almost exclusive contact with parents, and the intensity of the relationship tends to produce greater anxiety, higher conformity, and increased achievement orientation. A disproportionately large number of firstborns achieve eminence. Later, a child's contact with parents is diluted by his simultaneous relationships with older brothers and sisters. This multiple relationship seems to produce lower anxiety and achievement orientation but greater social orientation.

If we are lacking in the experience and emotional reserves which come with maturity we are likely to react to threatening situations with feelings of discouragement and despair, which may be expressed by withdrawal, helplessness, or striking out at the physical or social

environment with anger and hostility. The mature person can restrain his feelings and bring his experience and understanding to bear on the problem.

Normal anxiety

Anxiety affects our ability to function normally. There must be a certain amount of tension if there is to be any application of intellectual potential to the problem at hand. This degree of tension or anxiety, such as characterises the alert, or even moderately apprehensive person, may be called "normal anxiety".

Normal anxiety is associated with the most adequate performance. An increase is likely to be disturbing and disorganising, whereas if the level is too low the individual is unconcerned with the problem at hand and may not even percieve the existence of the problem.

Chronically high anxiety is neurotic anxiety where the reaction is out of all proportion to the threat and interferes particularly with interpersonal relationships. Some people seem to lack even normal anxiety and show no incentive to learn, show no concern for the rights and feelings of others, and are unconcerned about the future or the results of their actions. This pattern of behaviour is consistent with a psychopathic personality. Anxiety is, in fact, probably at the root of most neurotic and non-organic psychotic illness.

Because anxiety *is* painful and unpleasant, we go to some lengths to avoid it, and much of our everyday behaviour which may seem illogical or irrational makes sense when seen as attempts, usually unconscious in nature, to avoid situations that are potential sources of anxiety. This behaviour forms certain common patterns commonly called "defence mechanisms" whose main function is to reduce anxiety to a tolerable level – a sort of emotional analgesic for anxiety, some of which may facilitate learning but many of which may impede and retard learning.

Defence mechanisms

We all feel anxious about different things – a result of our difference in cultural and family backgrounds and social role expectations. Despite personal differences in the cause of our anxieties we all employ defence mechanisms as strategies for reducing our tensions.

Withdrawal is a very common defence mechanism, and is the most direct. If the situation looks as if it is too much to cope with, we simply get out of it or move away from it.

Sublimation consists of the transformation of unacceptable urges into acceptable activities. It can be a most healthy and creative mechanism.

Dissociation – unfavourable experiences or painful events are blocked off from full conscious awareness.

Conversion operates when a conflict or repressed idea manifests itself in bodily symptoms. This mechanism may be the basis of paralysis, abnormal motor movements, convulsions, deafness, loss of speech, and other sensory abnormalities. It provides only a temporary relief from problems.

Projection involves a distortion of reality wherein wishes and urges unacceptable to the self are ascribed to others. People often criticise faults in others, unaware that these are deficiencies in their own personalities.

Displacement is the substitution of another person or object for the one that is actually the source of anger, fear, or anxiety: eg, kicking the proverbial cat!

Denial is the refusal to admit that a situation exists or that an event happened.

Repression is an extreme form of denial wherein the feared event or circumstances are completely erased from awareness.

Regression is a return to an earlier, or more infantile, form of behaviour as a way of coping with a stressful situation.

Suspression is a conscious pushing aside of feelings or impulses. This is often aided by throwing ourselves into work or other activity; it usually offers only temporary relief.

Reaction formation consists of displaying the opposite behaviour to that which is felt and is unacceptable to the person. A basically insecure person may display a façade of aggressiveness.

Rationalisation is a very common adult defence mechanism, and children take a little longer to learn it. Logical reasons are constructed to explain the inexplic-

able or unacceptable actions, thus enabling a person to maintain his self-esteem, to save face, or to maintain peace of mind.

Intellectual control: eg. "Don't be silly, this is not an adult way to behave". Many consciously act out the roles they feel society expects of them. A useful form of control, but if used excessively then a fairly rigid, restricted, and colourless personality can result.

Permissiveness and anxiety

Permissiveness (defined as a non-controlling, undemanding climate) in an environment of detached warmth (the "democratic parent") seems very likely to produce fairly positive characteristics. But when it is accompanied by high hostility (the neglecting parent or society) permissiveness is more likely to result in high anxiety manifest in non-compliance and aggressiveness. Many studies of juvenile delinquents show that the delinquent's home environment has exactly this combination of permissiveness and hostility.

Relief of anxiety

"Facing up" to a threat and trying to deal with it as a problem to be solved, and not just avoided, calls for a considerable degree of maturity. The first step is that of finding ways to turn threats into challenges (or seeing problems as challenges, and of learning to turn our shortcomings into stepping stones).

There are many ways of relieving the physical and mental tension that goes with anxiety – cigarettes, alcohol, and drugs on the one hand, recreational activities, tension-relieving excercises and disciplines, such as yoga and meditation, on the other hand. However, it will be remembered that a normal amount of tension is seen as essential to human growth and development. Here, anxiety

is seen as energy to be used in the process of realising one's potential, as a means of attaining self-realisation. It can be set out graphically as follows.

Self-realisation — the release of human potential

The need is to develop two basic capacities – *knowing* and *loving* – which are used to reinforce one another.

Knowing – the unknown leads to *anxiety* – anxiety is *energy* without a *goal* – utilise the energy from anxiety by formulating and carrying out a *goal*. Utilising the energy from anxiety to realise a goal requires *courage*. Attraction to the *unknown potential* in yourself and in others is *faith*.

Loving – total, unconditional, unqualified acceptance. It is the hidden *potential* one is attracted to and loves and strives to bring out – uncovering and refining the hidden gems in each one of us (this is the real meaning of education which means "to draw out"). Also, the ability to be loved – to attract love and accept love. An unloving person not only blocks his own self-realisation but also prevents others from realising their potential.

Prejudice refers to a conflict in the expression of the loving and knowing capacities and is a definite blockage in the expression of human potential because the loving capacity is being used to impede the knowing capacity and is nearly always damaging to both the victim and to the person who is carrying it out.

In a fundamental sense, almost all neuroses and psychoses can be understood in terms of this kind of conflict. The goal of therapy is aimed at the removal of the blockage of becoming one's true self by enabling the person's loving capacity to support his knowing capacity.

Personality and Antisocial Disorders

By JOHN P. SPIEGEL, M.D.

Personality disorders — one of the four major themes of the Inter-American Conference on Mental Health of Children and Youth — constitute a very large and troublesome group of psychiatric conditions. The problems involved represent a severe challenge to the psychiatric profession and highlight some of the principal difficulties facing the profession in all areas of practice.

Because of their significance to the entire field of psychiatry, I want to review three of these problems:

1. The connection between diagnosis, labeling, and social control.

2. The connection between therapeutic approach and the values of the therapist.

3. The connection between antisocial behavior and social change, as represented by community protest, anti-regime violence, or similar forms of social disorder.

My concern with this third problem stems from my experience as director of the Lemberg Center for the Study of Violence at Brandeis University and from my studies of the riots and social disorders in the United States during the late 1960s and early 1970s.

What the participants saw as unfair distribution of political and economic power — and the related psychologic suffering of oppressed groups — was a constant feature of these events.*

The diagnostic approach to the classification of the personality disorders in the United States is, by general consensus, extremely unsatisfactory. The American Psychiatric Association's

---

* Because of the strong (though often subtle and concealed) influence of cultural values on the etiology, diagnosis, and treatment of personality disorders, my remarks apply only to mental health problems in the United States; I assume that cultural values — and value conflicts — play an equally important role in other countries.

1. PERSPECTIVES

Diagnostic and Statistical Manual of Mental Disorders lists 10 major categories: paranoid, cyclothymic, schizoid, explosive, obsessive-compulsive, hysterical, asthenic, antisocial, passive-aggressive, and inadequate personalities. In actual practice, a wider variety of terms is employed, such as borderline, depressive, sadomasochistic, and narcissistic. If we add the sexual deviations, alcoholism, and drug dependence to the list, it will be extended by some 20 diagnostic categories.

One of the problems is the difficulty of standardizing usage. The diagnosis conferred on a given patient sometimes seems a matter more of the tastes and predisposition of the individual psychiatrist than of scientific procedure. On a deeper level, this somewhat arbitrary collection of terms provides no information on the intensity or seriousness of the disorder. It indicates nothing about the preferred mode of treatment or about the relationship between diagnosis and prognosis.

All these matters of standardization — so important to the professional image of psychiatry in the eyes of an increasingly critical and sophisticated public — can be determined only by an intensive clinical examination of each patient. And the outcome of such an examination varies considerably from psychiatrist to psychiatrist, giving rise to the famous (or infamous) "battles of the experts" in court trials.

The lack of a validated connection between diagnosis, preferred mode of therapy, and prognosis is due to the lamentable scarcity of systematic research-based knowledge in this area. What is equally unfortunate but less obvious is the relationship between the diagnostic intent (that is, the covert purpose of the whole labeling system) and the burden of social control that is thereby imposed on psychiatrists.

It is not necessary to recall the moralistic past of the diagnostic system in order to demonstrate the weight of social disapproval inherent in the terminology. Such now-abandoned labels as "moral insanity" and "psychopathic personality" are neither more nor less revealing than the current "antisocial" and "passive-aggressive" personality labels. The pejorative connotation in the term "sexual deviations" is another example; while perhaps less stigmatizing than its precursor, "sexual perversions," it excludes the concept of culturally permitted sexual variations — thus signaling the social condemnation and contempt that are incurred by behavior assumed to be in opposition to the mainstream values of a particular culture.

In order to make my critique of this diagnostic system as pointed as possible, I would like to propose the following generalization: *Behavior that is in opposition to the values of a particular culture does not, in and of itself, constitute an illness, nor is it necessarily a sign of illness.*

I think that it is important to be clear about this, because the diagnostic system is applied so generously and so unscrupulously to society's outcasts and rebels that it tempts psychiatrists to play the game of casting out. And while it may be ego gratifying to serve as a kind of omniscient psychiatric trouble-shooter for society, it is not an appropriate professional role — at least, not when applied to socially provocative group behavior.

Two examples drawn at random from the "troubled '60s" illustrate how tempting and seductive this casting-out activity can be. One psychiatrist, writing about the "Beat Generation," implied that they chose the label "beatnik" with "defiant avidity" because of "an accusatory assumption on their part that they had been beaten into martyrdom." The implication was that, in the self-chosen role of victim, the beatnik displayed a masochistic personality disorder from which he believed he ought to be cured for the good of the country. The beatniks' relaxed and unorthodox way of life, therefore, could not be considered a valid comment on the overweening achievement values of the dominant culture or a valid protest against it.

The fact of the matter is that the word "beat" had a wholly different origin, and was as much thrust upon the members of this social movement by the mass media as it was seized by them once it had come to public attention. Had the movement persisted, it is quite likely that psychiatrists such as the one I mentioned would have tried to add the labels "beat personality" and (later) "hippie personality" to the list of personality disorders.

Another psychiatrist, testifying before a Congressional Committee about the student uprisings of the late 1960s, diagnosed the rebel leaders as paranoid characters. He described their followers as adolescents who had been deprived of emotional gratification and warmth by their parents and who were searching for objects — such as university administrations, the police, and the federal government — upon which to project their rage.

One main difficulty with diagnostic terms is that they are based essentially on a literary (some would say a phenomenologic or existential) approach. It is no accident that the names of two novelists, the Marquis de Sade and Leopold von Sacher-Masoch, have found their way into the diagnostic system. In these cases the labels were devised by Krafft-Ebing and refined by Freud, but it is obvious that anyone can play the game of inventing new diagnostic terms.

Another difficulty is the degree to which such coinages lend themselves to manipulation in the service of the administrative goals of society's institutions — what I have called "social control." For example, in the United States military services, personality disorders are regarded not as illnesses but as long-standing problems in adjustment. This point of view favors ease of administrative discharge of troublesome persons and protects the service from monetary claims for service-connected medical disabilities.

Despite all the problems with the use and abuse of the diagnostic system, if one looks behind the superficially provocative behavior of those who are unable or refuse to "adjust," one can discover a definable mental illness in *some but not all* of them. Whatever the external manifestations of their behavior may be, these persons are truly unhappy and dissatisfied with themselves and with their lives.

As a group, they have a condition that can be distinguished from psychoses by their adequate (sometimes superior) perception of reality. It can be distinguished from neuroses by the absence of internal conflict and by their tendency to blame all difficulties on their external environment. And it can be distinguished from organic conditions by the absence of any neurophysiologic defects.

Beyond these general distinguishing characteristics, the "illness" aspect of persons with personality disorders is signified by an ego structure that is extremely rigid. This is evidenced by their repetitious and often self-destructive behavior, by their lack of ability to adapt to new circumstances, and (really the same thing in different words) by their inability to learn or profit from experience.

Because of deprivation, neglect, cruelty, or inconsistency experienced during early childhood at the hands of his parents, the person suffering from a personality disorder has severe difficulties in interpersonal relations. He is unable to empathize with others in a sincere or spontaneous fashion and therefore is usually unable to develop persistent or loving relationships. Because of the disturbed family background and the early deprivations, such persons either are excessively dependent on others or else defend themselves against their dependent needs by exploitation, manipulation, fits of

"The strength of their need for narcissistic supplies makes intimate relationships almost intolerable"

explosive anger, or various forms of pseudo-independence. The immense strength of their need for continuous narcissistic supplies makes intimate relationships almost intolerable. Their fixed expectation, based on childhood experiences, is that no matter how trustworthy, sympathetic, or giving another person may appear to be on first contact, that person will ultimately betray, reject, or abandon the subject — thereby revealing either that the subject is basically unlovable and inferior, which is their secret but unacknowledged view of themselves, or that nobody can really be trusted, which is their usual, defensive view of personal relationships.

Basic to this tangle of trust and mistrust is the fixation on the problems of fault finding. The miseries of childhood and the conflicts and blaming procedures experienced in the family and transferred to and re-experienced in the adult world imply that difficulties in living and adapting cannot be considered simply as problems in human relations, to be solved in the best way possible. Rather, the unhappiness, loneliness, and isolation experienced by the subject must be someone's fault — at best a severe, unacceptable fault and at worst an unforgivable sin. To experience the fault as lying within the person, to make such an acknowledgment to oneself, would give rise to severe anxiety and depression. Better to project the blame to the external world. But since the fault is secretly perceived as lying within the ego, the projection is accompanied mainly by complaints of unfairness, frustration, or neglect. Self-justification through claims of victimization, rather than a realistic attempt to alter circumstances, constitutes the life-style of the subject.

If this is the *illness* underlying the kaleidoscopic behavioral phenomena of the personality disorders, the challenges to the therapist are manifold. The behavior is ego-syntonic and quite often pleasurable, at least at the moment of acting out. It is extremely difficult to obtain therapeutic leverage with a person who does not want to change his own behavior but, instead, wants the world to behave in more gratifying fashion toward him. This is where the connection between the therapeutic approach and the therapist's values, which I mentioned earlier, become important. If the therapist responds to the inevitable frustrations in treatment, the dependent demands, the constant overt or covert criticism, the unrealistic expectations, and the sense of being exploited by the patient with anger and rejection — responses that such patients are adept at eliciting — he will not be able to form a therapeutic alliance with the patient. Even if he attempts to conceal his actual feelings under the guise of "therapeutic neutrality," the patient will not be deceived. On the other hand, if he develops a maternal, overprotective, and oversympathetic response under the impulse to rescue the patient from his dreadful fate, or clings doggedly to a therapeutic tack when it is obviously not working, he cannot do the patient any good. Finally, if he secretly and vicariously enjoys hearing about the patient's acting-out behavior — his aggressiveness and defiance or his flamboyant sexual experiences — he cannot be of much help.

There is a certain amount of agreement in the United States that what is required is flexibility in the therapeutic approach to such patients. Intensive psychotherapy based on psychodynamic principles may work in some cases. If it does not, family therapy or couples therapy may be effective. In recent years, behavior therapy based on the principles of social learning has proved successful in some very difficult cases.

In any of these formats it is important not only that the therapist listen carefully to the patient's complaints but also that, in a carefully selective way, he reveal his own feelings about the patient's experiences and behavior in the therapeutic situation. The reason for adopting this as a therapeutic technique is that such patients frequently have a very narrow range of

---

"It is difficult to obtain therapeutic leverage with a person who does not want to change his own behavior"

---

social skills and great difficulty in identifying, naming, and acknowledging their own feelings. If anyone fails to perceive how he is actually feeling and reacting in a given situation, he is apt to behave in a narrow, fixed, repetitive, and socially ineffective manner. Furthermore, the acting-out behavior usually occurs when the patient feels himself to be in danger of being overwhelmed by a nameless emotion, whether

anger, sadness, or fear.

Therapeutic flexibility of this sort can be maintained only if the therapist is aware of his own culturally derived values, on the one hand, and of the possible validity of alternative values, on the other. He should be especially sensitive to both the creative and destructive potentiality of value conflicts. This insight enables him to identify with the variant or socially condemned

---

"Those engaged in social protest recognize no problem in themselves but complain about injustices of the system"

(by the majority culture) values to which such patients are responding and, at the same time, with the dominant cultural values that the patient appears to be rejecting or, at any rate, is unable to put into action. Through his ability to bridge value conflicts — to accept both sides as possibly valuable or interesting life-styles — the therapist helps the patient to recognize the conflict within himself and thus puts him on the road towards integrating what he has split up between himself and the outside world.

Should the therapist nevertheless take sides when a value conflict is clarified and exposed? Should he act as an agent of mainstream society, or should he present himself to the patient as neutral or merely as a mediator with respect to the conflict of values? Can he really decide what is best for the patient?

These are very tricky questions to which no firm answers can yet be given. My own opinion is that the therapist, no matter how sympathetic he may be to alternative value systems, must be clear within himself as to where his choices lie and be honest with the patient about his preferences. Only in this way can he represent a valid role model for the patient. Frankness of this sort still leaves the patient free to make his own choices; and if his ultimate solution is too much at variance with the key values of the therapist, the patient should be encouraged to look for another therapist. It often happens that just this freedom to choose and the crisis attendant upon the impending separation from the therapist enable the patient to make the emotionally significant connection with his childhood experiences and thus to begin to work on the resolution of his internal conflict.

The question of value conflicts brings us to

the third major problem for discussion that I mentioned at the beginning: the relation between antisocial behavior and social change. The behavior in question can range from civil disobedience through violent community confrontations to acts of terrorism. Are these the acts of sick people suffering from personality disorders, as implied by the two psychiatrists mentioned previously, or is the behavior a normal response to social injustice and the desire for social change?

The superficial connection is obvious. Those suffering from personality disorders recognize no intrinsic problem within themselves but constantly complain that they are victims of the behavior of other people. Those engaged in social protest also recognize no problem within themselves but complain about the injustices of the social system and about their inability to effect change except by engaging in potentially destructive antisocial behavior.

Most of the people who have participated in social protest in the United States are either adolescents or young adults. It is therefore seductively easy to attribute their behavior to adolescent identity problems if not to outright personality disorders. However, studies carried out at the Lemberg Center for the Study of Violence and elsewhere have shown that only a small minority of these youthful participants actually show evidence of serious personality disturbances.

Yet there is another and deeper connection between "activists" who demonstrate on behalf of social change and social justice and those who give clinical evidence of personality disorders. Both are responding in their own ways to the value conflicts characteristic of a particular society.

This comment requires me to say a word about the topic of cultural value conflicts as applied to mental health and illness. In the United States, cultural values — defined as a pattern of preference for life-styles, norms of behavior, and existential views of the nature of the world — vary and come into conflict because of three main considerations. First is the fact that our nation is composed of a mosaic of different ethnic and national groups that experience difficulties in correlating the values they brought from their countries of origin with the dominant value system of the United States. Second, the core Anglo-Saxon values of the politically dominant strata have always contained elements of strain. Typical in this connection is the inconsistency between our preaching of an egalitarian value system and our actual

practice, which institutionalizes hierarchical, elitist values featuring superior-inferior relationships, as witnessed in our treatment of minority groups and our handling of foreign relations. Many other aspects of institutional affairs — in the schools, in industry, and in community power structures — emphasize dominant-subordinate rather than egalitarian relationships. The third conflict-generating process derives from the fact that our mainstream values are themselves undergoing a fairly rapid change, partly as a result of the protests of the '60s. All these sources of strain are likely to produce a great deal of conflict between spouses and between parents and children, and thus in family life in general.

Dr. Raúl Hernández-Peón demonstrated, through his fundamental research on the physiology of the central nervous system, how CNS processes — particularly in the brain stem — are related to the mechanisms of attention and thus to the ways in which sensory inputs are filtered in or out in the course of organism-environment interactions. We can see by way of analogy that this is how values function in interpersonal relations. Values determine what is to be regarded as important and what is to be at best disregarded and at worst condemned. Values are the filtering mechanisms on the basis of which whole societies as well as subgroups are differentiated from one another. It is the incompatibility and conflict between value systems that make human relations so interesting in some social circumstances and so tragic in others.

We now come to consider how groups of young activists protesting on behalf of social change can be distinguished from young people displaying symptoms of antisocial personality disorders.

The demonstrators who get into legal difficulties are responding to the cultural value conflicts underlying issues of social justice — issues that first came to their attention forcibly in adolescence or early adulthood as the result of a social protest movement. These young people usually realize, retrospectively, that they have encountered the same value conflicts within their own families at an earlier time. But they had not suffered serious deprivation or neglect because of this.

The youngsters who get into trouble with the police because of severe personality disorders have experienced the same value conflicts in their families during childhood, but in a much more injurious form. Because of the conflicts between mother and father or between parents and child, the child's emotional and psychologic maturation has been seriously retarded and warped. The damage has been experienced very early. And neither during childhood nor in adolescence is the subject able to trace his difficulties to a conflict in values. He feels victimized but is unable to locate the source of

---

"Our mainstream values are themselves undergoing a fairly rapid change"

---

the difficulty except by blaming either himself or his parents and, later, by blaming whatever authority figure he encounters.

I have emphasized the importance of paying attention to value conflicts in the areas of diagnosis, treatment, and prevention. If we are to make much progress along these lines, an interdisciplinary effort will be required. We need the cooperation of sociologists, cultural anthropologists, political scientists, and attorneys in delineating the value conflicts affecting the various segments of the nation states.

The sooner we get on with this sort of interdisciplinary collaboration, the more we shall be able to do for the troubled youth of today.

The Effects of Allergy and Chemical Susceptibility on Children's Behavior

Parents and teachers are especially concerned when mental confusion, fatigue, irritability or sensory dysfunction take their toll on a child's school performance. Children who have thus been labeled as hyperactive, language or learning disabled, lazy, minimally brain injured or emotionally disturbed may in fact have a health problem. One type of health problem which is currently recognized has to do with the effects of allergy and chemical susceptibility on children's behavior.

Certain historical and exploratory research on the effects of allergy and chemical susceptibility on behavior in children has already been completed. Besides a need for much additional research data in this area, there is a serious need for a collation of the current available literature. Evidence will be offered indicating that many of the children diagnosed as "learning disabled" or having "minimal brain dysfunction" are in fact reacting maladaptively to ecological factors in their environment.

Definition of Terms

Most of the definitions of terms used will be explained as they appear in context; however, the following terms are offered here for clarification.

The term "allergy" has been traditionally and restrictively defined as those "cases in which a skin test (or other objective method) demonstrates an antigen — antibody reaction" (Speer, 1975a, p. 49). Use of the term allergy will take on a broader meaning here as it has for many of those familiar with the research in this field. A broader view would say, whether objective tests are positive or negative, any reaction that causes allergic-type manifestations may be termed allergy.

Learning disability. Any condition for which specific or gross ability deficits result in lower academic achievement than what would normally be expected considering intellectual ability.

Minimal brain dysfunction. A diagnostic classification characterized by any or all of the following: specific learning deficit (disability), perceptual motor deficit, general coordination deficit, hyperkinesis, impulsivity, emotional lability, short attention span — distractibility, "soft" neurological signs, borderline abnormal or abnormal electroencephalogram.

Most of the literature in the area of allergy and hypersensitivity-related behavior has come from the medical field, specifically from allergists and pediatric allergists. As early as 1898, Baker wrote an excellent description of a fatigue condition (apparently allergy-related) long before allergic disease was recognized. He differentiated this condition from normal fatigue, writing that no amount of sleep seemed to alleviate the pathologic type of fatigue. A few lines are quoted here:

With such children all the bodily positions are

Fred W. Fanning
The Univ. of Akron

Paul Cevasco
Cuyahoga Falls School

apt to be awkward . . . while the movements are . . . perhaps jerky, or fidgety, or irritable, from unnatural increase in reflex activity, headaches are often complained of . . . The subject instead of acting naturally in common matters, trifles with his luncheon, dawdles over every task, and engages in sports, if at all, with little or no zest or skill . . . He usually sleeps poorly, has nightmares . . . In the morning he is irritable, cross, and hysterical . . . It often appears that such children cannot concentrate the attention for any length of time, and cannot associate images and ideas well enough to learn much or to retain what they do succeed in learning . . . (Kittler, 1973, pp. 619-620).

At times allergic individuals' complaints seem so diffuse and bizarre as to resemble a highly developed neurosis or ongoing psychosis. Speer (1975b) reports that his study on the nature of multiple food allergy revealed patients' complaints of restlessness, anxiety, irritability, insomnia, weakness, muscle and joint aching and drowsiness. He states "Many of these patients had seen an internist or pediatrician for fatigue, a psychiatrist for tension, a neurologist for headache or an orthopedist for achiness" (Speer, 1975, p. 75).

An additional finding of this study showed that multiple food allergy was twice as common in boys as in girls (ages one through ten years), which roughly parallels the incidence of learning disabilities in boys and girls.

The Nature of Allergy Related Behavior Problems

For many years a major controversy has raged as to the primary or secondary nature of symptoms like those mentioned above. As with any bodily disease, allergy may result in secondary behavior problems. This may well be expected of a child who fights for his breath and suffers from irritated sensory tissue.

However, allergy may primarily affect a child's behavior (Shannon, 1922). In this instance, the brain and central nervous system act as complex allergic shock tissue, not unlike the skin tissue would react upon contact with poison ivy. Kaufman (1972, p. 118) states that, in certain people, "an allergic reaction — particularly food allergy — may affect the functioning of the central nervous system, causing impairment of and serious alterations in, the patient's usual thinking and feeling behavior."

Evidence that allergy affects brain functioning directly is offered by Baldwin and Kittler (1970) in a pilot study using 20 children with abnormal electroencephalograms and positive allergy skin tests to inhalants. After inhalant elimination and dietary restrictions were introduced, 1) nine electroencephalograms were read as normal, and two others improved from previous readings, 2) some children found to have average ability, initially, (by use of an intelligence test battery) but with serious learning problems, showed considerable improvement upon retesting, 3) those children initially tested as being retarded, showed no significant change in performance. Subjectively, diet restrictions appeared to improve some children's behavior.

Related to the nature of allergy-related behavior is the issue that deals with the misdiagnosis of allergy-caused behavior problems as those resulting from a primary psychiatric disorder. Tuft and Mueller (1970) state that when observable allergic symptoms (e.g., hives, atopic dermatitis, etc.) are not present, it is often difficult to say that food allergy is the possible cause rather than psychoneurosis. However, Mandell (1974) has found repeatedly that individuals suffering from allergy-caused behavior difficulties do not always possess traditional observable allergic manifestations.

An analysis of findings from a recent study by Klotz and Moeller (1974) revealed that psychiatrically disordered students have an increased allergic sensitivity. They state that by adding an allergic orientation in the diagnosis and treatment of these patients to other modalities, they have reduced the time necessary to return the patients as active functioning individuals in their home environment from 36 months to 9 months.

Clinical Ecology and Allergy

The pioneers in the study of allergy and hypersensitivity (ecologic) related behavioral manifestations appear to belong to a relatively small and new group of physicians who call themselves "clinical ecologists." Clinical ecology "is concerned with an almost unbelievable spectrum of physical and mental disorders that are due to reversible allergic and allergy — like susceptibilities, and addictive responses to biologically active substances in man's natural and synthetic environment" (Mandell, 1973, p. 1).

George Von Hilsheimer (1970), one of those associated with this group, warns that symptoms such as indigestion, sleepiness, hyperactivity, and signs of perceptual inability, as well as a poor or varying attention span may be signs of allergic reactions. He notes that ingestion of the most common offenders, peanuts, peanut butter, fish, pork, tomatoes, eggs and milk, can frequently result in drowsiness, depression, loss of vitality and strength, and perceptual debility.

The clinical ecologist attempts to find the offending allergen by use of "provocative testing". This involves administering an extract of the suspected allergen sublingually (under the tongue), subcutaneously; or intracutaneously, or a powdered allergen in its natural state (e.g. pollen, mold) is given by inhalation; the painless sublingual is apparently used most often (Mandell, 1969).

This method is much more reliable and useful than the conventional scratch testing (Buckley and Hawley, 1974; Philpott, 1974). Instead of a skin reaction, the physician might observe a behavioral manifestation ranging anywhere from hyperactivity to catatonia in the patient. Acute reactions from the allergens may be neutralized by administration of a very dilute solution of the allergen. Philpott (1974) reports that the neutralizing dose works in about 70 per cent of the cases.

The "rotary diversified diet" devised by Rinkel (Mandell, 1969) is also employed to evaluate the etiologic role of ingested foods. It is based on the premise that an allergen, not eaten for four to five days previous to ingestion, will cause an acute observable reaction. The diet is also used in the maintenance of some cyclic allergic states, enabling the individual to eat the offending food (in moderation).

Not only do children and adults suffer unknowingly from environmental factors, some even crave the very substance that is causing them harm. This is chronic food addiction: the person eats the food to which he is addicted in order to temporarily suppress the very symptoms that the food produced (Bigwood, 1972; Campbell, 1974). Food addiction is similar to alcoholic or narcotic addiction, also involving an uncomfortable withdrawal period of varying degrees (Mandell, 1974).

Harmful Chemicals in Food

Not everyone involved in the ecological treatment of behavior in children belongs to the group of "clinical ecologists". Dr. Benjamin Feingold's primary concern lies with the ecological treatment of hyperactive-learning disabled children (H-LD) that apparently are reacting to artificial colors and artificial flavors in their food. These two groups make up approximately 80 per cent of all the chemicals used in our food supply (Feingold, 1975a).

As is the case with many of those physicians involved in the ecological treatment of children's problem behavior, Dr. Feingold gradually came to realize that a behavioral change many times accompanied relief of physical allergic symptoms. He now focuses on the behaviors involved in the hyperactive-learning disabled child.

The term "hyperactive-learning disability" may be misleading but it refers to the most often encountered diagnostic pattern within the minimal brain dysfunction (MBD) category: "not all MBD's are hyperkinetic, while all H-LD's display the hyperactive pattern, minor to major" (Feingold, 1975b, p. 52).

Feingold states that his experience has shown 50 per cent of H-LD children to respond to strict elimination diets, and that "the younger the child the more complete the improvement" (Feingold, 1975a, p. 800). Feingold is one researcher who does not adhere to the provocative food testing approach and does not rely on hyposensitization techniques (he prefers the elimination diet).

A relatively high incidence of sensitivity to naturally occurring salicylates and particularly food dyes has been found by Hawley and Buckley (1974) in their clinical observations, while using the provocative allergen testing method. Unlike Benjamin Feingold, these physicians have made use of the provocative testing method, as well as observe the patient's reaction to specific elimination diets.

Since hypersensitivity to natural salicylates was first recognized by Feingold (1975b), Hawley and Buckley (1974) have noted that those children sensitive to the aniline dyes are occasionally sensitive to citrus fruit or apples (containing salicylates). Regarding treatment, they state they "have found that about half of over 150 hyperkinetic children tested with the sublingual dilutions of food dyes have some response to the test, indicating that a trial of the salicylate-free diet was indicated" (Hawley and Buckley, 1974, p. 31).

Air Pollutants

Another group of investigators has focused attention on the maladaptive reactions caused by environmental air pollution. The effects of air pollutants on neural and sensory functions in man vary widely. According to Ember (1975), even though the odorous pollutants may be a minor annoyance, they can lead to irritation, emotional upset, anorexia, and mental depression. Apparently the lipid soluble aerosols can enter the body and be absorbed in the lipids of the central nervous system. Here, their effects may persist long after the initial reagent has been removed. Examples of those pollutants having long term chronic effects are: organo-phosphate pesticides, and aerosols carrying the metals lead, mercury and cadmium (Ember, 1975).

Additionally, Ember (1975, p. 198) states "Two chemical messengers that act as a communication link between nerve cells have been reported to be decreased following ozone exposure." Also several electroencephalographic readouts have indicated a mild depression of cortical (higher brain) function.

A young girl's acute reaction to indoor and outdoor chemical air pollutants which resulted in cerebral disturbance involving abnormal behavioral and perceptual manifestations was noted in a case study cited by Mandell (1968).

A pioneer in the clinical ecology field, Theron Randolph (1970) states that domiciliary (within the home) and indoor air contaminants are more important than outdoor pollutants in the etiology of ecologic mental illness. He offers case studies which show how contaminants, as seemingly harmless as a gas furnace, cause reactions ranging from mental depression to hyperactivity in the chemically primarily of avoidance of the incriminated source.

Other researchers have investigated the dangers of petroleum-based products used in homes and schools. It has been observed that the resultant fumes can cause "nervousness, irritability, anti-social behavior, reduced reading comprehension, mental confusion, depression, headaches, asthma, hives and even an inability to learn" (Polluted Air, 1969). Aerosols are apparently the most offensive and include the following products: insecticide spray, paint spray, fixatives and snow spray, solvent for reproducing machines, germicidals, room deodorants, furniture treatment and disinfectant and deodorant sprays.

Conclusion

Much of the literature cited suggests that perhaps many of those children previously diagnosed as "learning disabled" or as having "minimal brain dysfunction" may be reacting maladaptively to ecological factors in their environment. More specifically, data was reported which supports the contention that allergy and chemical susceptibility can maladaptively effect children's behavior. However, available information in this area of research is still severely limited and must be broadly expanded if we are to better understand this type of environmental effect on children's behavior.

Reference List

Bigwood, C. The environment strikes back. *Harper's Bazaar*, June, 1972, pp. 70-71.

Buckley, R., & Hawley, C. Food dyes and hyperkinetic children. *Academic Therapy*, 1974, *10*(1), 27-32.

Campbell, M. B. Neurological and psychiatric aspects of allergy. *Otolaryngol Clinics of North America*, 1974, 7, pp. 805-835.

Ember, L. R. (Ed.). Caution: Air may be hazardous to health. *Environmental Service and Technology*, 1975, 9, pp. 198-199.

Feingold, B. F. Hyperkinesis and learning disabilities linked to artificial food flavors and colors. *American Journal of Nursing*, 1975, 75, pp. 797-803. (a)

Feingold, B. F. *Why your child is hyperactive*. New York: Random House, 1975. (b)

Kaufman, W. Some aspects of psychotherapy in allergic practice. *The Journal of Asthma Research*, 1972, *10*(2), 117-125.

Kittler, F. J. Allergy and behavior. In Speer, Robert & Dockham (Eds.), *Allergy and immunology in childhood*. Springfield, Illinois: Charles C. Thomas, 1973.

Kittler, F. J., & Baldwin, D. G. The role of allergic factors in the child with minimal brain dysfunction. *Annals of Allergy*, 1970, *28*, pp. 203-206.

Klotz, S. D., & Moeller, R. K. An apparent allergic mechanism in psychiatric patients. (Abstract). *Excerpta Medicia*, 1974 (Free Communications Abstracts).

Mandell, M. *Cerebral reactions in allergic patients*. Norwalk, Conn.: The New England Foundation for Allergic and Environmental Diseases, Inc., 1969.

Mandell, M. *An introduction to clinical ecology: Allergic, ecologic and addictive, factors in physical and mental disease*. Paper presented at second annual convention of the International Academy of Metabology, New York, March 23, 1973.

Mandell, M. Ecologic, allergic, and metabolic factors in the etiology of physical and mental disorders. In L. R. Pomeroy (Ed.). *New Dynamics of Preventive Medicine*. Miami: Symposia Specialists, 1974.

Philpott, W. H. Ecologic, orthomolecular, and behavioral contributions to psychiatry. *Journal of Orthomolecular psychiatry*, 1974, 3, pp. 356-370.

Polluted air at school. *Prevention*, June, 1969, pp. 41-44.

Randolph, T. G. Domiciliary chemical air pollution in the etiology of ecologic mental illness. *International Journal of Social Psychiatry*, 1970, *16*, pp. 243-265.

Speer, F. The allergic child. *American Family Physician*, 1975, *11*(2), 88-94. (a)

Speer, F. Multiple food allergy. *Annals of Allergy*, 1975, *34*(2), 71-76. (b)

Tuft, L., & Mueller, H. L. (Eds.). *Allergy in children*. Philadelphia: W. B. Saunders Co., 1970.

Von Hilsheimer, G. Education that works with "special" children. *Prevention*, July, 1970, pp. 61-

ANXIETY

Anxiety is closely related to the action of two natural chemicals in the brain; drugs that relieve anxiety may also make people unable to cope with change or adversity.

JEFFREY A. GRAY

Many people suffer from some form of extreme anxiety. Some experience sporadic attacks of panic for no apparent reason, others go around in a state of continual apprehension. Still others are afflicted with phobias, that is, persistent, excessive fears of objects or situations that most people would not consider significant sources of danger. The most common and crippling of these conditions is agoraphobia. A person with this phobia fears to go outside and may remain housebound for years. There is an important, if less obvious, element of anxiety in the obsessive-compulsive neurosis, in which a person feels a compulsive urge to perform some apparently unnecessary ritual, such as the repeated washing of perfectly clean hands. If the ritual is prevented, there is a great surge of anxiety. It is difficult to assess the number of people who suffer from these conditions. Many do not bother to consult a doctor, even though they are as severely affected as others who do. It has been estimated that there are four million phobics in Britain alone. If we add to these conditions the extremely

common reactive depression, in which anxiety is a prominent symptom, the number would be greatly swelled.

The usual way of controlling anxiety is with drugs, which cure none of the conditions described but that do help patients manage their anxiety. The drug with the longest pedigree—though it is usually prescribed by the patient, not the physician—is alcohol. These days a physician is more likely to prescribe one of the benzodiazepines, for example, Librium (chlordiazepoxide) or Valium (diazepam). Before these tranquilizers were developed in the 1950s, the medical profession relied chiefly on various barbiturates, such as Amytal (sodium amobarbital). The choice among these drugs is to a large extent arbitrary, although safety and convenience appear to favor the benzodiazepines. Experiments with animals show that all these drugs have similar effects on behavior. Collectively they are known as minor tranquilizers or antianxiety drugs, and their use in Western society is widespread and growing.

All of these drugs appear to relieve

anxiety, but there has been no understanding of how they work. Patients who take them say they are no longer beset with anxiety. With the help of the drugs, they are able to work, to sleep, and to go places they had feared to visit. But the effect of the drugs on the human body—especially on the nervous system—has been unknown. Any drug powerful enough to have such profound effects on emotions and behavior may also have other, unnoticed physiological effects that alter behavior in additional ways that neither the patient nor the doctor connects with the drug.

Because the problem seemed serious, we embarked on a series of studies to identify the precise effects of the drugs on the brain. We succeeded in isolating those effects, and in the process found that reliance on the drugs can have two serious consequences: When people lose their disabling anxieties they may also be losing their ability to cope with changes in their lives; what is more, the tranquilizers may make them likely to give up when faced with difficulties.

Alcohol and Amytal were the first an-

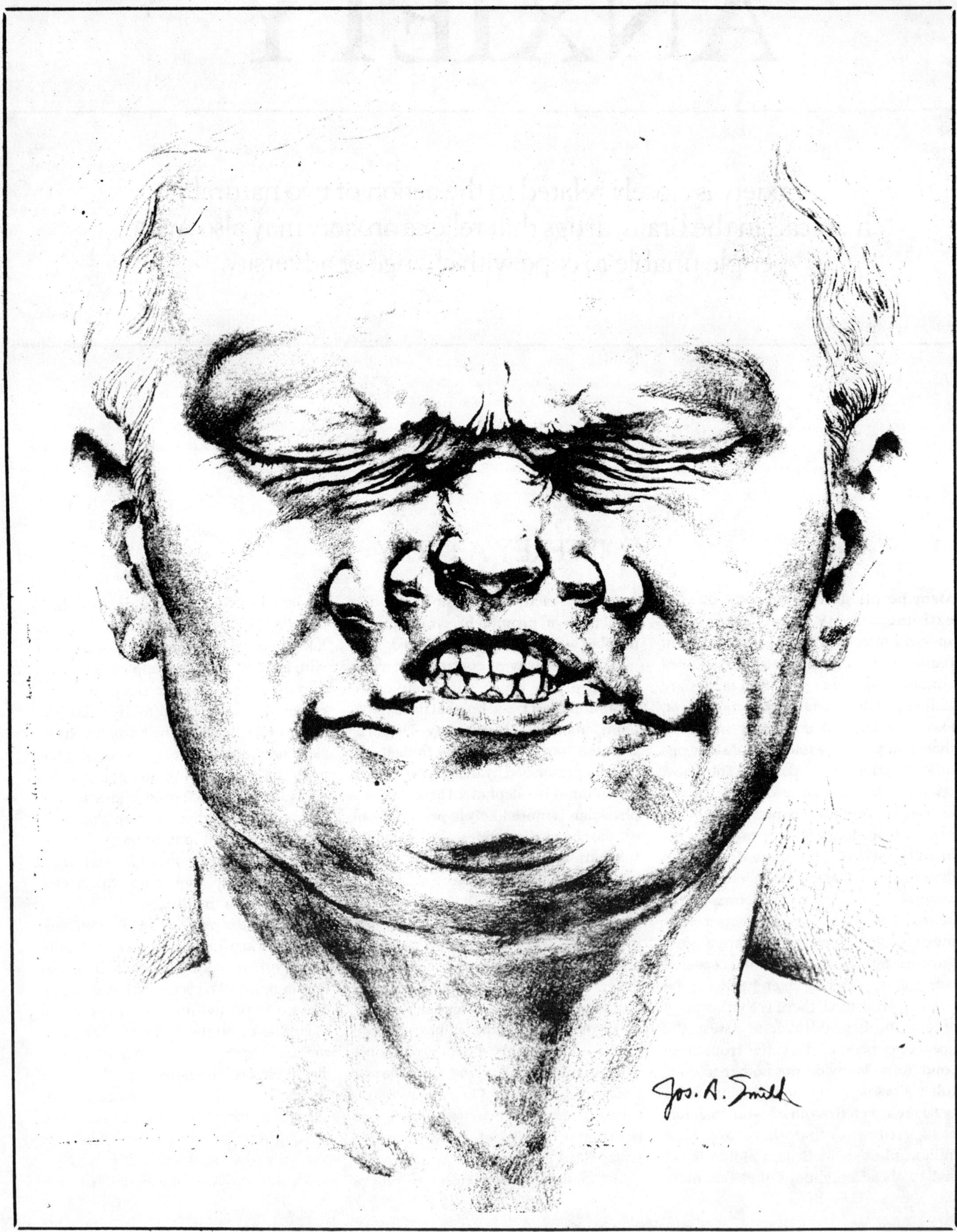
Jos. A. Smith

tianxiety drugs to come under laboratory scrutiny. In the late 1930s Neal Miller used the drugs with rats, and Jules Masserman used them with cats to study the psychological nature of anxiety. In the 1960s investigators began to look at drugs like Librium and Valium. By now there has been an enormous number of studies on the behavioral effects of all these drugs in a wide variety of species ranging from goldfish to chimpanzees. From these experiments it is clear that the behavioral effects of the antianxiety drugs are similar, no matter which drug is used or which species is studied. This similarity encourages the belief that, in the case of antianxiety drugs, it is possible to use studies of laboratory animals to predict the reactions of human beings. Since all species react similarly, it also suggests that the drugs act on a part of the brain that developed early in evolution. If so, anxiety is ancient and probably predates human beings.

Because these drugs are prescribed to lessen anxiety, they should make an animal less worried about danger. This prediction is easy to test. Suppose that we first train a rat to run down an alley for food and then begin to shock the animal each time it enters the box that contains its reward. When punished in this way, a sober animal soon learns to stop running to the box. But an animal injected with Amytal, Librium, or alcohol continues to go to the food despite the painful shock.

This phenomenon closely resembles the "Dutch courage" shown by soldiers who take a nip of whiskey before battle. Miller first reported Dutch courage in rats, and Masserman first reported it in cats; the experiments have since been repeated sufficiently often and in a sufficient variety of ways for it to be clear that Dutch courage is as universal a phenomenon in animals as it is in human beings. It is not absurd to suppose that animals experience an emotional state similar to human anxiety and that they respond in similar ways to treatment with antianxiety drugs.

Dutch courage is not due to a loss in the ability to feel pain, because drugged animals will flinch or jump at the same intensity of electric shock as sober ones. Nor do the drugs reduce aggressive behavior produced by painful sensations. If two rats are caged together and their feet are given painful shocks, they at once start fighting. Such fighting is not reduced — and may even be increased — by antianxiety drugs. It will of course surprise no one that alcohol does not reduce the aggressive response to a blow in the face, while it does reduce the fear of such a blow. But it is disturbing that this conclusion also applies to the other tranquilizers handed out so liberally by physicians. Margaret Lynch, Janet Lindsay, and Christopher Ounsted, working in a children's hospital in Oxford, have suggested that the recent spate of battered-baby cases may be due in part to this same pair of effects — reduced fear of the consequences of one's actions with no loss of aggression — in a parent chronically maintained on a drug like Librium or Valium.

The Dutch-courage experiment shows that it is difficult for an animal injected with an antianxiety drug to behave appropriately in anticipation of shock, but that behavior directly produced by shock (flinching, fighting) continues in the drugged animal. From this we might conclude that the antianxiety drugs dull the expectation of pain, but not pain itself. This is part of the truth, but not the whole of it. For if an animal can avoid a shock by doing something (running down the alley or jumping a barrier, for example), its behavior is unimpaired by the drugs. It is only when the avoidance of shock depends on *not* doing something (as in the Dutch-courage experiment) that the animal's behavior is altered by these drugs. Antianxiety drugs specifically prevent the animal from withholding an action that it has learned will bring pain. One might say the drugs make animals more impulsive.

This finding can in principle account for many of the effects of antianxiety drugs on human social behavior. As Miller remarked about alcohol, this drug "has a perplexing variety of effects, making some aggressive, others amorous, some tearful, and others talkative." If we suppose that after drinking alcohol or taking Librium or Amytal people behave in ways that were previously restrained by fear of the consequences, all these effects can be attributed to a single effect — the reduction of fear.

The experiments I have described so far have all depended on the use of painful stimuli, such as electric shocks. Yet it is comparatively rare for human fears to focus on impending pain (the dentist's chair is probably the most common exception to this rule). How, then, can we account for anxiety in the absence of threatened pain? Some fears, almost certainly, are innate and reflect ancient dangers to the survival of our species (the widespread fear of snakes is the most obvious example of this). But the majority require a more complex explanation, and one has emerged from research by Abram Amsel, who studied what happens when an animal fails to get an expected reward.

This situation arises when, after an animal has been rewarded with food or water for, say, pressing a lever, it presses the lever again and nothing happens. The effects of the omitted reward are clearly emotional. The animal becomes visibly disturbed (it may, for example, try to bite the experimenter or attack another animal) and shows in a variety of ways that it finds the experience of nonreward highly unpleasant. Animals that fail to get expected rewards and animals that have received painful shocks behave in very similar ways; for example, both become aggressive.

One effect of nonreward is that the animal eventually stops doing whatever once brought it the reward. But if the animal is first injected with one of the antianxiety drugs, it finds it much harder to give up this behavior (just as it finds it harder to give up punished behavior). In an experiment by Miller and his associates, rats were trained to run in an alley for a food reward. After this habit was well established, the food was removed from the goal box. Rats injected with Amytal and placed in the alley kept running to the empty goal box much longer than did undrugged rats. They acted, in other words, as though they found their failure to be rewarded less of a deterrent than do sober animals.

This kind of finding helps us understand why the antianxiety drugs have such pervasive and powerful effects on

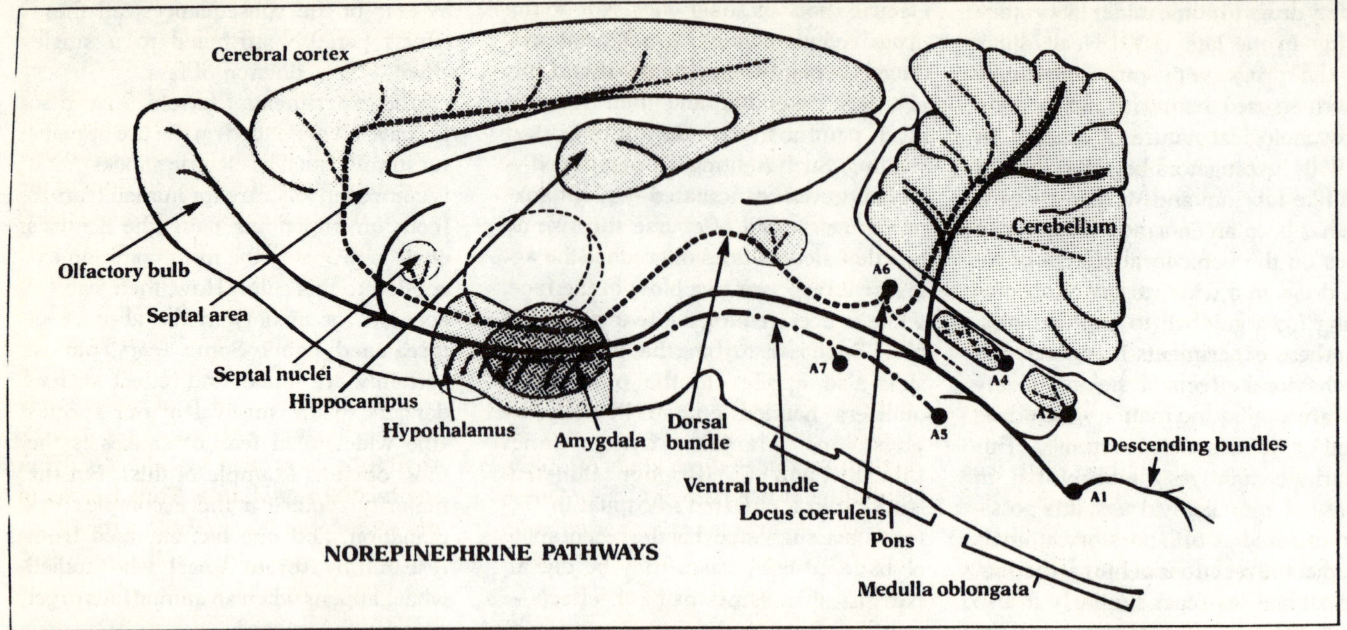

This map of a rat brain shows the long nerve fibers that transmit norepinephrine. The fibers extend from nerve cells clustered near the cerebellum (A1 through A7). Antianxiety drugs apparently interfere with the transmission of norepinephrine, which concentrates in the shaded areas, from neurons in the locus coeruleus (A6) to those in the hippocampus and septal areas.

human behavior. These drugs apparently do more than release behavior that is normally restrained by fear of pain; they also release behavior that is restrained by fear of failure, frustration, and disappointment. And there are few of us who do not harbor such fears, at least to some degree.

More complicated experiments show that, just as in the case of painful stimuli, antianxiety drugs do not lessen the impact of failure once the animal experiences it; instead, the drugged animal behaves as though it is less concerned by the possibility that it *might* fail to get a reward. As an illustration of this point, consider the way an animal behaves when a reward is unpredictable, sometimes present and sometimes absent. Rats trained to run down an alley for food that is only sometimes in the goal box come to run faster than rats trained to expect a reward at the end of every trip. Amsel has shown that the extra speed shown by rats that cannot depend on their reward reflects the increased emotional excitement that is generated by the possibility of disappointment. Notice that the rats run faster *before* they reach the goal box and discover whether they have been rewarded. As shown both in our laboratory and by

other researchers, antianxiety drugs block this effect of anticipated nonreward. Under the influence of Amytal or Librium, rats rewarded intermittently run no faster than rats that are always rewarded. They "keep their cool" when faced with possible failure.

But let us now change the experimental situation slightly by adding a second alley to the first and rewarding the rats in both goal boxes, giving them unpredictable rewards in the first alley and continual rewards in the second. Amsel and Jacqueline Roussel have shown that, in such a double runway, rats run faster in the second alley after they have found the first goal box empty than after they have found food there. This again reflects the emotional excitement generated by nonreward; but now the rats run faster *after* they have experienced failure. Under these conditions, rats injected with antianxiety drugs run just as fast as undrugged rats. Evidently these agents dampen the emotional excitement generated by the threat of failure, but not the excitement generated by failure itself. One might expect the antianxiety drugs to help a student during the period between taking an exam and hearing the results, but not necessarily to help him come to terms with a failing

mark.

The behavioral effects of the antianxiety drugs, as we have considered them so far, seem therapeutic. Under certain circumstances it could be valuable to care less about the threat of punishment or the possibility of failure. But our picture of these drugs would be incomplete if we omitted two negative features of their action.

The first of these is that the antianxiety drugs lessen an animal's ability to notice change in its environment and to respond to new events. Brendan McGonigle, for example, trained rats to discriminate between black and white doors, rewarding them with food when they ran through the right door. He then changed the pattern on the doors so the rats could solve the problem either by continuing to use the black-white cue or by using a new cue—horizontal or vertical stripes. Finally, he removed the black-white cue and left only the stripes. Drugged rats learned the original black-white discrimination just as well as sober ones, but they failed to notice the significance of the added stripes; in the final stage of the experiment, their performance broke down. This failure to notice significant changes in one's environment may be a factor in the increased likelihood of accidents that occurs after taking antianxiety drugs. Traffic accidents under the influence of alcohol are the most dramatic example of this.

The second negative aspect of the antianxiety drugs is that they prevent animals from learning to persist when faced with an adverse and unpredictable environment. If we train two groups of rats to run in an alley, giving one group rewards part of the time and the other rewards at the end of every run, and then stop the rewards altogether, the two groups behave differently. Although both groups eventually stop running to the empty goal box, the group that was rewarded only part of the time keeps running to the empty box much longer than the group that had learned to expect food on every trip. As argued by Amsel, this persistence results from the rats' development of tolerance for frustration. Robert Brown and Alan Wagner have shown that this tolerance for frustration even applies to electric shock: Rats trained with partial rewards and then shocked for entering the goal box continue to enter the box long after rats trained always to expect rewards have given up. The converse is also true. An animal that receives gradually increasing intensities of shock together with rewards will develop a tolerance for electric shock. If such rats are then put back in the alley and neither shocked nor rewarded, they continue running to the empty goal box longer than rats that were never shocked. It is probable that this persistence in the face of nonreward or shock is but one aspect of a general tolerance for stress that results when an animal is repeatedly exposed to unpleasant or painful events, a process Miller has called "toughening up."

But Joram Feldon and I have shown that this persistence never develops if the rats are trained with partial reward while under the influence of Amytal or Librium. And Nicola Davis and I have shown that Librium can block the development of tolerance for electric shock. Thus the antianxiety drugs prevent animals from "toughening up," from learning to persist in the face of adversity. There is clearly a moral here that every physician should bear in mind. The best way to help a failing marriage, for example, might not be to drug the partners, but to let them adapt to each other.

The various behavioral effects of the drugs I have described fit together nicely if the animal has what I have proposed as a "behavioral inhibition system." According to my hypothesis, activity in this system underlies the emotion of anxiety and is counteracted by the antianxiety drugs. The system is activated by three kinds of input: signals of impending punishment, signals of impending nonreward, and novel events. And the system produces three kinds of output: inhibition of behavior (as in the Dutch-courage experiment), increased emotional excitement or "arousal," and increased attention to novel events.

The behavioral inhibition system serves the animal by suppressing behavior that has become maladaptive while the animal scans its environment for new ways to meet an immediate challenge. But under conditions in which there is no better alternative than the old behavior, the behavioral inhibition system develops the animal's necessary added persistence.

If the behavioral inhibition system exists, it must be in the brain. A first clue to *where* in the brain comes from cases of brain damage (lesions) that result in behavior similar to that caused by antianxiety drugs. If the drugs act by impairing the function of a particular brain region, then destruction of that region should produce effects on behavior similar to those produced by these drugs. Two brain structures seem likely sites for the action of antianxiety drugs: the septal area and the hippocampus. We have recently completed a review of the numerous reports of the behavioral effects of lesions in these areas. Two key findings emerge. First, in the great majority of cases, lesions in both areas have strikingly similar effects; second, whenever the effects of the lesions do resemble each other, the direction of the behavioral change produced by the lesions is the same as that produced by the antianxiety drugs.

Faced with this pattern of data, the first question to ask is: Why do the behavioral effects of the two lesions resemble each other so closely? There is a ready answer. The septal area and the hippocampus are closely interrelated, both anatomically and physiologically. Cells in the medial septal area send their fibers to the hippocampus; conversely, one of the major direct projections of the hippocampus is to the lateral septal area. The hippocampus normally emits a pattern of high-voltage, rhythmic, slow brain waves ranging from about 4 to 12 cycles per second (hertz) known as the hippocampal theta rhythm. The function of this rhythm is a matter of considerable dispute, but it is well established that the rhythm is controlled by cells located in the medial septal area. Thus lesions in the septal area destroy both a major input to the hippocampus and a major output from it, as well as radically altering hippocampal electrical activity by permanently abolishing the theta rhythm.

It is natural to suppose, therefore, that the septal area and the hippocampus form part of a single functional "septohippocampal system." In 1970 I proposed that the antianxiety drugs alter behavior by acting on this system, and in particular, that they in some way impair septal control of the hippocampal theta rhythm.

A more precise hypothesis arose out of some simple experiments in which Gordon Ball and I recorded hippocampal electrical activity in an undrugged rat's brain while the animal, which was free-moving but connected to the recording apparatus by cable, ran in an alley for a water reward. We found that the rat displayed a theta rhythm throughout the experiment, but that the frequency of the hippocampal waves varied according to what it was doing or what was happening to it. When the animal drank, it produced low frequencies of theta (below about 7 hertz). When it was running down the alley toward the goal box, the animal produced high theta frequencies (above about 8.5 hertz). When the rat discovered an empty goal box, the omission of reward produced an intermediate frequency that, in a group of rats, averaged 7.7 hertz. This same frequency appeared when the rat explored a new environment.

Because of these findings, we had to give up the hypothesis that the antianx-

1. PERSPECTIVES

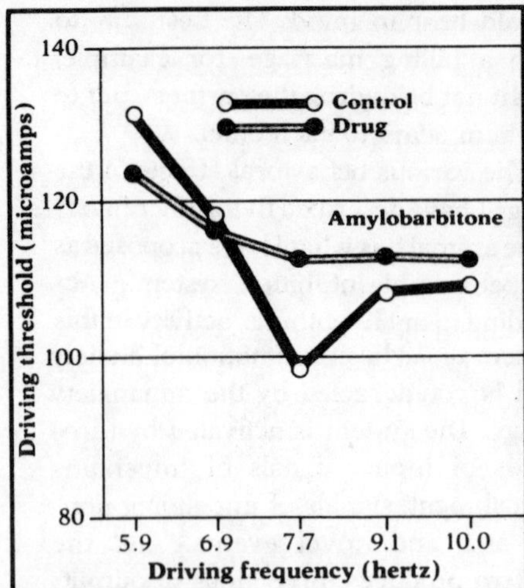

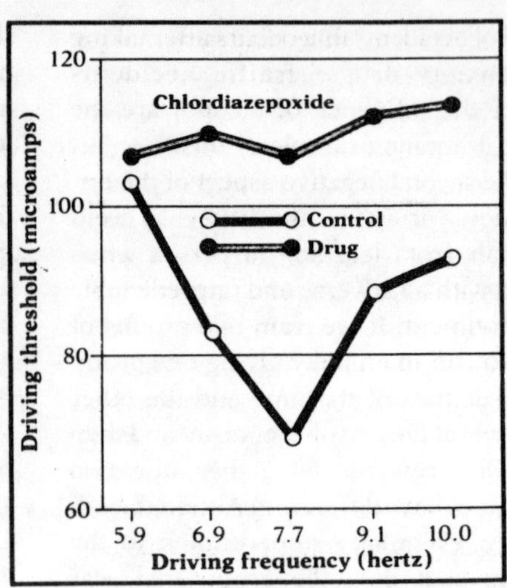

iety drugs impair general septal control of hippocampal theta. For if they did, the drugs would impair an animal's ability to approach a reward or to consume food or water, and they do not. Both running toward a water reward and drinking the water are accompanied by theta rhythm, the former at high frequencies, the latter at low. Our hypothesis necessarily became that antianxiety drugs impair septal control of hippocampal theta only in a small frequency band centered on 7.7 hertz (the frequency we had observed in response to nonreward and novelty, which we knew were affected by the drugs).

To test this prediction, we implanted a stimulating electrode in the medial septal area of each rat and a recording electrode in its hippocampus. We could now "drive" their hippocampal theta rhythm artificially, imposing any frequency we liked on the rhythm by delivering short pulses of electricity to the septal area. When we plotted the threshold current required to drive the theta rhythm in this way as a function of stimulation frequency, we obtained a characteristic curve—the theta-driving curve—that has a minimum threshold at exactly 7.7 hertz. Every one of a range of antianxiety drugs we have tested eliminates this minimum in the theta-driving curve by selectively increasing the threshold at 7.7 hertz. This result is a striking confirmation of our prediction.

Further confirmation that the theta rhythm at 7.7 hertz is related to anxiety came from experiments in which we drove this rhythm by electrical stimulation of the septal area and changed the rat's behavior in ways exactly opposite to the changes produced by the antianxiety drugs. (Perhaps we have discovered a way of making animals more anxious.)

Given these findings, we wondered how the antianxiety drugs perform this

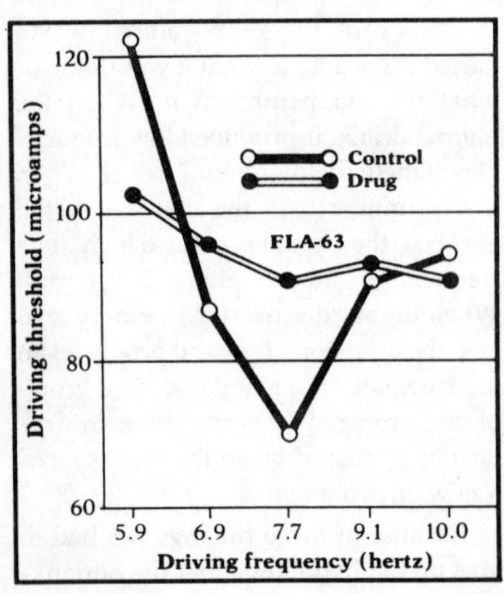

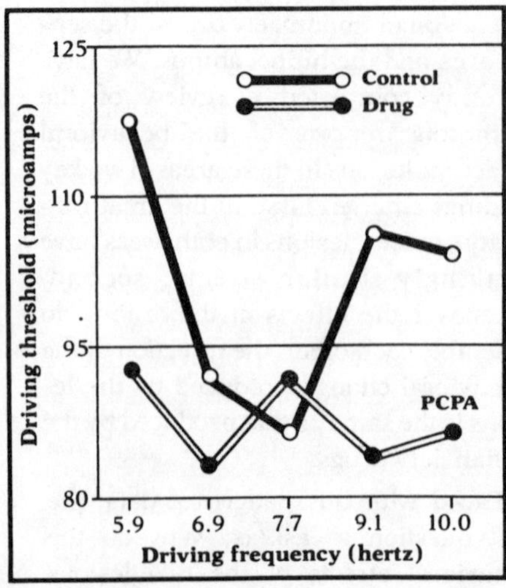

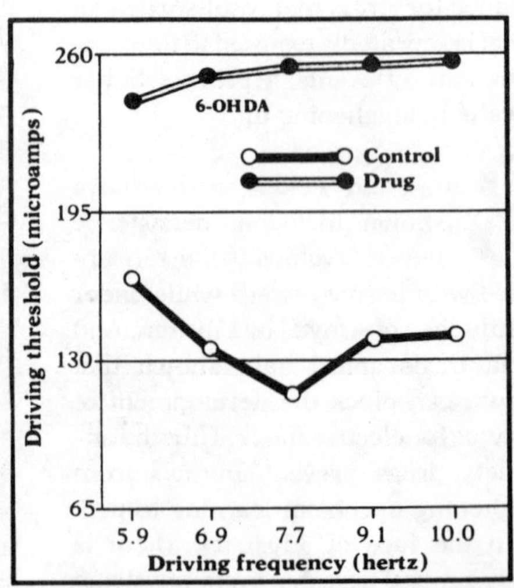

peculiar trick of selectively increasing the threshold at 7.7 hertz. In an effort to throw more light on this question, Neil McNaughton, David James, and I tried to mimic the effect of the antianxiety drugs on the theta-driving curve by using drugs with better-understood effects on chemicals in the brain.

The brain consists of millions of discrete elements (nerve cells, or neurons) connected in incredibly complex patterns. The small gap between neurons, which is their point of connection, is known as the synapse. Transmission of messages across the synapse is accomplished by a chemical (a neurotransmitter) that, when released by one neuron, triggers electrochemical activity in the next. A number of different chemicals are thought to perform this function in different parts of the brain. Pharmacologists have succeeded in synthesizing a number of drugs that can affect the action of neurotransmitters, and using some of them we investigated the possible role of neurotransmitters in the action of the antianxiety drugs.

Two of these neurotransmitters belong to a chemical family known as the monoamines: norepinephrine and serotonin. When we blocked the brain's synthesis of norepinephrine, the theta-driving curve showed a rise in the threshold at 7.7 hertz; this is precisely what happens when an animal takes antianxiety drugs. Blocking the synthesis of serotonin produced a mirror image of this effect. It lowered thresholds at every frequency except 7.7 hertz. Thus the normal shape of the theta-driving curve depends on the joint functioning of neural systems that use norepinephrine and serotonin to transmit messages across the synapse.

These results clearly pointed to a neural input using norepinephrine as its neurotransmitter to the hippocampus, the septal area, or both as the place where antianxiety drugs act on the brain. Such an input was not hard to find, for it had been described a decade before by a group of Swedish neuroanatomists using a technique known as fluorescence histochemistry. This process causes nerve fibers that contain norepinephrine to fluoresce brightly under the microscope. When they mapped a rat's

brain with this technique, they found a particular cluster of cell bodies, called the locus coeruleus, in the lower part of the brain. The cluster gives off long norepinephrine-containing fibers that travel to both the hippocampus and the septal area, as well as to other parts of the brain. These fibers ascend the brain in the dorsal noradrenergic bundle. This bundle of fibers, then, seemed the most likely site of the antianxiety drugs' action on the theta-driving curve.

To test this assumption Peter Kelly, Neil McNaughton, and I used a poison, 6-hydroxydopamine, that affects only fibers containing norepinephrine. By injecting this poison into the dorsal noradrenergic bundle, we destroyed this fiber tract with minimal damage to other neural systems. The lesion we created reduced the amount of hippocampal norepinephrine to only 3 percent of its normal level. If our hypothesis was right, it should also have removed the 7.7 hertz minimum from the theta-driving curve, as do the antianxiety drugs. This is what we found.

If these electrophysiological observations have anything to do with the behavioral effects of the antianxiety drugs, then our destruction of the dorsal noradrenergic bundle should also have changed behavior in the same manner as the drugs did. Animals whose brains have been so injured should not learn to persist in the face of adversity. Trained to run in the alley for food but rewarded only part of the time, they should stop running to the goal box soon after all rewards are withdrawn. When Susan Owen, Michael Boarder, Marianne Fillenz, and I tested rats under these conditions, the results were clear-cut. The rats did not persist but gave up as soon as did undamaged rats that had been rewarded each time they ran in the alley. In other experiments, we investigated reactions to novelty in the lesioned animals. These too were abolished, as they are by the antianxiety drugs.

These data point to the dorsal noradrenergic bundle, and particularly to its connections with the septo-hippocampal system, as the place where antianxiety drugs have an important effect. Looking at the results of other research strengthens our conclusions. Kjell

Fuxe's group in Sweden has shown that stress increases activity in neurons containing norepinephrine that are found in the higher parts of the brain, and that all major antianxiety drugs can eliminate this increased activity. Jay Weiss has demonstrated that levels of norepinephrine drop in the brains of rats exposed to intense shock or cold, as though the neural systems concerned are unable to keep up with the demands made on them. As repeated exposure leads animals to develop tolerance for these stresses, the levels of norepinephrine rise. Weiss has shown that Miller's toughening-up process, which follows repeated exposure to unpleasant events, is the result of an increased capacity in the animal's brain to synthesize norepinephrine so that it is better able to cope with excessive demand for the neurotransmitter.

Systems that use norepinephrine, then, are involved in the way the animal responds to a variety of stressful events (nonreward, novelty, shock, cold). But there is also evidence that suggests an important role for systems that use serotonin as the neurotransmitter. The pathways in the brain that carry serotonin follow much the same course as those that carry norepinephrine, and they too connect extensively with the septal area and the hippocampus. As we have seen, the normal shape of the theta-driving curve depends on the joint functioning of neurons that contain the two neurotransmitters. Fuxe's group has shown that stress increases the activity of neurons that contain serotonin and that this increase is counteracted by the antianxiety drugs—exactly the same pattern reported by his group for neurons that contain norepinephrine. Finally, Larry Stein in Philadelphia, as well as Nicholas Tye and Susan Iversen in Cambridge, England, have presented evidence implicating serotonin in animals' responses to punishment and in the behavioral effects of Valium and Librium. It seems likely that anxiety involves increased activity among neurons in the higher parts of the brain that contain both neurotransmitters, and that the connections of these kinds of neurons with the septo-hippocampal system play a particularly important role.

1. PERSPECTIVES

This excursion into the neuropsychology of anxiety in rats can give us important insights into the understanding of anxiety in human beings. The first concerns the connection between anxiety and depression. The two states are so close that psychiatrists often have great difficulty distinguishing between them. If we ask what gives rise to depression, we find an interesting answer: loss (of a loved one, a job, status, and so on). "Loss" may easily be translated into "removal of an accustomed source of reward," and this, as we have seen, acts on behavior much as punishment does and probably by means of the same physiological mechanisms. Thus it is possible that anxiety and depression are merely different names for the same fundamental state. The terms simply distinguish between the circumstances that have precipitated it: events associated with danger in the case of anxiety, events associated with the loss of reward in the case of depression. This inference is strengthened by the fact that the monoamines (norepinephrine and serotonin) have been implicated in depression as well as in anxiety.

Our increased understanding of anxiety may also help us to discover why certain people are particularly likely to display this emotion. It is known that individuals who suffer from phobias, anxiety states, reactive depression, etc., do not constitute a random sample of the population, but have enduring personality traits that both precede and outlast their illness. In the light of the experiments described in this article, I suggest that their predisposition toward anxiety and depression may consist in a high sensitivity to threats of danger or loss.

Finally, we have gained some insight into the costs and benefits of the antianxiety drugs themselves. These agents are valuable because they can reduce the emotional and behavioral effects of anticipated punishment, failure, frustration, and disappointment. But their value demands a price. Part of this price lies in the very therapeutic effects for which we value these drugs. A person who fails to give up behavior that is repeatedly punished may be courageous or inflexible, depending on the circumstances and on one's value judgments. But two other effects of the antianxiety drugs are more obviously harmful. They reduce a person's capacity to react to changes in the environment; and, what is most important, they keep a person from developing persistence in the face of unpredictable adversity. Since unpredictable adversity is one of the most predictable ingredients of life, this effect may make the price of the antianxiety drugs too high.

Medical Treatment Of Mental Illness

Pharmacotherapies revolutionize psychiatric care and present scientific and ethical challenges to scoeity.

Philip A. Berger

The author is an assistant professor in the Department of Psychiatry and Behavioral Sciences, Stanford University School of Medicine, Stanford, California 94305, and director of the Stanford Psychiatric Clinical Research Center, Palo Alto Veterans Administration Hospital, Palo Alto, California 94304.

Summary. Psychotherapeutic drugs have dramatically improved the prognosis for patients with severe mental illness. The drug treatments are not a panacea. The medications sometimes cause irreversible side effects, and they are not helpful for all patients. They allow large numbers of individuals to leave the hospital, but to return to communities that are often poorly prepared to provide continuing care. Despite their limitations, psychotherapeutic drugs relieve a great deal of human suffering. They also involve psychiatry in modern biological science. This has led to the continuing search for more effective medications based on the study of possible biochemical substrates of psychiatric disorders.

Effective pharmacological treatments for mental illness have existed only during the last quarter-century. This period has also witnessed a revolution in the care of patients with psychiatric disorders, and the number of patients in state and county mental hospitals has sharply declined. The introduction and evaluation of drug treatments required the development of more accurate methods of classification and of assessment of severity, and better criteria of improvement in mental patients. These more accurate methods could then be applied to nondrug treatments that were introduced in the optimistic period that followed the first successful drug trials. The resulting combination of drug therapy and psychological or socioenvironmental treatment is responsible for the vastly improved prognosis for patients with mental illness today (*1*).

Psychotherapeutic drugs have also helped wed some aspects of psychiatry with biological science, a source of significant therapeutic advances in the other medical specialities. Biological psychiatrists attempting to explain pharmacotherapies have also begun to investigate possible biochemical causes of mental illness.

The use of drug treatments for mental illness is not all positive: problems have arisen for patients, physicians, and society. The drugs are not ideal. Not all patients are helped, and many are only partially improved. Like other useful medications, the pharmacological agents used in mental illness can cause severe adverse reactions; some of these side effects are irreversible. Certain classes of drugs for psychiatric patients are toxic when taken in an overdose and thus can be used in suicide attempts. The use of psychotherapeutic drugs poses ethical questions for physicians and society. The symptoms of some mental disorders make it difficult for patients to understand their pharmacological treatments, and therefore they cannot base their decision on whether to take medications on a true understanding of the potential benefits and risks. Whether involuntary treatment of psychiatric patients is ever justified is the appropriate subject of vigorous debate. The factors that must be weighed include the patients' rights, the duties and responsibilities that a physician feels towards the patients, and the right of society to be protected from dangerous behaviors (*1*).

In this article I will discuss some of the practical, scientific, and ethical aspects of the medical treatment of mental illness. A description of the predrug era is followed by a discussion of the impact of recent therapeutic innovations. Three major psychiatric disorders are described: schizophrenia, depression, and mania. The important current drug treatments for these disorders are the antipsychotics for schizophrenia, tricyclic antidepressants or monoamine oxidase inhibitors for depression, and lithium salts for mania. Evidence for their efficacy, practical aspects of treatment, and critical evaluations of their hypothesized biochemical mechanisms of action are described. Finally, the ethical problems created by the drug treatments of mental disorders are outlined.

1. PERSPECTIVES

The Revolution in Psychiatric Care

Firsthand descriptions by physicians who worked with the mentally ill before the introduction of effective pharmacotherapies paint a dismal picture of the predrug era. There were few outpatient psychiatric clinics, and general medical hospitals rarely admitted patients with severe mental illness. Most patients were sent quickly to state mental hospitals, which were more like custodial facilities than medical treatment centers. Pessimism about psychiatric disorders was widespread, admissions increased, and discharges remained low.

Living areas in public mental hospitals were poorly furnished and crowded. Hallucinating patients paced the floor, or rocked in chairs, and talked to their "voices"; paranoid patients scanned the rooms, ever vigilant and ever fearful. Catatonic patients remained in fixed positions for days at a time, developing swollen limbs and pressure sores; withdrawn patients sat on wooden benches, year after year, doing nothing, while their physical health deteriorated. Manic patients joked, laughed, and moved about rapidly for days at a time until they collapsed, exhausted. Violent or agitated patients attacked other patients or staff members in response to idiosyncratic beliefs. Such patients were often kept in nearly empty "seclusion rooms," strapped to beds that were bolted to the floor or placed in warm baths or wrapped in wet sheets in an attempt to calm them (1, 2).

The physicians responsible for the treatment of patients in public mental hospitals were poorly equipped for the task. Before World War II, many of these physicians were trained in general medicine or neurology; during the postwar period some had also studied psychoanalytic psychotherapy. However, neither neurological diagnosis nor psychoanalysis had much to offer patients in public mental institutions. Thus, physicians acted mainly as custodians and administrators. Many of the people who worked in public mental hospitals were courageous and caring, but they faced an impossible task, not only because of the social stigma of mental illness, public apathy, and lack of adequate funds for patient facilities and staff, but also because there simply were few effective treatments for severe psychiatric disease (1, 2).

A dramatic change in the treatment of patients with mental illness began in the 1950's. For nearly 100 years, the number of patients in public mental institutions in the United States had increased by about 2 percent per year, reaching a peak of 559,000 in 1955 (Fig. 1) (3). Then in 1956, for the first time in history, more of these patients were discharged than admitted, a trend that continues despite a steady increase in both the admission rate and the national population. Today there are less than 200,000 patients in these institutions (3, 4). However, not even the majority of the individuals who leave public mental hospitals are free of psychiatric symptoms, and many continue to receive treatment in transitional facilities or outpatient clinics. Still, most are able to reestablish family relationships, find employment, and participate in community life (1, 4).

Conditions have also improved for patients in the hospitals. Very few patients require seclusion rooms and physical restraints; those who do usually respond rapidly to treatment. Most hospital wards are unlocked. Many are set up as "therapeutic communities," where patients and staff meet regularly to discuss all aspects of life in the hospital. Patients are treated with respect and encouraged to determine many of the conditions of their hospitalization. Increased patient government improves the hospital environment and also helps patients in the transition from hospitalization to home by making the hospital more like a family or a community. Other improvements in modern mental hospitals increase the similarities between the hospital and the rest of society. Plays, concerts, movies, sports equipment, and arts and crafts are available to most patients. Some psychiatric hospitals have small companies that contract to do piecework for local industries, so that patients can be economically productive even during their hospital stay (1).

These dramatic changes in the treatment of psychiatric patients are the result of many interrelated factors. Much of the momentum, however, came from the development and use of psychotherapeutic drugs. Use of these drugs led to a climate that favored innovation and encouraged the development and evaluation of other new therapeutic approaches. As with all important social changes, there have been some negative results from the discharge of large numbers of patients from public mental hospitals. In some areas, planning was inadequate for the return of psychiatric patients to the community (4, 5). Reich (6) reports that

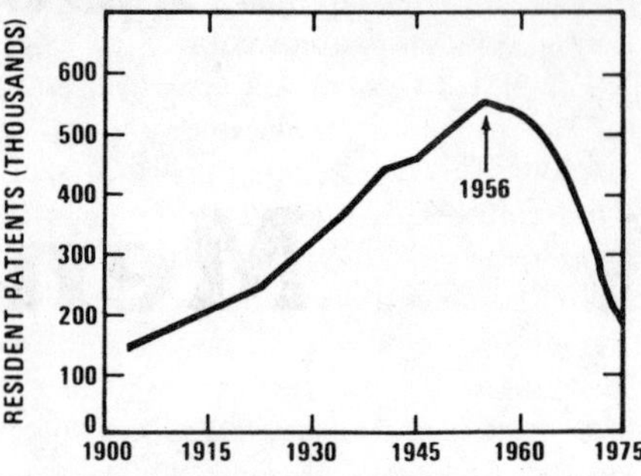

Fig. 1. Patient population in public mental institutions, 1900 through 1975 (3).

many patients discharged from New York State mental hospitals are living in cheap hotels, where they are robbed and abused by people who take advantage of their relative helplessness. Arnhoff (7) suggests that the impact of community treatment on the families of mental patients has not been carefully studied. He finds no convincing evidence that home or community treatment is better than hospital treatment in either its short- or its long-term effects (7).

The location of psychiatric treatment is certainly less important than its quality. While much remains to be done, it is clear that the quality of treatment for patients with severe mental illness has vastly improved since the introduction of psychotherapeutic drugs.

Schizophrenia

The schizophrenic syndrome usually begins in young adulthood. Symptoms include altered motor behavior, perceptual distortions, disturbed thinking, altered mood, and unusual interpersonal behavior. Occasionally, a schizophrenic syndrome appears suddenly; more commonly the symptoms have an insidious onset. In many cases the patient has a history of being somewhat withdrawn and introverted since childhood. In the prodromal phase of schizophrenia, commonplace reality may begin to seem strange. Patients often withdraw into themselves to focus on internal experiences. Commonly they feel depersonalized, as if their identity were being dissolved or lost. Those close to these individuals often have increasing difficulty empathizing with and understanding their unusual feelings, thoughts, and experiences. Normal diurnal rhythms of sleep, appetite, and sexual interest may be disrupted. Gradually, full-blown schizophrenic syndromes develop. Although symptoms vary from patient to patient, they usually make normal functioning difficult or impossible.

The motor behavior of schizophrenics ranges from total immobilization, called catatonia, to frenetic and purposeless activity often accompanied by peculiar mannerisms. Perceptual distortions include hallucinations, which can arise in any sensory modality, although auditory hallucinations ("hearing voices") are the most common. Frequently, the voices are threatening or obscene and may instruct the patient to perform specific acts. Sometimes patients hear their own thoughts out loud. Disturbances in thinking in schizophrenic patients lead to distorted concept formation, bizarre speech, and illogical thought patterns. The illogical thought patterns are often expressed as delusions, ideas that are false or improbable but that cannot be modified by persuasion or contradictory evidence. Common paranoid delusions lead schizophrenic patients to believe that they have been chosen for special missions or that they are the object of persecution by a group with complex plots against them. Some schizophrenics have the delusions that unseen forces are controlling their thoughts or behavior or "reading their minds." Delusions are reinforced by misinterpretations of reality. Thus schizophrenics often believe that items on television or in newspapers are cryptic messages confirming their beliefs.

Schizophrenic patients also have disorders of the thought process. This causes the speech pattern to wander and fail to lead to its apparent goal, a process called looseness of associations. Expressions of emotion in schizophrenic patients are often absent, blunted, or inappropriate to the content of the conversation. Sometimes schizophrenics are overwhelmed with intense anxiety or deep rage, unrelated to any obvious environmental stimuli.

In schizophrenic patients these profound disturbances in motor behavior, perceptions, thinking, and mood cause severe difficulties in everyday tasks and interpersonal relationships. Patients often behave in an impulsive, disorganized, or unusual manner. Schizophrenic patients are rarely dangerous, but they are unpredictable and may occasionally act violently if directed by "a voice," if they feel they must defend themselves against an imaginary enemy, or if they are overactive and severely disorganized (*1, 8*).

What is the incidence of schizophrenia? At present about 180,000 patients are hospitalized in the United States with the diagnosis of schizophrenia; another 800,000 are being treated as outpatients or have active symptoms but are not being treated. The number of individuals who develop schizophrenic symptoms each year is approximately 150 per 100,000. The chances that a person will be treated for schizophrenia in his lifetime have been estimated to be about 1 percent. About half of the available beds for the mentally ill and the mentally retarded, or about one-quarter of all available beds in hospitals, are occupied by patients with the diagnosis of schizophrenia. Despite the widely held belief that schizophrenia is more common in complex modern societies, the incidence of schizophrenia has been re' tively constant for the last 100 years in the United States. In addition, preliminary results of recent international collaborative studies show a similar incidence in all nations that have been studied (*9*).

Depression

The term depression is used to describe both a normal mood and a serious mental disorder. As a normal mood, depression refers to the transitory feelings of sadness, grief, disappointment, loneliness, or discouragement that everyone feels during the difficult times of life. As a mental disorder, depression is an illness with many symptoms, only one of which is sadness. Those with depression have changes in mood, thinking patterns, motor activity, and behavior. They also have somatic or physical symptoms and frequently have suicidal ideas that can lead to self-destructive behavior.

The mood of depressed individuals is variable but includes profound sadness and often a loss of the ability to feel pleasure. The ideas, activities, and relationships that usually bring pleasure can seem empty or hollow. The changes in thinking patterns lead to pessimism about the future and low self-esteem. Depressed people often deny their past accomplishments or feel unworthy of current achievements. Feelings of low self-esteem or worthlessness combine with pessimism to rob them of their motivation, making it difficult to maintain either jobs or interpersonal relationships. Often they feel guilty about not living up to the expectations of others. Guilt can be even more generalized, so that some depressed people may feel they have committed a sin or a crime and fear discovery or think they deserve punishment. Some severely depressed patients develop psychosis. A psychotic patient distorts or perceives reality incorrectly. This can lead to unusual beliefs or behaviors. For example, some depressed patients may feel they have actually become hollow inside, that their internal organs have "turned to dust." To give another example, a psychotically depressed individual may blame himself for a tragic world event such as a war or a flood. Many depressed people are fearful or anxious. They may be agitated and quite physically active but unable to concentrate on any task; or they may move very slowly, feel extremely weak, tired, and helpless, and have slow and labored thoughts that make it difficult to concentrate, to read, or even to form sentences for conversation.

Physical symptoms are often a prominent part of the depression syndrome. Those with severe depression often have no appetite and lose weight. Sleep disturbance is another common symptom, causing insomnia, restless nights, and early morning awakening. In severe depression a patient often wakes at 3 or 4 a.m. and is unable to get back to sleep. Some depressed patients also experience constipation, dry mouth, tight feelings in the chest, and aches and pains, particularly headaches and backaches. Many depressed people lose interest in sexual activity, and depressed women often have changes in their menstrual cycle.

Thoughts of death and suicide are the most dangerous symptom of severe depression. The hopelessness, guilt feelings, and low self-esteem can all contribute to suicidal thinking. Some patients see suicide as an escape from their psychic pain. Others feel there is no reason to go on living since things will never get better. Some believe that their death would relieve their family of the burden of caring for them; others feel that death is the appropriate punishment for their imagined sin or crime. Whatever the cognitive origin, suicide must be considered a possibility in anyone with depression.

Most depressed patients do not have a history of any other psychiatric illness. About one-fifth of depressed patients have episodes of both depression and mania and are called bipolar patients. Unipolar patients are those who suffer only recurrent depressive episodes. This distinction between bipolar and unipolar depression is increasingly important in both research and pharmacotherapy (*9*).

1. PERSPECTIVES

Mania

Mania is a severe emotional disorder that superficially appears to be the opposite of depression. Symptoms can be divided into changes in mood, thought, motor activity, and behavior. The mood is elated—sometimes euphoric, overconfident, or carefree. A manic individual is optimistic and may feel attractive, desirable, efficient, and alert. However, this mood often is brittle, and these individuals become irritable if frustrated. The thought patterns of manics are disturbed, with one thought rapidly following another in what is called flight of ideas. Ideas of potency, knowledge, and special abilities occur in severe mania. The motor activity of manics is also accelerated; they are restless and may work energetically, but may move from project to project, unable to complete any. Manic individuals may sleep little and eat less; like patients with severe depression, they tend to lose weight. Mild forms of mania, called hypomania, may serve a person well, since our society is more appreciative of, and even selects for success, people with some manic traits in preference to more depressive or contemplative individuals. In contrast, severe mania causes significant life disruptions and can be devastating to personal relationships and careers.

Some bipolar patients alternate between depression and mania. However, many have long periods of normal functioning in between episodes. In general, manic episodes are more common when bipolar patients are younger, while depression is more frequent with age. The duration of the episodes of bipolar illness varies. One common pattern is for depressive episodes to last about 6 months and manic episodes about 3 months. However, a few patients have been known to cycle from mania to depression in periods as short as 24 hours, while others have manic and depressed episodes that seem to last for years (10).

How common are depression and mania? The major problem in determining the incidence is the lack of a universal definition of depression or mania. The incidence of bipolar illness is about 300 per 100,000 or 0.3 percent. Perhaps 600,000 bipolar patients are identified and treated each year in the United States. The number of patients with severe unipolar depression is certainly much larger. According to the National Institute of Mental Health (NIMH) and other sources, some 1.5 million people are being treated for depression today. But perhaps three or even five times that number may actually need such treatment. Thus, there may be from 4.5 to 7.5 million individuals in the United States who are suffering the psychic pain, life disruptions, and risk of suicide associated with depression and who could benefit from treatment. The results from an NIMH and a British study suggest that perhaps as many as 15 percent of the population will have at least one depressive episode during their lifetime. There are at least 26,000 reported deaths by suicide each year, making it the tenth leading cause of death. Thus, depression and suicide are major public health concerns that require vigorous medical treatment (10, 11).

Antipsychotic Medications

The drug treatments of schizophrenia include substances from at least eight different chemical classes. The drugs are remarkable in their ability to counteract hallucinations, delusional thinking, assaultiveness, severe excitement or withdrawal, and unusual behavior and to facilitate the social adjustment of schizophrenic patients. Unfortunately, they are not effective in all patients and are only partially effective in others. They can also have troublesome and sometimes irreversible side effects (12).

Several important questions can be asked about the antipsychotics: Are they effective when compared to a placebo? Are they useful as maintenance treatments to prevent a return of schizophrenic symptoms? Do they produce serious or irreversible side effects? How do they work; what is the biochemical mechanism of their action on the brain?

The efficacy of the antipsychotic drugs in the treatment of schizophrenia has been established in numerous clinical trials. The drugs are effective in all subtypes of schizophrenia, at all stages of the illness, at all ages, and in every country where they have been studied (12). In the studies that established this efficacy the quantitative, double-blind, controlled research method was used. In this design, symptoms are quantitated by having one or more psychiatrists rate a patient's symptoms on standardized rating scales after a daily interview. The studies are double-blind in that both the investigator and the patient are unaware of what the patient is receiving, and they are controlled because one or more

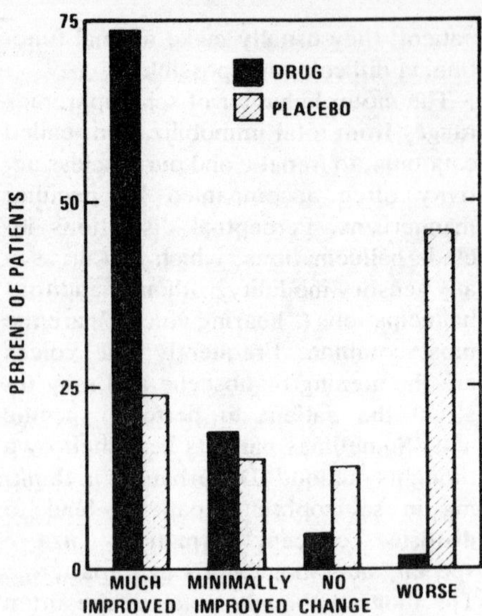

Fig. 2. Physicians' global ratings of patients' responses to treatment with antipsychotics or placebo (13).

drugs are compared to a medically inert placebo or to a drug with known efficacy.

Figure 2 summarizes some of the results of an NIMH collaborative study of the efficacy of the treatment of acute schizophrenia with antipsychotics (13). Approximately three-fourths of patients were ''much improved'' by antipsychotics during the 6-week study, while nearly half of the placebo group were ''worse.'' Double-blind, controlled studies have also been used to determine the efficacy of maintenance antipsychotic drugs in preventing the return of schizophrenic symptoms after an initial response to treatment.

A recent review summarized the 24 studies that met criteria for appropriate design (14). It was reported in this review that 698 of 1068 patients (65 percent) who received a placebo relapsed, compared to 639 of 2127 (30 percent) receiving maintenance antipsychotics; thus, the relapse rate in the drug-treated group was less than half that in the placebo group. Two conclusions can be drawn from this review of maintenance treatment. First, maintenance antipsychotics can prevent relapse in many but not all patients with schizophrenia. Second, since some patients do not relapse on placebo, these patients do not require maintenance treatment. Unfortunately, although some progress has been made, it is still not possible to predict with certainty which patients will relapse. The urgency of such a prediction is increased by several reversible but troublesome side effects, and by the one potentially irreversible side effect, caused by antipsychotics.

Antipsychotics are relatively safe, but they occasionally do produce troublesome side effects. Extrapyramidal motor reactions is the general term given to a wide variety of muscle or movement side effects sometimes caused by these medications. Some patients experience uncontrollable restlessness or muscle spasms in the neck, trunk, or eyes. Others develop muscle side effects that resemble the symptoms of Parkinson's disease, such as muscle rigidity, tremors, altered posture, and shuffling gait. Most of these extrapyramidal muscle reactions occur soon after antipsychotics are started and usually disappear spontaneously. They can also be controlled by the anticholinergic drugs that are used to treat Parkinson's disease (12).

Tardive dyskinesia is a movement disorder that is distinct from the early extrapyramidal reactions in several ways. It usually occurs only after prolonged treatment with antipsychotics. It does not usually respond to anticholinergic medications, and it is sometimes irreversible. Tardive dyskinesia consists of frequent, repetitive, involuntary movements of the lips, tongue, jaw, face, and sometimes of the trunk or limbs. These movements can be socially embarrassing and can make speech, eating, and sometimes even breathing difficult (15). The reported prevalence of tardive dyskinesia in hospitalized patients with mental illness varies between 0.5 and 40 percent, with a mean of about 15 percent (16). Differences in methods of case finding and definitions of the disorder make it difficult to accurately determine prevalence. However, the possibility that a patient will develop tardive dyskinesia makes the decision to place him on maintenance antipsychotics extremely difficult. The risk of and potential for life disruptions from a relapse of schizophrenic symptoms must be weighed against the risk of tardive dyskinesia.

Some patients probably should not be placed on maintenance antipsychotics. Patients with good social adjustment who develop schizophrenic symptoms suddenly in response to stress usually respond rapidly to antipsychotics and may never develop symptoms again. Hospitalized patients with chronic schizophrenic symptoms that respond only minimally to antipsychotics may not re-

quire drug maintenance. The gains from drug therapy in such patients are small. Relapse is not as much of a life problem as it would be for an employed outpatient, and the risk of tardive dyskinesia is great. However, for many patients the return of schizophrenic symptoms can cause severe life disruptions, and the benefits of maintenance antipsychotics would seem to outweigh the risk of tardive dyskinesia.

Antipsychotics and Brain Chemistry

A considerable body of evidence has accumulated showing that antipsychotic medications act by blocking the receptors of brain neurons that are stimulated by the neurotransmitter dopamine (17). Such chemical neurotransmitters are released by a small electrical potential in a neuron. The chemical diffuses across the microscopic gap, the synaptic cleft, that separates one neuron from another. The neurotransmitter then stimulates a receptor in the second neuron, causing it to increase its electrical activity.

Dopamine is presumed to serve as the neurotransmitter in at least three specific pathways in the brain: the nigrostriatal, the mesolimbic-mesocortical, and the tuberoinfundibular pathways (17, 18). The anatomic localization and some proposed functions for these pathways are listed in Table 1. Antipsychotic medications block dopamine receptors in all three; nigrostriatal blockade causes the extrapyramidal reactions, tuberoinfundibular blockade causes endocrine changes, and mesolimbic-mesocortical blockade is presumed to yield the antipsychotic activity of the medications (17). Seven separate types of evidence support the concept that antipsychotics

block dopamine receptors.

1) Antipsychotics increase the turnover (synthesis and breakdown) of dopamine, as demonstrated first by Carlsson and Lindqvist in 1963 (19). These investigators suggested that the increased turnover results from a feedback mechanism attempting to overcome dopamine receptor blockade. Increased turnover has also been shown in humans. However, one antipsychotic, clozapine, fails to have the expected effect on dopamine turnover in humans (20).

2) All antipsychotics except clozapine cause extrapyramidal reactions that sometimes mimic the symptoms of Parkinson's disease (21). Parkinson's disease results from degeneration of the nigrostriatal dopamine pathway, leading to a predominance of cholinergic over dopamine activity in this region (22). The similarity of antipsychotic-induced extrapyramidal reactions to the symptoms of Parkinson's disease suggests that antipsychotics inhibit dopamine activity in this nigrostriatal pathway. The improvement of both Parkinson's disease and extrapyramidal symptoms by anticholinergic drugs is further evidence of their similar biochemical mechanisms. The failure of clozapine to produce extrapyramidal reactions may be due to its potent anticholinergic activity (17).

3) Antipsychotics counteract the electrical response of neurons to the application of microscopic amounts of dopamine (23). The effects of amphetamine on neuronal activity are similar to the effects of dopamine. Antipsychotics also reverse the effects of amphetamine on the electrical activity of neurons (23).

4) In animals, antipsychotics reverse the behavioral effects of drugs that alter central dopamine activity. Amphetamine

Table 1. Dopamine pathways.

Pathway	Anatomic location	Hypothesized roles
Nigrostriatal	Substantia nigra (A9) to caudate-putamen (striatum)	Muscle and movement coordination Parkinson's disease Extrapyramidal symptoms of antipsychotics Animal stereotypy(?) Tardive dyskinesia(?)
Mesolimbic-mesocortical	Substantia nigra and area medial to substantia nigra (A9, A10) to limbic nucleii and cortical regions	Emotional tone(?) Antipsychotic action of neuroleptics(?) Amphetamine and L-dopa psychosis(?) Schizophrenia(?)
Tuberoinfundibular	Arcuate nucleus to median eminence	Modulation of some endocrine functions Antipsychotic drug action on prolactin

and apomorphine both cause altered behaviors in animals that are thought to be due to increased activity in brain dopamine pathways. These animal behaviors are reversed, blocked, or normalized by antipsychotics (*17, 24*).

5) Antipsychotics inhibit the activity of the enzyme dopamine-sensitive adenylate cyclase. Kebabian *et al.* (*25*) have suggested that this enzyme may be involved in the mechanism of dopamine receptors. Activity of this enzyme is increased in the presence of dopamine and decreased in the presence of antipsychotics. However, some antipsychotics, particularly butyrophenones, are less active against this enzyme than would be predicted from their clinical potency (*17, 25*).

6) Antipsychotics are found to inhibit the binding of dopamine to nerve cell membranes in laboratory preparations made from animal brain homogenates. Studies by Snyder (*26*) and Seeman *et al.* (*27*) suggest that the neurotransmitter may bind to the dopamine receptor in these preparations. The relative potency of antipsychotics in this system closely parallels both their clinical potency and their ability to inhibit dopamine-sensitive adenylate cyclase. Again, the butyrophenones inhibit dopamine binding less well than is predicted from clinical potency. However, all antipsychotics inhibit the binding of the butyrophenone haloperidol to nerve cell membranes, with a potency that parallels their clinical potency (*26*). Snyder (*26*) suggests that dopamine and haloperidol bind to discrete agonist and antagonist states of the dopamine receptor and that displacement of antagonist or haloperidol binding may be a better test of antipsychotic activity.

7) Antipsychotics stimulate the release of the hormone prolactin from the pituitary gland, and the tuberoinfundibular pathway plays a major inhibitory role in the regulation of prolactin release (*17, 28*). Sachar and his associates (*28*) report a close correlation between the prolactin response and the antipsychotic potency of the various chemical classes of antipsychotics.

Thus, there is considerable evidence that antipsychotics block brain dopamine receptors. This evidence led to the hypothesis that dopamine neuronal activity is excessive in schizophrenic patients, possibly in the mesolimbic-mesocortical pathway (*17*). This hypothesis of schizophrenia is supported by other indirect pharmacological evidence, but there is not yet any consistent direct evidence of altered brain dopamine metabolism or activity in schizophrenics (*29*).

Tardive dyskinesia is also thought to result from dopamine hyperactivity, but in the nigrostriatal pathway. The prolonged dopamine receptor blockade could lead to supersensitive receptors causing a relative predominance of dopamine over acetylcholine activity in this region (*30*). This imbalance in tardive dyskinesia would be the opposite of the imbalance in extrapyramidal reactions to antipsychotics and in Parkinson's disease, where acetylcholine is predominant. Since Parkinson's disease and extrapyramidal reactions respond to anticholinergics, tardive dyskinesia might reasonably respond to increasing acetylcholine activity. In preliminary studies the acetylcholine precursor choline chloride has been found to improve the movements of some patients with tardive dyskinesia (*31*). This finding supports the imbalance hypothesis of tardive dyskinesia and offers a potential treatment strategy for the disorder.

Antidepressant Medications

The two major types of drugs used to treat depression are the tricyclic antidepressants (tricyclics) and the monoamine oxidase inhibitors. Drugs from both pharmacological classes were first introduced in 1957, but monoamine oxidase inhibitors are used much less commonly than are tricyclics—they are generally thought to be less effective and more toxic. Tricyclics take 2 to 4 weeks to alter the symptoms of severe depression, but they are effective in about 70 percent of patients. In most cases tricyclics cause a complete remission of depressive symptoms; they improve mood, restore confidence, relieve the numerous physical symptoms, and eliminate suicidal thinking. Some patients may fail to respond to one tricyclic but will respond to another. In patients who remain depressed after a trial of two tricyclics, the monoamine oxidase inhibitors sometimes reverse depressive symptoms (*32*).

The same questions that were asked about the antipsychotics can be asked about the tricyclics: Are they effective in acute depressions or useful as maintenance treatments when compared to a placebo? Do they have dangerous or irreversible side effects? What is the biochemical mechanism of tricyclic action? The efficacy of tricyclics in the treatment of depression has been established in numerous clinical trials. In one recent literature review, which summarized only double-blind, placebo-controlled studies, tricyclics were found to be more effective than a placebo in 61 of 93 studies (*33*). The fact that 32 studies did not find tricyclics superior to a placebo may seem surprising. However, this is probably due to the high spontaneous remission rate in depression and the slow action of tricyclics. Mild depressions are more likely to remit spontaneously than severe depressions, but it has been estimated that about 30 percent of patients with severe depression recover without drug treatment. Studies that include patients with mild depression may have a placebo group with a remission rate nearly as high as that of the tricyclic group. Thus, tricyclics are more appropriately used to treat severe depression. Even though some of these patients would recover without drug treatment, the danger of suicide in severe depression makes tricyclic treatment not only important in relieving suffering, but also potentially lifesaving (*32*).

Three major collaborative studies, two in the United States and one in England, have found that tricyclics significantly reduced the relapse rate in patients who were initially treated with them (*34*). Since tricyclics have several potentially troublesome side effects, they probably should not be used as a maintenance treatment after recovery for a patient with a single depressive episode. However, for patients with repeated episodes of severe depression the side effects of tricyclic maintenance seem to be a small risk compared to the suffering and potential for suicide associated with multiple depressive episodes (*32*).

Tricyclics can be fatal when a large overdose is taken. This is an unfortunate characteristic for a drug used for the treatment of illness that can lead to suicide. Standard doses of tricyclics also cause several troublesome side effects, but they are usually not dangerous, except in patients with heart disease. Rarely, tricyclics can precipitate mania or schizophrenia in patients with a history of these illnesses. Tricyclics do not seem to cause the extrapyramidal motor reactions seen with the antipsychotics. Perhaps most importantly, tricyclics do not seem to cause tardive dyskinesia. Thus, the decision to place a patient on a maintenance drug is less complicated with tricyclics than with antipsychotics, except in patients with concurrent heart disease (*32*).

Despite an impressive quantity of data accumulated over the last 20 years, the exact mechanism of action of tricyclics is unknown (32). The most important hypothesis is that tricyclics increase the functional activity of the brain neurotransmitters norepinephrine and serotonin. Tricyclics are thought to potentiate norepinephrine and serotonin by preventing their uptake by the neuron that released them into the synaptic cleft. Their reuptake prevents these chemicals from continuing to act on the receptor on the second neuron and thus is one physiological mechanism for deactivating them. Reuptake blockade therefore should increase the concentration of norepinephrine and serotonin at the receptor (35). Reuptake blockade as a mode of action of tricyclics is suggested by numerous studies which show that these drugs inhibit the uptake of norepinephrine or serotonin injected into the rat brain (35).

The reuptake blockade of tricyclics forms part of the basis of the norepinephrine and serotonin hypothesis of affective disorders. This hypothesis, which is supported by several pharmacological and physiological findings, states that depression is due to a functional underactivity or deficiency of these neurotransmitters, while mania is associated with their functional hyperactivity (35). The other major class of antidepressants inhibits the action of the enzyme monoamine oxidase, which breaks down norepinephrine and serotonin, and thus monoamine oxidase inhibitors should also increase the concentration of the neurotransmitters (36). Reserpine is used to treat hypertension; it depletes brain norepinephrine and serotonin and causes a "depressionlike" syndrome in some patients. Some depressed patients seem to excrete lower amounts of 3-methyoxy-4-hydroxyphenylglycol, the most important breakdown product of norepinephrine. [Others have low spinal fluid concentrations of 5-hydroxyindoleacetic acid, the major metabolite of serotonin (35)]. Some depressed patients also have specific abnormalities in endocrine systems that are controlled by the hypothalamus and the pituitary gland (37). Hypothalamic-pituitary function also seems to be influenced by serotonin and norepinephrine activity (38).

Thus, there is some evidence that decreased norepinephrine or serotonin is associated with depression, but the hypothesis cannot be considered to be established. Much of the evidence is controversial. The true mechanism of action of either the monoamine oxidase inhibitors or the tricyclics is not known. Reserpine does not cause a depressionlike syndrome in everyone, and the similarity between this syndrome and clinical depression is the subject of debate. Not every depressed patient has low excretion of 3-methoxy-4-hydroxyphenylglycol, low concentrations of 5-hydroxyindoleacetic acid in the spinal fluid, or specific endocrine abnormalities (37).

A major problem for the norepinephrine-serotonin hypothesis of depression comes from the actions of tricyclics themselves. These medications immediately cause neurotransmitter reuptake blockade in animal studies, but they take 2 to 4 weeks to have antidepressant action in patients. The long-term effects of tricyclics on norepinephrine and serotonin are difficult to study and may not be the same as short-term ones. In addition, iprindole is an effective tricyclic that has been used in Europe and that does not seem to inhibit reuptake of norepinephrine or serotonin (37, 39). Thus, neither the biochemical basis of depression nor the mechanisms of action of antidepressants are known with certainty. The reuptake blockade of norepinephrine and serotonin by tricyclics and the norepinephrine-serotonin hypothesis of depression may be oversimplifications, but both hypotheses have helped organize important research on the biochemistry of the brain. More recent hypotheses of depression and of the biochemical mechanisms of tricyclics suggest an altered balance between the functional activities of two or more neurotransmitters, the possible involvement of acetylcholine in depression, and the hypothesis that depression and the action of tricyclics are the result of alterations in neurotransmitter receptors rather than the neurotransmitters themselves (37).

Lithium Carbonate

The discovery by John Cade in Australia in 1949 that lithium salts are effective antimanic agents marked the advent of modern psychopharmacology. Curiously, the drug was not introduced into the United States until 1969. Lithium is a unique drug for several reasons. It is highly specific in relieving manic symptoms—normalizing mood and slowing down thinking, motor activity, and other behaviors—all without causing oversedation. In addition, lithium seems to prevent or decrease the severity of both manic and depressive episodes in some bipolar patients. Finally, the lithium compounds used are simple inorganic salts that have no known function in normal physiology (40).

The efficacy of lithium in treating acute mania has been established in at least ten controlled studies (41). In general, these studies showed that lithium has more specific or unique effects in manic patients than do antipsychotics. However, lithium takes 4 to 10 days to begin to reduce manic symptoms. Thus, for some severely hyperactive and agitated patients with mania, the sedative and tranquilizing effects of the antipsychotics are necessary for 1 or 2 weeks (41).

Eight controlled, blind studies have shown that maintenance lithium either prevents or decreases the number of manic episodes in bipolar patients (42). Lithium also seems to prevent or decrease the number of depressive episodes in bipolar patients, and may prevent depressive episodes in some patients with severe recurrent unipolar depression (34). Since tricyclics also prevent depressive episodes in unipolar depressed patients and are the current treatment, controlled trials comparing lithium and tricyclics as maintenance treatments in unipolar depressed patients are urgently needed.

Unlike the antipsychotics and tricyclics, lithium seems to have a narrow range of effective concentrations in blood. Therefore, blood levels of lithium are measured frequently at first, but as the dose is established the interval between measurements can be extended to weeks or even months. Lithium can have numerous troublesome side effects on many organ systems, but most of these occur early in treatment, and no long-term or permanent side effects have been reported (40).

The biochemical mechanism of action of lithium on the brain is unknown. Lithium is distributed throughout the body and interacts with numerous biological systems, including the brain neurotransmitters norepinephrine and serotonin. The norepinephrine hypothesis of affective disorders proposes a norepinephrine overactivity in mania. Lithium decreases the electrically stimulated release of norepinephrine and seems to enhance its reuptake from the synaptic cleft (*37, 43*). This action is opposite to that of the tricyclics, and could explain the effect of lithium on mania. However, any biochemical hypothesis of the action of lithium must also explain its positive effect in some depressed patients (*37*). Thus, further studies of both the short- and long-term effects of lithium are needed to help clarify its mode of action.

Ethics and Psychopharmacology

Among the many ethical issues surrounding the use of psychotherapeutic agents, involuntary treatment is a particular subject of debate both within and outside the psychiatric profession. Should patients ever be given drug treatments without their consent? The exact legal mechanism varies, but severely disturbed patients often do receive such treatment. In California, patients must be a danger to themselves, a danger to others, or gravely disabled as a result of mental illness (*44*). Those who meet these criteria are often depressed patients with suicidal intentions or schizophrenic patients who are violent or unable to care for their basic needs.

Some argue that this involuntary treatment, although well intentioned, alters behavior by external means and that patients should have a right to refuse such treatment even when they are mentally ill (*45*). Szasz (*46*), an articulate spokesman for this viewpoint, believes that the government and the mental health profession have joined together, as did the state and the church in the past, to force people to conform to certain behaviors and beliefs (*45*). Szasz believes that individuals should be free to determine their own behavior, their own beliefs, and their own future, even if this behavior is potentially dangerous to the individual or to society. The logical consequence of this belief is that mental patients have the same rights and responsibilities as other members of the community. A psychiatric patient who harms someone should be tried and held responsible even if the action was due to a mental illness. Szasz's viewpoint has other logical consequences that are difficult for many people to accept. For instance, it suggests that a depressed patient should be allowed to commit suicide and a schizophrenic patient should be allowed to die from dehydration if he feels that fluids are poisoned (*1*).

In practice, many people feel that it is more humane to treat some patients without their consent. Suicidal feelings and delusional beliefs usually are temporary and respond to drug treatment. Patients are often grateful that their transient self-destructive or dangerous behavior was stopped. Suicidal thoughts and delusions are powerful controls over a person's behavior. Involuntarily treatment can remove these emotions and thus can be seen as liberating rather than restricting, since they can allow patients to return rapidly to their former lives, free of dangerous behaviors and self-destructive impulses (*1*).

There is no simple solution to the ethical dilemma of involuntary treatment. When used inappropriately, involuntary treatment can become one of the instruments a totalitarian state uses to control deviant behavior. When used in a humane manner, it can be lifesaving. Clearly, ethical inquiry must play a larger role in psychiatric treatment than it has in the past.

Conclusion

Remarkable progress has been made in the drug treatment of psychiatric disorders. Psychopharmacological agents are the cornerstone of the vastly improved mental health treatment structure for patients with schizophrenia, depression, and mania. The medications have also prompted psychiatrists to become more rigorous and quantitative in the diagnosis and longitudinal assessment of mental disorders. Perhaps most importantly, psychopharmacological agents have provided an interface between psychiatry and modern biological sciences. This has led to laboratory and clinical research that has improved our understanding of the human brain and of behavior and that offers hope for understanding the biochemical substrates of mental illness.

The pharmacotherapies themselves are far from ideal. Antipsychotics improve schizophrenic symptoms, but do not often "cure" the disease. Maintenance antipsychotics reduce the likelihood of a return of schizophrenic symptoms but add the risk of the sometimes irreversible movement disorder, tardive dyskinesia. Tricyclics do not seem to cause irreversible side effects and often reverse depressive symptoms, but they work slowly and are ineffective in 20 to 30 percent of patients. Tricyclics also can be fatal if taken in sufficiently large doses. Lithium salts can markedly improve the life of a manic-depressive patient, but they have troublesome side effects and do not help all patients. Thus, more effective and less toxic medications are an important goal of research in psychiatry. The combination of basic laboratory studies and carefully designed clinical evaluations is urgently needed to develop and test new medical treatments for mental illness.

Psychotherapeutic drugs are not a panacea. They allow a large number of psychiatric patients to be discharged, sometimes to communities that are poorly prepared to receive them and to provide the continuing care that many patients require. Further efforts are needed to determine the best ways to care for formerly hospitalized individuals and to help them become happy and productive members of society. Too often physicians rely solely on medications when psychological and socioenvironmental treatments are needed. Finally, the existence of potent psychotherapeutic drugs will continue to present ethical challenges to society.

References and Notes

1. P. A. Berger, B. Hamburg, D. A. Hamburg, *Daedalus* **106**, 261 (1977); J. Barchas, P. Berger, R. Ciaranello, G. Elliott, in *Psychopharmacology: From Theory to Practice*, J. D. Barchas, P. A. Berger, R. D. Ciaranello, G. R. Elliott, Eds. (Oxford, New York, 1977), p. 527.
2. F. J. Ayd, Jr., *Discoveries in Biological Psychiatry* (Lippincott, Philadelphia, 1970), p. 230.
3. E. L. Bassuk and S. Gerson, *Sci. Am.* **238**, 46 (February 1978).
4. M. Greenblatt, in *Psychopharmacology: A Generation of Progress*, M. A. Lipton, A. DiMascio, K. F. Killam, Eds. (Raven, New York, 1978), p. 1179.
5. M. Greenblatt, *N. Engl. J. Med.* **296**, 246 (1975).
6. R. Reich, *Bull. N.Y. State Dist. Branches Am. Psychiatr. Assoc.* **15**, 6 (1972).
7. F. N. Arnhoff, *Science* **188**, 1277 (1975).
8. L. C. Wynne and M. T. Singer, *Arch. Gen. Psychiatry* **9**, 191 (1963); S. Arieti, in *Psychopathology of Schizophrenia*, P. H. Hoch and J. Zubin, Eds. (Grune & Stratton, New York, 1966), p. 37; R. Cancro, *Dis. Nerv. Syst.* **29**, 846 (1968); W. T. Carpenter, J. Strauss, S. Maleh, *Arch. Gen. Psychiatry* **28**, 847 (1973); H. E. Lehmann, in *Comprehensive Textbook of Psychiatry*, A. M. Freedman, H. I. Kaplan, B. J. Sadock, Eds. (Williams & Wilkins, Baltimore, ed. 2, 1975), p. 890.
9. H. M. Babigian, in *Comprehensive Textbook of Psychiatry*, A. M. Freedman, H. I. Kaplan, B. J. Sadock, Eds. (Williams & Wilkins, Baltimore, ed. 2, 1975), p. 860; H. E. Lehmann, in *ibid.*, p. 851.
10. J. M. Mendels, *Concepts of Depression* (Wiley, New York, 1970); G. R. Klerman, in *Comprehensive Textbook of Psychiatry*, A. M. Freedman, H. I. Kaplan, B. J. Sadock, Eds. (Williams & Wilkins, Baltimore, ed. 2, 1975), p. 1003; F. F. Flach and S. C. Draghi, *The Nature and Treatment of Depression* (Wiley, New York, 1975); G. Usdin, *Depression: Clinical Biological and Psychological Perspectives* (Brunner/Mazel, New York, 1977); W. E. Fann, I. Karacan, A. D. Pokorny, R. L. Williams, Eds., *Phenomenology and Treatment of Depression* (Spectrum, New York, 1977).

11. N. Kline, *Dis. Nerv. Syst.* **37**, 10 (1976).
12. R. I. Shader and A. H. Jackson, in *Manual of Psychiatric Therapeutics*, R. Shader, Ed. (Little, Brown, Boston, 1975); p. 63; J. O. Cole, in *Drug Treatment of Mental Disorders*, L. Simpson, Ed. (Raven, New York, 1976), p. 13; L. E. Hollister, in *Psychopharmacology: From Theory to Practice*, J. D. Barchas, P. A. Berger, R. D. Ciaranello, G. R. Elliott, Eds. (Oxford, New York, 1977), p. 121.
13. J. Cole, S. Goldberg, G. Klerman, *Arch. Gen. Psychiatry* **10**, 246 (1964); R. F. Prien and J. Cole, *ibid.* **18**, 482 (1968); J. M. Davis, *Am. J. Psychiatry* **133**, 208 (1976).
14. J. M. Davis, *Am. J. Psychiatry* **132**, 1237 (1975).
15. E. G. DeFraites, K. L. Davis, P. A. Berger, *Biol. Psychiatry* **12**, 267 (1977); R. J. Balderessarini and D. Tarsy, in *Psychopharmacology: A Generation of Progress*, M. A. Lipton, A. DiMascio, K. F. Killam, Eds. (Raven, New York, 1978), p. 993.
16. W. E. Fann, J. M. Davis, D. S. Janowsky, *Dis. Nerv. Syst.* **33**, 182 (1972); R. J. Baldessarini, *Can. Psychiatr. Assoc. J.* **19**, 551 (1974).
17. P. A. Berger, G. R. Elliott, J. D. Barchas, in *Psychopharmacology: A Generation of Progress*, M. A. Lipton, A. DiMascio, K. F. Killam, Eds. (Raven, New York, 1978), p. 1071; A. Carlsson, *Am. J. Psychiatry* **135**, 164 (1978).
18. U. Ungerstedt, *Acta Physiol. Scand. Suppl. 367* (1971), pp. 1–48.
19. A. Carlsson and M. Lindqvist, *Acta Pharmacol. Toxicol.* **20**, 140 (1963).
20. J. Gerlach, K. Thorsen, R. Fog, *Psychopharmacologia* **40**, 341 (1975).
21. H. R. Bürki, E. Eichenberger, A. C. Sayers, T. C. White, *Pharmakopsychiatr. Neuro Psychopharmakol.* **8**, 115 (1975).
22. O. Hornykiewicz, *Klin. Wochenschr.* **75**, 309 (1963).
23. B. S. Bunney and G. K. Aghajanian, in *Predictability in Psychopharmacology: Preclinical and Clinical Correlations*, A. Sudilovsky, S. Gershon, B. Beer, Eds. (Raven, New York, 1975), p. 225.
24. J. D. Barchas, P. A. Berger, S. Matthysse, R. J. Wyatt, in *Principles of Psychopharmacology*, W. G. Clark and J. del Guidice, Eds. (Academic Press, New York, in press).
25. J. W. Kebabian, G. L. Petzgold, D. Greengard, *Proc. Natl. Acad. Sci. U.S.A.* **69**, 2145 (1972).
26. S. H. Snyder, *Am. J. Psychiatry* **133**, 197 (1976).
27. P. Seeman, M. Chou-Wong, J. Tadesco, K. Wong, *Proc. Natl. Acad. Sci. U.S.A.* **72**, 4376 (1975).
28. E. J. Sachar, P. H. Gruen, N. Altman, G. Langer, F. S. Halpern, M. Liefer, in *Neuroregulators and Psychiatric Disorders*, E. Usdin, D. A. Hamburg, J. D. Barchas, Eds. (Oxford, New York, 1977), p. 242.
29. J. D. Barchas, P. A. Berger, G. R. Elliott, E. Erdelyi, R. J. Wyatt, in *Biochemistry and Function of Monoamine Enzymes*, E. Usdin, N. Weiner, M. B. H. Youdin, Eds. (Dekker, New York, 1977), p. 863.
30. H. L. Klawans, Jr., *Am. J. Psychiatry* **130**, 82 (1973); K. L. Davis, L. E. Hollister, P. A. Berger, J. D. Barchas, *Psychopharmacol. Commun.* **1**, 533 (1975).
31. K. L. Davis, L. E. Hollister, P. A. Berger, *N. Engl. J. Med.* **293**, 152 (1975); K. L. Davis, L. E. Hollister, J. D. Barchas, P. A. Berger, *Life Sci.* **19**, 1507 (1976); J. H. Growdon, M. J. Hirsch, R. J. Wurtman, W. Wiener, *N. Engl. J. Med.* **297**, 524 (1977); K. L. Davis and P. A. Berger, *Biol. Psychiatry* **13**, 23 (1978).
32. J. J. Schildkraut and D. F. Klein, in *Manual of Psychiatric Therapeutics*, R. I. Shader, Ed. (Little, Brown, Boston, 1975), p. 39; J. M. Davis, in *Drug Treatment of Mental Disorders*, L. Simpson, Ed. (Raven, New York, 1976), p. 127; P. A. Berger, in *Psychopharmacology: From Theory to Practice*, J. D. Barchas, P. A. Berger, R. D. Ciaranello, G. R. Elliott, Eds. (Oxford, New York, 1977), p. 174.
33. J. B. Morris and A. T. Beck, *Arch Gen. Psychiatry* **30**, 667 (1974).
34. J. M. Davis, *Am. J. Psychiatry* **133**, 1 (1976).
35. J. J. Schildkraut, *ibid.* **122**, 509 (1965); W. E. Bunney and J. M. Davis, *Arch. Gen. Psychiatry* **13**, 483 (1965); P. A. Berger, in *Neurotransmitter Function*, W. S. Fields, Ed. (Grune & Stratton, New York, 1977), p. 305.
36. P. A. Berger and J. D. Barchas, in *Psychotherapeutic Drugs*, E. Usdin and I. S. Forrest, Eds. (Dekker, New York, 1977), p. 1173.
37. ______, in *Psychopharmacology: From Theory to Practice*, J. D. Barchas, P. A. Berger, R. D. Ciaranello, G. R. Elliott, Eds. (Oxford, New York, 1977), p. 151.
38. P. A. Berger, J. D. Barchas, J. Vernikos-Danellis, *Nature (London)* **248**, 424 (1974); B. S. Carroll and J. Mendels, in *Hormones, Behavior and Psychopathology*, E. J. Sachar, Ed. (Raven, New York, 1976), p. 193.
39. S. B. Ross, A. L. Renyi, S. O. Ogren, *Life Sci.* **10**, 1267 (1971); M. H. Bickel, in *Psychotherapeutic Drugs*, E. Usdin and I. S. Forrest, Eds. (Dekker, New York, 1977), p. 1131.
40. R. R. Fieve, in *Drug Treatment of Mental Disorders*, 1976), p. 193; R. L. Sack and E. DeFraites, in *Psychopharmacology: From Theory to Practice*, J. D. Barchas, P. A. Berger, R. D. Ciaranello, G. R. Elliott, Eds. (Oxford, New York, 1977), p. 208.
41. S. Gershon, in *Psychotherapeutic Drugs*, E. Usdin and I. S. Forrest, Eds. (Dekker, New York, 1977), p. 1377.
42. F. Quitkin, A. Rifkin, D. Klein, *Arch. Gen. Psychiatry* **33**, 337 (1976).
43. S. M. Schanberg, J. J. Schildkraut, I. J. Kopin, *Biochem. Pharmacol.* **16**, 393 (1967); R. I. Katz, T. N. Chase, I. J. Kopin, *Science* **162**, 466 (1968).
44. The California Community Mental Health Services Act (Lantermann-Petris-Short Act), division 5, part I, chaps. 1, 2, and 3.
45. T. A. Gonda and M. B. Waitzkin, *Curr. Concepts Psychiatry* **1**, 5 (1976).
46. T. Szasz, *Law, Liberty, Psychiatry* (Macmillan, New York, 1963).
47. I thank J. D. Barchas, G. R. Elliott, and S. I. Watson for helpful discussions and J. S. Magliozzi for manuscript preparation. Supported by National Institute of Mental Health Specialized Research Center grant MH-30854 and the Medical Research Service of the Veterans Administration.

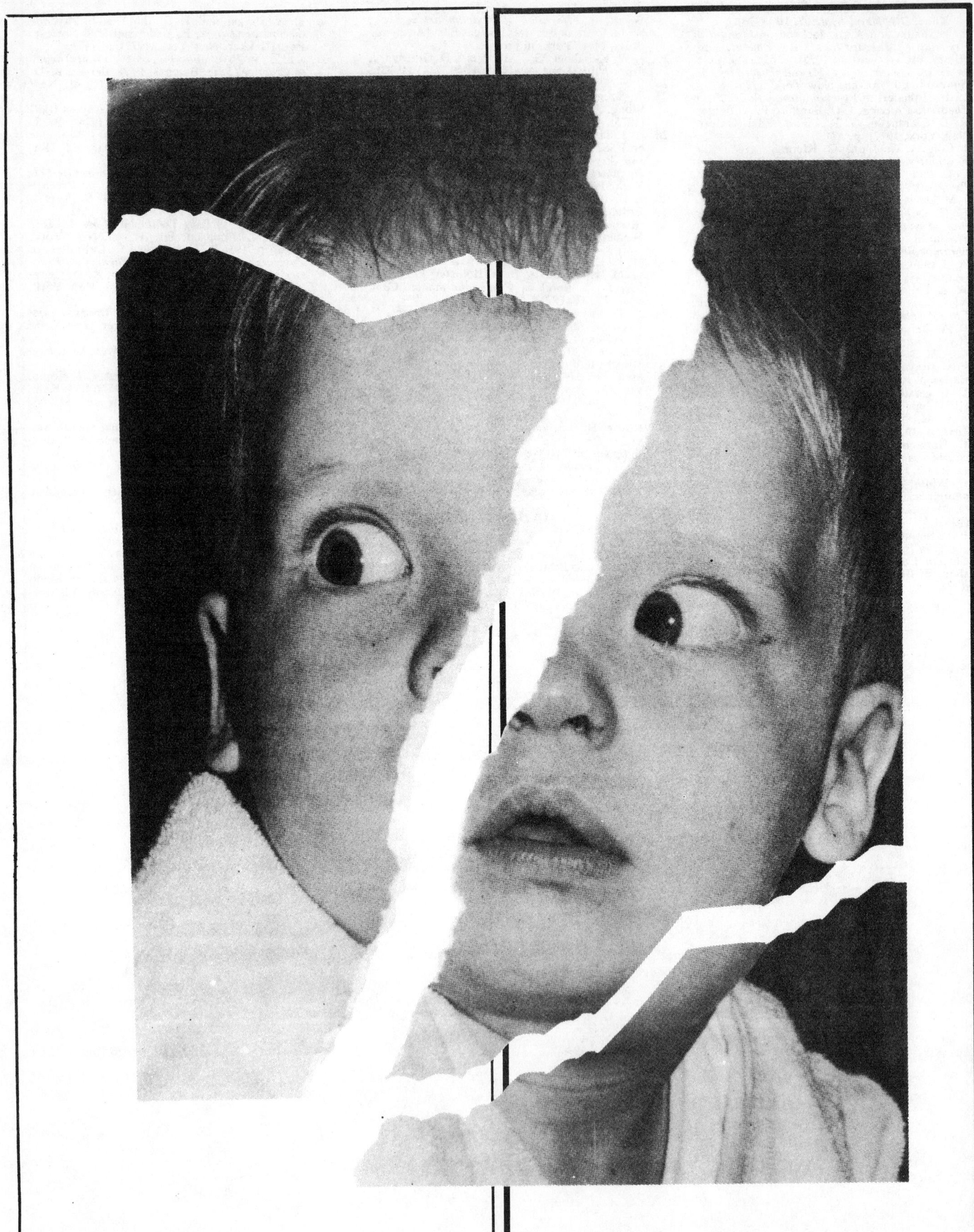

Prenatal through Infancy

(0-2 years)

Researchers in the field of child behavior have long ago documented the individual differences in children's behavior from the time of birth. Their activity levels, mobility, frequency and duration of crying, eating habits, and sleep-wake cycle vary considerably. This normal variation in behavior makes identification of abnormal behavior in this stage very difficult.

Intensity of behavior is an indication that there is a problem; a great shift in patterns of behavior is another indicator of trouble. These signs can be spotted in the 0-2 year age range.

Depression, aggression and hostility all can have their roots in infancy. All three deviant behaviors are environmentally produced; they are either adapted as behaviors modelled after their caretakers, or as responses to unfavorable living and growing conditions.

Parents, or caretakers, are the first role models that toddlers have. They do not interact enough with a peer group, nor are they cognizant enough of peer group behavior to imitate their behavior consistently. The most reinforcing model is the adult. When the adult, parent or caretaker, is aggressive or hostile, the child imitates the outward manifestations of this behavior. The toddler grabs things, hits people and yells without malice. The malice comes with development. This behavior can be ameliorated by reinforcing prosocial and altruistic actions.

Depression is a behavior that can also be learned from a role model; more often, though, it is a reaction to environmental conditions. Harsh conditions or lack of stimulation can cause depressive reactions in infants. Their cries become less intense when no one responds; their babbling less frequent when no one answers. This behavior can be reversed by correcting the environmental faults, however, when depression in infancy is a coping mechanism, it is used as a coping mechanism throughout life.

In this section a case study of a phobic toddler is presented. It is rare that phobia is diagnosed in a child of sixteen months, however, as this article indicates, it does occur.

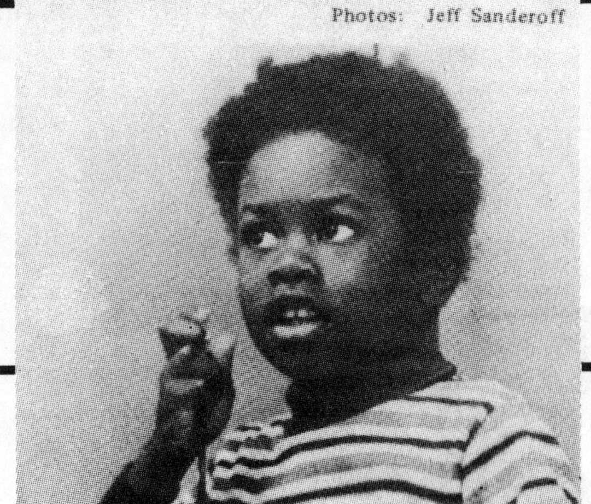

Phobic Symptoms in a Toddler

Early Intervention Can Forestall

Serious Developments

John B. Reinhart, M.D.,* Dorothy Pisula, Ph.D.†

DISTURBED and potentially disturbed young children are typically first seen by pediatricians rather than by child psychiatrists. As evidence gathers of early onset of functions of the mind, it becomes important that observations of mental deviations and carrying out of early intervention become a part of pediatric practice. This case report illustrates these points.

Observations of psychic activity in very young children have not often been recorded. With infants, accounts of dream activity have been written and seem quite valid.[1,2] Phobic states and conversion reactions reviewed by Proctor[3] and Rock[4] include some preschool children. Schnurmann[5] describes a 2.5-month-old girl who developed nightmares and a fear of dogs related to her becoming aware of sexual differences and to her mother's illness and absence. Freud's[6] analysis of "little Hans" was the first report of the treatment of a phobia in childhood, of a little boy just under 5 years of age.

---

* Director, Division of Behavioral Sciences, Children's Hospital of Pittsburgh, 125 De Soto Street, Pittsburgh, Pa. 15213; Professor, Pediatrics and Child Psychiatry, University of Pittsburgh, School of Medicine, Pittsburgh, Pa. 15213.

† Chief Psychologist, Department of Psychology, Children's Hospital of Pittsburgh, 125 De Soto Street, Pittsburgh, Pa. 15213.

Case Record

One of us (JBR) was asked to consult with a family about their 22-month-old daughter who for 6 months after the birth of a male sibling had developed a fear of the bath, a fear of falling and hurting herself, and an unwillingness to use her hands, holding them clenched to her side. Endeavors by her pediatrician to treat the problem by seditives, tranquilizers, and reassurance had been ineffective. A family friend suggested psychiatric consultation.

When the patient's mother gave the above brief history over the phone, we suggested that the problem seemed one of sibling rivalry and that her angry feelings toward the new baby might be interpreted to this little girl. It was also suggested that she might have become aware of sexual differences and have feelings about this. The mother had some doubt about the suggestions, but agreed to them and was given an appointment for the following week.

Later, Mary's parents told of their telling her "you're not worried about your boo-boo, you're worried about hurting your baby brother, and we won't let that happen." They told, "she stopped in the middle of a scream and her eyes got big, and ever since she's used her hands. She also seems happier than she's been in months!"

Mary's parents were in their thirties. Mary was her mother's second pregnancy, the first having ended in a miscarriage. Pregnancy and delivery were not remarkable. Mary was an 8+ lb baby whose only difficulty was some colic in the first

Phobic Symptoms in a Toddler, John B. Reinhart and Dorothy Pisula, *Clinical Pediatrics*, Vol. 16, No. 12, Dec. 1977. ©1977 by J. P. Lippincott Company.

3 months. She was advanced in her motor and language development, of pleasant disposition, and nondemanding. She was seen as a very bright, "adult behaving" girl with a pleasant disposition. She was always aware of "things out of place" and was concerned about torn pages in her books and other deviations from routine. Her mother's second pregnancy was not remarkable. Mary had been told that a new baby was expected. In addition to her parents, Mary was being cared for by a woman who lived in the home and helped with the housework, and there was a teenage babysitter who sat on weekends. She expressed no upset about her parents leaving her when cared for by these two people. She had no feeding or sleeping difficulties. Toilet training had begun and Mary was compliant about 50 per cent of the time.

The present illness began on the evening that Mary's mother went into labor. About 7:30 that evening father took mother to the hospital after mother's "water broke." The father's aunt came in to take care of Mary and gave her a bath. On the next day Mary suffered a rather serious scratch, "a deep abrasion." That evening her father bathed her, as was the routine, and Mary did not seem upset. Over the next few days, however, Mary began to be more and more resistant to her baths until her father, in exasperation, gave her a spanking. Thereafter he was able to give her a bath without much difficulty, but she often fussed about anyone else giving her a bath. The abrasion took 4 weeks to heal. During this time Mary's previous preoccupation with things out of place, missing or hurt increased. When her mother had a small boil on her chin Mary could hardly look at it. She began to be very fearful of falling and hurting herself and her usual pleasant disposition became a worried and unhappy one. Her toilet training lapsed. About a week before the mother's telephone call, Mary had a second serious scratch, again on the little finger. She then refused to use this hand and soon refused to use either hand and tried to eat off her plate without using her hands.

Parents' History. Mary's father was the second of two children, an "only child," the first child having died at the age of a few days. His father died of a coronary attack in 1955 and his mother was in good health. She tended to be controlling but the family relationship was good.

Mary's mother was the youngest of three; her siblings were a good deal older and she thought she "might have been spoiled." She saw her daughter's behavior much as she imagined hers as a child, and her husband who knew her as a neighbor in childhood agreed. She had a successful career and had married after the death of her mother.

Follow-Up Study on Mary. Six weeks after consultation Mary's mother sent the following note: "Over a month has passed since we saw you, and I am very pleased to report that Mary is doing much better. Occasionally we still have 'upheavals,' but they are certainly fewer in number and much less severe. She seems to be happy most of the time—almost like her old self. She even has accepted the idea of placing a band-aid on her finger if it has been scraped and the 'boo-boo' trauma seems to be passing. She is playing a lot with her brother, and at times appears fond of him (he's almost 8

months now). In general all is much better."

When Mary was 4 years and 3 months her parents were seen again in consultation. They had noted that Mary was getting more jealous of her brother. In early summer, she had pushed her brother in the pool and he had swallowed water and had to be resuscitated. That night she had wet her bed for the first time in over a year. Since then she had not wanted to go into the water, was extremely fearful, insisted on a safety tube and refused any attempts to learn to swim. Two weeks prior to the consultation while her brother was climbing on the garage door, Mary "accidentally" pushed the automatic switch of the garage door and he had gone up with the door, narrowly escaping a serious injury. Again that night Mary wet her bed.

At home Mary was described as "aggressive, domineering, and bossy." Outside of the home and at school her behavior and achievement were excellent.

Additional past history revealed two potentially traumatic events. In the summer after her second birthday, because of persistent hoarseness, her pediatrician had advised laryngoscopy. This was done as an outpatient but Mary did have general anesthesia. Separated from her mother, and in response to her query about her absence, the anesthetist is reported to have said "your mother is on the moon." From that time she had been extremely fearful and phobic about any examination of her mouth or throat. Also, in the late summer of that year, her father had a number of anginal attacks.

Through the next few years she still had difficulty in dealing with her aggressive and angry feelings and when they escaped control she regressed in behavior (enuresis) and developed a phobic state again (for water), but she could respond to encouragement from her mother.

Parents were urged once again to talk with their daughter about her angry killing wishes toward her brother and to let her know that they would not permit her to hurt her brother. In a telephone call 3 months later we were advised that things were going along fine. A day or two after the consultation Mary's mother talked with her as instructed and following that, her behavior improved and her bedwetting stopped completely. She had started school and was doing quite well.

In a follow-up telephone call Mary's mother told that Mary was being more open in talking about her feelings and that the physical aggressiveness was ceasing. Mary had had a "fantastic" school experience. At the beginning she had tremendous hesitation to draw and use her hands but after the first 2 months of school this gradually disappeared. She still tends to dominate her brother.

When Mary was 5½ years old, her mother called because of concern about Mary who had just started the first grade. The teacher reported that she kept up with her work well, but felt that she was easily upset and somewhat immature. She was overly concerned for approval of the teacher. She seemed to be getting along better with her brother, but she seemed to be worrying too much. One office visit was held with the psychiatrist. That en-

---

Such direct intervention need not be done by a psychiatrist but can be taken care of by an interested pediatrician who is knowledgeable in child development from a psychologic standpoint.

---

tire summer she was fearful of and refused to go to the swimming pool.

In the following summer, Mary and her parents were seen at the request of the authors. Things had been going quite well. Early in the school year she would wet her pants in the cafeteria at school because she was fearful of asking permission to leave. After discussion with her mother about the importance of "emergency absences" Mary was able to approach the authorities and from that time on had no further difficulty. Her behavior still tended to be egocentric and she had no hesitation in interrupting her mother when she was talking with other adults. Her grandmother also felt that she was "sassy," but her parents seemed to handle these episodes with relative equanimity.

Mary and her mother began to take horseback-riding lessons. Soon after the parents insisted that she take swimming lessons. There was apprehension at first, but in 2 months, with encouragement, she jumped in and began to swim. Since then she has enjoyed swimming and has no fear of the water. The family told of the current saying, "We've thrown the words 'I can't' in the garbage can." Mary's brother still seemed an easy going, bright, persistent 5 year old with a high frustration tolerance. He was beginning to be more adept at protecting himself in dealing with his older sister both verbally and physically. As for the future, her mother said that Mary was interested in getting married, was quite feminine, and wanted to have babies—only girls—and if she had boys she would continue to have babies until she had a girl and then she would stop.

At six years, Mary was an attractive girl with no problems in separating from her parents who tended to exaggerate her stories of her abilities but in all respects was seen as normal.

Psychologic Examinations

In these, Mary was socially responsive, outgoing, verbally fluent and her visible behavior communicated an attitude of zest, vivacity and readiness to respond. She scored well above the average for her age in understanding of verbal and arithmetical concepts, average or a little below in her grasp of concepts of spatial relations. On the Wechsler Intelligence Scale for Children her Verbal I.Q. was 123, Performance I.Q. 99. Her reproduction of the designs of the Bender Gestalt Test were less integrated than the average for her age.

With designs that were particularly difficult for her, she made a simplified design suggesting some regression. On the Rorschach test she had a wealth of associations of a global, nonspecific form. The overall picture suggested an ambitious, productive, responsive approach with little attention to detail. She read with good comprehension at third grade level. On the Thematic Apperception Test fantasy primarily and almost exclusively centered on family interrelations and role definition. There are themes of sibling rivalry and loss of family, especially of parents. In view of Mary's history of sibling rivalry one fantasy seems of particular interest:

One day an ugly man was in the forest. He scared everyone to death. They screamed and yelled "Oh, look at that, he is so ugly I think I will run away from home." This little boy was so scared his mother told him to go away and make his own home and then the boy made his own home out of bricks and the boy is very curious because his mother said that. Well, so the boy went home and the ugly thing was dead.

Asked to explain a little more how it would be that the mother would send the boy away from home, Mary explained as though the logic was obvious, "Well, if the boy stayed at home this ugly thing might punish him and he would not be able to punish him if he was not there so the mother told him to go away."

In her test performance Mary did not show the same confidence and self-assertion as in her general behavior. She showed a high degree of verbal fluency in familiar tasks and in those well rooted in previously formed associations. She was, however, extremely resistant to trial and error with unfamiliar or unpracticed tasks and showed distress in the form of sighing, refusals, restlessness, and immobility. She had difficulty changing her set and restructuring a problem to deal with it in a different way if her first effort was not successful.

Mary's parents reported that these test findings were consistent with earlier tests. They had been alerted earlier to the discrepancy between verbal excellence and relative lag in spatial conceptualization and some suggestion had been made that perhaps Mary had a perceptual deficit. Mary's schoolteacher spoke of her as one of the most delightful, outgoing children in the class, a good student and a joy to teach; her one disturbing characteristic was the need to always be right, with a show of anxiety or of avoidance in situations where she could not be sure she would be right.

The test picture of this little girl at age 6, confirmed by reports of her parents and teacher, is that she is very bright, other oriented, has an excessive need to be right, learns fast from imitation but does little trial and error experimentation, and whose cognitive style is ambitious but global and not particularly differentiated.

Discussion

That Mary's symptom disappeared following her mother's interpretation to her of her angry feelings to her brother seems obvious. Whether she responded to the words or the music, the content or the feeling, is not certain. From the cognitive style and general personality attributes she shows at age six one may try to reconstruct what might have been the developmental integrations at age 16 to 22 months and how these may have related to her symptoms. Her present test performance—with its emphasis on verbal fluency, the relative lag in spatial conceptualization, the emphasis on rightness, the field dependency—suggests an extreme form of what has been identified as a pattern of tested abilities more common among little girls than among little boys. So excessive is this "feminine" direction of the pattern in Mary's case, that it actually inhibits optimal performance by its restrictiveness at some times. Being sure of herself as a girl evidently has been something of a special challenge for her.[8]

At the time of her first symptoms, this little girl in a culturally enriched environment where there was a heavy emphasis on verbal interrelations, in her development of conceptual constancies of physical objects must have been beginning to stabilize some sense of gender indentity. When the label "girl" was beginning to have some special meaning for herself, a combination of events occurred that may well have led to an extreme fascination and threat about her own anatomic constancy and about herself. She injured her hand and the laceration persisted as a reminder. Her mother left, to return with a new brother. How Mary perceived her own wound or in what way she perceived her new brother as specifically different is unknown. Very probably her lacerated hand captured some degree of attention and certainly the reports about the new brother and his arrival home with mother would require that the label "boy" as distinct from girl would have to be restructured into her image of herself and of others.

In her current story of a boy who is required to leave home in order to be protected from the "ugly thing," it is tempting to see a hypothetic version of what might have been going on in her own understanding and feeling at age 16 to 22 months when she had temporarily lost her mother, had a wound to herself, and a new brother. The resolution of her symptoms with the interpretation suggests that her paralysis or inhibition of use of her hands may have been a way of protecting her brother against the action of her own, "ugly thing"— her aggressive feelings. Her paralysis also may

have been a way of disowning the injured member in this little girl struggling to maintain self consistency.

Through the next few years she still had difficulty in dealing with her aggressive and angry feelings and when they escaped control she regressed in behavior (enuresis) and developed a phobic state again (for water), but she could respond to encouragement from her mother, and her fear of water was conquered by her parents insisting and encouraging her to take swimming lessons.

Nevertheless, the "accidents" to her brother in the wading pool and with the garage door demonstrate why there is a need to protect preschool children from themselves and their peers.

In response to her anesthesia and laryngoscopy and threatened "loss" of her mother she became phobic about examination of her mouth; and this persisted, though diminishing somewhat, over the next 4 years.

That her father's illness over a 2-month period was not disruptive may be attributed to her mother's presence and support and the fact that her father's response to treatment was good.

Recapitulation

This story of a little girl who developed phobic symptoms between her 16 and 22 months, who improved with interpretation of her feelings to her, shows her to have low tolerance to frustration, moderately high intensity, and to be not as persistent as her brother. But she was not severely negative, had a positive approach, pleasant mood, and was relatively adaptable, regular and not distractible. In terms of Thomas et al.[10] she did not fit into a high-risk group in terms of expectation of severe behavior disturbances.

Her fear of water seems related to her baths, her mother's sudden disappearance to have a baby and later to her pushing her brother into the pool. Either of these two incidents could have explained why Mary feared water. One is reminded of Bowlby's comments[10] about how Schreber's delusions could have been more easily understood if one had the data concerning his father's techniques for educating children.

The symptom of inhibition of the use of her hands at the age of 22 months was similar to the observation of her resistance to using her hands in her first few months of kindergarten experience. This disappeared as she became more comfortable with her teacher and school itself.

Follow-up over the next 4 years and psychologic examination at age 6 years shows a development pattern in which some variation of the original symptoms recurring at times of stress can be resolved by relatively brief direct intervention. Such direct intervention need not be done by a psychiatrist, but can be taken care of by an interested pediatrician who is knowledgeable in child development from a psychologic standpoint.

References

1. Grotjahn, M.: Dream observations in a two year four month old baby. Psychoanal. Q. **7**: 507, 1938.
2. Erickson, M.: On the possible occurrence of a dream in an eight month old infant. Psychoanal. Q. **10**: 382, 1941.
3. Proctor, J. T.: Hysteria in childhood. Am. J. Orthopsychiatry **28**: 394, 1958.
4. Rock, N. L.: Conversion reactions in childhood. J. Am. Acad. Child Psychiatry **10**: 65, 1971.
5. Schnurmann, A.: Observations of a phobia. Psychoanal. Study Child **3–4**: 243, 1949.
6. Freud, S.: Analysis of phobia in a five year old boy (1909). *In*: Collected Works, vol. 3, pp. 149–289, New York Basic Books 1959.
7. Maccoby, E.: Sex differences in intellectual functioning. *In*: The Development of Sex Differences, E. Maccoby, Ed. Stanford University Press 1966, pp. 25–55.
8. Kohlberg, L.: A cognitive-developmental analysis of children's sex-role concepts and attitudes. *In*: The Development of Sex Differences, E. Maccoby, Ed. Stanford University Press 1966, pp. 82–173.
9. Bowlby, J.: Attachment and Loss, vol. II Separation. New York, Basic Books Inc., 1973, pp. 176–177.
10. Thomas, A., Chess, S., Birch, H. C., *et al.*: Behavioral Individuality in Early Childhood. New York University Press 1963.

ANNOTATION

Depressive Disorder in Childhood

Dr. John Pearce

Guy's Hospital, St. Thomas Street, London S.E.1.

INTRODUCTION

CONCEPTS of health and illness vary from one clinician to another and depend on training, experience and personal philosophy as well as the fashionable attitudes of society. The confusion which surrounds the topic "depression" in children reflects these differences of outlook. "Depression" can have at least three different meanings:

1. A normal lowering of mood; an expected emotional response to adversity.
2. An abnormality of mood which is a handicap and constitutes a specific disorder or syndrome.
3. An illness characterized by a depressed mood qualitatively different from usual with a recognized aetiology and prognosis.

Most of the literature on depression does not specify which type of "depression" is being referred to.

Despondency in children was recognized by medical writers in the 17th century and by the mid-nineteenth century suicide and melancholia were noted in children. It was not until the early 20th century that manic-depressive psychosis was reported in children (Walk, 1964). This was followed by the identification of specific infantile forms of depression such as "anaclitic depression" (Spitz, 1946) in 15% of children under one year old separated from their mothers in a Nursery.

It is now generally accepted that children do experience depression as a mood change, but there is less agreement on whether they can suffer from a 'depressive disorder or illness and on how this may present at different ages.

WHAT CONSTITUTES A DEPRESSIVE DISORDER IN CHILDHOOD?

Clear diagnostic criteria are necessary before it is possible to talk of incidence, aetiology and prognosis. A recent study of 547 children aged 1–17 years old attending a Child Psychiatric Department showed that 23% had the *symptom* of depression. This was significantly and positively associated with the following symptoms: anxiety, sleep disturbance, irritability, suicidal thoughts, eating disturbances, school refusal, phobias, alimentary disorders, obsessions and hypochondriasis. It was concluded that a reasonable definition of depressive disorder would be as follows:

1. The association of depression, sadness, unhappiness, misery or tearfulness with at least two of the above symptoms.
2. The lowered mood should be present for at least four weeks and represent a change from normality.
3. The symptoms must be severe enough to interfere with the child's everyday

social and/or cognitive functioning (Pearce, 1974). Very similar criteria have earlier been stated by Weinberg *et al.*, (1973).

INCIDENCE

In a survey of school age children Shepherd *et al.* (1971) found an incidence of 4% abnormal mood changes and 10% excessive crying with varying frequency according to age. The Isle of Wight epidemiological study (Rutter *et al.*, 1970) identified a one year prevalence of affective disorder of 1·4 per 1000 in 10 and 11 year old children. The data for 14–15 year olds showed a three-fold increase in the prevalence of depressive disorder (Rutter *et al.*, 1976).

Amongst children referred for psychiatric help approximately 15–20% can be expected to have a depressive disorder using the diagnostic criteria defined above (Pearce, 1974). In an Educational Diagnostic Centre, Weinberg *et al.* (1973) found that 58% of 72 prepubertal children were suffering from a depressive disorder and three-quarters of these had a first or second degree relative who had been treated with ECT and/or medication for a depressive illness.

SYMPTOMS OF DEPRESSIVE DISORDER

Children generally have difficulty describing their own emotional state and it is overt behaviour noted by adults which draws attention to a depressed child. However, careful questioning of the child often elicits depressive symptoms which have been missed.

Almost every symptom possible has been claimed to be associated with depression in children. However, the more usual features are as follows: A sad, unhappy or miserable looking child who may or may not complain of his feelings but will convey his depression in his behaviour, e.g. crying, lethargy, social withdrawal, listlessness. Complaints of aches and pains are frequent and may take on a hypochondrical quality. Sleeping and eating disturbances are frequently present as is irritability and a low tolerance of frustration. Physical aggression, however, is unusual. Anxiety is a common if not constant feature of the depressed child and may take on obsessional or phobic characteristics. As in adults, the relationship between depression, aggression and anxiety is a complex one.

Altered perception may occur in depressed children and usually consists of over-valued ideas of being unwanted and unloved, accompanied by low self-esteem. Morbid thoughts including suicidal ideas are surprisingly common in depressed children; approximately 30% express suicidal thoughts (Pearce, 1974). Completed, suicide is however a very rare event in childhood before the age of 14 yr (Shaffer 1974). Less than 50% of suicidal children have a depressive disorder (Mattson *et al.*, 1969). In most cases there is a complex interaction between depression, aggression, and socio-cultural factors.

The child with a depressive disorder must be distinguished from the child who is reacting in a "normal" and "healthy" way to sad life events, and from the child whose usual style of behaviour includes features which occur in depression. There is no doubt that the seriously depressed child can be very disturbed but the presence of frank delusions or hallucinations would suggest another diagnosis such as organic psychosis or schizophrenia.

MASKED DEPRESSION

Depression in children is sometimes said to be "masked" or take on an "equivalent" form (Glaser, 1967). This has caused confusion since the terms suggest that there is depressive symptomatology without evidence of depressive affect. In fact lowering of mood is almost invariably to be found if sought for by careful interview or special means such as drawings and play activity. Of course the younger the child the more mood fluctuates and the depressive phases may be easily missed. Maturation brings with it an increasing persistence of mood states which makes them easier to identify. This raises the question whether the manifestations of depression vary with different stages of development. What evidence there is suggests that although symptom patterns change with age, the difference is one of frequency rather than of symptoms.

AETIOLOGY

Family influences are important in the development of childhood depressive disorder (Freud, 1965). Reports showing an increased rate of depression in parents are frequent (Frommer, 1968). The significance of this is not clear and Rutter (1966) was unable to show a specific link between depression in the parent and depression in the child. Probably genetic influences, social learning and adverse parent–child interaction each play a part.

In a review of psychoanalytic theories of depression in children Rie (1966) found general agreement that loss of a loved object either in fantasy or reality has a precipitating role in depression. Sandler and Joffe (1965) concluded from a clinical study of 100 depressed children that loss is an important aetiological factor. An important contribution of psychoanalytic theories has been to put depressive disorders in a developmental context. The concept of time and therefore the possibility of feeling hopeless is seen as an ego function. Guilt and repression of aggression are super-ego functions. Thus the presentation of depression will depend on the developmental level the child has reached.

Most of the evidence available indicates that early separation experiences are followed by a higher rate of depressive disorders in later adolescence or adulthood, rather than immediately following the loss (Rutter, 1972). However Caplan and Douglas (1969) found twice the rate of parental "loss" in a group of children with depressed mood (mean age $11\frac{1}{2}$ yr) compared with the controls. Loss of parents as a result of marital disharmony appears to lead to a higher incidence of depressive disorder than loss through death.

Anything which predisposes to low self-esteem, such as poor academic attainment, rejection and scapegoating, is likely to cause depression, but there is no evidence that these stresses are in any way specific. Depression can be seen as just one possible response to an adverse stimulus. Anxious, sensitive children with neurotic personality traits seem to be particularly vulnerable to depression (Lokare, 1971).

The influence of cerebral biochemistry in the aetiology of depressive affect in children is not known. The definite increase in depression which occurs after puberty mainly in girls suggests that hormonal influences play a part. It can be concluded that there is no single cause of depressive disorder. Each child's depression results from an interaction between internally and externally generated factors.

MANAGEMENT OF THE DEPRESSED CHILD

As yet there is no conclusive evidence that any treatment has a specific anti-depressant effect, because suitably controlled studies are lacking. Frommer (1967) been a proponent of anti-depressant medication for childhood depression and there is now a growing recognition that these drugs are of significant benefit in certain cases. They are indicated where it is apparent, because of the severity and persistence of the depression, that other treatment alone is not going to be sufficient.

Adverse environmental influences play a major part in precipitating childhood depressive disorder. The emphasis of therapy should therefore be directed towards providing conditions at home, at school and in the community where the child may flourish. This will often include treating the parents' depression and working closely with the school.

The establishment of a psychotherapeutic relationship with depressed children is important as they usually feel isolated and misunderstood. Individual, family or group psychotherapy can be helpful in some cases, but the specific indications for this type of treatment have not yet been clearly worked out.

As in other childhood psychiatric disorders, the complexity of the dynamic interaction between the individual child and the environment requires an eclectic approach (Graham, 1974). The aim of any treatment should be to help the child, and family, to find ways of coping with depression and understanding it so that any future episodes of depression can be dealt with using the individual's own resources.

THE IMPLICATIONS OF DEPRESSION

A depressive disorder can set up many new and often unhealthy patterns of behaviour and relationships. These may become self-perpetuating and it would be unwise to expect them to resolve spontaneously (Frommer, 1967). Nissen (1971) reported a follow-up study of depressed children over 26 years and found an increased incidence of depression and other psychiatric and psychosomatic illness.

Zeitlin (1972) noted three interesting associations between childhood and adult disorders. Enuresis was less likely than other child psychiatric disorders to be followed by psychiatric illness as an adult, but when it did depression almost invariably resulted. Zeitlin also found that when children with conduct disorder later presented with a neurotic disorder as adults this was always depressive in type. In the same study Zeitlin reported that a poor prognosis in terms of adult psychiatric disorder was linked with the following symptoms: restlessness, tempers, obsessions, sleep disturbance, peer isolation, somatic complaints, tension, and gratification habits, all of which are frequently associated with depression in children.

The evidence therefore suggests that childhood depressive disorder has a serious significance for the child and should not be regarded as a transient phase of normal experience and development.

CONCLUSION

The development of a depressive disorder is governed by many different factors which include the child's maturity, vulnerability, the nature of the adverse stresses and the amount of support the child is able to receive from the environment. As the child grows he gradually develops a concept of self and reality which depends to a large extent on the love, care and positive attention he receives. With the developing awareness of reality, the child's mood becomes less transient and given sufficient stress and vulnerability, a persistent depressive disorder can occur and has characteristic associated symptoms which vary with age, sex, personality and previous experience. No age is immune from depression but to develop a depressive disorder as an infant requires unusually powerful adverse circumstances. Increasing maturity lowers the threshold for depressive disorder and the biological and psychological changes of puberty lower the threshold still further. However it is not until later in adolescence that the very specific response of manic depressive psychosis arises.

There are still many areas where research is urgently needed, but depressive disorder can now be identified and can be expected to occur in 10–20% of children attending a psychiatric clinic. Without appropriate treatment, the child's depression may have serious repercussions in adult life.

Aggression and Hostility in Young Children

BETTYE M. CALDWELL

How does aggressive behavior develop? What are some effective methods for dealing with such behavior? How can we help young children acquire more prosocial behaviors, such as cooperation and altruism?

I have been active in early childhood education for half a generation now, and during that time I have seen my own professional interests turn almost 180°—from a primary concern with cognitive development (though that was never my only concern in working with young children) to an overriding obsession with how to foster the development of other-oriented, altruistic behavior in young children. This turn-around might not have occurred were it not for my personal style of working, namely, to be right in the thick of the action with teachers and children.

But what is there about my present life that has catalyzed this metamorphosis? For the past five-and-a-half years I have been the director of the Center for Early Development and Education. This is a research project funded during the first five years by the Office of Child Development and sponsored jointly by the University of Arkansas and the Little Rock School District. This year our funds come from the Carnegie Corporation; the Rockefeller Brothers' Fund; Title XX of the Social Security Act; plus financial support from our sponsors, the University of Arkansas at Little Rock and the Little Rock School District. The project originated out of my strong conviction that the experiences a child has during the first five years determine to a great extent later success or failure and the concomitant

Reprinted by permission from *Young Children*, Vol. 32, No. 2 (Jan. 1977), pp. 4-13. ©1977, National Association for the Education for Young Children, 1834 Connecticut Avenue, N.W., Washington, D. C. 20009.

conviction that in the case of intervention with low socioeconomic children, there must be continuity between those first five years and later school experience if the early gains are to be maintained. We are housed in a Little Rock public elementary school, and our program of day care, health and family services, and home intervention is directed toward all children ages six months through fifth grade who attend Kramer School. Within that larger context, the particular experience which is most responsible for my own metamorphosis is that of being a public school principal—these three years have had tremendous and far reaching consequences in my way of viewing early childhood education and child development.

Just how has this way of life so significantly altered the way I feel about children and the process of education?

For one thing, I am now convinced that those of us in early childhood education have been unduly arrogant in our attitudes toward elementary education. There was certainly great arrogance (although perhaps unwitting and implicit) on my part in the thinking that led to the development of the Kramer Project. I was saying in effect, "Those of us who represent early childhood education could take care of America's children if you uncreative people in elementary education just wouldn't mess them up when we have finished with them."

Also I was saying—and there was nothing implicit in this, for I said it openly—"The techniques that we use in early childhood education would help to 'humanize' the schools if you would just watch us and learn from us. *(Why lines, physical punishment, schedules to go to the bathroom, desks in a row?)*" One of the things I have learned is that every one of those seemingly "inhuman" customs had its origins not in the emotional pathology of a distorted teacher but most likely in the gropings of a highly dedicated teacher trying to minimize the careless accidents and de-

liberate provocations that can be caused by children who have not, during earlier developmental periods, acquired sufficient self-control as to render such seemingly archaic customs unnecessary.

For another thing, I am persuaded by authors such as Toffler (1970) that changes are occurring in our society at an unassimilable rate, and that children are not exempt from the impact of these changes. For example, they are not immune to the impact of the media with its change in acceptable themes. The media demonstrate that "good guys" don't always win, and that quarrels are usually resolved by aggression and cunning. What does "All in the Family" teach about family life? Or about the equality of the sexes? What do children learn from the daily news? They learn that Whites and Blacks are fighting in Boston, but they do not learn that 20,000 children are being bused in Little Rock (where, supposedly, it all started) without incident.

There are many other opportunities for indirect or incidental social learning also—from Watergate, from the words emanating from a thousand songs that demand instant gratification, from such slogans as "do your own thing," from meetings in which adults might not be able to speak because of being shouted down, from direct and indirect forms of racial discrimination that persist in every segment of life, and from international indications that one can only settle disputes by resorting to aggression. While we need to be concerned about aggression and hostility in young children, we need even more to be concerned about these same behaviors in adults, and about the omnipresent indicators that ours is a society that apparently values such behavior.

What Do We Know about Aggression in Young Children

It is always disturbing to have someone say something like, "We really don't know too much about aggression and hostility in young children" —especially when you live with it every day. I am certain that every teacher and every aide is more of an expert on this subject than most of the researchers. But we necessarily have to say that about aggression, especially in young children, for a semantic reason if no other—namely, aggression is usually defined as behavior (verbal or physical) that has injury of a person or object as its *intent*. It can sometimes be very conjectural to try to assign intent to a young child's behavior. Did the baby who bit another child "intend" to hurt the other child, or was it to soothe aching gums? Did the toddler who pushed another child down in her eagerness to obtain a toy, causing the other child to cry, "intend" to hurt the pushed-down child or merely to get the toy? Does the child who calls his teacher a dirty name intend to defame her or to study her reaction for future reference or to try out words in an attempt to understand their meaning? Obviously, determination of intent is very difficult when we are concerned with very young children. Thus more people now are willing to define behavior as aggressive if it merely has the capacity to hurt or injure or damage, regardless of intent. The word hostility is even more difficult to define with reference to children, but most of us know what we mean by the term—the angry child whose behavior leaves little room for doubt as to its intent.

Although I do not like to labor too long on definitions, I think one more distinction is worth making. This is what Feshbach (1970) has called the difference between instrumental and hostile aggression. Instrumental aggression is the sort which is aimed at the retrieval of an object, territory, or privilege, i.e., that which results when a goal is blocked. Hostile aggression, on the other hand, is oriented to another person, as a person, following

some sort of ego threat or a perception that another person has behaved intentionally: "He did it on purpose."

There is some evidence (Hartup 1974) that of these two forms, instrumental aggression is far more common in young children. In fact, the decline in overall aggression with age is largely a function of the decline with age in instrumental aggression. In one of the older studies concerned with children's aggression (Dawe 1934), most of the aggression shown by children from about eighteen months to almost six years of age was instigated by disputes over possessions, with the tendency most prevalent among the younger subjects. During these years person-directed, retaliatory, and hostile outbursts increased with age.

Another finding from these skimpy developmental studies of aggression was that the most aggressive children are sometimes the children who also show the greatest amount of prosocial (positive) behavior. This suggests that some children are simply more actively social than others; they engage in more of all types of interpersonal behavior. In spite of scattered "facts" of this sort, we still know precious little about age changes in aggressive behavior. Even more important, we know very little about time trends in incidence of aggressive behavior.

I think one thing we need to do in order to better understand aggression in young children is to develop some new ways of thinking about it. Because of the semantic problems centering around intent, I think it would be better to look at aggression as another manifestation of self versus other. That is, quite apart from whether the biting baby wanted to hurt his victim, we know that he was concerned with gratification of a self-based need. The child who suddenly took a toy from another might not even have noticed that another child was at that moment playing with it, so focused was she on her own desire to possess and manipulate the toy.

Elaine M. Ward

We need to be as concerned about the development in children of a healthy "other" concept as we do about the development of a healthy "self" concept. But how many of us are concerned with this task in our curricula? Not enough, I fear. We desperately need suggestions as to ways to help children develop empathy and concern for others, and our good thinkers need to be giving weight to this need equal to that of the importance of the self-concept.

Practical Suggestions for Those Who Must Cope

Those of us working with children cannot wait until all the data are accumulated and our good thinkers have reached their final conclusions. We are forced to deal with aggression daily and to use whatever bits and pieces of evidence are available to us at the present time—whether or not it is still inconclusive. We must evaluate the data as it comes in and do the best we can to wisely choose our methods of coping with the aggression expressed by the children in our programs. Therefore, I want to discuss some practical guidelines for all of us who must deal with aggression daily. Some of the guidelines are fairly well supported by research findings; others are based more on my personal way of viewing the problem and my attempts at seeking a solution.

Physical punishment of aggression is not the answer. One generalization that emerges with consistency is that there is a close relationship between high use of severe physical punishment by parents and high incidence of aggression by their children. "Spare the rod and spoil the child" is not borne out by data. However, it is difficult to get causative data. Though the two variables, physical punishment by parents and aggression by children, are closely related, it is still somewhat open to debate whether physical punishment "causes" the higher incidence of aggression. It might be possible to argue that high aggression on the part of the child causes more severe punishment by the parents and not vice versa. At this time we simply cannot say. We do know, however, that they are correlated. Further, it seems logical that the adult who uses physical punishment to deal with physical aggression is communicating: "You are just not big enough to get away with it and I am." The adult also is demonstrating to the child a certain belief in aggression as a viable solution to problems.

Ignoring aggression in children is not the answer. This is something I encouraged students and teachers to do for years. Ample testimony to my approach could be found by counting the number of times children at Kramer have been heard to say, "Mrs. Caldwell won't do nothing to you." I am now convinced that this is the wrong thing to do. Ignoring aggression will not make it disappear. The danger, it seems, in not responding to a child's aggressiveness is that the child may regard the watching adult's failure to deal with the aggressive behavior as adult approval of those actions. Siegel and Kohn (1970) have conducted an experiment which seems to support this interpretation of an adult's permissiveness by children. Working with pairs of preschool age children, they allowed half of the pairs to play with various toys for two sessions in the presence of a permissive (and noncondemning) adult; the other half of the pairs played in a similar setting but with no one else in the room. Most of the children in the adult-present condition exhibited more aggression in the second session than in the first; all of the children in the adult-absent condition decreased in aggression in the second session. The adult's permissiveness apparently was viewed by the children as approval of their aggressive behavior and therefore that behavior increased rather than decreased.

Permitting aggression or hostility to be expressed, and assuming that this will "discharge" the tension, will not work. Much of our current popular psychology, however, continues to promote this viewpoint. An article in a popular magazine recently listed the following consequences which can supposedly result from ignoring anger: taut, angry muscles; malfunctioning internal organs; migraine headaches; hives; pimples; itchy rashes; common colds; problems both mild and serious with the bladder, the stomach, and the bowels; ulcers; colitis; heart attacks; being accident prone; disastrous love affairs; and depression. Advice to openly express your anger and hostility in order to remain healthy and happy has been given for years and is still being given by some. Not only is the expression of anger and hostility supposedly preventive but it is also viewed by some as curative.

Yet this position is questionable in light of recent research findings. Berkowitz (1974) after an extensive review of research conducted on controlling aggression in young children concludes:

> He [the child] should not be encouraged to attack someone to express his hostility in the hope that he will drain some hypothetical energy reservoir. The catharsis notion is an outmoded theoretical conception lacking adequate empirical support which also has potentially dangerous social implications. Violence ultimately produces more violence. (p. 135)

With this principle in mind, there is one hint as to when "punishment" (but not aggressive punishment) should occur. According to a study done by Walters, Parke, and Cane (1965), it is most effective to punish or rebuke a would-be aggressor immediately after the aggressor has initiated the aggressive behavior rather than after the attack is completed or the goal is obtained. In their study, Walters, Parke, and Cane rebuked one half of a group of boys each time they reached for an attractive toy. For the other half of the boys, punishment (again in the form of a verbal reproof) came after the toy had been touched. Later the boys were allowed to play in the room with the desired toy but this time with the punishing agent absent. Those boys who had been rebuked before touching the toy demonstrated a greater ability to resist the temptation when left alone with the forbidden toy.

In order to minimize aggression, we need parent cooperation. One of my colleagues, Richard Elardo, and I conducted a study designed to determine whether or not teachers in day care programs and the parents of the children enrolled held differing values with respect to various areas of children's behavior. According to our research, one of the few important differences between parental values and teachers' values was in the area of aggressive behavior. Parents tended to believe that young children should be aggressive and fight in school, so others will not think they are sissies or cowards.

I have seen evidence of this attitude on the part of parents at our own school. We have had parents pick their son up from school and then drive around the school campus looking for another child who supposedly had insulted their son—in order that when the other boy was located, the son could get out of the car and beat the boy up. Similarly, we had a child whose parents had "dared" him to come home from school without having beaten up the little boy who threw sand in his sister's eyes while they were playing together the previous weekend.

Unfortunately, the school will remain ineffective in its efforts to control aggression in children as long as the parents support and even encourage such behavior in their children. If we are to minimize aggression, the school and the parents must work together.

In order to control aggression, we must strengthen altruism; we must emphasize helpfulness and cooperation as highly valued behaviors. In order to do this, however, we must have a society committed to these values. In 1974 I was a member of a U.S. delegation to the People's Republic of China. Our delegation spent most of its time observing in the Chinese kindergartens, which are for children between the ages of three and seven years. I saw no incidents of aggression on the part of the Chinese children. They did not push, shove, hit, kick, or in any way show hostility toward other students; further, there were no verbal attacks made against one another. The children were helpful and cooperative toward their classmates. At first I was somewhat amazed, but later such behaviors seemed the natural consequence of the societal values. The motto which guides the Chinese is "Serve the people!" and, as far as I could tell, the motto had become a way of life. The highest virtue is service to another person or to the collective, and the worst offense is selfishness.

Our society, I fear, lacks this emphasis on service and concern for other people. We, as a society, value competition and self-advancement. We profess belief in helping others, but usually it is considered secondary to the belief that people must help themselves. If we are to foster altruism in children, our society must esteem this quality. Even if the school and the individual parents agree, little will be achieved until the whole society values helpfulness and cooperation, and other attitudes which are inconsistent with aggression and hostility.

Non-permissiveness in our attitudes toward aggression may be as important as punishment for aggressiveness. We need to learn to communicate the attitude that says, "That sort of behavior is simply not going to be tolerated here." This was one of the major findings of the longitudinal study conducted by Sears, Maccoby, and Levin (1957) on patterns of child-rearing.

Our findings suggest that the way for parents to produce a non-aggressive child is to make abundantly clear that aggression is frowned upon, and to stop aggression when it occurs, but to avoid punishing the child for his aggression. Punishment seems to have complex effects. While undoubtedly it often stops a particular form of aggression, at least momentarily, it appears to generate more hostility in the child and lead to further aggressive outbursts at some other time or place. . . . Thus, the most peaceful home is one in which the mother believes aggression is not desirable and under no circumstances is ever to be expressed toward her, but who relies mainly on nonpunitive forms of control. The homes where the children show angry, aggressive outbursts frequently are likely to be homes in which the mother has a relatively tolerant (or careless!) attitude toward such behavior, or where she administers severe punishment for it, or both. (p. 266)

From my experience, I think the statement above would be just as true if we were to go back through it and every time the authors use the word "home" we were to substitute the word "classroom" and every time they use the word "parents" or "mother" we were to substitute the word "teacher." In our schools, we must communicate to the children a low tolerance of aggression while also using nonpunitive techniques for controlling it. Certainly this will not be an easy task. But all the evidence we have on the subject indicates that this is the most effective means for achieving our goal.

We must help children de-escalate their aggressive behavior. This is for me a relatively new concept which is of importance in helping to minimize aggressive behavior in children. It was born in this practical life I lead —observing the children at their play and observing how it is that most of the aggressive behavior develops. I couldn't begin to count the number of times I have seen a group of children running after each other, playing "monster," or "superman," or any of

the other chasing games. Eventually one of the children gets knocked down, or trips, and gets hurt. The child becomes angry and blames a playmate—and the play becomes a fight. The same pattern is typical of play in the sandbox. The children begin innocently making pies, cakes, etc., until someone breaks a cake or pie and the "baker" gets mad and another fight occurs. Whenever these incidents occur and the question "why?" is posed to the children someone will answer, "We were just playing." Think how many times you have heard that explanation. I have come to realize how very often that is correct. Play, which began as positive social interaction, simply escalated too fast and in a manner not anticipated (and often not desired) by the children involved.

Our mistake is that we ususally read intent into the resultant aggressive behavior and reason: "The child should not get away with such behavior; he should be punished." We build intent into their actions, even though it might not have been there with the children (the tripping of a child or the breaking of a mud pie from the children's viewpoint were unintended accidents resulting from too much enthusiasm). If we can avoid being judgmental and simply help the children de-escalate back to the level of play, we will possibly have helped more than if we mete out punishment.

Children need to learn different alternatives to problem situations. It is relatively common for a child to tell me, "I hit him 'cause there wasn't nothin' else to do." Children do have a more limited repertoire of behaviors than adults. But it is up to us to work at providing more desirable alternatives for them. Unless we can help a child realize there are a variety of options, some more desirable than others, we cannot expect behavior to change.

We need to be more willing to play with children and to help them learn to play. How many children in your school know all the verses to London

Elaine M. Ward

Bridge? How many jump rope to the verses we chanted as children? (All their memorization is taken up with commercials.) Or how many of you rationalize that children need to be alone during free play time? The more adults withdraw from children, the more they expose them to peer influence. And the more children interact in the absence of adults (whose behavior they could model), the more likely they are to engage in fights and quarrels over property and privileges.

Summary

Our number one objective as teachers should be to facilitate the development of children's behavior that is cooperative and supportive of one another, altruistic and prosocial rather than aggressive. Those of us who work with children know that we must cope with a great deal of aggressive behavior, which is essentially self-centered. Although this is a phenomenon of our age and our culture, it is quite possible that we have been contributing our share to the apparent increase in such behavior. The isolation of our educational endeavors from schools for older children has in the past deprived us of the opportunity to follow the careers of children and obtain the necessary feedback we should have to enable us to adapt our own techniques to the realities of life histories.

For over a generation now we have been taught essentially to let children express their aggression both to "get it out of their system" and to prevent the development of symptoms of emotional dysfunction. As we now look at this practice, it appears to have been misleading. Aggression breeds not contentment and subsequent cooperation; aggression breeds more aggression. Severe punishment for aggression—especially punishment that mirrors the aggressive act itself —apparently does little to decrease the frequency of such behavior.

Nor does ignoring such behavior help; unfortunately, it does not just go away, and there is very little evidence that a child "grows out of it." Apparently children simply grow into more sophisticated manifestations of aggressive behavior, unless the environment in which the child is developing (home, school, community, nation) communicates that such behavior is not valued, and will not be tolerated. If that environment values cooperation and service to others, and if all segments of society support one another in that valuation, apparently children can learn to develop self-control and concern for others.

We, as parents and teachers, need to give some thought to helping children learn to de-escalate their aggressiveness back down to the level of play, where much of the behavior starts. De-escalating play is different from defusing the hostility which is often theorized as causing aggressiveness. As part of this de-escalation, a plea was made for more, rather than less, involvement of adults with children in their play. The price of liberty is supposed to be eternal vigilance. Vigilance by and extended contact with adults who model nonaggressive behavior is indeed one necessary precondition for the development of children who can cooperate with one another and with adults—and be happy in the process.

References

Berkowitz, L. "Control of Aggression." In *Review of Child Development Research, Vol. III*, edited by B. Caldwell and H. Ricciuti, pp. 95-140. Chicago: University of Chicago Press, 1973.

Dawe, H. C. "An Analysis of Two Hundred Quarrels of Preschool Children." *Child Development,* 1934, pp. 139-157.

Elardo, R., and Caldwell, B. M. "Value Imposition in Early Education: Fact or Fancy." *Child Care Quarterly,* 1973, pp. 6-13.

Feshbach, S. "Aggression." In *Carmichael's Manual of Child Psychology,* edited by P. H. Mussen, pp. 159-259. New York: John Wiley & Sons, 1970.

Hartup, W. W. "Aggression in Childhood: Developmental Perspectives." *American Psychologist,* 1974, pp. 336-341.

Sears, R. R.; Maccoby, E. E.; and Levin, H. *Patterns of Child Rearing.* Evanston, Ill.: Row, Peterson, and Co., 1957.

Siegel, A. E., and Kohn, L. G. "Permissiveness, Permission, and Aggression: The Effects of Adult Presence or Absence on Aggression in Children." In *Child Development and Behavior,* edited by F. Rebelsky and L. Dorman, pp. 234-242. New York: Alfred A. Knopf, 1970.

Toffler, A. *Future Shock.* New York: Random House, 1970.

Walters, R. H.; Parke, R. D.; and Cane, V. A. "Timing of Punishment and the Observation of Consequences to Others as Determinants of Response Inhibition." *Journal of Experimental Child Psychology,* 1965, pp. 10-30.

Early Identification and Preschool

(2-5 years)

As late as the 1960's, young children with behavior problems or emotional disorders were not being diagnosed. The traditional assumption had been that the disorder was caused by the parents - with an emphasis on mother-blame. Parents, ashamed and guilt-ridden, did not bring their deviant children to the attention of a professional. This is no longer true.

The most common disorders being diagnosed in young children are autism, hyperactivity, and anti-social behavior. The etiology of autism has been believed to be cold, uncaring parents, specifically the mother. This theory has been abandoned. Though much research has been done in the field, the cause of autism is unknown. The method of treatment varies from pharmacological or chemotherapy to behavior modification. The one point of agreement is that early diagnosis and early placement (not necessarily residential placement) is essential for progress.

Hyperactivity is a behavior disorder with a variety of causes. The overly active youngster is showing a "symptom" by his/her frenetic activity, not a "disease." Food allergies, specific learning disabilities, biochemical imbalances and environmental conditions are all problems where the symptom might be hyperactive behavior. Treatment of this disorder, or symptom, in early childhood is essential. If not corrected, the hyperative youngster shows a lack of self-esteem and learning difficulties once they reach school age. Treatment of this behavior disorder depends upon its cause: the treatment could be a special diet, vitamin therapy, behavior modification or play therapy.

Anti-social behavior in young children, aggression or withdrawal, is not uncommon. These behavior problems cannot be helped by dynamic therapy - usually, behavior modification or role modelling in preschool, through the use of mainstreaming are the therapies of choice.

A THREE-YEAR FOLLOW-UP OF HYPERACTIVE PRESCHOOLERS INTO ELEMENTARY SCHOOL

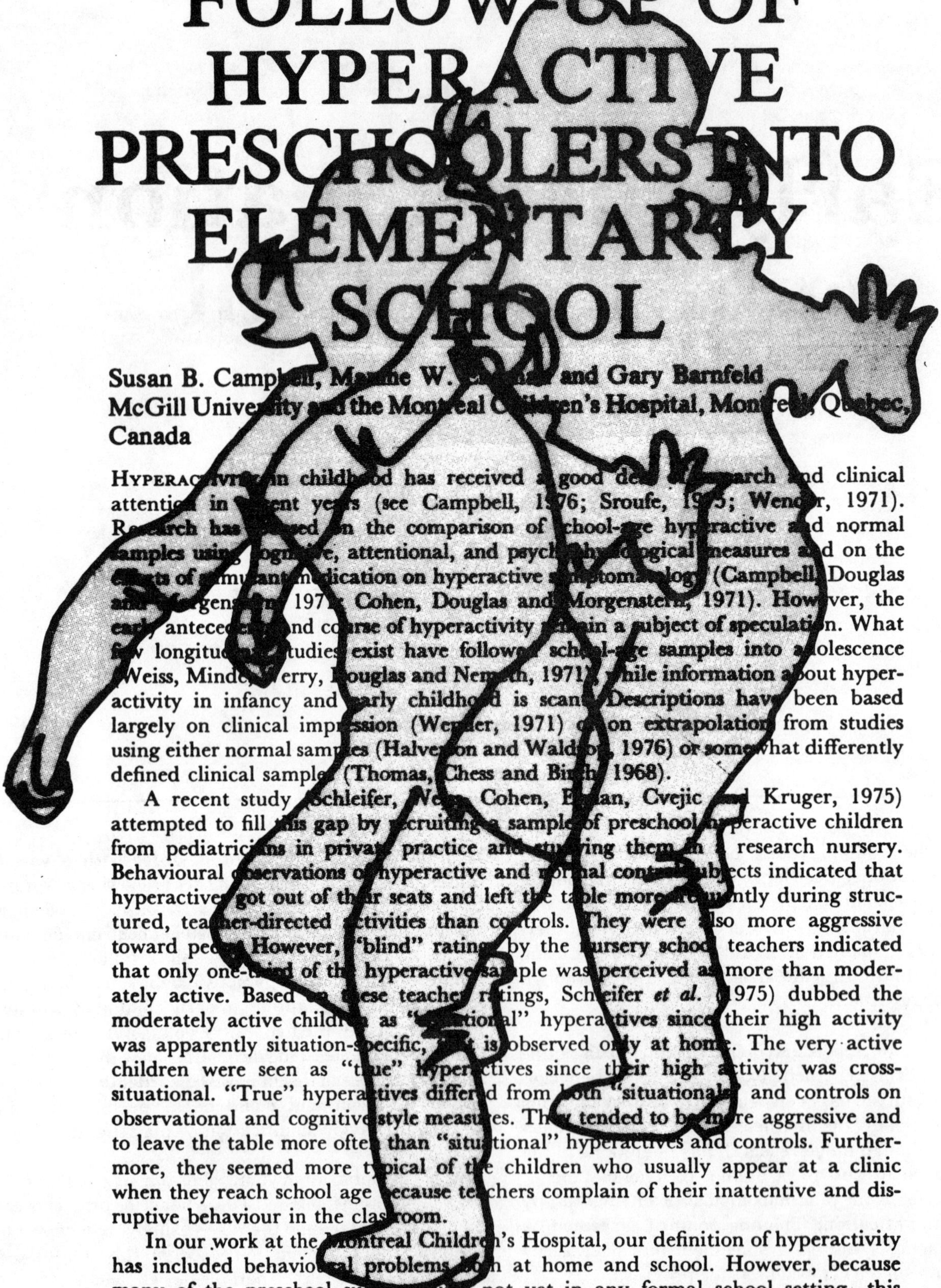

Susan B. Campbell, Maxine W. Endman and Gary Barnfeld
McGill University and the Montreal Children's Hospital, Montreal, Quebec, Canada

Hyperactivity in childhood has received a good deal of research and clinical attention in recent years (see Campbell, 1976; Sroufe, 1975; Wender, 1971). Research has focused on the comparison of school-age hyperactive and normal samples using cognitive, attentional, and psychophysiological measures and on the effects of stimulant medication on hyperactive symptomatology (Campbell, Douglas and Morgenstern, 1971; Cohen, Douglas and Morgenstern, 1971). However, the early antecedents and course of hyperactivity remain a subject of speculation. What few longitudinal studies exist have followed school-age samples into adolescence (Weiss, Minde, Werry, Douglas and Nemeth, 1971), while information about hyperactivity in infancy and early childhood is scant. Descriptions have been based largely on clinical impression (Wender, 1971) or on extrapolation from studies using either normal samples (Halverson and Waldrop, 1976) or somewhat differently defined clinical samples (Thomas, Chess and Birch, 1968).

A recent study (Schleifer, Weiss, Cohen, Elman, Cvejic and Kruger, 1975) attempted to fill this gap by recruiting a sample of preschool hyperactive children from pediatricians in private practice and studying them in a research nursery. Behavioural observations of hyperactive and normal control subjects indicated that hyperactives got out of their seats and left the table more frequently during structured, teacher-directed activities than controls. They were also more aggressive toward peers. However, "blind" ratings by the nursery school teachers indicated that only one-third of the hyperactive sample was perceived as more than moderately active. Based on these teacher ratings, Schleifer *et al.* (1975) dubbed the moderately active children as "situational" hyperactives since their high activity was apparently situation-specific, that is observed only at home. The very active children were seen as "true" hyperactives since their high activity was cross-situational. "True" hyperactives differed from both "situationals" and controls on observational and cognitive-style measures. They tended to be more aggressive and to leave the table more often than "situational" hyperactives and controls. Furthermore, they seemed more typical of the children who usually appear at a clinic when they reach school age because teachers complain of their inattentive and disruptive behaviour in the classroom.

In our work at the Montreal Children's Hospital, our definition of hyperactivity has included behavioural problems both at home and school. However, because many of the preschool subjects were not yet in any formal school setting, this

A Three-Year Follow-Up of Hyperactive Preschoolers into Elementary School, Susan B. Campbell, Maxine W. Endman and Gary Bernfeld, *Journal of Child Psychology and Psychiatry*, Vol. 18, 1977. ©1977 by Pergamon Press Ltd.

criterion could not be met. This may account for the apparently different composition of this sample in which two-thirds were not judged severe behaviour problems in the research nursery although mothers complained of difficult behaviour at home. Since school age hyperactives typically have greater difficulty at school than at home, this discrepancy between the preschool sample and older samples was particularly intriguing. Moreover, because the Schleifer *et al.* (1975) study had suggested the possibility that two distinct subgroups of hyperactive children had been identified in the preschool years, it seemed important to follow these children to determine whether they remained hyperactive and whether there was a difference in outcome between "true" and "situational" hyperactive subgroups. The first phase of this follow-up study involved measures of cognitive style, observations of mother–child interaction in a problem-solving situation, maternal reports of behaviour problems, and a measure of moral judgement (Campbell, Schleifer, Weiss and Perlman, 1977). Results pointed to the heterogeneity of the clinical sample. On most measures of mother–child interaction and cognitive functioning, "situational" hyperactives and controls did not differ, while "true" hyperactives requested more feedback from their mothers, talked more in a problem-solving situation, and made more immature moral judgements. However, maternal reports of behaviour problems demonstrated that mothers of both subgroups of hyperactives continued to perceive their children as problems, with both groups showing large differences from controls on ratings of impulsive–hyperactive and conduct problem behaviour.

Thus, the first phase of the follow-up indicated that both "true" and "situational" subgroups were reported to be problems at home, although laboratory measures continued to differentiate them. It was, therefore, unclear whether the "situational" group actually continued to have more difficulties than controls or whether maternal reports reflected inaccurate maternal perceptions of behaviour. In an effort to answer this question, a second follow-up study was designed to provide observations of classroom behaviour and data from teachers on the adjustment of these children in school. It was assumed that if problems were persistent they would be apparent in the classroom. Moreover, school data would provide information on these youngsters independent of maternal perceptions of child behaviour.

In addition to observations of classroom behaviour, teachers' reports were obtained on the Teacher Rating Scale, a measure of child psychopathology (Conners, 1969), and children were administered the Coopersmith Self-Esteem Inventory (Coopersmith, 1967). It was hypothesized that true hyperactive children would engage in more disruptive, off-task, and out-of-seat behaviour and elicit more directions and negative feedback from teachers than control children from their own classrooms and controls and "situational" hyperactives from the original study. They were also expected to be rated by their teachers as more hyperactive and inattentive than the other groups. Moreover, it was assumed that both hyperactive subgroups would show lower self-esteem than controls, with "situational" hyperactives reporting particularly low self-esteem in relation to home and family and the "true" group expressing lower self-esteem in relation to school.

METHOD

Subjects

Of the original 54 subjects in the preschool study, only 31 could be traced for the second follow-up, 15 hyperactives and 16 controls. Of the 23 subjects who were lost, nine hyperactives and four controls had left the province. Three control families could not be traced. Parents of three hyperactives and three controls refused permission for observers to go into their child's school; finally, one hyperactive female subject was in an institution for the emotionally disturbed, following hospitalization of her mother in a psychiatric facility. Despite this large attrition rate over the three year period since original contact with these families, the initial and follow-up samples appear essentially similar in terms of age, intelligence, and hyperactivity ratings of the children at intake as well as social class. Hyperactivity ratings were initially completed using the Werry–Weiss–Peters Activity Scale (Werry, 1968), while socioeconomic ratings were based on the Hollingshead Scale (Hollingshead, 1957). Original and follow-up sample characteristics are summarized in Table 1.

The hyperactive follow-up sample consisted of three girls and 12 boys ranging in age from 6 years 11 months to 8 years 7 months. Six were in grade one classrooms, seven in grade two classrooms, and two were in special classes for learning disabilities. Of the 16 children in the control group, all but

TABLE 1. CHARACTERISTICS OF ORIGINAL AND FOLLOW-UP SAMPLES

	Hyperactive		Control	
	Mean	S.D.	Mean	S.D.
Original sample	$N = 28$		$N = 26$	
Age at intake	47·23	5·80	47·28	5·91
Binet I.Q. at $4\frac{1}{2}$	102·96	11·11	104·33	10·40
Social class	32·41	15·94	24·27	15·04
Hyperactivity score	47·50	9·53	26·38	5·13
Follow-up sample	$N = 15$		$N = 16$	
Age at intake	46·67	5·65	47·56	6·57
Age at follow-up	92·07	7·54	92·00	8·12
Binet I.Q. at $4\frac{1}{2}$	104·40	11·11	110·91	11·25
WISC I.Q. at $6\frac{1}{2}$	116·67	13·93	121·93	10·24
Social class	33·07	17·01	27·14	17·14
Hyperactivity score	47·87	8·22	27·06	6·08

two were male. They ranged in age from 6 years 5 months to 8 years 8 months. One child was in kindergarten, five children were in grade one, eight in grade 2, one in grade 3, and one was in a special class for children with learning disabilities. Of the 15 children in the hyperactive group, three girls and five boys had been classified as "situational", with the remaining seven boys classed as "true" hyperactives.

The groups were matched on age, WISC I.Q. at $6\frac{1}{2}$, and social class. Means and standard deviations of these data are reported in Table 1. Differences between hyperactive and control groups on age ($t = 0·98$), I.Q. ($t = 0·24$), and social class ($t = 0·34$) were not statistically significant. Similarly, one-way analyses of variance indicated that when "true" and "situational" subgroups were separated, the groups were still well matched on these demographic variables. The parents of two hyperactive children were separated. None of the hyperactive children was on medication at the time of the study. More details of treatment are provided in an earlier publication (Campbell *et al.*, 1977).

Procedure

All subjects were observed in their regular classrooms by observers who were "blind" to group membership. In addition to the target child, a child of the same sex was chosen at random to serve as a classroom control. Since children were in schools throughout the city and classes varied in degree of structure from traditional to open area, these additional groups were necessary to control for the potentially confounding effects of differences among classrooms. However, distributions of subjects across types of classrooms turned out to be the same. Eight controls and seven hyperactives were in traditional classes, four subjects in each group were in open area classes, and four children in each group were in classes which were intermediate in degree of structure. Children were not aware they were being observed. Teachers were told that target subjects were participants in a longitudinal study of child development. No mention was made of problem behaviour and teachers were not informed which child had been chosen as the classroom control in order to avoid any bias in selection. Thus, a total of 62 subjects was observed, the 31 children from the follow-up sample and their 31 same sex classroom controls.

Observations were carried out during a regular academic period for both the target subject and the classroom control, in two alternating 15 min blocks, for a total of 30 min of observation per child. Observers were "blind" to the group membership of the target child. Both teacher and child behaviours were coded in 10 sec blocks on predefined behavioural categories using a time-sampling approach. Subjects were observed for 10 sec and behaviours were then coded in the next 10 sec. A stopwatch was started at the beginning of each 15 min period. Inter-observer reliability was computed on a random sample of 16 subjects, using the formula agreements divided by agreements plus disagreements. Reliability was high, ranging from 85·8% to 100% with a mean of 92·3%. Coding categories are defined below with interobserver reliability in parenthesis.

Child behaviours

In-seat, off-task: Child has remained in his seat, but is not attending to the class activity and/or teacher's instructions (85·8%).

Out-of-seat, off-task: Child has lifted himself from his seat and is not attending to the classroom activity and/or teacher's instructions (88·5%).

Attention-soliciting: Child requests teacher's attention in an appropriate manner such as raising hand (90%).

Disruptive behaviour toward teacher: Physical or verbal behaviour which disturbs teacher's on-going activity such as calling out inappropriately or going to teacher's desk (93·8%).

Disruptive behaviour toward peer: Physical or verbal behaviour which disturbs another child inappropriately such as teasing, talking to, or poking peer (91·4%).

Disrupts class: Inappropriate physical or verbal behaviour as above, but which disturbs three or more peers (100%).

Teacher behaviours

Positive feedback: Praise or encouraging statements to child about his/her performance or behaviour (89·6%).

Negative feedback: Expression of disapproval to child about behaviour or performance; reprimands (100%).

Directions: Instructions to child; reminders to attend or persist which are not evaluative in nature (91·4%).

After the observations were completed, teachers were asked to complete the Conners Teacher Rating Scale (Conners, 1969) on the target child. Teachers were asked to rate each of 39 behaviours as "not at all a problem" to "very much a problem" on a four point scale.

The target child was then taken to a testing room and individually administered the Coopersmith Self-Esteem Inventory (Coopersmith, 1967). The examiner said: "I would like to get to know you a bit better. To help me do this I would like you to answer a few questions about yourself. One thing that I want you to remember is that this has nothing to do with school; there are no right or wrong answers. I will read you a sentence and I want you to think very hard if this sentence says something true of you or false of you. Do you understand?" The 52 items were then read to the subject and responses recorded.

RESULTS

Data analyses were carried out for the total hyperactive group and with the hyperactive group split into "true" and "situational" subgroups. Although results were essentially parallel, some additional trends were observed in the data when the hyperactive subgroups were combined. Thus, data will be reported for the comparison among "true", "situational", and control groups for all variables and some additional trends in hyperactive–control comparisons will be noted.

Classroom observations

As mentioned above, a classroom control of the same sex as the target child was selected at random and observed in order to control for variations in class structure. Raw data were subjected to a square root transformation to normalize the distributions and then a 2×3 nested analysis of variance, assessing group and classroom effects was carried out for each of the child and teacher behaviours. Newman–Keuls tests were then used to compare the means when a significant F ratio was obtained. Because the comparison was nested within classrooms, interaction effects were of interest which would indicate differences between groups within a classroom, that is hyperactive subgroups and classroom controls, as well as between subgroups from the initial study. However, no significant interactions were obtained, though several unexpected main effects were significant.

A significant classroom effect was obtained for the variable negative feedback ($F = 4·75$, $d.f. = 2/56$, $p < 0·01$). Teachers from classrooms with both "true" and "situational" subjects gave significantly more negative feedback to both target subjects and their classroom controls than did teachers of control children from the original sample and their controls. Newman–Keuls tests indicated that both these differences were significant at better than the 0·05 level. Thus, hyperactive subjects in both groups received more negative feedback than the original controls. However, their in-class controls also received more negative teacher attention, suggesting that the presence of a hyperactive child in a classroom leads to more negative teacher–child interaction.

Similar analyses of child behaviours likewise failed to demonstrate significant interaction effects. However, a main effect for classrooms was obtained for disrupts class ($F = 3·56$, $d.f. = 2/56$, $p < 0·05$), with Newman–Keuls tests indicating that "true" hyperactives and their classroom controls were more disruptive than the other groups ($p < 0·05$). A similar trend emerged for the variable disruptive behaviour toward teacher ($F = 2·40$, $d.f. = 2/56$, $p = 0·09$) and although this difference failed to attain a satisfactory level of significance, means on this variable were highest for "situational" subjects and their classroom controls. These findings likewise suggest that the presence of a hyperactive child in the classroom appears to influence teacher–child interaction between both normal and problem children. Off-task behaviours, attention-soliciting, and disruptive behaviour toward peers failed to differentiate the groups.

Although no main or interaction effects were obtained for the variable out-of-seat, off-task, *a priori* *t*-tests (Winer, 1962) indicated that "true" hyperactives were more often out-of-seat and off-task than "situational" hyperactives ($t = 4.38$, $d.f. = 13$, $p < 0.01$) and control children from their own classrooms ($t = 3.39$, $d.f. = 12$, $p < 0.01$).

A significant main effect for the variable positive feedback ($F = 8.74$, $d.f. = 1/56$, $p < 0.01$) indicated that target subjects in all three groups received more positive feedback than classroom controls. Teacher directions similarly showed a main effect with target subjects receiving more directions than classroom controls ($F = 13.23$, $d.f. = 1/56$, $p < 0.001$). Thus, teachers provided more directions and positive feedback to subjects they knew were being observed. These findings are summarized in Table 2.

The analyses reported above took into account only frequency of occurrence of each behaviour. In addition, several simple sequence analyses were carried out to determine whether particular child behaviours appeared to elicit specific teacher behaviours differentially. For the sequences of interest, the child behaviour which preceded teacher behaviour, either in the same or previous 10 sec block was calculated for each subject. Only sequences which occurred with sufficient frequency to be analyzed will be discussed further.

These data were similarly subjected to a 2 × 3 nested ANOVA. Target subjects in all three groups were more likely than controls to elicit directions from their teachers when they engaged in out-of-seat, off-task behaviour ($F = 7.46$, $d.f. = 1/56$, $p < 0.01$), attention-soliciting behaviour ($F = 5.74$, $d.f. = 1/56$, $p < 0.02$), and disruptive behaviour toward peers ($F = 5.64$, $d.f. = 1/56$, $p < 0.02$). This was true despite the finding, reported above, that target subjects and classroom controls did not differ significantly in the frequency of occurrence of these behaviours, suggesting that teachers were attending to such behaviour significantly more often in target subjects. On the other hand, in-seat, off-task behaviour and non-disruptive behaviour (i.e. behaviours not coded) did not differentially elicit directions from teachers. Target subjects in all three groups also received more positive feedback after attention-soliciting behaviour ($F = 6.11$, $d.f. = 1/56$, $p < 0.02$). Finally, a significant interaction ($F = 3.63$, $d.f. = 2/56$, $p < 0.05$), was obtained for the sequence attention-soliciting followed by negative feedback from teacher. Comparisons between the means using a Newman–Keuls procedure indicated that "situational" hyperactives elicited more negative feedback after attention-soliciting behaviour than "true" hyperactives and controls from the original sample, as well as controls from their own classrooms ($p < 0.05$ for all comparisons). These data are summarized in Table 2.

Teacher Rating Scales

This measure was obtained only for target subjects. Means and standard deviations for the four factor scores computed according to standard instructions (Conners, 1969) are summarized in Table 3. A one-way analysis of variance indicated significant group differences on the Inattentive–Passive ($F = 3.98$, $d.f. = 2/28$, $p < 0.05$) and Hyperactivity ($F = 6.71$, $d.f. = 2/28$, $p < 0.01$) factors. Newman–Keuls tests revealed that "true" hyperactives were significantly more inattentive than controls ($p < 0.05$) and "situational" hyperactives ($p < 0.05$). Contrary to expectation, however, teachers rated both the "situational" and "true" hyperactive subgroups as significantly more hyperactive than controls ($p < 0.05$ for both). The Conduct Problem and Tension–Anxiety factors did not differentiate the groups.

Self-esteem

The Coopersmith Self-Esteem Inventory was scored according to standard instructions (Coopersmith, 1967) and scores were analyzed for the subscales Social Self, Home and Parents, School and Academic, and General Self as well as the Lie

TABLE 2. MEANS AND STANDARD DEVIATIONS OF OBSERVATIONAL VARIABLES FOR TARGET SUBJECTS AND CLASSROOM CONTROLS

	True $N = 7$		Classroom Control $N = 7$		Situational $N = 8$		Classroom control $N = 8$		Control $N = 16$		Classroom control $N = 16$	
	Mean	S.D.	Mean	S.D.	Mean	S.D.	Mean	S.D.	Mean	S.D.	Mean	S.D.
Teacher behaviours												
Positive feedback	2·71	3·90	0·29	0·49	0·75	0·70	0·25	0·70	1·00	1·60	0·25	0·44
Negative feedback	0·57	0·53	1·00	1·52	0·75	1·16	0·63	1·06	0·13	0·34	0·13	0·34
Directions	8·71	8·17	4·57	4·79	6·81	2·59	3·38	3·02	4·88	4·52	1·50	1·71
Child behaviours												
In-seat, off-task	12·50	12·37	10·71	6·45	13·31	7·73	10·25	4·20	12·03	6·83	13·91	11·10
Out-of-seat, off-task	22·14	17·91	14·14	10·85	11·94	11·38	9·50	9·25	12·41	10·88	9·97	10·14
Attention-soliciting	7·07	9·90	3·14	1·67	6·69	6·29	5·63	6·41	6·53	7·20	4·25	3·45
Disrupts class	0·43	0·78	0·29	0·49	0·00	0·00	0·00	0·00	0·13	0·34	0·06	0·25
Disrupts peer	11·86	10·47	10·14	7·35	11·75	9·66	11·00	12·16	13·13	11·32	12·00	9·14
Disrupts teacher	0·00	0·00	0·00	0·00	0·38	0·74	0·25	0·46	0·16	0·50	0·06	0·25
Sequences												
In-seat, directions	0·43	0·79	0·00	0·00	0·75	1·75	0·13	0·35	0·25	0·77	0·13	0·50
Out-of-seat, directions	3·71	5·35	1·43	2·00	2·00	2·00	0·88	0·83	2·00	2·48	0·31	0·60
Attention-soliciting, directions	3·57	5·68	1·43	1·81	1·88	2·03	0·89	0·82	1·88	2·31	0·44	0·63
Disrupts peer, directions	0·57	0·79	0·00	0·00	0·13	0·35	0·25	0·46	0·44	0·81	0·00	0·00
Non-disrupt, directions	3·71	6·87	2·86	3·34	3·25	2·38	1·63	2·77	1·56	2·19	0·88	1·45
Out-of-seat, positive feedback	0·43	0·79	0·14	0·38	0·25	0·46	0·00	0·00	0·19	0·54	0·13	0·34
Attention, positive feedback	0·57	0·71	0·00	0·00	0·38	0·52	0·00	0·00	0·31	0·87	0·00	0·00
Attention, negative feedback	0·00	0·00	0·14	0·38	0·25	0·46	0·00	0·00	0·00	0·00	0·00	0·00

Note: Means and standard deviations of raw data.

TABLE 3. MEANS AND STANDARD DEVIATIONS OF TEACHER RATING SCALE AND SELF-ESTEEM VARIABLES FOR TARGET SUBJECTS

Variable	True		Situational		Control	
	Mean	S.D.	Mean	S.D.	Mean	S.D.
Teacher rating scale						
Conduct problem	4·00	7·43	7·50	9·10	2·13	6·71
Inattentive–passive	9·14	3·67	4·87	2·99	4·12	4·47
Tension–anxiety	5·85	2·67	4·37	2·82	4·00	2·96
Hyperactivity	9·42	6·80	9·00	5·52	2·87	3·22
Self-esteem						
Social	9·42	5·00	9·75	2·92	11·12	3·34
Home–parents	10·85	2·79	9·50	3·16	10·00	3·18
School–academic	10·57	4·72	9·25	4·40	12·12	2·57
General self	34·00	12·75	29·25	6·67	38·12	9·04
Lie scale	5·28	2·14	5·50	2·39	4·87	1·85
Total	64·85	22·89	57·75	13·02	71·62	15·30

Scale and Total Score. Means and standard deviations are presented in Table 3. One-way analyses of variance indicated no significant differences despite the tendency for "situational" hyperactives to show slightly lower School, General, and Total self-esteem. When the hyperactive subgroups are combined, these trends approach significance for School and Academic Self ($t = 1·76$, $d.f. = 29$, $p = 0·09$), General Self ($t = 1·96$, $d.f. = 29$, $p = 0·06$), and Total Self-Esteem ($t = 1·77$, $d.f. = 29$, $p = 0·09$) with hyperactive subjects indicating a poorer self-concept than controls.

DISCUSSION

These results indicate that children identified as hyperactive in the preschool years continue to have difficulties when they reach elementary school. Both classroom observations and teacher ratings continue to differentiate "true" and "situational" hyperactive subjects from the original control sample. In addition, several differences between "true" and "situational" subgroups suggest that this distinction, originally made on the basis of preschool behaviour (Schleifer *et al.*, 1975), has some prognostic utility.

Classroom observations indicate that hyperactive subgroups elicit more negative feedback from their teachers and engage in more disruptive behaviour than controls from the original sample. They are also rated by their teachers as more hyperactive than controls, consistent with maternal ratings obtained at ages 4 (Schleifer *et al.*, 1975) and 6½ (Campbell *et al.*, 1977). This suggests that both the "situational" and "true" groups are indeed more difficult to manage than controls and that maternal ratings of behaviour problems reflect actual problems and not merely inappropriate expectations of child behaviour. In addition, hyperactive subjects, as a group, show a tendency to report somewhat lower self-esteem than controls, a not surprising finding in view of maternal reports of more difficult behaviour from infancy (Campbell, 1976) and the present observation that they receive more negative feedback from teachers. However, these results are contrary to the speculations of Campbell *et al.* (1977) that "situational" hyperactives may come from less tolerant homes than "true" hyperactives and controls; since "situational" subjects do not appear to perceive their parents as more punitive or rejecting it is not likely that their parents are intolerant of normal, but exuberant behaviour.

Comparisons between hyperactive subgroups indicate that "true" hyperactives continue to have somewhat more problems than the "situational" group. They are rated by teachers as more inattentive and are also out-of-seat and off-task more of the time. "Situationals" and controls, however, do not differ on these two measures. Teacher ratings suggest that "situationals" are as fidgety and disruptive as "trues" but not as inattentive. Moreover, teacher ratings appear to parallel classroom observations since both hyperactive subgroups were noted to engage in disruptive behaviour, while out-of-seat, off-task behaviour differentiated "true" from "situational" hyperactives. Thus, consistent with the initial finding that "true" hyperactives left the table more frequently during structured activities than "situationals" and controls (Schleifer *et al.*, 1975), "true" hyperactives continue to leave their seats more often in the elementrary school classroom. Given the convergence of classroom observations and teacher ratings, it appears that nursery school behaviour is predictive of later classroom behaviour, in keeping with the findings of Halverson and Waldrop (1976) with a normal sample. Moreover, active and aggressive behaviour in the preschool appears to have some prognostic validity, with less active and aggressive youngsters within the hyperactive group showing fewer problems in elementary school than the more active and aggressive subgroup. Thus, consistent with both original data and 6½ year follow-up data, "situational" hyperactives continue to have more difficulties than controls, but fewer than children designated "true" hyperactives.

Comparisons among classroom controls and original subgroups suggest that the presence of a hyperactive child in the classroom may influence interaction patterns within the classroom as a whole. Despite the fact that the degree of class structure was relatively evenly distributed across the groups, both groups of hyperactive subjects and their classroom controls received more negative feedback from the teacher and engaged in more disruptive behaviour than did the original control group and their classroom controls. This may suggest that the presence of a hyperactive child in the classroom leads to more negative interaction between teacher and pupils. One possibility is that disruptive behaviour, once initiated by the hyperactive youngster, becomes contagious with peers also becoming disruptive. In other words, the disruptive behaviour of the hyperactive child may have a disinhibiting effect on non-hyperactive peers, with difficult behaviour leading to teacher reprimands in an escalating fashion. Unfortunately, interaction between hyperactive subjects and classroom controls was not specifically coded, so it is not possible to determine from these data whether, in fact, disruptive behaviour from classroom controls was instigated by the behaviour of hyperactive subjects. However, this finding does permit the speculation that the presence of a hyperactive child affects the ecology of a classroom, and suggests directions for further research.

Additional main effects indicated that target subjects, both hyperactive and control, received more teacher directions and positive feedback than their classroom controls. Sequence analyses also indicated that directions from the teacher more frequently followed out-of-seat behaviour, attention-soliciting, and disruptive behaviour toward peers in the target population than their in-class controls. Further, target subjects received more positive feedback after attention-soliciting behaviour. These findings indicate that teacher behaviour is influenced by the presence of an observer in that more positive, structuring behaviours are directed toward the child being observed, regardless of clinical status. Moreover, target subjects were more likely than classroom controls to be reinforced for inappropriate behaviour. Out-of-seat, off-task and disuptive behaviour toward peer were more likely to be followed by teacher attention in the form of directions. On the other hand, negative feedback seemed to be less selectively influenced by knowledge of the observer's focus since hyperactive children and their classroom controls received equal amounts. Moreover, "situational" hyperactives received significantly more negative feedback in response to attention-soliciting, suggesting that observer presence did not inhibit teachers from reprimanding target children. However, these data indicate the importance of observing more than one child in a classroom simultaneously and of controlling for teacher awareness. Initially, we had hoped to avoid bias in the selection of a classroom control, but this inadvertently influenced teacher behaviour.

In summary, children designated hyperactive in the preschool years continue to manifest problems in elementary school as measured by classroom observations and teacher ratings. They also appear to have somewhat lower self-esteem than controls. Moreover, the distinction between "true" and "situational" hyperactives, initially made on the basis of preschool behaviour, appears to have some prognostic utility since "true" hyperactives were more often out-of-seat and off-task and were rated as more inattentive than "situational" hyperactives. Furthermore, the stability of hyperactive behaviour in this age group suggests that earlier identification and remediation may be possible. In addition, it is worth noting the high attrition rate, particularly among the "situationals", which suggests that we may indeed be dealing with distinct etiological subgroups of reactive and constitutional hyperactivity.

SUMMARY

Hyperactive and control children, originally observed in a research nursery at age 4 and then followed-up at $6\frac{1}{2}$, were observed in their elementary school classrooms at $7\frac{1}{2}$. Hyperactive children received more negative feedback from teachers, engaged in more disruptive behaviour, were rated by their teachers as more hyperactive, and expressed somewhat lower self-esteem than controls. However, comparisons between classrooms with hyperactive and control children suggested that the presence of a hyperactive child may influence interaction patterns between the teacher and the class as a whole. Moreover, observer presence influenced teachers' positive behaviours toward the child being observed.

Activity Group Therapy for Emotionally Disturbed Children

Agnes M. Plenk

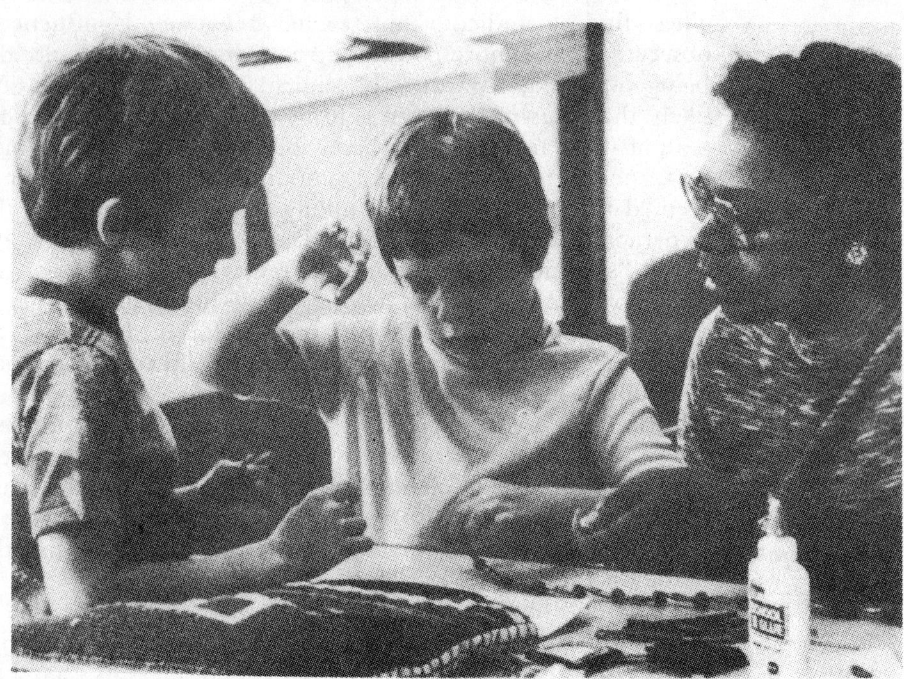

ABSTRACT

Treatment services for preschool children with emotional problems is a neglected area in the network of mental health facilities. This might be partly due to pressures of schools and courts to treat the large number of disturbed children in the latency and adolescent age groups and partly to the lack of adequate models. One agency offering comprehensive services for children between the ages of two to five and in operation since 1962 is described in the following article. Though structure of the agency, funding and admission procedures are mentioned, major emphasis is on the theoretical and practical application of activity group therapy to this age group. Case studies are used to illustrate the most frequent symptoms encountered and the treatment followed.

66   Activity Group Therapy for Emotionally Disturbed Pre-School Children, Agnes M. Plenk, *Behavioral Disorders*, Vol. 3, No. 3, May 1978. ©1978 by The Council for Children with Behavioral Disorders, The Council for Exceptional Children.

The Children's Center was founded in 1962 by the present executive director in response to community needs. It has developed over the last sixteen years into a comprehensive treatment center for pre-school children (ages 2–6) with emotional problems. Evaluation services, day treatment, short-term outpatient groups, and a residential facility are provided for the children. The largest number of clients we have are the children attending day treatment. This paper deals essentially with this treatment modality. The children attend the Centers daily for a 3-hour period, 5-days a week, 12 months a year. Parents attend weekly or bi-weekly individual or group counseling sessions; parent education classes, consultation to day care centers and training for graduate and undergraduate students are also provided. Total enrollment in two day treatment centers is 140 families. During fiscal 1976, the total number of families treated at some time during the year was 284. The staff consists of 14 full-time and 21 part-time clinical and clerical professionals, 20 students, as well as 100 volunteers.

A separate residential facility serves 7 children, 7 days a week. Its goal of treatment in most cases is restoration of the child to his family, or if this is not possible, into a long-term foster home. In this new environment, the children cope with their previous behavior patterns while experiencing and learning more appropriate living skills. The child's expectations of adults and of himself must undergo major changes before he or she can rejoin the natural family unit. All the children in the residential facility also attend the day treatment center for half a day.

The primary referral sources are physicians, pre-schools, day care centers, social agencies, and former clients. All children between the ages of two and six with a primary diagnosis of behavioral difficulties are eligible for treatment. Children referred through the Utah State Division of Family Services are transported under Title XIX provisions; parents not on public assistance form carpools. With the opening of the second day treatment Center in a somewhat distant but high risk part of the Valley, traveling time has been substantially reduced, though transportation is still a problem.

The Center is maintained by "contracts for service" with different agencies, i.e. State Division of Family Services and several school districts. Third-party payments, partial fees by parents, United Way funds, private and foundation contributions, and income from projects provide additional revenue.

THE CHILDREN

For a number of reasons, mainly conditions for funding, children have to be labeled and classified into diagnostic groups. It has taken considerable time to convert adult categories into useable children's classifications, and many child therapists are justifiably concerned about using psychiatric terminology with 2-year-olds. The category of developmental deviation, indicating poor or minimal functioning without a specific etiology, seems often to serve well in this dilemma.

Children in this group frequently have delayed speech, poor self-care skills, a short attention span, and a variety of intellectual deficits. Their interpersonal relationships are often immature, showing strong dependency needs and little motivation for making changes leading to greater independence and autonomy. Differential diagnosis between developmental deviation and mental retardation is at times a real challenge and can only be made after careful observation, psychological testing and response to treatment, particularly as family and developmental histories are often sketchy.

> Peter, age 4½, was referred to the Center by the Utah State Protective Services Division on suspicion of abuse by his natural mother. He showed severe delay in speech, was indiscriminately dependent on whoever took care of him, and made only slow changes despite residential care. After six months, his self-care skills were age appropriate, dependent behavior was cooperative. However, intellectual functioning and language output were still delayed; the diagnosis was changed to mild retardation, and he was referred to special education in his school district.

The largest number of children are referred for personality disorders, either oppositional or tension discharge type. The latter show aggressive, destructive, acting-out patterns which have led to serious difficulties at home or in day care centers and nursery schools. These children have been unable to form relationships of trust either with adults or peers. They are frequently manipulative and appear incapable of genuine feeling. They often show extreme hoarding behaviors, need immediate gratification, and are suspicious of adult intervention. Many have experienced frequent separations, rejection, abuse, and neglect.

> Mary Ann, age 3, on her first day at the Center, approached the table for snack with both arms loaded with toys, pulling a buggy and pushing a small scooter. She carefully placed all the loot on her lap and underneath her chair; and when served with cookies, immediately broke them into small pieces, shoveling them into her mouth. It took several weeks to convince her that toys and food were always available. Some time later, she was finally able to verbalize her concern: "We'll have cookies again, won't we?"

The group of children referred to as "oppositional" show a variety of negative symptoms; frequently, lack of toilet training, withholding of speech and stools, and being extremely controlling of other family members.

Young children are most sensitive to change and often "adjust" with maladaptive behavior patterns. The diagnosis of reactive disorders fits these children and the Center admits them only when the symptom has maintained itself for some time. Little girls often react to their parents' divorce with controlling, angry actions usually directed against the mother, whose own depression, isolation and anger feed into this behavior, leading to a short-term need for intervention. In our experience, boys whose parents are divorced, particularly if they are the oldest male child in the family, become anxious, withdrawn day dreamers with sleeping and eating problems, often because they are dealing with tremendous guilt and unresolved oedipal conflicts. In working with these children, mothers' treatment is of utmost importance, combined with careful choice of group therapists.

> Shane, age 5, was brought to the Center by his mother. He would not go to sleep until midnight, refused foods he had loved previously, and despite his superior intelligence, was "failing" in kindergarten. Both parents were supported in discussing with Shane the reasons for their divorce, setting realistic limits on his behavior at home and in school, and reinforcing his many exceptional abilities. He was assigned to an outpatient group with a male therapist who could provide short-term, non-threatening transitional first aid, and a female therapist who could absorb, interpret, and redirect some of Shane's unexpressed anger. The school's cooperation was obtained. Shane's non-participation in routine was overlooked, and creative ideas were reinforced. This increased his peer relationships and made use of his exceptional intellectual endowment. After a short time, sleeping and eating problems disappeared, relationship to his mother improved considerably, functioning in school became adequate, but Shane's ability to communicate with his father remained poor. We suspect that this will take individual psychotherapy when Shane reaches pre-puberty.

Only a small group of children come to us with problems of internalized anxiety. The neurotic child is usually not referred at such an early age. These children oververbalize, intellectualize, and thus appear in early childhood as particularly brilliant and only slowly come to grips with their underlying feelings of hostility and anger. Reality oriented alternatives leading to more appropriate group interaction are the first step in rehabilitation.

Each year, a small number of children come to the Center who show extreme emotional withdrawal, preoccupation with their own bodies, insistence on sameness, mood swings, and lack of speech. Facial grimaces, unusual hand movements, and indifference to pain appear in varying degrees. Whether these children's difficulty is due to biologic or environmental causes is still a major controversy; we assume at this time that a constitutional predisposition combined with ensuing environmental circumstances creates the most baffling of all childhood disorders: early infantile autism.

> Troy, admitted into day treatment at age 5, had been seen at the Center a year earlier, but staff recommendations were not accepted by the parents. Speech consisted of meaningless appearing phrases, frequently television commercials; play was totally isolated, and new experiences were actively resisted. Toilet training was sporadic, considerably more consistent at the Center than at home. Both parents attended a group for parents of autistic children. After the first few months, Troy needed constant adult attention to prevent violent outbursts. From his earlier sedentary, apathetic behavior, he changed into a hyperactive, isolated, but constantly moving force. Speech became more meaningful, participation in group activities increased, but Troy's fixed smile and unpredictable attacks, particularly on female therapists and volunteers, severely limited their therapeutic effectiveness. After a while, despite the improvement Troy had made, his maintenance in the group proved to be a problem. He had minimal emotional responses to conditioning techniques such as "time out," and even fewer to interpretations, though it greatly increased his intellectual output. With continuing bizarre behaviors at home, hospitalization at a local children's inpatient ward was the final resort after a particularly dangerous attack on another child. During hospitalization, intellectual and

self-care skills remained improved and the family recovered, but only minimal inroads were made in Troy's affective outbursts despite consistent behavior management. After three months of hospitalization, he returned to the Center, and an individual male therapist was also assigned to him. Troy was placed into a different play group than previously and was able to maintain himself somewhat more adequately. Physical attacks on adults diminished considerably, but Troy now attacked the most vulnerable and least well defended children. He was terminated the following fall and enrolled in a special, self-contained small classroom for the emotionally handicapped in the public school system. He continued with weekly individual therapy sessions. Except for two major outbursts in school, when he attacked and bit a child, he has been able to maintain himself, form a growing attachment to his therapist and express some quite appropriate feelings to him.

EVALUATION

Prior to admission, all children undergo a ten-day assessment process consisting of psychological testing with old and new instruments (Plenk & Jones, 1967), a home visit, and a ten-day observation period. Careful notes are kept, and a checklist of behavior is completed, frequently including base line data of specific behavior monitored during the second week in the group. A developmental and family history and sometimes a psychiatric interview are then combined with the test findings and the group observations. A profile is compiled and an intervention plan developed specifying target behaviors (Rose, 1972). Long-term, overall goals are expressed in dynamic terms, while short-term mini-goals are formulated on observable, measurable behaviors and are re-evaluated quarterly.

> Mary, age 2½, was referred to the Agency by the Utah Division of Family Services. Major concerns were prolonged (two hours) tantrums several times daily. Mother could not pinpoint antecedents, and was responding with harsh punishment. After all assessment procedures, a long-term goal was established: development of trust. Mini-goals were: 1) increase in spontaneous speech to four-word sentences, 2) positive sharing experience with one child, three times daily, and 3) diminishing of target behavior by fifty percent in both number and length of tantrums.

Traditional psychotherapy has been accused of vague generalizations in treatment outcomes, and our goal setting procedure might appear static and pedestrian. It was originally initiated in the wake of computerized accountability, but has proven to be valuable for therapists, parents, and ultimately for the children. It seems more sophisticated to deal with large scale generalities than specific treatment goals, but the latter have the advantage of observable concreteness.

GROUPING

The children are placed in groups of eight or nine, a size which we have found to be just right for our type of intervention. This group is large enough to encourage the formation of flexible subgroups, but small enough to permit individual input by the therapists. We have also discovered that though nine disturbed youngsters might at times be a handful, it encourages use of group dynamics rather than individual therapy in a group setting. Major considerations for grouping are activity level, impulse control, self care skills, and verbal communication development. A combination of acting out and withdrawn children, mute and wordy ones, boys and girls, seems to work best within our eclectic treatment model. Limiting the group to a homogeneous character would deprive the children of one of the most effective agents of change, namely, peer modeling. The timid and withdrawn child needs to see and experience that acting out behaviour will not result in punishment, or have dire, long lasting consequences, and the acting out child will hopefully model some of the alternate behaviors employed by the more controlled members of the group. Peer influence, verbal or non-verbal, frequently permits the therapist to be less active in intervention, and therefore, to save him or herself for the next step, that of suggesting alternate modes of behavior. We have learned from experience to place only one autistic or psychotic child in each group; partly because these children require one-to-one input much of the time and partly because their progress is so slow and defeating that it either discourages the staff, or assumes such fascination that the other children are neglected.

Another important consideration for grouping is level of functioning which in many ways is more important than chronological age. Success experiences leading to an improved self concept are of utmost importance for the children at the Center, and placement has to be arranged accordingly. The total composition of the group has to permit success and, at the same time, provide challenge and room for growth.

THERAPY MODEL

The therapy model at The Children's Center is child centered. All families come to us because the children are hurting, and though this is affecting the family, they come not because of their own pain. Frequently, parents are unable to see their part in the child's difficulties and are angry and amazed at their offspring. Therefore, the immediate need is two-fold: the parents and the child must learn to see human behavior in its totality as interactions within a given environment rather than as isolated incidents unconnected from each other, and they must be motivated to make the necessary changes.

To achieve this goal, we use an eclectic, pragmatic approach to child therapy and a reality based technique with parents. The life space interview (Redl, 1966), social learning theory (Bandura, Ross and Ross, 1963), White's (1960) ideas about competency and Erikson's (1950) timetable of biological and cultural developmental stages, form the basis of our approach. Activity groups lend themselves particularly well to a combination of techniques permitting the children to investigate the social environment, learn what one can expect of people and what one has to contribute, explore and expand options of change in comfortably safe surroundings with actively involved adults.

GROUP THERAPY

In working therapeutically with young children, modification of usual psychotherapeutic processes is necessary. Rather than listening, summarizing, reformulating, and presenting alternatives, the therapist of young children needs to base intervention on observation of the child in play, in managing daily routine, and in acceptance of new experiences. Play is for the young child the major vehicle of expression of his feelings about himself, significant others, and the world around him. Violence, police, paramedics, and the "six million dollar man," have taken the place of "three little pigs going to market," and the "little engine that could." For intervention to be effective, observation is followed by a definite treatment plan which is a combination of behavior management, on-the-spot interpretations, modeling, and verbalizing alternate behaviors to help solve inner conflicts which hamper adequate coping. The general aim is to enhance or create coping strategies in both parents and children, rather than resolving pathologies.

We are assuming that children whose emotional control is poor have already experienced failure and rejection from significant people in their earliest environment. These experiences create a poor self concept and prevent the child from using the many positive experiences essential for healthy personality development. It is just because of this failure experience that we have chosen a group intervention model for habilitation rather than the more traditional individual method. It is too much to ask the child, in our opinion, to immediately relate to another adult, usually again a female, on an intimate basis, particularly if mother claims love, allegiance, and compliance. Therefore, the group model with fewer interpersonal demands is at times more successful.

In a group situation, emotional experiences are available on a variety of levels in an environment open to experimentation and "fail safe." The children have the choice of relating on the intensity level for which they are ready: choosing peers, volunteers who change daily but return weekly, or one of the two constant therapists. The child chooses someone to relate to based on his or her age, emotional state, and level of pathology. Some children, however, resist involvement for a long time, remaining physically and emotionally isolated, needing additional support outside the group.

Johnnie, age 3½, had been placed in custody of The Division of Family Services twice and had been in four foster homes prior to admission to the Center. Though exceedingly bright and charming, he had no impulse control and insisted on immediate gratification. He manipulated peers and volunteers and pushed therapists into rewarding negative behavior with attention, as he was unable to accept praise for positive behavior. Johnnie's behavior improved in the foster home but varied greatly in the group. He not only responded to stimulation in the group, but more often than not, was the instigator of trouble. Prior to his return home, individual therapy was added to the total intervention plan. Noticeable improvement occurred until mother became pregnant. During the nine months of a high-risk pregnancy, Johnnie was in constant panic, fearing desertion. He tested limits imaginatively and needed continuous proof that despite the new arrival, he was acceptable and would remain at home. He refused to come to the Center for his group sessions but continued in individual therapy. He was successfully enrolled in a Headstart Program when the family left to join the stepfather in the Service. We still hear from Johnnie and his mother, and though he is doing quite well in school, he has problems at home and is in treatment again at a community mental health center.

THERAPEUTIC ROLES

For many children brought up in a family of constant issue-taking, the volunteer is the most helpful initial therapeutic agent. Not that they are more permissive than the therapists, but the mere fact that they have to be faced only once a week permits greater risk-taking. Interventions can be carried out in small steps and are often accepted without the volunteer's interpretations. The therapists are the major facilitators in the group. It is their personality, training, and experience which creates the therapeutic atmosphere in each group. Goals and strategies are only as good as the people carrying them out. Our groups are not controlled laboratory situations, but kaleidoscopes of realistic happenings. Flexibility and ability of the therapist to enter into the child's play and empathize with him on his level is essential. Intellectualization and adult value judgments are not helpful when dealing with young disturbed children. Appropriate provisions must be made to permit expression of feeling. Our culture often labels as "naughty" those actions which provide outlets for frustration. Though we make endless rules for young children under the guise of safety, respect, morals, etc., we unfortunately permit no "back talk", no acting out of any negative feeling. As a matter of fact, we usually don't even acknowledge the existence of negative feelings in children, and act surprised and hurt when they are not eternally grateful.

How can we help children express their feelings? Certainly, the ultimate goal is to verbalize, but until this happens, the child must feel comfortable with the physical expression of positive and negative feelings. Pounding clay, cutting play dough, hammering, throwing bean bags, clapping hands, stamping feet can all be expressions of affect. It is essential for children to feel comfortable showing appropriate affect, and the same comfort must be shown by the therapists in expressing positive as well as negative feelings. Therapists need spontaneity, immediacy, and a sense of humor to encourage expression of feeling on the part of the children.

LIMIT SETTING

Within our framework, "comfortably safe surroundings" means limit setting rather than total permissiveness. "The child has a right to know what he feels, but this does not carry with it any right to act out his feelings blindly" (Kubie, 1960). The majority of the children lack adequate ego controls and have only limited capacities to deal with internal impulses and external demands. It is, therefore, essential that limits are set to offer opportunities for ego growth. Disturbed young children are easily overstimulated and have low temptation resistance. It seems important to have carefully selected props in support of the limits to be set. Research available at this time (Sears, Maccoby, & Levin, 1957) shows that permissiveness is often associated with a high aggression level; children receiving the signal, "go ahead," feel that they have to fulfill the expectancy and usually do. The non-permissive adult on the other hand, has the expectation that the child will not be aggressive, and in many instances this provides the child with the necessary boundary. Therapists who lack confidence in themselves will foster more aggressive behavior in children. For some of our children, it is the exploitation of every weakness in the adult which pushes them to disintegrative anti-social behavior. The ensuing impotence of the therapist adds fuel to the fire, and sometimes only a change in therapists can save such a situation.

Limit setting, however, has to be rational rather than arbitrary, issue oriented rather than absolute, responsive to the rights of all rather than generally authoritarian, and conducive to verbal give-and-take rather than inhibitive. If these guidelines can be followed, limit setting will lead to conscience development rather than increased hostility. To the confusion of many, the Center has only few limits: children are not permitted to hurt themselves or others, willfully destroy property, or leave the premises. All other limits are set to meet the children's individual needs, varying specifically with the growth of inner controls and internalization of the group's and the therapist's values. The real dangers in limit setting are the possibility of punitiveness, the lack of realization that punishment has only a surface behavioral effect, and the awareness that one of the side effects of punishment is a return to earlier symptoms. Redl (1966) has developed criteria for intervention which have stood the course of time well. Some of the more important ones are: to arrest the contagion chain, to avoid conflict with the outside world and evident danger, and to avoid overstimulation. He cautions against intervention when it might strengthen the behavior, when it is not observed by the therapist, when the appropriate timing is missed, and when it would ruin the relationship between child and therapist.

CONSULTATION AND IN-SERVICE TRAINING

The structure of the Agency provides for close backup services and intensive weekly staff meetings. Regular bi-weekly supervisory meetings are scheduled with senior staff members, and each child's achievement of mini-goals or lack of progress is discussed. In addition, mini-staffs are frequently scheduled which include all involved agency personnel and professionals from referring agencies to jointly develop new ideas or strategies. The senior staff members spend time in the observation rooms or in the rooms with the children and are intimately acquainted with needs and problems of each child. Parents' therapists attend supervisory meetings to help in the mutual understanding of the total system in which the child functions. With the growth of the Agency, personal communication has become more difficult.

CORE THERAPEUTIC ISSUES

Core therapeutic issues at the Center are partially determined by the age group we handle and by our treatment philosophy. The children in treatment at the Center have not been able to correlate their increasing capacities with the demands of their social environment.

Early physical or emotional deprivation prevents the infant's solution of the first core issue: trust vs. mistrust (Erikson, 1950). Children not having experienced positive nurturing are often suspicious, manipulative, angry and frequently in a continuous panic. They demand material things without ever having enough, or sit apathetically having given up the fight for life. Intervention strategies to make up for this deficit demand accepting, supportive, nurturing adults who with much physical outreach attempt to construct the earlier missed experiences. We do not try to regress the children to early infantile stages, nor do we try to become parent substitutes. But we do try to meet each child's need by convincing him or her that there is meaning in what we are doing. It seems in many instances the diluted attention in a group therapy situation speeds up development of missed stages, avoiding guilt feelings due to strong feelings of transference. At times, dependency situations are created by inexperienced therapists which confuse and hamstring the children. It is particularly important for the supervisor to be aware of this possibility and help the therapist avoid any detriment to the child.

Another major developmental stage frequently not mastered by our patients is autonomy vs. shame and guilt (Erikson, 1950). Trouble is expressed mostly in lack of toilet training, withholding of stools, withholding of language and withholding of oneself as a relating, giving individual. Though we consider difficulties in toilet training from a dynamic viewpoint, we treat it behaviorally. We attempt to remove the process from emotional entanglements and try to resolve the issue more objectively with behavior management techniques, peer modeling and social reinforcement. As we never use aversive techniques, it usually takes a while, but the ensuing sense of achievement in the child at times generalizes into other areas of functioning. A baseline is established and step-by-step procedures to be followed by everyone in the room are posted. Primary reinforcers are used as rewards. Home training is correlated if the family is not too dysfunctional or uncooperative. Procedures of rather firm but fair outer controls seem essential at this stage to form a balance permitting the development of inner controls.

The overly aggressive, oppositional child frequently has not solved the conflicts of outer vs. inner control and continues to struggle with dimensions of initiative. He is many times unable to gauge whether his initiative is acceptable or will lead to conflict and ensuing guilt. Such guilt might prove paralyzing and result in low self esteem, inability to take risks, and poor cognitive functioning. Vigorous physical and intellectual activity with room for exploration and experimentation under the guidance of a rewarding adult is needed to free some of our children of already developed guilt and help others to gain control by achievement and competence. Again, the role of the therapist and the other adults in the room is essential. He or she must be ready to provide competency oriented programming to assure successful and rewarding experiences for our already confused children. A permissive peer group without an adequate model cannot achieve this essential change to ready the child for school. Bandura, Ross and Ross (1963) have shown that children model and identify with the rewarding adult: the one in charge.

A good deal of thought is given to match the child and his need to the therapist and his or her strengths. The administrative structure of the Center which provides eight simultaneous groups makes this feasible.

PROGRAMMING

We are trying to combine the best from established nursery school programs with newer findings in child development. A particular emphasis is to adapt a curriculum oriented to the middle class to the needs of other groups. As our program is directed toward change of maladaptive patterns to more personally useful ones, we need to provide success experiences. Careful programming is the means to this end. It is essential to be aware of each child's level of skill, motivation and control prior to planning the group's day. We are making use of Vinter's (1974) and Trieschmann, Whittaker and Brendtro's (1969) clever analysis of program components and have adjusted them for a younger age group. The one universally helpful and fun-filled activity is water play. We have a built-in water table in every therapy room and use it daily during free play. It is failure proof, sex and culture free, and leads to all sorts of adventures: from Piaget-like insights to working through the perils of a shampoo. Language skills are stressed in all groups, and a speech therapist works with individual children and coordinates language programs in each group. Dance therapy has proven helpful with some of our most withdrawn children, but too stimulating for those with poor impulse control. Much of the program, again, depends on the skill of presentation, the selection of materials, and the structure of the total day by the therapist.

GENERALIZATION OF COOPERATIVE BEHAVIOR ACROSS CLASSROOM SITUATIONS

James John Reisinger, Ph.D.
Children's Memorial Hospital
Northwestern University Medical School
Chicago

Three behavior-disordered preschoolers who had low rates of cooperative behavior served as subjects in a classroom setting. Observations were made throughout phases of Baseline, Intervention I, Reversal, and Intervention II, and within a multiple baseline design. For participation in a low-frequency assembly task, children gained access time to high-frequency activities. Data were also collected during free-play occasions during which contingencies were not manipulated. Results indicated an increase in cooperative behavior and proximity within task-specific (e.g., assembly) situations. There was additional evidence of generalization of such behavior during free-play periods. The outcomes indicate the feasibility of group behavior change by simple systematic contingency rearrangement of existing classroom activities. Results also support generalization of programmed gains to nonprogrammed behavior classes within the same environment.

The utility of behavior change procedures to shape adaptive classroom behavior has been regularly reported in the literature (Barrish, Saunders, & Wolf, 1969; Schwartz & Hawkins, 1970; Walker, Hops, & Feigenbaum, 1976). As appropriate teacher contingencies are applied, children increase their attention to designated tasks and decrease their rate of disruptive behavior. A teacher may alter individual or group behavior by attending to desired behavior and ignoring undesired behavior (Hall, Panyan, Raben, & Broden, 1968; Madsen, Becker, & Thomas, 1968), shaping individual behavior (Broden, Bruce, Mitchell, Carter, & Hall, 1970), or by dispensing tangible, secondary reinforcers (e.g., tokens) contingent on acceptable behavior (Frederiksen & Frederiksen, 1975; Miller & Schneider, 1970).

While demonstrations of intervention continue, efficacy of effect beyond their immediate applications (i.e., generalization) is frequently not known. Baer, Wolf, and Risley (1968) advocated the programming of generalization, but it has often been assumed to be a "naturally" occurring event. Only within the last 5 years has there been a notable increase in attention to it. Yet, to be effective, positive behavior change must often occur across time, persons, and settings. Also, change effects should sometimes spread to a variety of related behaviors (Stokes & Baer, 1977).

For purposes of definition, generalization was taken to mean the occurrence of relevant behavior under different, nontraining conditions (i.e., across subjects, settings, people, behaviors, and/or time) without the scheduling of the

Generalization of Cooperative Behavior Across Classroom Situations, James John Reisinger, *The Journal of Special Education*, Vol. 12, No. 2, Summer 1978. ©1978 by Buttonwood Farms, Inc.

same events which had been performed in the training conditions (Stokes &
Baer, 1977).

The current study focused on the generalization of cooperative behavior and
proximity to peer across classroom situations and with a population of antisocial, disruptive preschoolers. Specifically, the study tested the feasibility of increasing rates of cooperative child behavior within a structured, task-specific
situation. Concurrent data collected for the target children in a free-play
situation were intended to assess the extent of generalization within the same
environment, but to less structured activities.

METHOD

Setting

The study was conducted in the preschool classroom module of the Holy
Spirit Hospital Early Intervention Program (EIP). The EIP system (Reisinger &
Hoffman, Note 1) is essentially a replication of the Regional Intervention Project (Ora & Reisinger, Note 2). The program charged no fees, required parent
involvement on the operations level, and served behaviorally disordered preschool children. The EIP comprehensive model's operation, organization,
and theoretical rationale have been previously described (see Reisinger, 1976).
Reisinger, 1976).

Classroom sessions, each 3 hours in duration, were conducted 4 mornings
per week. Regular scheduled activities included Group Welcome Exercise,
Language Work, Fine-Motor Training, Free Play, Snack, Story Time, Art, and
Group Good-Bye Exercise. The classroom was equipped with toys and supplies
common to a nursery school. The staff consisted of one teacher. The study was
implemented during the fine-motor period (by use of a task-specific training
procedure), and data collection extended to free play.

Subjects

The classroom population consisted of 8 children (5 boys and 3 girls) whose
ages ranged from 3.5 to 4.5 years. Their intelligence was within normal limits
and physical examinations yielded no evidence of organic concerns. Children
lived at home within intact, middle-class families. A variety of behavioral deficits were represented, including speech delay and low social interaction skills.
Also, all children were noted to engage in various disruptive, oppositional behaviors.

Three target children were chosen based on lowest rates of cooperative behavior and proximity to their peers, i.e., they were often noted to be more than
3 ft from any other children.

Observation procedures

The categories for rating were based in part on those used by Hart,
Reynolds, Baer, Brawley, and Harris (1968). Cooperative behavior was defined
as: (a) a child handing an object to another child; (b) a child physically supporting another child; (c) a child helping another by putting away, bringing, or
building something; or (d) two children sharing a task, such as coloring the
same book, using the same bucket, assemblying the same puzzle, etc. Proximity
was defined as one child being within 3 ft of another child. In-task-area was
determined by whether both children (i.e., target child and a partner) remained within a designated area of the classroom.

Tasks were of the assembly type (e.g., puzzles). They were selected because
their structure lent itself to developing cooperative behavior. That is, both children were able to be actively involved in completion of the same task.

Activities to be used as reinforcers were ascertained by direct observation of
the class. Prior to initiation of baselines, various activities were available to the
class noncontingently. Such activities were already a part of the usual classroom

agenda. Thus, during regular class routine, children's participation times per activity were recorded. The rationale was that if the majority of children participated in certain activities over time, such relatively high-frequency activities could function as positive reinforcers for low-frequency cooperative behavior. The activities employed as reinforcers were access to the water tub with toys and access to Play-Doh.

For task-specific observations, all rating categories were utilized; in free play, the in-task-area category was irrelevant. Whenever feasible, two persons were used to observe sessions. They were selected from any combination of trained persons who were available at the particular time. A group of six parents and undergraduates constituted the pool of observers. Observers were located adjacent to the classroom and were separated from it by a one-way mirror. Each wore earphones, and a wood screen was positioned between observers to help insure independent judgments. Each observer was equipped with a stop-watch to monitor intervals and session durations.

The same scale was used for rating categories in both task-specific and free-play situations. During each 10-minute observation per child, the occurrence of behavior categories was noted in 10-second intervals. For free-play observations, frequencies of proximity and cooperative behavior were examined between target children and other children. Observation sessions were 5 minutes per target child. Free play permitted all children to select any activities within the classroom. Such observations were conducted each day following task-specific periods and through all phases of the study.

In addition, data were collected for rates of verbal contacts to and from target children. Verbal contacts were defined as any exchange of words to a target child, from a target child, and involving any other child. The proximity definition was observed to qualify this construct. A verbal contact was scored only once per 10-second interval regardless of the duration within an interval.

Observer agreement was determined for each rating category individually by dividing the number of agreements by the number of agreements plus disagreements. Agreements were scored when two observers recorded the same category within the same 10-second interval. Disagreements occurred when only one observer recorded a category. Nonoccurrence of a category, although agreed on by both observers, was not considered in tabulations of agreements.

Experimental procedures

The study included four phases: Baseline, Intervention (i.e., access to high-frequency activities contingent on performance of low-frequency behavior), Reversal, and Reinstatement of Intervention. The design also incorporated the multiple baseline.

Three target children were observed for two 5-minute periods (i.e., task-specific and free play) each day for 35 days. A task-specific observation was arranged by seating two children (target and nontarget) at a circular table and positioning a task between them so that it was equally accessible to each. Instructions were given, and the observation time began as the teacher left the task area. Tasks were selected so that they could not be completed within the time alloted.

Baseline (task-specific). The teacher requested the children to help one another in assembly of the task. Each child was provided parts of the task and told not to leave the table until the teacher returned. If a child assigned to task left the designated area, the teacher was permitted one command indicating return to task. A child not responding appropriately was ignored until the observation time had elapsed. At the conclusion of the observation, the teacher had the task-specific children join the class. No praise was provided for remaining in the task area or for performance. The remainder of the children were occupied in another section of the classroom while task-specific observations were conducted.

Intervention I (activity as reinforcement). Instructions were identical to

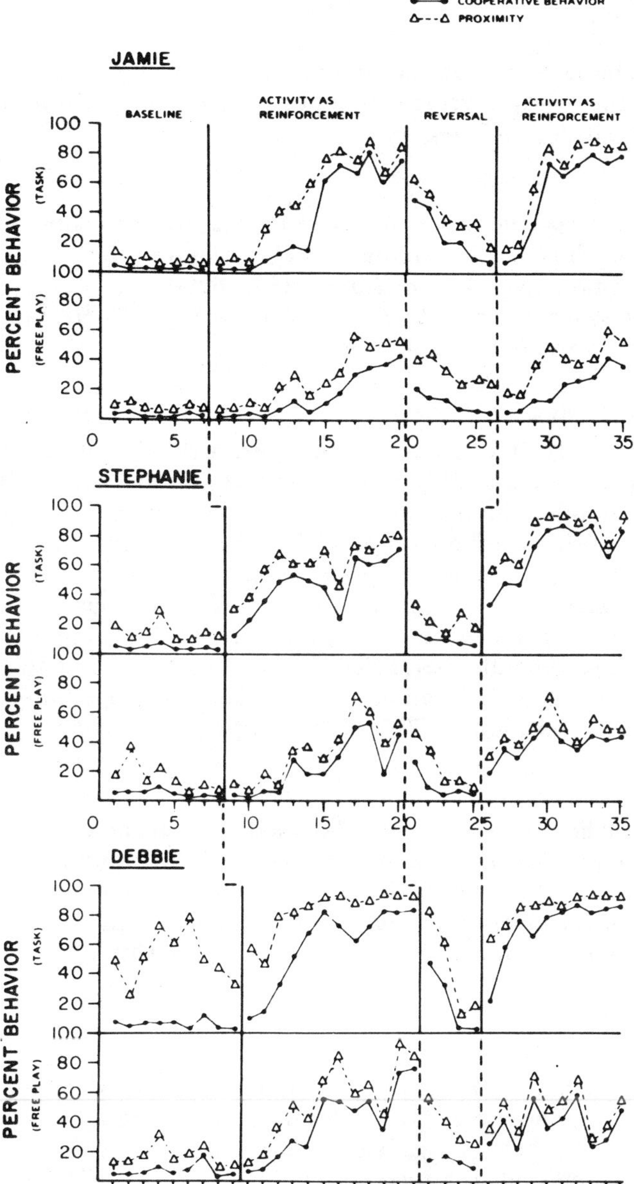

Figure 1. Cooperative behavior and proximity for three target children as measured across task-specific and free-play situations in the classroom. Daily observations were recorded through conditions of Baseline, Intervention (activity as reinforcement), Reversal, and Reinstatement of Intervention.

baseline except that children were made aware of the contingencies (access to high-frequency activity for performance at task together). At the conclusion of the observation period each day, time of access to reinforcers was determined in proportion to time engaged in cooperative behavior. That is, 100% cooperative behavior on 5 minutes of task-specific work resulted in 5 minutes access to the high-frequency (reinforcement) activities.

Reversal. Instructions to continue task work were given. However, children were told that they could not earn time to play with water or Play-Doh.

Intervention II (activity as reinforcement). Contingencies were reinstated.

RESULTS

Reliability

Reliability checks were conducted for more than 80% of the observations. Throughout the study, agreement among observers consistently remained above 87%, regardless of category.

Baselines

Data from task-specific observations yielded a rate of cooperative behavior near 5% across children. Proximity was also relatively low (i.e., usually 5%–10%), the exception being Debbie (range 23%–82%).

Free-play measures were uniformly low (i.e., usually 2%–7%) for cooperative behavior and for proximity of all children.

Intervention I (activity as reinforcement)

Access time to high-frequency activities was provided contingent on cooperation at low-frequency assembly tasks. Increases in cooperative behavior and proximity were evident immediately, or within a maximum of four sessions. By the conclusion of this intervention condition, the behaviors reached 77%–84%, 72%–81%, and 82%–92%, per respective child.

While there were no intervention procedures for free play, records indicated increases in cooperative behavior and proximity. Such changes, while less consistent and stable, generally paralleled those related to use of the intervention procedure. At the final observation, the frequency of cooperation and proximity was 42%–54%, 43%–50%, 77%–84%, per respective child.

Reversal

The task-specific reversal was accompanied by reductions in both behaviors being monitored across children. The final day of this condition found rates to be 7%–16%, 4%–14%, and 1%–19%. Again, without contingencies being altered in free play, cooperative behavior decreased with proximity. The corresponding data points showed 4%–21%, 2%–6%, and 10%–20%.

Intervention II (activity as reinforcement)

Reinstitution of contingencies resulted in rapid returns to previous level of behavior improvement. The final intervention session's data for cooperative behavior and proximity were 80%–87%, 82%–91%, and 82%–89%. Similarly, free-play data showed trends again reflecting the task-specific outcomes.

As could be predicted, the increases in free-play cooperative behavior and proximity were accompanied by increases in incidents of verbal contacts to and from all target children. Such increases, across children and observations corresponding to both intervention conditions, ranged from 15% to 40%. If computations were based on only the last four sessions of both conditions, the range would indicate 33%–62% increases in verbal exchange.

DISCUSSION

The introduction of contingencies — participation in a low-frequency behavior allowing access to a high-frequency behavior — resulted in marked increases in cooperative child behavior and proximity to peers. Use of a reversal procedure served to illustrate functional control over such changes in both behaviors. In addition, child behavior was tracked from programmed circumstances (i.e., task-specific) to nonstructured activities (i.e., free play). Positive changes subsequently noted support the conclusion of generalization across activities within the same classroom environment. Variations in verbal contacts within free-play observations also paralleled contingency modifications within task-specific sessions. While activity as reinforcement contingencies were not in effect during free-play sessions, continuations of cooperative behavior were accompanied by increased positive verbal exchanges. A similar pattern of developing social interaction on the verbal level was also noted during task-specific sessions.

Data indicated a parallel and highly positive relationship between the two dependent measures. To increase cooperative child behavior, as defined in this study, increases in proximity were also necessary. Proximity could have been increased without similar changes in cooperation. To develop the change in both measures, positive reinforcement was not supplied for proximity alone, but only as it was a necessary subbehavior of cooperation. That is, proximity, which was noted simultaneously with cooperative behavior, resulted in reinforcement of both behaviors.

The procedure for intervention makes efficient use of teacher time. The need for contingent personal attention is reduced by use of other reinforcements already existing in the standard classroom. Teachers might therefore systematically reorganize the usual environmental conditions so as to constructively shape child behavior. Such action seems especially appropriate when goals involve group behavior change and when logistics prohibit primary use of such techniques as differential reinforcement.

Also, since cooperation and proximity occurred across situations, there is an implication for generalization. Although some investigations have begun to focus on generalization across environments (e.g., Reisinger, Frangia, & Hoffman, 1976; Reisinger & Ora, 1977), findings within environments, with few exceptions (e.g., Miller & Sloane, 1976), remain sparse. In this study, two behaviors generalized to new circumstances within the same environment but without a planned behavior maintenance procedure. This outcome initially implies that some behaviors might be expected to continue in the absence of an extension of the original sustaining contingencies. However, there are various alternate explanations to suggest that generalization should not be left to the fate of "natural" events. For instance, it would be plausible to assume the existence of a behavioral trap (Baer, Rowbury, & Goetz, 1975). That is, child behavior may well have generalized because it was positively reinforced in the new situation, not by high-frequency activities but, for example, by peer interaction patterns themselves. The current investigation yields no direct evidence here, but the impact of peer reinforcement has been previously documented (e.g., Johnston & Johnston, 1972; Solomon & Wahler, 1973; Wahler, 1967) and provides one feasible explanation for the observed generalization. Further detailed study is necessary for conclusive statements about the specific cause(s) for generalization.

Mainstreaming Young Emotionally Disturbed Children: Rationale and Restraints

Samuel J. Meisels and Seymour J. Friedland

ABSTRACT

Young emotionally disturbed children have only recently been intentionally integrated into regular classrooms. In this paper, reasons are presented concerning why young behaviorally disordered children have not previously been identified or assisted in participating in mainstreamed classrooms. It is argued that in order for these children to profit from the experience of the regular classroom, two general conditions must be met. First, the regular classroom structure, typical teacher behaviors and established patterns of relationships with parents must be modified. Second, the potential of a modified regular classroom to meet all of the therapeutic needs of young disturbed children should be carefully assessed. The addition of a specialized clinical milieu may be a necessary concomitant of mainstreaming for many children with behavioral disorders.

INTRODUCTION

The integration of handicapped children into regular classrooms has taken place without sufficient attention being devoted to individual differences in the populations of handicapped children. Early emphasis was placed on integrating retarded children in elementary schools (Birch, 1974; Dunn, 1968; Hammons, 1974) and models developed for this specific age group and handicapping condition were then assumed to be applicable to all age groups and disabilities (Reger, 1974; Wynne, Dakof and Ulfeder, 1975). However, preschool and kindergarten children pose very different problems and issues from those posed by elementary-aged children. Similarly, emotionally disturbed children present issues and challenges that are different from those of mentally retarded or physically handicapped children. This paper examines some of the unique issues of integrating or mainstreaming preschool and kindergarten emotionally disturbed children.

ISSUES UNIQUE TO THE YOUNG EMOTIONALLY DISTURBED CHILD

Until the 1960's school-aged emotionally disturbed children received very little attention or support in public schools. Trippe (1963) reports that behaviorally disordered children were all but completely ignored in public school classrooms if their behavior was compliant. Non-compliant, emotionally disturbed children generally were not permitted to enroll in public school programs. Paul (1977) notes that these children were frequently "left in psychiatric hospitals . . . because there was no appropriate educational program in the schools, misplaced in classes for the retarded, or excluded from school altogether because of behavior problems and the school's inability to cope with or respond to their needs" (pp. 8–9).

Even fewer educational options were available for preschool and kindergarten-aged children with behavior disorders. In general, the development of early intervention

Mainstreaming Young Emotionally Disturbed Children: Rationale and Restraints, Samuel J. Meisels and Seymour J. Friedland, *Behavioral Disorders*, Vol. 3, No. 3, May 1978. ©1978 by The Council for Children with Behavioral Disorders, The Council for Exceptional Children.

programs for young emotionally disturbed children was not considered urgent. Some of the factors that contributed to this neglect can be identified. First, the early dominance of maturational psychologists such as Gesell (1940) led to a view of young children as inexorably governed by physical timeclocks that could not be tampered with significantly, either for purposes of acceleration or remediation. This view of the immutable progression of nature negated the importance or need for programs designed to identify and remediate deficits at an early age.

A second reason young emotionally disturbed children were not identified or assisted in their development originates with one of the most significant characteristics of this age group. Development is rapid during this period. Changes in cognitive, physical and emotional skills occur during very short periods of time. This factor promotes the notion that it is sensible to wait and see if a deficit will disappear or be "outgrown," rather than deciding to label and intervene early. Third, much of the behavior seen in preschool children is generally considered reactive; that is, it is explained as a product of the immediate situation (Group for the Advancement of Psychiatry, 1966). This view leads to the assumption that behavioral deficits appearing early in development do not represent enduring traits, but responses to immediate environmental events. Such a view suggests that most disturbances in young children may be transient, thus minimizing the importance of early intervention. Finally, there has been a tendency in clinical diagnosis to assume that if a child displays apparently permanent, non-reactive difficulties, then these difficulties must be generated by physical factors. Hence, the emotional disorder is interpreted as an organic deficit. An excellent example of this phenomenon is the diagnosis of Minimal Brain Dysfunction so widely applied to preschool children who display antisocial behavior.

Thus, a dichotomous approach to providing educational services for children has evolved. On the one hand, because of the extreme nature of their disorders, preschool children with psychotic tendencies or autistic characteristics are usually placed in segregated programs. In contrast, children who show less severe signs of disturbance are frequently not clearly identified or provided with specialized services. Since their condition is seen as temporary, due to maturational or environmental factors, or is mistakenly identified as organic, these children are placed in regular preschool and kindergarten programs, not because of the value of integration, but because of the difficulty of making an early diagnosis of emotional disturbance. In examining "integrated" programs for young emotionally disturbed children, one is thus frequently discussing programming for a population that may not be clearly defined and whose deficit may not really be acknowledged as a disability.

It is the contention of this paper that the purposeful and conscious integration or mainstreaming of mildly and moderately disturbed children into the regular classroom can be valuable. In the following section the rationale for mainstreaming young emotionally disturbed children is given. The next section identifies some modifications of the mainstream that may promote a more successful experience for behaviorally disordered children. The final section identifies some constraints of the regular classroom that should be considered when mainstreaming young emotionally disturbed children.

RATIONALE: BENEFICIAL FEATURES OF REGULAR CLASSROOMS FOR EMOTIONALLY DISTURBED CHILDREN

In a paper that explores the implications for teacher training entailed by mainstreaming emotionally disturbed children, Fink (1977) notes that there are several advantages of special class placement which should not be abandoned in the movement toward mainstreaming. In Fink's view, behaviorally disordered children who participate in special educational programs benefit from "The Three R's of Special Education": 1) respite, 2) repair, and 3) renewal.

In Fink's terms, the emotionally disturbed child enrolled in a special class can obtain *respite* from the network of tension, stress and discomfort in which he finds himself. Such experience also makes possible the *repair* and development of skills, and ultimately provides an experience of *renewal* of the whole person.

These features of the special class can also play a significant role in an integrated preschool or kindergarten classroom. Respite takes several forms for young behaviorally disordered children in mainstreamed classrooms. If the child is a member of an unstable or inconsistent family group, the regularity, stability and potentially nurturant qualities of an organized preschool or kindergarten program staffed by able and dependable teachers may be extremely beneficial. Similarly, if the child is treated "like other children," and is systematically exposed to a set of relatively common expectations and limits, he may experience some relief or respite from his own inability to govern his impulses and manage his behavior.

The quality of respite in the mainstreamed classroom overlaps with that of repair. In the integrated classroom an emotionally disturbed child may have opportunities to be exposed to corrective emotional experiences. The provocative child may discover that not all adults react with rejection and anger to his or her behavior. The child with little basic trust may find adults who are responsive and who can be involved in reciprocal relationships. The depressed child may be stimulated by the affective investment of non-disabled children. These experiences offer an opportunity for emotional repair to young disturbed children.

Finally, the integrated early childhood program offers numerous opportunities for renewal of the whole person. A competent early childhood program is designed to help children obtain a strong sense of selfhood and ego. As Fink (1977) notes, renewal draws upon respite from stress and repair of significant intellectual and interpersonal skills. Regular early childhood programs provide numerous opportunities for children to experience success, as well as reinforcement of positive behaviors and exposure to pleasurable interpersonal experiences. Taken together, these experiences have the potential of improving a disturbed child's sense of self and the role he can play in the world.

These features of regular early childhood programs are paralleled by three other characteristics of integrated programs: 1) maturation, 2) mastery and 3) modelling. Maturation refers to the wide range of normality represented in most preschool and kindergarten programs. Children under the age of six mature at dramatically different rates, hence justifying a range of behavior that is not typically expected in classrooms for older elementary-aged children. This range of normality permits the integration of disturbed children to take place without these children's behaviors being isolated or highlighted as exceptionally bizarre or atypical.

Another aspect of early childhood programs that is beneficial for mainstreaming is the orientation of these programs toward mastery experiences. Many early childhood programs are formally or informally criterion-referenced, in the sense that a child's performance or behavior is referenced to a specific task or content area, rather than to the child's relative position to other children in some undifferentiated normative grouping (Meisels, 1976). The typical early childhood and kindergarten program is not deficit-oriented; rather, it is oriented toward encouraging children to attain a degree of knowledge or level of performance that is individually appropriate. Children who display various levels of mastery can still be reinforced and respected for the abilities that they demonstrate. The wide range of activities that may be considered mastery experiences in early childhood programs could contribute to a disturbed child's potential experience of effectance, autonomy and competence (see White, 1959).

Finally, the integrated classroom offers emotionally disturbed children opportunities to interact with positive role models as well as occasions to serve as positive models for other children. Bandura (1973) has shown that under certain circumstances, negative behavior is modelled more readily and more frequently than positive behavior. This is one reason classrooms composed entirely of behaviorally disordered children may frequently have a negative impact on the children enrolled in these programs. Several researchers, including Csapo (1972), Hartup (1970), Guralnick (1976) and Solomon and Wahler (1973) have shown that with systematic planning, exposure of special needs children to positive non-handicapped role models will result in a marked increase in socially positive behaviors on the part of special needs children. The integrated classroom, with its focus on normality and on "typical" behavior, is thus capable of providing emotionally disturbed children with experience with positive peer models.

Integrated classrooms also provide opportunities for emotionally disturbed children to serve as positive role models for their nondisturbed peers. Given the ability of the majority of the children in an integrated classroom to respond favorably to positive, competent and purposeful activity, when disturbed children display mastery and effectance, they are likely to be reinforced for these actions by their peers. This reinforcement may take the form of other children directly imitating their actions, desiring to spend time with them, or including them in their spontaneous play groups.

Thus, there is a place for emotionally disturbed children in mainstreamed early childhood programs. However, not all of a disturbed child's needs can be met in the regular classroom unless that program is modified in certain significant respects.

MODIFYING THE MAINSTREAM

Behaviorally disordered children present a number of distinct characteristics that distinguish them from other children. These characteristics differ in quality and intensity from one child to another. In order to create an educational setting that is appropriate for these children, a number of modifications in the regular classroom may have to be made by the teacher. Several examples of classroom adaptations follow.

1. *Classroom schedule*: In order for an emotionally disturbed child to be successfully integrated, teachers may have to adjust their classroom routines to create a sense of greater stability and predictability. A definite classroom schedule may have to be formulated—at least for the children with special needs—and then followed with regularity. Abrupt or unusual transitions may prove particularly difficult for children who have serious problems paying attention and trusting others (Swap, 1974). Such children should receive special preparation and attention at transitional points (e.g., at clean-up, snack time, end of the day or end of an activity), and may profit from a ritual such as an early warning, a timer, or a special place or cushion in the classroom.

2. *Classroom objectives*: In general, goals and outcome objectives formulated for use with emotionally disturbed children are process-oriented rather than product-oriented. Although skill development is crucial in order for these children to experience control and mastery (Hewett, 1968; Wood, 1972), academic skills may not be primary objectives for the child, or they may have to be pursued in a modified form. Wood (1975) notes that before a child is able to respond to the environment with *success*, first the child must be able to respond with *pleasure*. This entails learning to trust one's own body and skills, to use words to satisfy needs, to trust an adult sufficiently to respond to him, and to respond to the environment with active awareness and integration. These objectives may be achieved more effectively and efficiently through the "climate" of a classroom, rather than through a uniform progression of activities.

3. *Unusual behaviors*: Children with behavioral disorders frequently display a disproportionate amount of disruptive behavior (Pastor and Swap, in press). Teachers who integrate emotionally disturbed children into their classes must be willing to accept more disruptive behavior in their classrooms than would typically be expected. These teachers must also learn how to help children who are acting out, who are disruptive or who are prone to tantrums. Some techniques which are useful include knowing how to hold and restrain these children, how to implement selective segregation or "time out" from the classroom, and how to help these children acquire inner controls and the ability to verbalize.

Children who display profound isolation and withdrawal can also prove disruptive in the classroom. Teachers must learn how to intervene in the behavior of these children by interrupting their withdrawn behavior and insisting on classroom participation that is consistent with their capabilities.

4. *New teaching skills*: The previous sections identify a number of skills of individualization that may have to be learned for the first time by a regular classroom teacher. Although individualized programming is a fairly common concomitant of early childhood programs, behavior modification techniques are not typically used in regular classrooms for young children. Since many emotionally disturbed children require consistent and dependable rewards for modifying their behavior, it would be helpful for teachers who integrate disturbed children into their classrooms to have an awareness of the effects of interpersonal and environmental reinforcement on young children.

The teacher's approach to limit-setting may also have to be modified. Limits, rules and restrictions should be devised and applied with clarity, consistency and attention to consequences. The teacher may also have to review the physical arrangement of the classroom. Some children who are impulsive and disruptive respond favorably to a classroom that contains a number of small, safe places in which functions are clear and boundaries determined.

Finally, teachers who are working with emotionally disturbed children may have to learn to cope with primitive issues with which they might be uncomfortable. Issues such as death, aggression, sexuality or elimination may arise at any time. Teachers have to be familiar with their feelings concerning these issues and must be prepared to help children cope with and begin to govern their own potentially powerful feelings.

It is important to note that non-disturbed children may also engage in unusual or disruptive behavior some of the time. Thus, the techniques developed or refined specifically for mainstreamed emotionally disturbed children will probably have general usefulness for teachers in their work with all the children in their classrooms.

5. *Peer relationships in the classroom*: Young children are frequently frightened by children who act differently from them, particularly if they are exposed to angry, disruptive, acting-out behavior. Teachers in integrated settings will have to learn techniques of explaining and interpreting children's actions in behaviorally observable terms so that non-disturbed children will be able to mediate and understand some of this behavior. Other useful techniques for maximizing positive interactions between special needs children and other children include: arranging with parents for children to play together outside of school; establishing respect for individuals as a prime classroom value; creating a safe, protected environment so that children can risk forming relationships; explaining individual differences to children in a neutral, value-free manner; and designing and guiding positive interactions between children based on a common interest or curricular experience (see Meisels, 1977).

6. *Parent relationships*: Teachers also have to learn to work effectively with the parents of emotionally disturbed children. Their children are frequently a source of stress for them, and they—as is the case with most parents of special needs children—should be given advice about how to manage their child at home and how to support their child's growth and development.

Frequently, if the child is receiving therapy, the parents are also involved in some form of counseling or therapy. This type of arrangement is usually considered optimal, because it enables the parents to become closely involved with the child's therapeutic program. However, it may have effects on the teacher-parent relationship. For example, the participation of a clinical "authority" may dilute the teacher's authority. When conflicting messages come from the teacher and the therapist, the credibility of the teacher may decline. Moreover, since the focus of therapy is typically on the maladaptive aspects of relationships between the child and family, the more generally adaptive experiences in the classroom may not be valued as highly by the parents. In order to avoid some of these misunderstandings, teachers, parents and therapists should stay in close communication with one another and should make a significant effort to support and respect each's contribution to the child's well-being.

RESTRAINTS: THERAPEUTIC NEEDS THAT CANNOT BE MET IN THE INTEGRATED CLASSROOM

Due to its structure and intrinsic nature, the regular classroom usually cannot meet a number of therapeutic needs of young emotionally disturbed children. Failure to recognize the limitations of the regular classroom may result in the inappropriate attempt to incorporate techniques developed for the clinical situation into the regular classroom. What follows is a discussion of those therapeutic needs of the preschool child that usually cannot be met in the regular classroom.

The disturbing behavior of many emotionally disturbed children often takes the form of acting and functioning at developmental levels well below chronological age. For example, the excessive clinging and crying that is most often found in the toddler may be a prominent characteristic of the emotionally disturbed three-or four-year old. For many disturbed children there may be therapeutic value in functioning at this regressed level. The opportunity to act in such a regressed manner in a safe environment may provide the child with the experience of satisfying specific needs and impulses within a context that is low in anxiety. Children who engage in a great deal of clinging and crying may discover that attachment and attention can result from such behaviors and that they need not perpetually experience frustration in the face of basic dependency needs. Such experiences may then allow the child to progress to more mature ways of relating to others. The overly-socialized child with a harsh superego may benefit from being regressed from rule games into symbolic and practice play (Friedland and Shilkret, 1977). Children who are having difficulty in the later stages of identification may need to experiment with developmentally earlier tasks concerning the expression and inhibition of feelings. Permission for regressed behavior and the fostering of regression are common techniques of the clinical situation. Because of the physical organization of the therapeutic setting and because of the clinician's ability to monitor the child, therapists can tolerate a level of regression in clinical situations that is unacceptable in the classroom. No matter how permissive a classroom, highly regressed behavior will be disruptive and can frequently be destructive, leading to the danger of affective contagion, of harm to other children and of heightened guilt and fear in the child. For many emotionally disturbed children, there may be a need to provide other therapeutic situations, such as play therapy, that can allow for therapeutic regression.

Another example of disturbed behavior that is inappropriate for the classroom focuses on the expression of particularly threatening play themes. By means of proper equipment, spatial design and teacher intervention, most well-designed preschool or kindergarten classrooms facilitate play representing a number of critical developmental issues. Identity issues, fears and controls are confronted as an everyday occurrence in the dress-up corner. Yet, there may be some themes of importance to the emotionally disturbed child that may be disturbing or traumatic to other children because of their content and manner of portrayal. The explicit confrontation of issues concerning death, separation, elimination, annihilation, and anger may be overwhelming to the observing or participating non-disturbed child. However, such working-through in play may be essential for a disturbed child. This represents another circumstance in which the individual therapy situation may be a necessary concomitant of the integrated program.

Many young emotionally disturbed children require a suspension of the ongoing process of life in order to establish controls, get distance from anxiety-provoking stimuli, and experiment with new coping devices. These therapeutic experiences usually require a place and time that is set apart distinctly from everyday life. Often, the artificiality of the treatment room and situation provides such a vehicle. By delimiting the therapeutic situation in time, housing it in a building that the child attends only for a single purpose, and restricting the nature of available materials, a separation from and suspension of the common and the familiar is suggested to the child. In contrast, the classroom is usually designed as a microcosm of the familiar and common world of the child. Its adult staffing, grouping of children, and carefully selected furnishings frequently are attempts to promote the notion of a miniature representation of the society at large. Many emotionally disturbed children may, for therapeutic reasons, require a temporary release from this type of experience. The sole use of the integrated classroom as a treatment setting would impede the progress of such children.

Finally, the integrated program may not be able to meet some of the therapeutic needs presented by the parents of the disturbed child. Frequently, the treatment of the child may require changes in patterns of parenting, and an acceptance by the parents of some of the negative feelings and behaviors presented by their child. The traditional perception of the educational institution and classroom as child-focused mitigates against establishing contracts with parents that would be of therapeutic value to the child. The clinical situation can more typically make such demands. The parents of the disturbed child have explicitly brought their child to a change-agent who may then openly expect parental involvement. In contrast, the integrated classroom may be so quickly assimilated to the parent's concept of the typical classroom, that expectations of change may not be appropriate. For such changes to take place, a partnership between teachers, parents and therapists is usually a prerequisite.

CONCLUSION

The integrated classroom is an effective educational setting for many young mildly or moderately emotionally disturbed children. There are a number of reasons for integrating disturbed children in early childhood programs. The success of this integration, however, rests generally on two conditions. First, the mainstreamed classroom must be modified for the emotionally disturbed child in terms of structure, teacher behavior and expectations and parent-teacher relationships. Second, since the regular classroom program may be unable to meet all of the behaviorally disordered child's needs, the addition of a clinical or therapeutic milieu should be carefully considered.

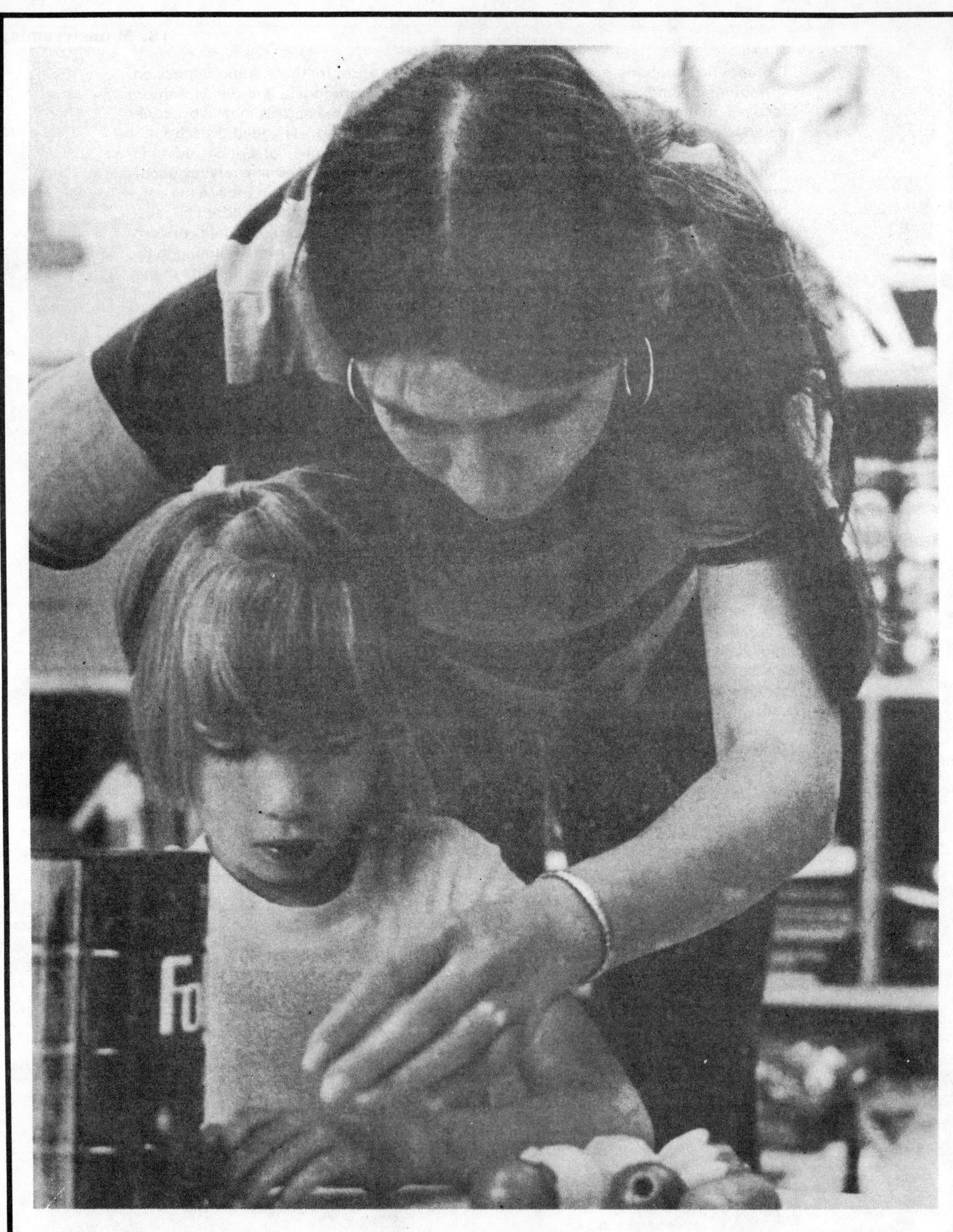

Cognitive Development

(5-12 years)

Behaviorally disordered children develop learning problems once they enter school. Although the majority of these children have normal IQs and no discernible sign of a learning disability, they fall behind their peers in school. Their abnormal behavior interferes with their learning. The more bizarre the behavior, the greater the interference with their learning.

Some children develop problems upon entering school; this has been labelled "school phobia." In actuality the disorder is a separation anxiety - fear of leaving mother, or primary caretaker. This fear, when closely examined, is usually fostered, consciously or unconsciously, by the mother. Most therapies are successful in treating this disorder. Included in this section is the use of hypnotic intervention to treat school phobia, but in order for it not to recur, the parent must also be treated.

Emotionally disturbed children perceive themselves as disliked, and have low self-esteem. These feelings become a self-fulfilling prophecy. They do not have many friends because they do not feel that they can have friends. Their behavior is rejecting, and their statements to others are usually negative. When studied, behavior disordered children seem to cause others to reject them.

It has been accepted by many researchers that psychotic, autistic, children are of normal or above-normal intelligence. These children consistently scored low on intelligence tests or they were found to be untestable. Researchers, however, believed that their bizarre behavior masked their "true" IQ. Ahmad Baker, "Cognitive Functioning of Psychotic Children: A Reappraisal," challenges the assumption of normal innate intelligence. He claims that previous research does not support the premise.

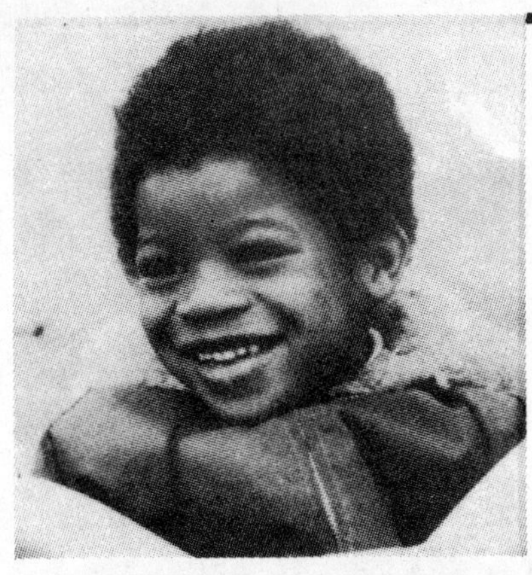

The Assessment of the Child at School Entry

Martin C.O. Bax, M.B.

From the Thomas Coram Research Unit, London University, London, England

Most learning and behavior disorders in school children present as "crisis situations," when anxious parents or exasperated teachers suddenly call for medical or psychological help with a child aged 9, 10, or 11 who is in severe difficulties. It is not surprising that remedial efforts to help these children are often unsuccessful. It seems likely that if we could identify the children earlier and try to help them before they get into difficulties, the results would be much better. However, the correlation between abnormalities found in babies in the newborn period or in the early years of life, although significant, are quite low, and we cannot identify with any degree of reliability children who may have school difficulties at this earlier age. On the other hand, we have shown that a thorough assessment of the child at school entry will allow one to identify quite a large proportion of the children who are going to get into difficulties.[1] A careful assessment, therefore, of children at school entry is an essential part of educational pediatrics.

There are a number of other reasons why preschool assessments cannot identify potential problems. The main one is that there are a number of functions emerging about age 5 or 6 which cannot be adequately studied in the early years. A further, and very important, reason for putting a great deal of emphasis on the initial examination at school is that whatever administrative arrangements, under the various systems of medicine that operate in different countries, are made in the preschool period to see children, it is difficult to be certain of seeing all the children. It is just those children who are not brought by their parents for regular preschool examinations who are most likely to be among those who run into difficulties. School must be attended by all children and the well-organized medical care system can see that the potential of every single child has been investigated.

HISTORY

Doctors and other experts in child development who have seen the child earlier in his life may warn the pediatrician who examines the child at school entry of any prior problems and alert him to potential risks. However, administrative arrangements, particularly in the urban areas of most big cities, are such that one cannot guarantee that this information is in front of one. One depends, therefore, to a large extent, on information from the mother, and history-taking should be based on a thorough knowledge on the sort of information parents can give reliably and what information may be unreliable.[2]

The assessment of the child's behavior which must be based at this age on parental reports together with any available experience of teachers of the child in the nursery (or other preschool provision) requires skill. In our experience middle-class parents tend to overestimate the neurotic tendencies of their children, whereas working-class parents underestimate them. Antisocial behavior, on the other hand, will be identified in all social classes. We have used a version of the Rutter behavioral scale, which we have adapted for use with 5-year-olds, and found it useful.[3]

One should bear in mind that children who demonstrate difficult, neurotic, or antisocial behavior in the home may not display this behavior in school, and the correlation between behavior as assessed by teachers and by parents is not very high at later ages. Apart from the use of the scale, most physicians will also inquire into sleeping and feeding habits and look for overt signs of behavior disturbance such as temper tantrums. It is possible, with a pre-designed questionnaire, to get a trained medical auxiliary—a school nurse, in the United Kingdom—to take the medical history, but the doctor should check this himself and particularly explore areas where the teacher has reported abnormalities. It

The Assessment of the Child at School Entry, Martin C. O. Bax, *Pediatrics*, Vol. 58, No. 3, Sept. 1976. ©1978 by The American Academy of Pediatrics, Inc.

is important to remember that illnesses, apart from their intrinsic significance, may have had long-term effects on the child's behavior, and separation experiences such as hospitalization can be significant, and the doctor again has to make a judgment as to how important such episodes have been.

EXAMINATION

We have trained school nurses to weigh and measure the child and also to carry out tests of visual acuity. Many school entrants can use the Snellen charts, and where the letters are unfamiliar the child may "draw" the shape in the air. If he fails at this, letter-matching charts which are based on Snellen letters are a great advance, in our view, over various other nonliterate tests such as the E test. I shall not detail the pediatric examination of the child but again draw attention to the fact that a physical abnormality, such as the discovery of a congenital heart lesion, should alert the doctor to make a more careful study of the child because handicaps are often multiple. For instance, we have shown that children with undescended testes are more likely to have a neurodevelopmental disorder.[1] Another group of children who have been reported as potentially abnormal are those with squints[2]: approximately one third of squinting children have a more generalized disorder, while perhaps two thirds have a "simple strabismus." The assessment of the central nervous system is important, and although we ask the nurse to do the visual acuity we ourselves always look carefully at eye movements, particularly at upward gaze, but don't routinely carry out a cover test as the significance of a latent squint remains doubtful. The movements of the face can be noted and asymmetries are particularly important. Tone and power can readily be assessed once the child is relaxed and reflexes elicited.

We don't believe that the plantar response is a useful routine test in the ordinary child, who dislikes it, and in consequence its results may confuse the doctor more than they assist him. The traditional finger-nose test, together with other observations of fine motor movements during the developmental examination, will serve to identify minor cases of ataxia. The items I have suggested above, together with careful observation of the child while he moves, should identify minor hemiplegias and neurological asymmetry, which are probably the most common neurological findings noted in the ordinary school population.

DEVELOPMENTAL EXAMINATION

Gross motor movements are assessed by watching the child walk and asking him to hop. At 5, little girls hop significantly better than little boys, but both sexes find it difficult to hop up and down on the spot or within a circle which the examiner can draw on the ground; they hop better along a line. I expect to see seven hops, but expect quite a number of 5-year-old boys to fail and rather fewer of the girls. By 6 both sexes should be able to hop. Heel-toe walking along a line is another useful test of gross motor function at this age, but again a perfect performance is not achieved by all 5-year-old children. Few can carry out the test backwards, that is to say placing one foot behind the other, a skill which is not acquired until 7.

Fine motor movements can be assessed in many ways and the examiner should remember that it is the quality of the performance that should be noted as well as the quantitative measure that may be used. I get the child to lightly pat the back of the hand and we count the number of pats given in five seconds and observe the regularity of the movement. Twelve rhythmical pats in five seconds should be achieved and there will be some difference between the dominant and the nondominant side. Other examiners prefer to get the child to build with bricks, but again watch the quality here rather than count the number of bricks in the tower! Purdue pegboards and threading beads are also useful tests.[3] The doctor will select his own favorite.

The grip at this age should, of course, be the traditional tripod grip. An idiosyncratic grip of a pencil or pen is not uncommon, probably occurring in about one in 20 of the population, but it should allow the child to make fine, discrete movements with the pencil. Fisted grips or grips high up the pencil, described as awkward, are of possible significance. If the child is shy or alarmed, he may not perform at his best level, and the doctor should always be looking for the optimal performance and ignore initial clumsy attempts. Once the pencil is in the hand one goes on to copying tasks, which we discuss below.

HEARING, SPEECH, AND LANGUAGE

In many parts of the world children will have routine pure-tone audiograms early in their school years. While this practice should of course be encouraged, the doctor should always carry out a hearing test himself. He should make certain that the child not only has intact hearing, which implies stimulation of the cochlea as a result of sound waves falling on it and the transmission of a nervous impulse to the cerebral cortex, but also intact listening, which involves the decoding of that signal so that it becomes meaningful to the child. The inability to decode an incoming auditory signal has been referred to by various names such as central deafness, but I prefer to talk of auditory imperception. The ability to carry out this decoding normally develops at the same time as do speech and language, namely, during the first and second years of life. The 3-year-old child, however, will still prefer to communicate with you close to and in an *en face* position, so that he can carefully listen to what you are saying and at the same time use visual cues from your face to help him decode the communication you are making. It is not uncommon to find children with delayed development of auditory perception, and in our own studies about one half the children who fail our screening test have a hearing loss and one half have a problem with auditory perception. The tests we use are either the Reed test, which involves standing six feet behind the child first on one side then on the other, and while one ear is occluded, asking him to point at pictures when they are named in a whispered voice. There are also similar pictures suitable for testing in the Stycar sets, and by using appropriate sets of pictures it is possible to pick up high-pitched as well as low-pitched hearing problems. An occasional, more severly retarded child will have difficulty with these tests, and one may have to fall back in the clinical situation on distraction techniques and want to send the child for full assessment at a speech and hearing clinic.

As linguists write more and more about the development of language in the child, the complexities of terminology which the clinician has to struggle with become greater and greater. However, for our present purposes it seems reasonable to talk about language as "the inner symbolization of thought," and to describe speech as a medium for expressing it. There are of course other media for expressing language, such as the written word and various touch and sign systems. Speech and language development in the child again usually go hand in hand, and delayed speech development is often, though not invariably, associated with some language deficit. The more speech problems a child has, the more likely these are to persist and the more likely they are to be associated with a language problem.

In the young child, I routinely record the following six consonants: *s, l, k, sh, th,* and *r,* and ask the child to say single words containing these consonantal sounds, and listen for them in continuous speech. In continuous speech one looks for reversals and substitutions which, of course, may occur even when the child has the ability to make the sounds correctly in single words.

It is helpful for the doctor to have watched colleagues in speech pathology and psychology administer some of the speech and language tests they commonly use.[1] The doctor will be struck by the time required to carry out a comprehensive study of the child's language. In evaluating, the Illinois Test of Psycholinguistic Abilities is among the best known. The Reynell Test is particularly useful with children under 6, and I have recently shown that a doctor's clinical testing can correlate highly with the results of such tests.

The clinician does not have time to make a formal assessment of language, but hopefully during the examination most children will talk to the doctor about what he is doing, and the doctor can ask him questions about his home life and about common everyday occurrences. It is important for the doctor to know the sort of thing that 5- and 6-year-old children know about and talk about in the area where he is working. In the center of London I have found children quite commonly referring to pictures of trees as flowers, and using this word for most vegetation, whereas in rural areas this could be suggestive of some delay in language development. Urban children will, however, be good at distinguishing between cars, buses, trucks, and motorcycles, and discussion of these topics will be rewarding. For children who find it difficult to get talking, I routinely carry various types of picture material and puzzles of common, everyday topics on which the child should initiate language. One can go on and do some more formal language tests such as the Peabody picture vocabulary test, but probably the rather crude assessment outlined above is just as effective and will serve to pick out the children whose language is markedly delayed. It is the abnormal child one is looking for, rather than trying to produce a description of the range of normal intellectual development in the whole population, which is an appropriate task for the psychologist. The doctor ought to sort out the 4% or 5% of 5-year-old children who will need to be more fully assessed.

PERCEPTUAL AND INTELLECTUAL DEVELOPMENT

The doctor should not attempt to assess the child's precise intellectual level. He is looking for the child with abnormalities, and a few simple tests will serve to pick out these children at this age. Intelligence, of course, is closely linked with speech and language development and during the course of evaluating the former in a child with speech and language abnormality the doctor will have begun to assess whether the latter is due to a specific problem in the speech and language area, or part of a more global intellectual delay. In terms of perception, I always ask the child to copy a circle, square, triangle, and cross. At around 5, many children will not draw an adequate triangle. The commonest error is to draw first a vertical line and then a horizontal line, then start a second vertical line which is joined to the top of the first vertical line in a circular manner. Obviously, one can ask the child to draw other objects and the draw-a-man test is one that some people use at this age. It is worth pointing out that the correlations between draw-a-man results and intelligence are not very high. Another perceptual test with which I have had considerable experience in screening school entrants is the series of Berges-Lezine tests of imitation of gestures.[8] These have the advantage that they require no equipment and are therefore easily used in the field situation. Our reliability studies of them have not, however, been very satisfactory, but in terms of validity we have shown that failure on items 5 and 6 involving imitation of hand movements[8] correlates highly with failure on a whole battery of neurodevelopmental tests.

Pulling together the different elements in the examination at this stage, the doctor should be able to decide whether the child is within normal range of intelligence, whether he is in the subnormal range, or whether he needs further assessment. Intellectual assessment may, of course, be hampered by behavior problems.

BEHAVIOR

It is difficult to assess a child's behavior in the context of a fairly short medical interview and it is worth remembering the great variation in behavior that normal children will display. Aggressive behavior towards the doctor is uncommon, but may be an indication of serious behavioral difficulties; on the other hand, shy and withdrawn behavior is probably not significant and in part may reflect the doctor's lack of skill in forming a relationship with a young child. Nevertheless, we routinely do record our impressions of the child's behavior and together with the history obtained from the parents, our feelings about the child at this time. As yet, we are not certain of the long-term value of such subjective assessments.

The problem for the doctor is what to do when he has completed his assessment. Thankfully 80% to 90% of children will, of course, be normal, but according to the area one is working in, 10% or more will have done poorly during the screening examination and will need further and fuller assessment. Even when this is done, the doctor may be in great difficulties with his psychological colleagues as to how to advise the school to proceed. The correlations between findings by psychologists and physicians, though significant, are not one to one; that is to say, even a child with gross neurological problems such as cerebral palsy will not necessarily have a learning problem. I have seen children with severe perceptuomotor problems of a degree which seemed to me to be clear evidence of brain damage and who, I predicted, would have gross reading difficulties, only to find them reading at a superior level within a year. This is not to say that there is not a relationship between neurodevelopmental findings and subsequent school performance: there is, and the doctor should watch these children very carefully at regular intervals and be prepared to intervene with help as soon as it becomes clear that the particular child is one whose neurodevelopmental status is going to make his functioning in school difficult.

Methods of help vary from country to country, and indeed from school to school, and in the child's best interests the doctor and his psychological colleagues will make the best use of those pairs of hands available. In my own experience medication has little to offer in the way of help either to the children who present primarily as having learning difficulties, or those whose behavior is the outstanding problem. Virtually no children in normal schools should, I believe, be on drug treatment, though a number in special schools may be helped by it.

REFERENCES

1. Bax MCO, Whitmore K: Neurodevelopmental screening in the school-entrant medical examination. Lancet 2:368, 1973.
2. Donoghue EC, Shakespeare. RA: The reliability of pediatric case-history milestones. Dev Med Child Neurol 9:64, 1967.
3. Rutter M, Tizard J, Whitmore K: Education, Health and Behaviour. London, Longmans/Green, 1970.
4. Sheridan D: Vision screening for very young or handicapped children in aspects of developmental and paediatric ophthalmology. Heinemann/Lippincott, 1969.
5. Venables WA: The incidence of squint in minimally handicapped children. Br Orthopaediatr J 24:53, 1967.
6. Holt KS: The Assessment of Cerebral Palsy. London, Lloyd/Luke, 1965.
7. Mittler P: The Child with Delayed Speech. London, Heinemann/Lippincott, 1970.
8. Berges T, Lezine I: The imitation of gestures: A technique for study of the body schema and praxis of children three to six years of age. Clin Dev Med 1965, No. 18.

HYPNOTIC INTERVENTION WITH SCHOOL PHOBIC CHILDREN

Evelyn D. Lawlor
Post Graduate Center for Mental Health, New York, N.Y.

ABSTRACT

CASE studies are used to illustrate the use of hypnosis in working with children who exhibit symptoms of "school phobia". Responses thus obtained during and after hypnosis are utilized to uncover underlying conflicts and fears.

The literature (Adler and Ansbacher, 1967; Friedman, 1963; Kessler, 1966; Caplan, 1961; Johnson, 1941, 1957, etc.) confirms findings that children have fears they are unable to bring to consciousness and talk about. Typical are fears of abandonment by parents; fears of disaster befalling parents, especially the mother; feared based on destructive wishes toward siblings due to severe rivalry for the mother's love and attention; fear that exhibiting angry feelings will be punished by the parents; and fears of annihilation and starvation.

Hypnosis has aided in restoring these children to a school environment more quickly than more traditional methods. One case is reported with excerpts from a session. The perceptions uncovered through such hypnosis may be utilized with children in various school settings.

Reviewed by Dr. Lewis Wolberg, Post Graduate Centre for Mental Health, New York, N. Y.

School Phobia according to the reports in the literature is more prevalent among girls than boys. In my experience as a school nurse, teacher and school psychologist, I have found almost equal numbers of each sex.

Children may be realistically fearful of school, if the mother has threatened to leave them there because they were "bad" or had displeased her in some way.

The term school phobia is a misnomer. In the majority of cases, there is no fear of school *per se,* but a fear of leaving home because of the child's own destructive fantasies.

In many instances, what appears to be school phobia may be a power struggle between parent and child. The child feels it is being overpowered by the parent, and forced to do something it is not "ready" for. It then tries to prove it can be more powerful than the parent, and resorts to feigned illnesses and thus may control the situation.

Even though the child may be well prepared to enter school, there still remains the need to test the mother to see whether she really means what she says by sending the child out among strangers and the unknown outside world. If the parent gives in the first time, the child will repeat this behaviour in an effort to maintain the status quo, to remain home with mother. The mother may then feels guilty and fear that the child may suffer more by going to school. As a result, we find some children kept at home until seven or eight years of age. The older the child is at entry, the more difficult is its separation and adjustment process.

Another factor is the mother's emotional dependence on the child. The mother may be fearful of separating from the child because of her own needs and destructive fantasies. The child senses the mother's anxiety, and responds with the fantasy that the school is a fearful place, therefore it is better to remain safely at home.

Hypnosis in two of the cases discussed help achieve meaningful communication and change with more economy of time than traditional methods of counseling.

The following are case presentations of children referred to the psychologist as being school phobic. They complained of varied symptoms such as headaches, nausea, vomiting and general weakness. They clung to their mothers, displayed temper tantrums and exhibited withdrawal symptoms.

Three of the children had been referred from a parochial school, another from a public school. The parents in each case were seen in separate conferences and complete histories taken.

The technique of using hypnosis was explained to the parents and to the children. The parents wholeheartedly agreed, as they felt desperate, and were willing to try anything at this point.

All of the children had been dropped from school, with the exception of the one in public school. The reasons given for exclusion were immaturity and inability to adjust to the school environment.

The Case of John C., Parochial School

John, a five year old, was the eldest in a family of three boys. The younger siblings were one and three years old respectively. The mother stated that John had developed normally until he began school.

On his first day, John was very quiet and seemed overawed by the sensation of being one in a class of 50 little strangers. It was reported that he refused to participate in any group or class activities.

On the second day, John began to cry when getting ready for school. He dawdled and said he couldn't dress himself, which he had been doing since he was four years of age. The mother became very impatient ad shouted at him to hurry. She had dressed and fed the younger children, and still John had not finished dressing. At this point the mother exploded and was very rough in handling him. She literally pushed the food down his throat and rushed him out so he could go to school with a neighbour's children.

The mother was called to school later in the morning to take him home; he had had projectile vomiting and had splattered the children near him. They became upset, began to cry and wanted their mothers.

The next morning John said he was sick and unable to get out of bed. He had no temperature, no sniffles and no cough. The mother demanded that he get up or she would give him a spanking. This brought results, but due to his heavy sobbing he was unable to eat breakfast. The mother again sent him to school with the other children.

The mother was again called to school; John had soiled his pants. She went to school and brought him home, but was not in the least sympathetic. She was advised to keep him home for a few days and to try again.

Several days later, she took him back with the same results. The mother was advised to get some help for John. She was referred to me, and I suggested hypnosis to which the parents agreed.

I went to' the home for the interview, as I thought John would be more comfortable and less anxious. The mother arranged for us to be alone in a room. John liked this special attention.

I had him draw a picture of himself, and then one of the family. He depicted himself as a tiny figure at the bottom of the page. He was not in the family picture. When asked where he was, he turned the paper over and there was his picture. I asked him questions about his family and he said he felt he didn't belong.

John was friendly and co-operative, but could shed no light on his reaction to school. Hypnosis was quickly induced by having John fixate his eyes on the beam of a pencil flashlight. The following is an excerpt of the first session with him :

Th : What is your name?
John : John C......

Th : How old are you?
John : I'm five years old.

Th : What school do you attend?
John : H...... R......

Th : What grade are you in?
John : Kindergarten.

Th : Who is your teacher?
John : Sister M......

Th : Tell me how you feel about going to school.
John : I don't like it.

Th : It seems that something bothers you about going to school.
John : I don't like it. I'm not afraid.

Th : Not afraid?
John : Unh, unh.

Th : Tell me about not being afraid.
John : They fight. I don't fight. I walk away.

Th : Who are they?
John : The children.

Th : Something upsets you about leaving home.
John : Yuh, I don't want to leave home.

Th :	Tell me about it.	John :	I'm afraid.
Th :	Afraid?	John :	Of something happening.
Th :	Like what?	John :	To my mother and the babies.
Th :	Something happening to mother and the babies?	John :	A car will hit my mother when she crosses the street.
Th :	Yes, go on.	John :	She might get hit......
Th :	Uh,huh, and then?	John :	The carriage will get smashed up and......
Th :	Can you tell me more?	John :	I'm afraid of not seeing my mother any more.
Th :	You see her every day.	John :	I know, she might leave me and I'll be all alone.
Th :	Where would she go?	John :	She'll take the babies for a walk and she'll not come home.
Th :	Did this ever happen?	John :	Unh, unh.
Th :	When you were a baby she took you for walks.	John :	Uh, huh, but there's two of them now.
Th :	You mean, you were the only one then?	John :	Uh, huh.
Th :	You want to be the one and only one then?	John :	Uh,huh. She doesn't have time to play with me.
Th :	You'are a big boy. What about your friends?	John :	I don't like the kids. They like to fight.
Th :	How about going back to school?	John :	I can't. I have to stay at home.
Th :	Why?	John :	I have to take care of my mother.
Th :	Doesn't your father do that?	John :	No, he goes to work.
Th :	How can you take care of her?	John :	I'll kill anybody who tries to hurt my mother.
Th :	Tell me more about that.	John :	She'll go away and not come back.
Th :	Who went away and didn't come back?	John :	My grandmother.
Th :	Your grandmother?	John :	Uh, huh, God took her away.

The mother was amazed to hear John tell about these fears. The grandmother had died shortly before John entered school. He had been told she went to heaven, that he wouldn't see her any more, and God had taken her to live with Him.

From this session we get a perception of some of John's fantasies. He is in rivalry with both of his younger siblings for the mother's attention. We see some of the hostile and destructive wishes for mother and siblings. There is also an implied oedipal problem; whether he can take over Daddy's job of taking care of his mother; his wish to be powerful and strong.

The school informed the mother they felt John was too immature to return and suggested he be kept home until entrance into the first grade.

The following were suggested and followed through by the mother :

1. John was given duties in the home to help her.
2. He was entered in the nursery school at the apartment house where he lived for half a day.
3. The mother obtained books and worked with him in the afternoon while the siblings took their naps.
4. The mother arranged with the neighbours to look after John if she happened to be at the store when he came home.
5. The father was encouraged to take time to play with John when he was home on weekends.

In three subsequent sessions, John was able to verbalize his hostile feelings toward the siblings for taking his place, and towards his parents for bringing them home. He said his mother should throw them both out of the window.

Shortly after this, I had John draw another picture of the family. On it he drew his father and mother with the two younger siblings shown miniscule at the bottom of the page. His mother and I used this picture to explain what a family, is, how each person has a place in it, and how much each needs the other.

The parents were advised not to show partiality in granting favours, as one of John's fantasies was that of being rejected. The mother was helped in continuing to build John's concept of himself as that of someone growing up; that he would be six years old in September and that children of his age go to school every day.

As the year progressed, John's anxieties concerning the safety of his mother and the babies lessened. He began to play with other children his age, and learned to enjoy all kinds of activities. The following September John entered a school that was nearer his home. He adjusted well and no more phobic symptoms were evidenced.

The Case of Andrea B., Parochial School

Andrea, a four and a half year old, was an only child of unstable young parents. The mother had shown signs of being mentally ill for some time and subsequently committed suicide by jumping out of a window. Andrea was in the apartment at the time and witnessed this event. She remained there alone until the father came home later in the evening.

When the father arrived, the superintendent of the building took him to the back yard where his wife's body lay, as the coroner had not yet arrived. The father called a young lady, apparently his girl friend, who came to stay in the apartment to care for Andrea.

Andrea had begun kindergarten three weeks before the demise of her mother. In school, the teacher reported that Andrea was unable to sit in her seat; that she was hyperactive, disruptive and destructive. She required an inordinate amount of attention, more than the teacher could give in a class of 50 children.

A few weeks after the mother's suicide, Andrea's behaviour underwent a drastic change. She began to soil her clothes. Instead of being hyperactive she became severely withdrawn. She would sit in her seat, close her eyes, rock vigorously back and forth and suck her thumb. If stopped, she would scream hysterically. The father and girl friend were not sympathetic to her needs. When called to school to take her home, they would slap and embarrass her in front of the teacher and children in the class.

The principal discharged Andrea from school and advised the father to get help for her. The father was referred to me and he agreed to hypnotic sessions.

At the first session, I had Andrea draw a picture of herself and another of her family. Significantly, she drew only herself for her family. She explained that since her mother had gone to heaven and her father goes to work, she was all alone.

Hypnosis was easily induced through eye fixation on a twirling red satin ball. Under trance, Andrea related her fears of being alone, and of going to school. The nun's habits were long, black and flowing, and she equated them with being witches. She said they screamed at her and punished her; therefore she wanted to stay home and wait for her "Mummy". She had been told that her "Mummy" had gone to heaven, but this had little meaning for her. Andrea said she had been "bad", that the witches were going to put her away all by herself. She also brought out a fantasy that because she was bad her mother had gone away and left her. She said if she had been a good girl, maybe "Mummy" would have stayed with her.

The father, hearing this, realized he had not provided a secure environment for Andrea after this traumatic episode. He felt he should not have taken in a strange person so soon after his wife's demise. This young woman was a girl friend, and this relationship caused Andrea to feel excluded.

The father's married sister, whose only child was a girl six months Andrea's senior, was willing to take Andrea to live with her. This woman was a very warm person, and able to provide Andrea with the emotional security she needed.

Andrea was entered in a nursery school for the remainder of the school year. Although withdrawn at first, she began to relate and play with other children. She made a good adjustment.

At five and a half, Andrea was re-entered in the same parochial school she first attended, but began to show the same symptoms exhibited previously. She became frightened and hysterical when a nun came near her, and she had to be removed from the class.

Her father then brought her back for another hypnotic session. This time, she brought out her fear of never seeing her mother again, fear of abandonment and fear of the witches dressed in black. She vividly related her experience at the mother's funeral when relatives dressed in black told her that "Mummy" had gone, never to come back. She also related the hysterical outbursts exhibited by family members. Andrea also verbalized her "sad" and "bad" feelings about the way her father and his girl friend had treated her.

Conferences were held with the aunt and uncle to inform them of Andrea's fears. Ways were suggested to relieve her anxiety and to help her adjust in the new environments. The suggestion was taken that she be placed in the public school which her cousin attended.

Apparently, the father did not want the responsibility of Andrea and asked the aunt and uncle to adopt her which they agreed to do. Andrea adjusted well in her new home and school, and developed into a happy child.

The Case of Angela R., Public School

Angela, an only child, was six and in the first grade of public school. She was a beautiful child, but grossly overweight.

On her first visit to school, she clung to her mother, refusing to let her out of her sight. The mother was allowed to sit in the back of the room for the first few weeks. This was very disruptive to the teacher and class. Every time Angela drew a line on a paper she would run back and show it to her mother. This behaviour affected the other children who began to cry for their mothers.

It was suggested that the mother bring Angela to the classroom and leave her on the line with the class. Instead of doing so, the mother remained in the hall outside of the classroom door and peeped in occasionally. Whenever Angela caught a glimpse of her mother, she would hold her stomach and scream as if in severe pain. The mother would then rush into the room and hold her.

After this happened several times, the daughter was sent to her family doctor with a note. He found nothing physically wrong with her and suggested that Angela return to school.

The teacher reported the child to the guidance office, stating that it was impossible to keep her in the classroom because of the mother's interference.

The guidance counsellor had a conference with the mother and Angela. It was learned that the mother had encouraged Angela to stay home at least two times a week. The mother was advised that Angela must attend school daily. With the new arrangement, the mother was to leave Angela on the line with the class in the school yard and return to take her home for lunch.

However, Angela began to get "sick" on the line. She would threaten, "I'm going to vomit on them" (meaning the other children). The mother would be asked to come and Angela would cling to her and cry.

In a conference with the mother, I learned that she was dependent on Angela for emotional support. This existed because the mother had four miscarriages before having Angela, and was fearful of something disastrous happening to her if she were not around. I asked her what she imagined could happen to Angela. The mother related her fears that Angela might become sick in school and die before she could be taken to a doctor or hospital; that some child might hurt her; that she might be sexually attacked by one of the "junkies" in the neighbourhood. It was pointed out that because of the way she protected Angela there was little chance of such things happening. She admitted that to be so.

When Angela was interviewed, she said she liked school and was not afraid to stay in the classroom. She related fears of something happening to her mother. What were these fears? Fears of her mother dying, of being abandoned and of starving to death. In subsequent sessions Angela reluctantly brought out her feelings of anger towards her mother for keeping her a baby. She felt guilty over this and expressed the view that maybe she was a "bad" girl. I said this was understandable because she felt she wanted to do things six year old children were capable of doing and that she felt frustrated by being prevented from doing them.

The mother was helped to see that her fears and anxieties were being transferred to Angela, and that each was controlling the other through emotional dependence. The mother felt her fears were justified because several little girls in her building had been molested. Again, I helped her see that if she brought Angela to school, came for her and took her back home, this was unlikely to happen.

The father criticized the mother severely for her over-indulgence and infantilization of Angela. He also told her that idolizing Angela and worshipping her was wrong, and God might take her away because of this. The father was seen and the fears of both mother and child explained to him. He was also able to verbalize his hostility to both Angela and his wife. He felt that Angela was monopolizing his wife and that he was being neglected. He was also made to understand that threats by him were not helpful in the situation.

Angela, being bi-lingual, was made the leader of a group of Spanish-speaking children in the class. She was also called upon as an interpreter for children in the Kindergarten. She became proud of her status and impatient with her mother for wanting to keep her home.

The mother was advised to let Angela help with some of the household chores and be permitted to feed and dress herself. The mother also realized how this could help Angela grow up. The mother began to cry and said she was "losing her baby". It took her a long time to realize that Angela was no longer a baby and that she could not hold back the child's growth.

The mother was referred to the Early Childhood Co-ordinator, who placed her in the parent volunteer programme.

Angela became very happy in this altered school situation and progressed rapidly in her studies.

DISCUSSION

Separation anxiety and fears were evident in all of these children, each exhibiting various aspects of these phenomona.

The first two children were helped through hypnosis and manipulation of the environment. The third child was aided by manipulation of the environment and through confrontation with both mother and child.

In John's case, the mother was willing to separate herself from him, and showed no compunction about "pushing him out". John's strong feelings of rivalry towards his siblings and his destructive fantasies as to what would happen to their mother and to them made it necessary for him to stay home. (Fenichel, 1945).

John was defending himself by regression; he exhibited increased dependence on his mother while displacing hostile wishes through overconcern (Fenichel, 1945). He believed that through magical thinking and staying home to watch he could prevent his fantasies from materializing.

His mother was not fearful of separating from him but her insistence on his going to school increased the fear of separation from her, which he viewed as a traumatic event (Friedman, 1963).

As he became able to verbalize and put these fears outside of himself as well as to free himself of anxiety due to unconscious guilt, changes in his adjustment were rapid.

Andrea's phobia was a result of the dreaded aspect of a school situation which she associated with her mother's death (Friedman, 1963). The black habits of the nuns were a contributing factor to her anxiety. Other factors were having seen her mother jump out of the window and subjection to the highly emotional experience of attending her mother's funeral. She also identified the nuns with witches who would punish her because she was a "bad little girl".

As a result of the fear of separation, she wanted to remain home in the hope that her mother would reappear (A. M. Johnson, 1941). The basis of her concern was complete abandonment by her parents, inability to express feelings of anger towards her father and possibly towards her mother (Fenichel, 1945).

After verbalizing her fears, transferring to another school and being placed with her aunt, she began to accept her mother's absence and the growth in her own personality could be seen.

Angela, according to her own statement, was ready and willing to separate from her mother. The mother herself thought of the school as a cold, impersonal place (Eisenberg, 1958) and sympathized excessively with the child's complaints. Angela sensed that her mother wanted her to remain at home. Her mother made Angela feel guilty for wanting to leave her, so Angela tended to go along with this. Angela feared loss of love, abandonment and possible starvation if she did not give in to her mother's emotional demands (A. S. Johnson, 1941).

The mother had poorly resolved dependence on her child. She demonstrated acute anxiety and fantasized violence happening to Angela if left in school. Her fears were also concerned with Angela's dying from lack of care or being a victim of violence from the outside world. Some of her fears may have been due to her own anger towards Angela for wanting to leave her which the mother could not express.

The mother tried to exploit the child's dependence with the result that separation became a traumatic experience for both (Friedman, 1948). The mother herself was unable to tolerate any thought of separation.

After the fears and anxieties of both were somewhat resolved and energies directed towards constructive activities, the mother was able to let Angela develop and grow in a more normal way.

Preventive Measures

It is difficult for adults to comprehend the nearly unbearable anxiety a young child suffers when separating from a parent. The experience is often traumatic to such children, especially when a mother is emotionally dependent on them, and measures should be taken to help them cope.

In talks with parents, we try to explain how they should prepare themselves and their children for entrance into school. We encourage parents to visit the school and classroom with the child well in advance of the first day of school.

We find that many children who are emotionally disturbed can attend school, but when they are ready to return home, anxiety overwhelms them if the mother is not immediately visible. This can often be a basis for the development of school phobia.

In talks with parents we tell them they cannot always promise to be available at the exact time the child needs them. Instructions should include the following:

1. Whenever the parent is late in arriving at the school to pick up a child, the child should wait in the office.
2. The parent should arrange to have a neighbour take the child home if she will be later than is customary.
3. If a child arrives home and the mother is not there, the child should be instructed to go to a neighbour's house until she arrives.
4. The mother should leave an emergency number in the office of the school to call if she will be very late in arriving.

Briefly stated, it is very important to relieve children of undue anxiety. Otherwise their fantasies may overwhelm them and hysteria may result.

BIBLIOGRAPHY

1. Adler, Alfred: *Individual Psychology* Ed. by Heinz and Rowena Ansbacher. New York: Harper Torch Books, 1967, 45-184.
2. Coolidge, J. C. et al.: "Patterns of Aggression in School Phobia". *Psychoanalytic Study of the Child*, Vol. XVII. New York: International Universities Press, 1962.
3. Eisenberg, Leon: "School Phobia": A Study of Communication of Anxiety, *American Journal of Psychiatry*, Vol. CXIV, 1958, 712-718.
4. Fenichel, Otto: "Anxiety Reactions". *Psychoanalytic Theory of the Neuroses*. New York: W. W. Norton, Inc., 1945, pp 181-545.
5. Friedman, Paul: "School Phobia". *American Handbook of Psychiatry*. New York: Basic Books, 1963, pp 301-303.
6. Gardner, George E., Waldfogel, Samuel: "Intervention in Crises as a Method of Primary Prevention". In *Prevention of Mental Disorders in Children*, Ed. Gerald Caplan. New York: Basic Books, 1961, pp 307-16.
7. Johnson, A. M., et al.: "School Phobia". *American Journal of Orthopsychiatry*, Vol. XI, 1941, pp 702-711.
8. Johnson, A. M.: "School Phobia". *American Journal of Orthopsychiatry*, Vol. XVII. 1957, pp 307-309.
9. Kessler, Jane: "School Phobia" *Psychopathology of Childhood*. New Jersey: Prentice-Hall, Englewood Cliffs, 1966, pp 237-243.
10. Lippman, H. S.: *Treatment of the Child in Emotional Conflict*, New York: McGraw Hill Book Company, 1956.
11. Lawlor, E. D.: Unpublished Case Reports, 1969-72.

Cognitive Functioning of Psychotic Children: A Reappraisal

AHMAD M. BAKER

Abstract: A discussion of the relative cognitive functioning of psychotic children is presented in terms of previous research and theoretical assumptions. The premise that psychotic children possess normal innate intelligence is challenged by the emergence of recent research dealing with measurement and stability of psychotic children's cognitive level. An analysis of recent and relevant research suggests that psychotic children do not differ from mentally retarded children in terms of cognitive functioning. It is proposed, therefore, that a reappraisal be made of the existing assumptions about psychotic children's intelligence level and that those assumptions be modified in order to make them congruent with empirical investigation.

MAUDLEY'S recognition over a century ago of the existence of "insanity in early life" has led to the differentiation of a group of conditions characterized by childhood mental disturbances. In 1911 Bleuler grouped a cluster of related conditions (dementia praecox) under the rubric, *schizophrenias*; but it was not until 1933 that Potter differentiated schizophrenia as a condition in its own entity. Potter's criteria for diagnosis were (a) a generalized reaction of interest from the environment; (b) dereistic thinking, feeling, and acting; (c) disturbances of thought manifested by perseveration, diminution, and incoherence; (d) distortion of affect; and (e) vacillation of behavior from incessant activity to complete immobilization. Childhood schizophrenia remained the global diagnosis of infantile mental disturbances until Kanner in 1943 delineated the syndrome of behaviors he termed *early infantile autism*. This childhood disturbance is characterized by such behaviors as limited emotional attachments to the parents and other individuals, ritualistic and compulsive behavior, and an early age of onset. Although Kanner (1943) implied that autistic children had "good cognitive potentialities," most of the research that has been concerned with cognitive development of severely disturbed children suggests that they are retarded. This paper will attempt to review some of the relevant research supporting this hypothesis.

4. 5 - 12 YEARS

Challenging the Assumption of Normal Intelligence

The assumption that psychotic children possess innate normal intelligence has been predicated on two factors: (a) clinical subjective data and interpretation of some disturbed children's idiosyncratic behavior (e.g., manifestation of unusual feats of memory by some autistic children) as an indicator of untapped intelligence and (b) the disturbed child's lack of physical anomalies associated with severe retardation. Rutter and Lockyer (1967), however, found that only 25% of psychotic children had an IQ within the normal range. Their study was corroborated by Pollack (1967), who reviewed 13 studies involving a total of 306 psychotic children in which IQ had been formally measured. Pollack's study revealed that one-third to one-half of psychotic children had IQ's below 70, two-thirds below 80, and less than one-fourth above 90. The poor performance of psychotic children on intelligence tests has been attributed to specific language deficits rather than to a global deficiency of intelligence (Lockyer & Rutter, 1970). Recent research, however, suggests that psychotic children, especially autistics, manifest linguistically, and possibly etiologically, distinct subgroups (Simmons & Baltax, 1975).

In an attempt to compare the intelligence of autistic and retarded children, Wolf, Wenar, and Rottenberg (1972) selected 32 autistic children and 35 mentally retarded children and examined their ability to vocalize, communicate, and establish relationships with adults, in addition to their desire for mastery and their psychosexual development. Results of the study indicated that the mentally retarded group was rated as functioning at a significantly higher level in all areas except mastery. When the scores of the mentally retarded children with Down's syndrome ($N=11$) were excluded from the data, the two groups did not differ significantly in terms of mastery or psychosexual development. The significant differences that were obtained for the remaining groups also were suspect. IQ scores were available for all but one of the mentally retarded subjects. On the other hand, none of the autistic children were evaluated because they were labeled as "untestable," indicating that their cognitive functioning, as a group, may have been lower than that of the mentally retarded group. This possibility is strengthened further if one examines the IQ scores of the Down's syndrome mentally retarded group and compares them with the IQ scores of mentally retarded children not having Down's syndrome. The Down's syndrome group had a mean IQ of 38, compared with 27 for the remaining mentally retarded subjects, an indication that the most severely retarded children were comparable to the autistic children.

In their study of special educational treatments of autistic children, Rutter and Bartak (1973) conducted followup studies of three autistic classes in which different treatment strategies (psychotherapeutic, structured, and permissive) were in use. Although the autistic children in the structured classroom made the most academic achievement following a 3 year period, their IQ scores were found to be the best predictors of their educational, social, and speech progress. It must be noted that the mean IQ of the children in the structured unit was 66, as compared with 52 for the children in the psychotherapeutic unit and 48 for the children in the permissive unit. In addition, it was noted that those children who were judged to be the most disturbed and least responsive during the initial assessment period tended to be the most disturbed and least responsive during the followup assessment period 3 years later. The Rutter and Bartak study clearly demonstrated that the severity and prognosis of a mental disturbance are related to the child's cognitive functioning level.

The intellectual functioning of autistic children and its comparison with other groups of children have been studied by DeMyer and her associates. Three of their studies deserve noting. In the first study, DeMyer, Barton, and Norton (1972) developed a test battery that they used to compare the adaptive, verbal, and motor profiles of psychotic and nonpsychotic subnormal children. The battery consisted of five major tasks: (a) intellectual (visual and verbal memory, problem solving, number concepts, and self awareness); (b) language (receptive, expressive, and comprehensive); (c) motor (gross lower extremities, gross upper extremities, and fine upper extremities); (d) perceptual motor (paper/pencil skills, fitting and assembling skills); and (e) perceptual (color, size, and form). Their subjects consisted of 81 boys and 16 girls who were referred to the Clinical Research Center for Early Childhood Schizophrenia. The diagnostic groups were composed of 3 normal children (mean IQ = 103.0), 29 nonpsychotic subnormal children (mean IQ = 70.3), 11 early schizophrenic children (mean IQ = 58.5), 19 primary functioning autistic children (mean IQ = 47.3), and 35 secondary functioning autistic children (mean IQ = 28.9). The children were independently diagnosed by two psychiatrists with a 92% agreement. The children in the three psychotic categories were characterized by reduced speech for communication, emotional withdrawal, and nonfunctional object use.

Results of the study revealed that the normal subjects, despite their small number, significantly differed from all four pathological groups on all tasks except ball play, in which normal and nonpsychotic subnormal subjects did not significantly differ. However, psychotic and nonpsychotic subnormal subjects demonstrated subnormal performances in all other areas, with the autistic and psychotic groups having the most depressed scores. The authors presented evidence to suggest that the basis for the poor performance displayed by the autistic, psychotic, and nonpsychotic subnormal children was a central nervous system dysfunction rather than inadequate environmental stimulation during the first year of life.

In an attempt to determine the most valid indicator of an autistic child's prognosis, DeMyer, Barton, DeMyer, Norton, Allen, and Steele (1973) evaluated a followup study of 85 autistic boys and 35 girls, along with 26 nonpsychotic mentally retarded children. Their results indicated that the general prognosis for autistic children is poor (1% to 2% recover to normal); the lower the child's IQ, the poorer the prognosis becomes. Their results indicated that approximately 5% to 10% of autistic children score within the normal IQ range (IQ of 85 or above), 12% to 20% within the mildly retarded range (IQ of 50 to 67), and 43% to 68% within the moderately to profoundly retarded range (IQ of below 50). It also was pointed out that the causes of autistic children's retardation was probably due to biological factors. They presented evidence which indicated that autistic children suffer from more gross EEG abnormalities than nonpsychotic mental retardates. Furthermore, they cited some electrophysiological studies that locate the brain as the site of the abnormality. The evidence in the DeMyer studies serves as a major refutation of the assumption that autistic and psychotic children possess average innate intellectual capacity.

IQ Stability

In order to study the stability of autistic children's IQ's and the effect of that stability on their progress, DeMyer, Barton, Kimberlin, Allen, Yang, and Steele (1974) compared the IQ scores of 115 autistic and 47 subnormal children over a mean 6 year period. Their results showed that 94% of the 115 autistic children they studied had IQ's of 67 or below, with the greatest number being in the moderately or severely retarded range. Furthermore, it was found that the stability of autistic children's IQ scores was not substantially different from that of the general population. However, closer examination of the data revealed that autistic children having an initial IQ in the 55 to 60 range benefited from treatment and achieved higher IQ's at followup. Autistic children having an initial IQ of 40 or below did not benefit from treatment, and their IQ scores did not change at followup, except for those children whose IQ scores were the lowest—their scores

decreased at followup. The researchers concluded that IQ can serve as a prognosticating tool in determining how well an autistic child can benefit from treatment. They suggested an IQ of 50 as a guideline in separating autistic children who can or cannot benefit from treatment strategies. In addition, it was borne out that severely disturbed children also are severely retarded.

Early Studies

The suspicion that psychotic children possessed inferior intellectual development had been raised by earlier studies. Eaton and Menolascino (1966) evaluated 32 children displaying psychotic behavior: 24 were diagnosed as having chronic brain syndrome with psychoses, 6 were schizophrenic, and 2 displayed early infantile autism. Intellectual assessment of the children revealed that 8 were mildly retarded, 7 were moderately retarded, and 3 were severely retarded. The remaining children were considered to be too disturbed to be assessed adequately. The Eaton and Menolascino study demonstrated that of the 32 psychotic children they studied, at least 75% were retarded in varying degrees.

Another early attempt to compare psychotic children with mentally retarded children was done by Gillies (1965). He matched 28 psychotic children with 28 subnormal children and administered to them the following tests: Peabody, Seguin Formboard or Wallen Formboard, Performance WISC, Vineland, and Goodenough. Psychotic children scored lower than the retarded children on vocabulary age and social age. The discrepancy between verbal and nonverbal scores was greater for the psychotic children than for the retarded children, and social ages were significantly lower than the nonverbal ages for the psychotic group but not for the subnormal group.

Some researchers have attempted to divide the varying degrees of retardation among psychotic children on the basis of the condition's origin. Goldfarb (1961), placing psychotic children into organic and nonorganic groups, found the IQ distribution in a group of 24 psychotic children to be bimodal. Psychotic children classified as organic had a mean IQ of 62, while the nonorganic group had a mean IQ of 92. Goldberg and Soper (1963) found that IQ scores of psychotic children were correlated with their neurological indexes; that is, children manifesting the greatest number of neurological signs indicative of brain dysfunction had the lowest IQ's. They considered their results to confirm Goldfarb's findings.

Although many researchers admit that retardation accompanies psychoses, some continue to suggest that the retardations are qualitatively different. Rimland (1964) developed the

argument that autistic children possess islets of normal and near normal intelligence or special abilities of the *idiot savant* kind. It must be noted that Rimland's evidence is of an anecdotal nature, and little formal study has been conducted to test this hypothesis. Goldberg and Soper (1963), however, found that only 20% of their children exhibited this phenomenon. Pollack (1967) cited a study by Cullies, who investigated the performance of psychotic and retarded children on verbal and performance tasks. He found that psychotic and retarded children did not differ significantly on all the tasks. He further argued that possessing certain abilities is not confined to psychotic children; it is often cited as diagnostic of brain damage.

Need for Research and Reappraisal

The study of childhood mental disturbances, although a relatively recent phenomenon, has been extensive. However, most of the studies have been concerned mainly with treatment methods of psychotic children and their comparative effects. Many of these studies can be classified as descriptive rather than experimental. Hence, there exists a paucity of research on the comparative cognitive development of psychotic children. It has been argued that the lack of research in this area is due to the fact that severely disturbed children are untestable. The research by DeMyer and her associates renders this argument benign. By selecting eclectically, they were able to administer tasks that measured the cognitive functioning of severely disturbed children.

Although some researchers (e.g., Prior & Chen, 1975) continue to persist in their attempt to prove that severely disturbed children possess normal innate intelligence, most of the research that has addressed this issue points to the contrary. Empirical investigation has concluded that psychotic children who test retarded, for all practical purposes, are retarded.

References

DeMyer, M. K., Barton, S., DeMyer, W. E., Norton, J. A., Allen, J., & Steele, R. Prognosis in autism: A follow-up study. *Journal of Autism and Childhood Schizophrenia*, 1973, 3, 199-246.

DeMyer, M. K., Barton, S., Kimberlin, C., Allen, J., Yang, E., & Steele, R. The measured intelligence of autistic children. *Journal of Autism and Childhood Schizophrenia*, 1974, 4, 42-60.

DeMyer, M. K., Barton, S., & Norton, J. A. A comparison of adaptive, verbal, and motor profiles of psychotic and nonpsychotic children. *Journal of Autism and Childhood Schizophrenia*, 1972, 2, 359-377.

Eaton, L., & Menolascino, F. J. Psychotic reactions of childhood—Experiences of mental retardation pilot project. *Journal of Nervous and Mental Disease*, 1966, 143, 55-67.

Gillies, S. M. Some abilities of psychotic children and subnormal subjects. *Journal of Mental Deficiency Research*, 1965, 9, 89-101.

Goldberg, B., & Soper, J. Childhood psychosis or mental retardation: A diagnostic dilemma. *Canadian Medical Association Journal*, 1963, 89, 1015-1019.

Goldfarb, W. *Childhood schizophrenia*. Cambridge MA: Harvard University Press, 1961.

Kanner, L. Autistic disturbances of affective contact. *Nervous Child*, 1943, 2, 217-250.

Lockyer, L., & Rutter, M. Five to fifteen year follow-up study of infantile psychosis: IV. Patterns of cognitive ability. *British Journal of Social and Clinical Psychology*, 1970, 9, 152-163.

Pollack, M. Mental subnormality and "childhood schizophrenia." In J. Zubin (Ed.), *Psychopathology of mental development*. New York: Grune & Stratton, 1967.

POTENTIAL AND ACTUAL INSTRUCTIONAL LEVELS OF EMOTIONALLY DISTURBED CHILDREN

SUSAN C. ROBERTS, LYNDAL M. BULLOCK AND R. KEITH BROWN
Barry College, Miami Shores, Florida 33161

An investigation was conducted in Florida to determine the reading and arithmetic achievement levels of emotionally disturbed children in special public school programs. The data revealed a two-year deficit in both academic areas when chronological age was taken into consideration. The greatest proportion of classes were self-contained, although the largest number of children were being served in resource programs. Self-contained classrooms generally appeared to be serving the children with the most severe academic deficiencies. The results of the investigation have important implications for diagnosis and remediation components in teacher training programs. Teachers must learn how to appropriately assess their pupils' strengths and weaknesses prior to implementing remedial programs for them.

In recent years much effort has been directed toward ascertaining the academic achievement levels of emotionally disturbed children. It has generally been found that these children score higher in reading than in arithmetic and that their performance in both subject areas is below expectation when chronological and mental age are used for making such judgment.

Shimota (1964) found almost one-third of a sample of institutionalized disturbed adolescents disabled in reading. Reading disability was defined as tested skill, 25 percent or more below grade expectation based on age and I.Q. Motto and Latham (1966) reported that children who remained in a school in a hospital setting longer than ten months benefitted from their educational experience at the level expected for their mental ages, while those who attended for shorter periods of time, did not. Short-term institutionalization for disturbed children involves, first, an adjustment to the hospital situation with unfamiliar books and teachers, and soon thereafter, a readjustment to the former home/school setup.

Stennett (1966) found that emotionally disturbed children tend to get farther behind their classmates in achievement as they progress through the elementary grades. "Although some of these children do 'recover spontaneously', the group trend is clearly for them to get 'stuck' on a track which leads to increasingly severe educational deficits (Stennett, 1966, p. 447)." Boys showed this trend more dramatically.

Bullock and Brown (1972) asked teachers of special public school classes for the emotionally disturbed to indicate each pupil's chronological age as well as his reading and arithmetic instructional levels. The data were divided into three parts according to type of program: resource room, self-contained, and "other" (crisis, itinerant, itinerant-resource). The mean potential instructional level as determined by chronological age for all the children was 4.31. In contrast, the mean reading and arithmetic levels were 2.44 and 2.54 respectively, indicating a deficit of approximately two years in both academic areas.

In the investigation conducted in Florida, ninety-eight percent of the children in resource rooms were in grades K-6, yet over 99% were functioning in the K-6 range in reading and arithmetic. Fifteen children in resource rooms were in grades 7 and 8, however, only four were reading at or above this level and none were at or above this level in arithmetic. Both the continually widening gap between potential and actual instructional level and the higher achievement in reading than arithmetic as reported in the literature are evident among the children served in resource programs.

Ninety percent of the children in self-contained classrooms were performing in the K-6 range in reading and arithmetic, whereas according to chronological age, only 71% were really in grades K-6. Two thirds of the youngsters in grades 7-12 were performing below the secondary level in both academic subjects. The higher percentage of secondary school age children at their appropriate grade level in self-contained classrooms, when compared with the students in resource rooms, may be attributed to the full-time placement in a special class offering maximum extra assistance of the former group.

Fifty-eight percent of the children in "other" programs were in grades K-6, however, over three-fourths of all those in "other" programs were achieving in the K-6 range in reading and over four-fifths were achieving in this range in arithmetic. Almost half the secondary school age students were performing in the 7-12 grade range in both academic subjects. The children served in crisis, itinerant, and itinerant-resource programs are expected to have fewer academic difficulties than those in self-contained and resource classes.

Resource rooms were serving the largest proportion (48%) of the total number of emotionally disturbed children, as well as the lowest proportion of secondary school-age children. The problems as a result of departmentalization involved in the administration and coordination of the efforts of resource rooms in secondary schools is undoubtedly the reason that only a few such plans have been implemented. Self-contained classrooms were serving 13% more children than were "other" programs; yet, whereas 28% of the children in self-contained classrooms were of secondary school age, 42% of the children in "other" programs were of secondary school age. Children in the latter group were functioning more closely to their appropriate age-grade level than were children in the former group. This supports the contention that special self-contained classrooms best meet the needs of emotionally disturbed students with severe academic problems, while those youngsters with comparatively mild academic deficits are best assigned to special teachers on an intermittent or part-time schedule.

Teachers of emotionally disturbed children in public school programs should not assume that their pupils are functioning equally well in all academic areas or that they are working at the grade level commensurate with their chronological age. Teachers must be able to interpret data from psychological evaluations done by qualified personnel within the school system, mental health centers, and guidance clinics and derive implications from them for maximum efficiency in determining short-range as well as long-range educational objectives. Individual subtest scores, rather than overall or composite scores, must be carefully examined in light of the whole child and his day-to-day performance in the classroom. The psychological data obtained from one testing session should not be considered in isolation.

The findings of the Florida study imply the importance of the diagnosis and remediation components in teacher training programs. Teachers should be able to administer reliable, valid instruments to determine their pupils' strengths and weaknesses in academic subjects and cognitive processes. These steps are essential to ascertaining at which levels the child is functioning and through which channels he may best be taught. Assessment must take place prior to planning individualized sequential programs utilizing educational materials appropriate to each child's interest level and ability. Following this procedure will result in higher achieving, better adjusted children in our schools.

References

Bullock, L. M., and Brown, R. K. Educational provisions for emotionally disturbed children: A status report. Florida Educational Research Development Commission, 1972.

Motto, J. J., and Latham, L. An analysis of children's educational achievement and related variables in a state psychiatric hospital. *Exceptional Children*, 1966, 32, 619-623.

Shimota, H. E. Reading skills in emotionally disturbed institutionalized adolescents. *Journal of Educational Research*, 1964, 58, 106-111.

Stennett, R. G. Emotional handicap in the elementary years: Phase or disease. *American Journal of Orthopsychiatary*, 1966, 36, 444-448.

Friendship Claims and Communications of Disturbed and Normal Children

John M. Reisman and Susan I. Shorr

John M. Reisman is Professor of Psychology and Director of Clinical Training at DePaul University. He received his Ph.D. from Michigan State University in 1958 and was Chief Psychologist of the Rochester Child Guidance Clinic from 1959-69. He is the author of *A History of Clinical Psychology* and *Principles of Psychotherapy With Children,* and is scheduled to soon have published *The Anatomy of Friendship.*

Susan Shorr is a doctoral student in clinical-community psychology at DePaul University. She received her bachelor's degree from the University of Michigan in 1975. Her current interests include the study of child abuse and parent-child interactions.

ABSTRACT

Sixteen emotionally disturbed children from a day treatment program and sixteen normal children matched for age and sex were interviewed and asked how many friends they had. Each child was also asked to respond to a communication task involving a hypothetical friend's personal problem. Normal and disturbed children did not differ in the mean number of friends claimed, but there was a tendency for disturbed children to report having fewer than two friends more often than normals. Disturbed children performed less effectively and at a lower developmental level on the communication task. There was no relationship between friendship claims and performance in communication. Few questions were asked by the disturbed children, as compared to the normals, suggesting an area for training that might improve the competence of these youngsters.

Emotional disturbance in children has frequently been associated with poor peer relations. Hartup (1976) cited several studies which demonstrated a relationship between popularity with peers and emotional well-being and concluded that peer rejection is a most sensitive indicator of disturbance. Various behavioral correlates, including general emotional adjustment, anxiety, dependence, and aggres-

sion, have been found to be associated with peer rejection (Hartup, 1970).

The significance of peer relations in emotional development is further illustrated in the research conducted by Roff and his associates (Roff, 1961, 1963; Roff, Knight, & Wertheim, 1976; Roff, Sells & Golden, 1972). In retrospective studies Roff and his coworkers found that poor peer adjustment in childhood was significantly related to adult disorders, including psychosis, neurosis, and conduct problems. Moreover, Roff, Knight, and Wertheim (1976) found that disturbance in peer relationships during childhood was one of the few retrospective correlates of adult schizophrenia.

Rolf (1976), using social competence data, found that peer-rated social incompetence and the presence of externalizing behavior disorders are the best predictors of high risk cases of poor adult outcome. Investigatory studies of peer relations typically utilize sociometric techniques based on reports from peers or teachers. Using the Bower Class Play Sociometric Device (Bower, 1969), in which classmates assign one another to roles in a purported play, Cowen et al. (1973) found that, when compared to clinicians' predictions and teacher ratings, peer ratings of social competence were by far the most powerful predictors of later behavior disorders and the need for further psychiatric treatment.

Further, disturbed children have been found to perform differently from normal children on cognitive tasks involving interpersonal relationships. In particular, their conceptions of friendship seem less mature (Selman, 1976; Hayden,

Nasby, & Davids, 1977), and their solutions to interpersonal problems are more forceful and impulsive, with fewer requests for information concerning the circumstances of the problem (Spivack & Shure, 1974). Also treatment programs have been instituted which have had as a major aim the improvement in social behaviors through the provision of corrective relationships (Powers & Witmer, 1951; Goodman, 1972; McWilliams & Finkel, 1973).

These studies have led to a characterization of emotionally disturbed children as a homogenous group of peer-rejected individuals. The only distinction made in this regard is whether these children admit or deny and distort their poor peer relationships (Freud, 1965; Bower, 1969), presumably those who do the latter are more disturbed than the former. However, research has yet to determine whether emotionally disturbed children themselves recognize disturbances in their peer relationships, and if this recognition is associated with severity of disturbance. Moreover, there has been little research to determine if this characterization of peer rejection is appropriate to emotionally disturbed children in instutions or settings where they constitute the population, as compared to the usual situation in which an emotionally disturbed child is in a classroom of normal children.

The purpose of the present study was to investigate peer relations in emotionally disturbed and normal children by interviews of the children and by presenting them with a cognitive task in which they were required to verbally express how they would respond to statements of a friend describing a personal problem in school. It was hypothesized that: (a) Emotionally disturbed children in a special school would claim to have fewer friends than normal children; (b) Emotionally disturbed children would ask fewer questions and deal less effectively with the communication task than normal children; and (c) Emotionally disturbed children who are distorting or denying the number of their friends will ask fewer questions and deal less effectively with the communication task than emotionally disturbed children whose friendship estimates are consensually validated.

Method

Thirty-two children ranging in age from seven to twelve years participated in the study. Half (nine girls and seven boys) were severely emotionally disturbed, but not considered psychotic. They had been diagnosed by a psychiatrist as part of an extensive evaluation to determine their suitability for a special program and the need for their exclusion from public school. Despite their disturbance, they were not regarded as functioning at retarded levels. These 16 children were recruited from a population of 26 who attended a day treatment program for emotionally disturbed children in which the average stay is three to four years. All were considered by their teachers to be very much in need of the program, and prior to the initiation of the study its design was discussed and modified to minimize the possibilities of distressing the youngsters.

Each of the 16 disturbed children was matched with a normal child on the basis of age and sex ($M = 9.6$ years for females in both groups; $M = 10.5$ years for males). The normal children were drawn from grades 2-6 of two parochial schools located in the same area of the city as the day treatment program. They were recruited from those who teachers judged to be developing normally and without significant psychological problems. Further, interviewers were instructed to exclude any "normal" child who did not wish to participate or who gave any evidence of psychological disturbance, though such a circumstance did not occur. The parents of both groups of children, as well as the children themselves, were solicited for their cooperation in the study.

Each normal and disturbed child was interviewed individually at school for 10-15 minutes by a graduate student in clinical psychology. It was explained that we were interested in learning about the child's friends and friendship. Although all the normal children were interviewed alone, the teachers of the disturbed children thought it best to remain with each child during the course of the interview to make the situation a more comfortable one and to be available should the child become distressed.

During the course of interview, background information was obtained (grade, age, birthdate) and the child was asked: Do you have any friends? How many friends do you have? If in response to the number of friends, the child gave an indefinite or highly improbable figure, e.g., "Lots," "Hundreds," he or she was urged to give a specific or reasonable number.

The child was then asked to name his friends, as a check on the validity of the numerical estimate, and was asked to indicate what he liked or valued about friendship or having friends. Although there were discrepancies between a large number of friends claimed by a child and the number of names produced, the rho was .76, indicating a significant degree of correspondence between the two sets of data.

The statements about what is valued in friendship were categorized independently and blindly by both authors into three groups on the basis of Aristotle's system in Book VIII of his *Nichomachean Ethics:* Pleasure — friends are valued as playmates or as sources of entertainment; Utility — friends are valued for their helpfulness or usefulness in dealing with problems; and Virtue — friends are valued for their admirable qualities, such as loyalty and dependability (Murstein &Spitz, 1973-4). The authors practiced categorizing batches of 20 responses from another study on friendship until there was over 90% agreement. This level of agreement was attained in three batches; there was 97% agreement in categorizing the responses in this study.

The second part of the interview consisted of a communication task in which the respondent was asked to imagine that a good friend had come to see him or her and had started to talk about a problem. The child was asked to verbally respond to each of the friend's ten statements as read by the interviewer from the following script: "I don't like school. This teacher doesn't like me. The work is very hard. I'm getting yelled at for everything I do. It's really getting me down. I don't think I'm as smart as the others. I feel like running away. What do you think I should do? I like what you said. I feel better now." If during any part of the interview a child appeared distressed, the interview was terminated and resumed at a subsequent session. Although such an interruption was not necessary for the normal children, it did prove needed for two disturbed children.

Responses were categorized independently and blindly by the two authors using a system described by Reisman and Yamokoski (1974): Empathic, Responsive, Interrogative, Expository, Interpretative, Suggestions, Self-Disclosure, Evaluations, and Other statements. There was 87% agreement between the authors in categorizing the responses, with two categories being of major interest in connection with this study; Interrogative — any question or request for additional information; Other — irrelevant statements, changes of topic, and inability to respond.

An evaluation of responses to the question in the script, "What do you think I should do?," was based on Loevinger's model of ego development. A description of the model and a review of the research generated by it are presented by Hauser (1976). Again there was blind, independent scoring of the responses by the authors, with 90% agreement. Only three of Loevinger's six levels were found among the children in the study. They were: Level 1 — Impulsive or inability to respond, the child urges aggression or withdrawal or cannot produce a response; Level 2 — Conformity or dependence, the child recommends staying, seeking help from teachers, parents, or friends; Level 3 — Conscientiousness, the child urges the friend to study harder, pay attention, or bring the work in on time, implying self-criticalness and self-help.

About three months after meeting with the emotionally disturbed children, their teachers were asked to estimate the number of friends they thought each child had, at home and at school. Davids & Parenti (1958a) found such estimates to be significantly related to popularity. Although there had been concern about obtaining this information from the teachers who were present during the child's interview, there turned out to be virtually no relationship between the two sets of estimates ($rho = .27$). Denial was operationally defined as a difference in the estimate of friends between teacher and child that was at least three times greater or smaller. Employing this definition, a Denial Group ($N = 6$) and a No Denial Group ($N = 10$) were formed within the disturbed sample. For both groups the mean number of friends estimated by teachers was 5. The No Denial Group also had a mean number of friends claimed that was 5, but the Denial Group claimed a mean number of 37 friends. Clearly the two groups differed, as intended, on the number of friends they claimed as compared to the number of friends their teachers thought them to have.

Results

Hypothesis One: There was no significant difference in the mean number of friends claimed between the normal ($M = 18$) and disturbed ($M = 17$) groups, nor was there a significant difference in the variances between the groups. However it was noted that many disturbed children claimed to have few friends, two or less. When the data were analyzed by a split for two or less friends claimed, there was a tendency for more members of the disturbed group to report having few friends ($N = 5$) as compared to the normal group ($N = 1$; $X^2 = 3.28$; $p < .10 > .05$). Thus although normal and disturbed children do not differ in the mean number of friends claimed, there appeared to be a tendency for disturbed children to report to have few friends more often than normal children.

Table 1
Mean Number of Responses

Type of Response	Disturbed Children ($N = 16$)	Normal Children ($N = 16$)	t
Empathic	0	0	—
Responsive	0	0	—
Interrogative	.63	1.81	2.24*
Expository	1.25	3.25	2.88*
Interpretative	0	0	—
Suggestion	3.38	3.31	N.S.
Self-Disclosure	1.19	.38	1.40
Evaluation	1.81	1.69	N.S.
Other	2.12	.38	2.60*
Total	10.38	10.82	N.S.

*$p < .05$.

Hypothesis Two: Disturbed children asked significantly fewer questions (Interrogative statements) in their responses to the communication task than did normal children. The disturbed children also produced fewer Expository responses (expert-like statements) and more Other responses (irrelevant statements or an inability to respond) than did the normal children. Finally, a sign test indicated significantly more disturbed children responded at a lower developmental level to the question "What do you think I shoud do?" than their matched controls ($p < .05$). The responses of the disturbed group tended to be at levels one (Impulsive) and two (Conformity). In contrast, the responses of the normal children were at levels two and three (Conscientiousness). Thus, this hypothesis was supported.

Hypothesis Three: There were no significant differences between the Denial Group and No Denial group in the number of questions asked, number of "Other" responses given, or level of response to the question "What do you think I should do?" Thus, there was no support for this hypothesis.

Nor were any significant differences found on these variables between those disturbed children falling above and below the median of the number of friends claimed. Evidently, categorization on the basis of number of friends claimed and Denial-No Denial of friends did not differentiate the performances on this cognitive task within this disturbed group of children.

Discussion

The findings of this study provide some support for contentions of perceived differences in friendship patterns between disturbed and normal children. Within a disturbed group, there were more children who were aware of having few friends, though this result was obscured in the group data by those who claimed to have many friends. It should be emphasized that these findings were obtained from a group of disturbed children attending a special educational program, and that possibly peer-rejection would have been more in evidence had the children been in regular classrooms. Similarly, Davids and Parenti (1958b) found there were degrees of popularity among a group of institutionalized disturbed boys, though even the most popular of these boys might have been rejected in a normal group setting. It would be of considerable interest to repeat this study using disturbed children who have not been excluded from public school so as to assess the effects of the normal classroom setting upon the child's friendship claims and functioning.

The lack of relationship between indices of performance on a communication task and friendship claims suggests that within a disturbed group peer acceptance and rejection are unrelated to subtle immaturities in communication skills, though these skills do discriminate between disturbed and normal children and may be related to acceptance within a "normal" group. Further, if one were to take measures of disturbance which are correlated with normal peer acceptance, it is possible a relation would be found between these measures and claimed number of friends. Davids (1972) reported a negative relationship between popularity among a group of disturbed boys and indicators of pathology, such as unpredictable aggression and withdrawal.

Both the normal and disturbed children tended to handle the communication task by being authoritative and giving direct bits of advice. However, the disturbed children asked fewer questions, less often expressed expert opinions, more often did not know how to respond, and gave solutions to the interpersonal problem that were less mature than the normals, suggesting a deficit of skills in this area. These findings are similar to those of Selman (1976), Hayden, Nasby, & Davids (1977), and Spivack and Shure (1974), who also reported less effective, differentiated, or developed (mature) social skills among the disturbed.

In particular, the few questions raised by the disturbed group in their performance on the communication task suggests these children may act in situations on the basis of limited and minimal information thus adding to the impression of their ineptitude and impulsivity. A profitable area for further inquiry would be to explore the consequences of increasing their questioning as a means to delay actions and to acquire appropriate information so situations can be dealt with more effectively.

The Medicine Pots——
A Motivation Operation

Letti L. Clark

"It's nice that kids get to make so many things in art these days. We didn't have these opportunities when I was in school."

Art teachers across the country hear echoes of this thinking. Ironically, though, the *making of things* in an art class is *not* the most important happening or the greatest humanizing opportunity which is presented.

So often, by the time many students reach the upper elementary grades, they are experiencing central school system dysfunction. They have been put down, shut up, forced into, bawled out, embarrassed in-front-of and held behind so often that they are exhibiting symptoms of ego-collapse and educational shutdown. The art interval offers an anecdotal opportunity to recondition the broken spirit and medicate the ill-functioning self concept. Here a child has the chance to be an individual. A bruised self-image can be treated.

What do you do with a child who has an established record of failure and comes to you in a condition of ego arrest? How do you motivate a child who already has ceased his academic breathing? The problem is common. The solution is not simple.

At our school during a recent unit on ceramics, I witnessed the return to life of several students, non-achievers, who were led to believe that they could succeed instead of fail in a pot-building assignment. The believing did not come easy. The resistance was strong. When you have experienced failure so many times it is very dangerous and threatening to show your feelings and extend your hopes with the possibility of again meeting defeat. A believing environment had to be carefully and slowly created for the patients in this operation.

Before actually beginning work with the clay, the students were given a contract which clearly set forth the A, B and C grade requirements. To help the formation of a believable plan, a chart was furnished which listed all the possible combinations of pot building methods and decorating techniques along with the number of firings required for each. Using this information the students attempted to estimate the amount of time necessary for each step of the work. Their expected rate of progress was then plotted on their personal project calendar, which showed the number of working days available. Vacation days were designated as well as the days on which the kiln would be fired. At first this process, which admittedly was very complicated, confused even the quickest students. Very soon, however, the confusion cleared and the students began working with a directed purpose which had not been in evidence previously. The plan that each student made was kept in the room and was available during each working period. Most students consulted their plan daily.

Initially the non-achievers required a good deal of individual attention. Noticeably though, before long, they began realizing that they were making it. The idea even occurred to some that if they could work a little faster they would be able to earn the next higher grade. All of the students were encouraged during their routine consultation with the teacher. The students who were less secure about their ability to succeed were given more attention and positively reinforced more often. The initial horseplay which was paraded to mask feelings of inadequacy and pos-

108   Reprinted from *School Arts*, Vol. 76, No. 6, Feb., 1977 with permission of Davis Publications, Inc. ©1977 Davis Publications.

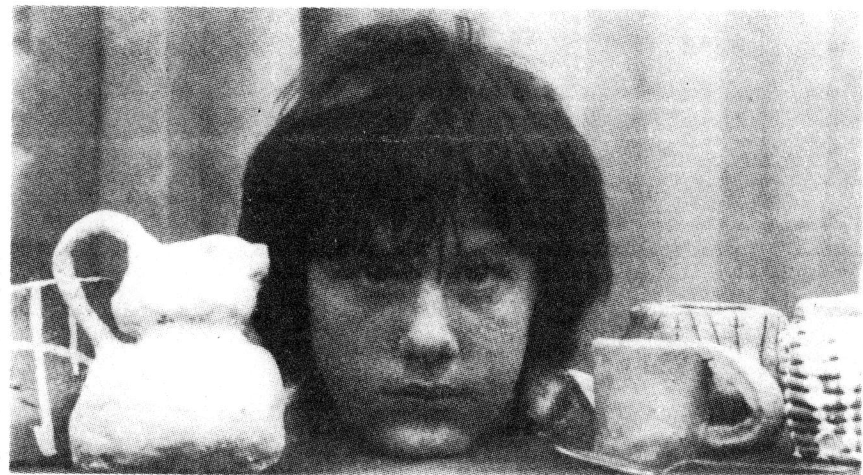

sible defeat, were ignored. The social interactions between students and teacher were carefully limited to positive exchanges concerning the student's work progress.

In a very short time ceramic engineers began to dominate the room. Small successes began to be realized. These small successes fostered larger ones and damaged concepts of self experienced recovery as the students worked with confidence guided by their calendars.

The pot making operation was successful for this eighth grade group which consisted of students who were performing with an extremely varied amount of success academically. The achievers continue to achieve and the non-achievers blossomed under the therapeutic encouragement which enabled them first to trust, next to believe success a possibility and finally to succeed. Our ceramic pots truly were *medicine pots*.

Letti L. Clark is an art teacher, State Street Middle School, Alliance, Ohio.

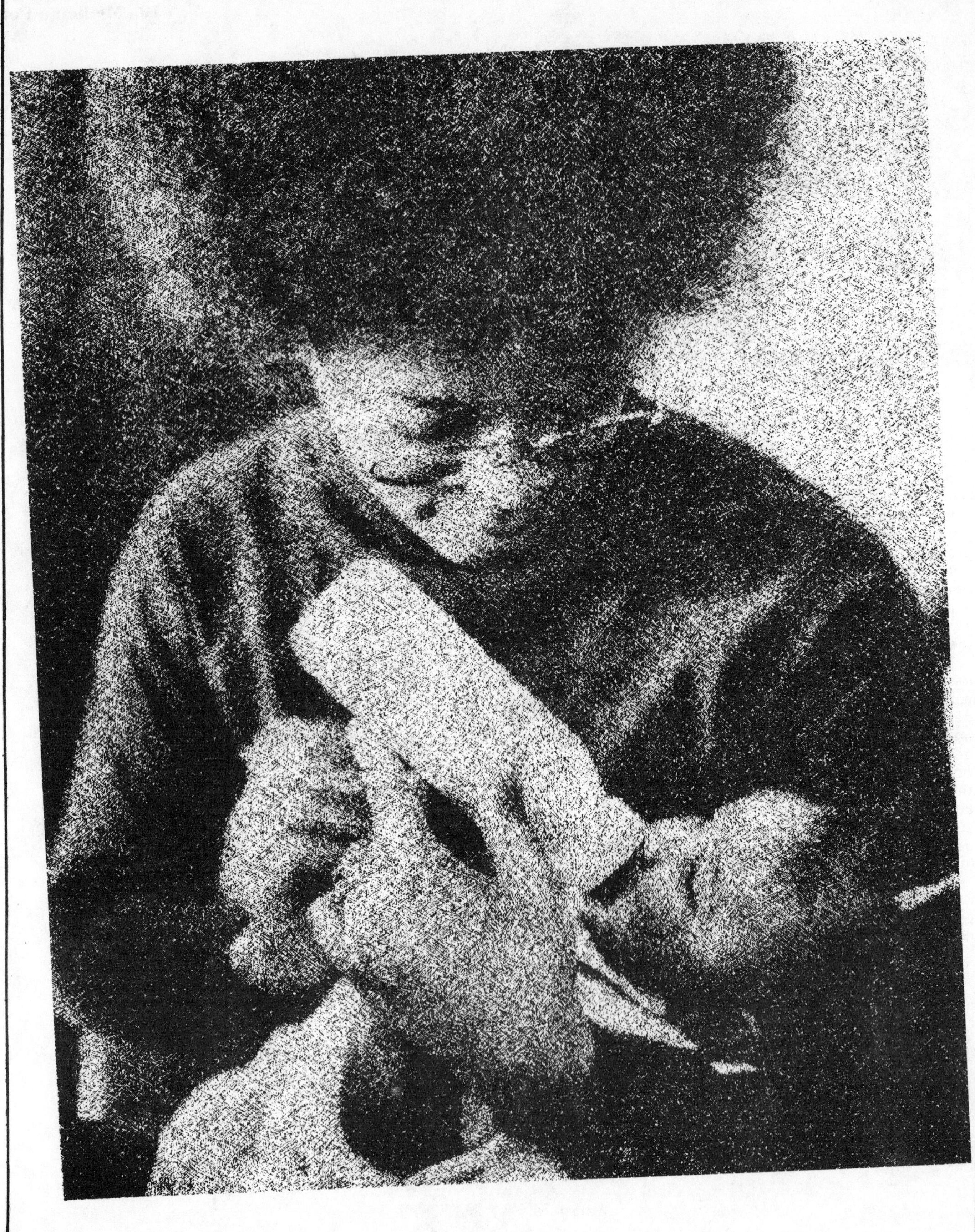

Parenting

Parents of behaviorally disordered children need psychological support. They suffer from guilt because society has marked them as "failures" as parents. They are incapable of "controlling" their children. The old adage of "children should be seen and not heard" - and certainly *not* be disruptive - still holds true, to some degree, today. If these parents are to be of help to their children, they must have professional assurance that they are not wholly at fault.

The parents of autistic children have taken the blame for being cold and unresponsive for years. They have born the guilt of being the cause of their child's behavior problem. Though the etiology of autism is still unknown, parents are being freed from the guilt. The schools, teachers and therapists should make an effort to include parents in the child's behavioral planning so that the parents can help maintain a consistent total environment. When parents are included the child benefits, the planners benefit and the parents benefit. The child's behavior is handled consistently at home and in school. The planners receive the benefit of knowing how the child reacts to the behavioral plan outside of his sphere of control. The parents are treated as an important part of a team, freed from guilt, and given training on how to handle their difficult child.

There are times when the problems of the deviant child are so severe - they are totally out of control and are a danger to self and/or others - that the parents cannot cope. The only alternative the parents have - and they see it as a difficult decision but their's and the child's only chance - is institutionalization. With this move most parents are not seeking to "punish" their children, they are truly desirous of help. Society, however, does not accept this and tends to "condemn" the parents for being too lenient (or too strict) to allow the child's behavior to deteriorate to that extent. The law also, in effect, condemns the parents. A new ruling allows children in institutions "due process," which could legally release them from their placement. The catch is that the parents must be willing to provide their children with a place to live. (The children must have some type of home.) What is really happening is that parents are being condemned by their children and society and being forced to make the difficult decision of whether or not to place their child *twice*.

THE AGGRESSIVE CHILD

by Luleen S. Anderson

Luleen S. Anderson, Ph.D., is co-ordinator of Psychological Services and Elementary Guidance for the Quincy Public Schools, Quincy, Massachusetts.

One of the most frequently expressed concerns of elementary school teachers is how to manage the aggressive "behavior problem" child in their classrooms. The overly aggressive child has been described as one who disrupts his own academic progress, the learning efforts of his classmates and his relationships with others.[1] A teacher may struggle daily with such a child, searching in vain for help in changing his or her behavior.

The aggressive child who alternately angers and upsets the teacher is caught up in a vicious cycle, one that is counter-productive both for the young student and the teacher. Parents, too, struggle with such aggressive behavior and worry about how to discipline and manage their child.

This article will focus on helping adults to understand the role of anger in young children (preschool through elementary school age) and its rela-

tionship to learning, as well as on specific approaches and techniques for managing aggression in young children. The emphasis is on the acceptance of angry feelings in children—and ourselves—and on developing strategies for teaching children more effective mastery of their angry feelings, mastery which enhances their self-esteem. The article will not discuss child development or the various theories of aggression, nor will it discuss the use of drug therapy or children for whom neurological or organic problems are primary.

Handling children's anger can be perplexing, draining and anger-provoking for adults. In fact, one of the major problems in dealing with anger in children is *our* difficulty in handling the anger that their feelings stir up in *us*. Haim Ginot explained that we as teachers, counselors, parents or administrators need to remind ourselves that we were not always taught how

to deal with anger as a fact of life during our own childhoods.[2] We were led to believe then that to be angry was to be bad, and we were often made to feel guilty for experiencing anger and sinful for expressing it.

A major difficulty in dealing with anger in children can be eliminated if we can rid ourselves of the notion that anger is bad and therefore we—or the children in our care—are bad if we or they experience or express it. Instead, we should recognize that healthy, appropriately expressed and constructively directed anger is critical to the righting of wrongs—and to academic achievement. (Children who are at risk as learners are often those who have not been able to sublimate their aggressive energies to make them work for them.) Our goal is not to repress or destroy angry feelings in children—or in ourselves—but rather to be accepting of these feelings and committed to helping channel and

The Aggressive Child, Luleen S. Anderson, *Children Today*, Vol. 7, No. 1, Jan.-Feb. 1978. ©1978 U. S. Department of Health, Education and Welfare, Children's Bureau.

direct them to constructive ends.

At home or in a classroom, a parent's or teacher's attitude toward children must include a willingness to allow them (and himself or herself) to feel *all* their feelings. The helping adult's skills will then be directed toward demonstrating to children acceptable ways of expressing their feelings. Strong feelings cannot be denied. They must be recognized and treated with respect, and their power acknowledged and diverted with skill and ingenuity.

Approaches to handling angry outbursts will vary according to our understanding of what motivated an outburst. Angry outbursts should not always be viewed as a sign of pathology; it should be recognized—as Blanck and Blanck suggest—that the aggressive drive is in the service of separation/individuation. While the aim of affection is to unite, the aim of aggression is to separate—to develop one's independence, autonomy and individualism.[3] Therefore, aggression that serves psychological growth is not necessarily negative or hostile. Indeed, in adequately functioning children with healthy egos, anger is often prompted by a situation.

In order to respond effectively to aggressive behavior in children we need to have some ideas about what may have triggered an outburst. Writers on this subject have suggested that anger may be a defense to ward off painful feelings; that it may be associated with failure, low self-esteem and feelings of isolation; or that it may be related to anxiety about situations over which the child has no control. (Many children experience anger and anxiety simultaneously.)

It has also been suggested that angry defiance may be associated with feelings of dependency, and that anger may be associated with sadness and depression. In childhood, anger and sadness are very close to one another and it is important to remember that much of what an adult experiences as sadness is expressed by a child as anger.

Before we look at specific techniques for the management of aggressive/angry outbursts, several points should be highlighted:

• We should distinguish between anger, a temporary emotional state provoked typically by frustration, and aggression, which is often used as a synonym for destructiveness—the attempt to hurt a person or to destroy property.

• Tamed aggression is not hostile if it serves in helping to establish a child's sense of identity. Neither should aggression be confused with activity. Erikson describes aggressivity as connoting those aspects of the aggressive drive which are growth-promoting and self-assertive, rather than hostile and destructive.

• Anger and aggression do not have to be dirty words. The origin of the word aggression—*ad-gradior*—is "I move forwards." Thus, the traditional meaning includes dynamism, self-assertiveness and expansiveness. In other words, in looking at aggressive behavior in children, we must be careful to distinguish between behavior that indicates emotional problems and behavior that is developmentally appropriate.

How can this issue be approached—and what possible intervention strategies may be considered? Fritz Redl suggests four options to consider in view of the complexities of children's behavior:[4]

Permitting some behavior. "I accept fully" (within certain limits) means that the child is allowed to enjoy the behavior without anxiety or guilt.

Tolerating certain behaviors. This is different from permitting or ignoring. "I hope very soon you won't need to do this, but in the meantime . . ."

Interfering with (interrupting) surface behavior, using a wide range of techniques or approaches.

Preventive planning—avoiding a disruptive behavior by developing a better procedure or strategy in advance.

I have found a number of "interference techniques" to be helpful in working with the aggressive child. Before sharing these, however, I would like to point out that techniques cannot be employed effectively without an underlying philosophy of child development, and that our task is to provide *active tutoring* to children in the development of ego strength. Therefore, our interventions should be geared toward giving momentary support to a child's ego when it faces a task beyond its coping abilities. As one bright 7-year-old said to his counselor, "I know it's O.K. to feel angry, but you still haven't told me what to do with these feelings!"

It is also important to understand the complexity of human behavior and to realize that while we are attempting to change highly unacceptable surface behavior, we also are trying to understand what motivated it.

Finally, our actions should be motivated by the need to *protect* and to *teach*, not by a desire to punish.[5] Parents and teachers must show a child that they accept his or her feelings, while suggesting other options for handling and/or expressing the feelings. An adult might say, for example, "Let me tell you what some boys would do in a situation like this . . ." It is not enough to tell children what behaviors we find unacceptable; we must also teach them acceptable ways of coping, and ways must be found to communicate our expectations of children. Contrary to popular opinion, punishment is not the most effective tool for communicating expectations.

Responding to the Aggressive Child

These techniques should not be seen as a "bag of tricks" which can substitute for educational and therapeutic processes. They are best viewed as strategies which may be helpful when they are used within the psychological framework outlined earlier. Many of the following techniques are found in *The Aggressive Child* by Redl and Wineman:[6]

• *Catch the child being good.* Tell the child what behaviors please you. Respond to his positive efforts and reinforce good behavior. In interactions with children, we often talk more about what is wrong than what is right. Children's self-image and self-esteem are enhanced by the positive feedback we give to them. How a child sees and feels about himself is a powerful determinant of his behavior, just as all of us, regardless of age or position in life, are influenced by our views of ourselves.

An observing and sensitive parent will find countless opportunities during the day to make such comments as, "I like the way you came in for dinner without being reminded."; "I appreciate your hanging up your clothes even though you were in a hurry to get out to play."; "You were really patient while I was on the phone."; "Thanks for sharing your snack with your sister. I like the way you're able to think of others."; and "Thank you for telling the truth about what really happened."

Similarly, teachers who are appreciative and respect children will ease up on negative statements and include in their interactions with children such statements as, "I know it was difficult for you to wait your turn and I'm pleased that you could do it.";

"Thanks for sitting in your seat quietly."; "You were thoughtful in offering to help Johnny with his spelling."; and "You worked hard on that project and I admire your effort."

• *Planned ignoring*—not of a child but of a behavior that is inappropriate but within the range of tolerability. The "ignoring" has to be planned and systematic, with the goal of having the child recognize that the behavior is inappropriate. It takes great skill to know when and what to ignore, and when to stop ignoring. There are a wide range of behaviors that can be ignored so that a child can stop himself, thus retaining his autonomy.

• *Provide physical outlets and other alternatives.* Especially in educational settings, it is important for children to have opportunities for physical exercise and movement.

• *Manipulate the environment.* Aggressive behavior can be produced by placing children in tough, tempting situations. Rules and regulations, as well as physical space, may be too stringent or tight for certain groups and situations. We should try to plan the environment so that certain things don't happen, or at least to reduce the probability of their happening. We're asking for trouble when we leave a baseball bat lying on the living room couch, for example, or take a class into the gym for a program before the athletic equipment has been put away.

• *Verbalize* your acceptance of the child's angry feelings, but offer other suggestions for expressing them. Teach children to put their angry feelings into words, rather than their fists.

• *Use proximity and touch control*—move physically closer to the child as a means of curbing the impulse. Young children are often calmed by having an adult nearby to act as an external ego. (This is a very important concept with ego-disturbed children. How close is close? Some children are frightened by being touched. The age and background of the child are important in deciding how much physical contact to initiate.)

• *Express interest in the child's activities.* Children naturally try to involve adults in what they are doing, often to the adult's annoyance at being interrupted in his or her activity. Very young children (and children who are emotionally deprived or ego-damaged) seem to need much more adult involvement in their interests. A child about to use a toy or tool in a way that will lead to conflict is sometimes easily diverted by an adult who expresses interest in having it shown to him, or in having the child point out its uses and advantages. Many a young child has been spared being hit with a toy that another frustrated youngster is having trouble with when an alert teacher or parent has moved in quickly to say, for example, "Tommy, I see you're playing with the locomotive; help me figure out how it works." An outburst from an older child struggling with a difficult reading selection can be thwarted by a caring adult who moves near the child to say, "Show me which words are giving you trouble."

• *Be ready to show affection.* Sometimes all that is needed for a child to regain control in the face of anxiety is a sudden hug or other impulsive show of affection. Children with serious emotional problems, however, may have trouble accepting the more traditional forms of affection, or even admitting their need for them.

• *Re-group and/or restructure* the group constellation. Abandon a "problem" activity and substitute, temporarily, a more desirable one. This act should not be interpreted by the children as punitive.

• Clostly related to the re-grouping or restructuring approach is the technique of *removing the source* of anger and frustration when the feelings it produces stem from a problem-solving block rather than from pathology.

•*Ease tension through humor.* Kidding the child out of a temper tantrum or outburst offers the child an opportunity to "save face." However, it is important to distinguish between face-saving humor and sarcasm or teasing ridicule.

• *Appeal directly to the child.* Tell him or her how you feel and ask for consideration. This method is often effective with children who know how to behave appropriately and who have solid relationships with adults. It is less useful, however, with children who have little appreciation for appropriate behavior, or who see adults as enemies. Young children like to be called upon to be helpful, and they can often respond sympathetically when told of an adult's need for special consideration. For example, a parent may gain a child's cooperation by saying, "I know that noise you're making doesn't usually bother me, but today I've got a headache, so could you find something else you'd enjoy doing?" Children respect a teacher—and see her as more human—if she can say honestly, "Can you please not ask me anything for a few minutes this morning? I'm upset because I had a flat tire on the way to school and I got soaked changing it."

• *Interpret situations*—help the child understand why a particular situation may be stressful, or help him to see his own motivation, as well as the motivation of others, as a source of the problem. We often fail to appreciate how easily very young children can begin to react positively once they understand a provoking situation. Among other goals, we want to correct the child's false assumptions (that people don't like him, or that he's stupid, for example) so the provoking behavior will not be necessary.

• *Use physical restraint.* Occasionally a child may lose control so completely that he has to be physically restrained or removed from the scene to prevent him from hurting himself or severely disrupting the group, or to "save face" for the child. The adult and child can talk about the incident later. This approach should not be viewed by the child as punishment but as a means of saying, "You can't do that." Some children need reassurance that they will be controlled when they lose their self-control. In such situations an adult cannot afford to lose his or her temper—and unfriendly remarks by other children should not be tolerated.

• *Encourage* the child to see his strengths as well as his weaknesses. Help the child to see that the gap between where he is and where he wants to be is not so great that he can't try to bridge it.

• *Use promises and rewards.* Promises of future pleasure can be used both to initiate and to stop behavior. This approach is not as simple as it sounds, and it should not be equated with bribery. We must know what the child likes—what brings him pleasure—and we must deliver on our promises: "When you finish this paper, you can listen to some music."; "If we finish this project by two o'clock, we'll have some free time."; or "When you finish cleaning your room we'll make cookies."

• *Say "NO"!* Limits should be clearly defined, and children's freedom to function within those limits should be respected. However, we often forget that a "no" at the proper time can be critical.

• *Build a positive self-image*—encourage the child to see himself as a valued and valuable person. Help him to accept himself, to fight discouragement and to feel encouraged about himself and his potential.

• *Use punishment cautiously.* There is a clouded area between the practice of punishment when it reflects hostility toward a child and when it is used as an educational tool. As an educational tool, punishment should be seen as negative reinforcement. Such punishment may include the provision of a "time out" period and the *temporary* withholding from the child of an adult's attention and/or affection.

• *Model appropriate behavior.* Teachers especially should be aware of the powerful influence they can exert on a child's or group's behavior through modeling.

• *Teach children to express themselves verbally.* Verbalizing helps a child to establish control and thus reduces acting out behavior. Encourage the child by saying, for example, "*Tell* him you don't like his taking your pencil," and "*Tell* her in words that you don't feel like sharing just now."

The Role of Discipline

One of the most difficult tasks of parenting and of teaching is finding the appropriate balance between freedom and discipline. It is unfortunate that, to many of us, discipline and punishment are synonomous. Good discipline is harmonious with the fostering of good mental health. Tanner and Lindgren point out that the issue in good discipline is not just to have the child suppress a desire or behavior while the adult is present, because he is afraid of the adult, but rather to have the child reject them out of his own sense of selfhood.[7] We want children to become self-disciplined, to develop inner controls which will guide and monitor their behavior when they are not under supervision. Unfortunately, adults often lose sight of this goal and settle for control through fear—getting children to behave for fear of what we will do to them if they don't.

Good discipline includes creating an atmosphere of quiet firmness, clarity and conscientiousness, using praise and reasoning. Bad discipline involves punishment which is unduly harsh and/or inappropriate, and it is often associated with verbal ridicule and attacks on the child's integrity.

Jane Kessler points out that a child learns to be the person he is in three ways: through his inheritance, including his genetic make-up, which makes him unique; by what we as parents and teachers teach him; and, possibly most important, by how we as teachers and parents think and feel about ourselves and the things we teach him.[8]

As one fourth grade teacher put it: "One of the most important goals we strive for as parents, educators and mental health professionals is to help children develop respect for themselves and others. In order to accomplish this goal we must see children as worthy human beings and be sincere in dealing with them."

In any discussion on handling anger in children, we should first ask ourselves what our goals are. My goals for children include wanting them to grow up prepared to experience and to cope with the richness and complexities of *all* human emotions and to be able to accept and to master their feelings in order to utilize them in flexible, constructive, comfortable and creative ways. Arriving at this goal takes years of patient practice. It is a vital process in which parents, teachers and all caring adults can play a crucial and exciting role.

[1] Robert Woody, *Behavioral Problem Children in the Schools*, New York, Appleton-Century-Crofts, 1969.

[2] Haim Ginot, *Between Parent and Child*, New York, Macmillan Co., 1965.

[3] Gertrude Blanck and Rubin Blanck, *Ego Psychology: Theory and Practice*, New York, Columbia University Press, 1974.

[4] Fritz Redl and David Wineman, *The Aggressive Child*, Glencoe, Ill., Free Press, 1963.

[5] Margaret Frank, "Modifications of Activity Groups Therapy: Responses of Ego-Impoverished Children," *Clinical Social Work Journal*, Vol. 4, 1976.

[6] Redl and Wineman, op. cit.

[7] Laurel Tanner and Clay Lindgren, *Classroom Teaching and Learning: A Mental Health Approach*, New York, Holt, Rinehart and Winston, Inc., 1971.

[8] Jane Kessler, *Psychopathology of Childhood*, Englewood Cliffs, N.J., Prentice-Hall, 1966.

Autism

The State Fails to Respond

Penny-Pinching in A Land of Plenty

The State's services for families with autistic children are woefully inadequate, a result of "systematic thoughtlessness."

By Robert Palm

Autism. Its Greek root indicates an absorption into the self, a turning away from worldly things to focus instead on the buzz and clamor of one's own mind. For an estimated 1,500 autistic children and adults in Connecticut, the disability probably means a solitude that will haunt them for life. Autism is only recently understood: an untold number of last generation's children are now autistic adults, locked away in state mental institutions. The autistic children of today have a better chance of passage through this limbo, but most often, their parents are caught in a hell of anguished frustration.

Tremendous strides have been made in the diagnosis and education of autistic children in the 35 years since the disorder was identified. But professionals who work with autistic children point out that:

—Connecticut, a wealthy state which has two of the best private facilities in the country for the autistic, is woefully inadequate in providing public residential centers for autistic youngsters.

—No single state agency takes responsibility for providing desperately needed services, with the result that autistic children are often hopscotched from program to program, to their serious detriment.

—The parents of autistic chidlren, their lives already tragically disrupted, face the further burden of having to battle penny-pinching local school boards for treatment which exceeds the minimum requirements of state law. This adversarial role costs the parents thousands of dollars in legal expenses, and puts an unbearable strain on the family.

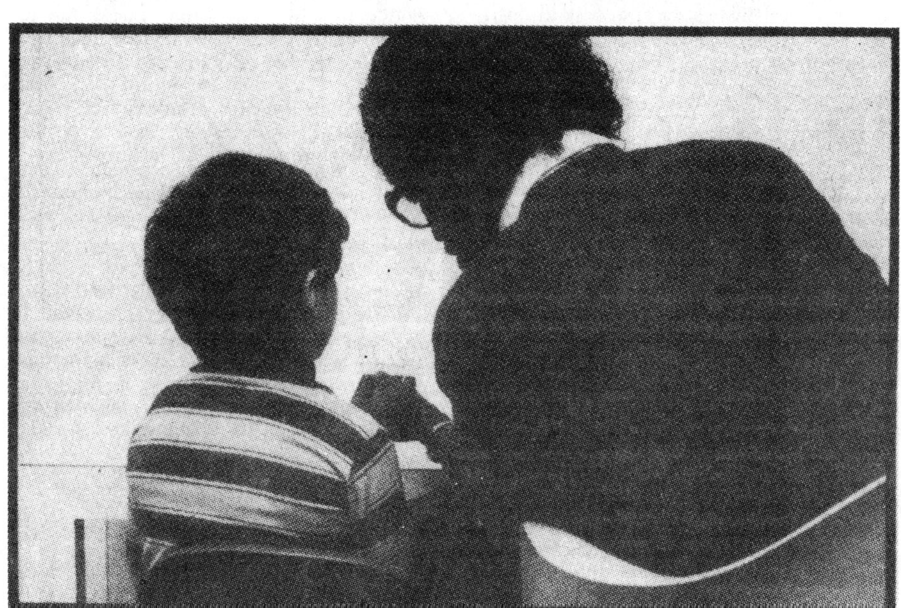

Learning to use language is often the most difficult task for autistic youngsters, although some eventually learn to speak well enough. Strangely, personal pronouns are alien to these children, whose realm of experience is largely within. (photo courtesy The Foundation School)

The Child

A ten-year-old we'll call Roger is walking on tiptoes around the fenced perimeter of the playground at the Foundation School in Orange. He never speaks to the other children in the special school, some of whom are autistic, some of whom are emotionally disabled. He has a fine head of raven hair, and a delicately honed face that someday may be handsome. When the tumble of the other children cuts too near him, he swerves away like a little bumper car, his gaze sweeping the playground, yet rarely alighting onto one object for very long. When recess is over, he sits cross-legged on the floor, awaiting his ride home, and fiddles endlessly with the handle of his lunchbox.

Another autistic boy swoops from teacher to teacher, his pale blue eyes imploring them to swing him high into the air. They oblige, but first ask that he say the word "up": he mumbles a syllable that sounds close enough, and up into the air he goes.

"He could have anything he wants, if only he'd say certain words," murmurs Jack Bell, the school's director. But the simplest words in the English language are as foreign to many autistic children as the revolution in Iran. A sad paradox is that for these children whose whole universe is contained within themselves, the word least likely to emerge is the pronoun "I."

5. PARENTING

The First Years

To understand the agony of parents' later struggles with the inertia and sometimes callousness of the state's educational and mental health systems, it helps to know what they go through in the terrible first years of the child's disorder.

The autistic child is often the first born. A chill creeps into the mother's tenderness and joy as she realizes that her infant seldom looks at her while she is feeding him; that his attention fades in and out, as if she weren't there; that when he looks at his mother, there is no apparent return of affection; that she is, in fact, holding a little stranger in her arms.

Later, the child may be unusually docile, or he may cry inconsolably for hours. He may stare interminably at one particular toy, or at his fingers, or at a speck of dust. Or he may spend hours banging his head against the crib.

According to Dr. Donald J. Cohen, of Yale's Child Study Center, such symptoms of autism become apparent usually by the time the child is a year old, and almost always by age two. By that time, the child's parents will have begun a seemingly endless search for a pediatrician who can tell them what's wrong. An untold number of autistic children, say authorities on the subject, are misdiagnosed as mentally retarded, schizophrenic, or emotionally disturbed. Compounding the problem is the way in which organic diseases, such as brain damage from lead poisoning and congenital rubella, mimic the symptoms of autism.

Hours and hours of clinical testing follow: hearing tests, blood screenings, skull X-rays, electroencephalograms, examination of the cerebrospinal fluid, and more. When the child is three, the state will pay for special training, and, with luck and persistence, the parents can get their child into one of the top-notch regional or private programs. During the next three years, it's pre-school programs with medical evaluation. Then, at age six, into a regular school program for the handicapped.

"But it's not so easy," says Cohen. "Very often, the parents have to fight all the way for a suitable program for their child."

The Search for Residential Program

Not that good special education programs don't exist. Particularly for young children, regional programs like Area Cooperative Educational Services in North Haven—in which various towns share resources—provide admirable training and education. But when a severely autistic child gets older and less manageable, many parents find themselves up against a wall of resistance. Then, the search for a good residential program becomes a yearly ordeal of wondering whether the local school board will pay for the child's enrollment next year, and the year after.

Times, obviously, are tough. The demands on school boards and administrations are many, especially in these days of competitive lobbying by dozens of hitherto unrecognized needy groups,

handicapped or not. The autistic are small in number, although their need is overwhelming. Some educators, school board members, bureaucrats, legislators, and staff members have been tireless in promoting the rights of autistic children. Others have been more interested in balancing budgets; many more have been caught uncomfortably between controlling costs and helping the children.

According to Dr. Cohen, it is not uncommon for school officials to pull a child out of an excellent school like Benhaven and place him in a "better" setting, "which to them means cheaper. The whole purpose, although perhaps it's not conscious, is to beat down the parents," Cohen says with some bitterness.

Exhausted by the rigors of caring for a child who may have no control over his bodily functions, who may throw fits of violent rage, whose lone amusement might be chewing the curtains into shreds, the parents are apt to cave in to the school board and accept "adequate" services—those provided by a stingy interpretation of the letter of the law.

State laws say that every child must receive the type of education from which he or she will receive the most benefit. The interpretation of those laws, however, is the rub. What may be "adequate" for a mildly handicapped child is glaringly inadequate for the needs of a severely autistic child. When a child of 10 still has to be toilet trained, when he still can't speak more than a few repetitive phrases, when he has to be restrained from trying to pull the skin off his elbows, then services provided for the "normally" handicapped just aren't enough.

"A Peculiar Type of Cheapness"

"It gets down to a peculiar type of cheapness," says Dr. Cohen of the resistance by some local school boards to pay for special programs. State and federal agencies, through complicated reimbursement plans, send a good portion of the money back to the towns, anyway. But the more fiscally conservative board members still are galled that the money came from the school budget, but is returned instead to the town's general fund. So the $15,000 or $25,000 spent on one autistic child *seems* like a lot of money, money that could have been saved or spent on something else.

Dr. Achille Riello, director of special education services for the New Haven public schools, asserts that the New Haven Board of Education has "a very clear policy" that all handicapped children receive the services they need. This year's school budget provides some $6 million for special education, with more than $1 million of that spent on programs for local youths in outside facilities.

In Hartford, Larry Volpe of the school system's Pupil Appraisal Team points to a three-stage mechanism by which autistic and other handicapped children are placed in the appropriate program. He notes that although autism is a devastating condition, the number of afflicted children is small. "We've been pretty lucky," he says.

But in Dr. Cohen's view of overall state

services, "it's a systematic thoughtlessness in which all the cards are stacked against the parents."

Parents of autistic children have been pushing for years to get schooling 12 months a year for their kids, for example. A whole school year's worth of progress can be wiped out during the long summer vacation, or even during the shorter holidays. Yet the legal school calendar becomes a shield behind which school administrators can deny the parents' requests.

And it is nearly impossible for teachers to be able to work 12 months a year. A woman in Fairfield County rubs her hands wearily; they are bitten and bruised from her autistic students, who themselves are seemingly oblivious to physical pain, and who may inflict injury on others without realizing it. Yet, she says, if more funds were available, teachers could be found to work with the children during the holiday months.

"Respite" Care Needed

Because of the arduousness of training and caring for these children, parents need a respite, a time when they are relieved for a few days or weeks from their all-consuming burden. Respite homes are needed so that parents can restore their sanity, their marriages, and provide for a short while an undisrupted environment for their other children.

"It sounds trivial," says Dr. Cohen, "but it's a major issue." The need for respite care was pointed out in 1973 by a study committee appointed by then Gov. Thomas Meskill. "The opportunity for the family to be free of the responsibility for an autistic child for a few weeks, a couple of times a year not only benefits them but also the afflicted child, and may be the vital factor that determines whether the child is maintained at home or is institutionalized," the report notes. "The Committee knows of only one respite home in the state that is specifically for autistic children. This provides the State with an excellent model, but unfortunately it is only available to a small number of children."

That situation has improved little since then. Meanwhile, of far greater urgency is the need for residential homes. When the autistic child reaches the age of 13 or 14, the most serious in an endless series of crises develops. Larger and stronger now, the child's tantrums and sudden rages can be so devastating that reluctantly, the parents start looking for a residency program. Again, they often find themselves hunting from pillar to post, torn all the while by the heartbreak of "giving up" their child, and beset by guilt and self-doubt.

Rich Connecticut Sends Kids Away

Of the 60 programs in the state for the handicapped, 10 have some facilities and staff for the autistic. Less than half of those make provisions for residency: Benhaven, the model program that the rest of the nation looks to, has room for less than half a dozen patients on a live-in basis. As a result, many autistic children requiring residential care are sent out of state, to New Hampshire, Vermont, Florida: unfortunately, facilities in those states and others are being filled up, and now Connecticut children are often sent back here, and the whole frustrating procedure begins anew.

The lack of residency programs, he feels, stems partly from the confusion that until recently surrounded the diagnosis of autistic children. Because the disorder can resemble a whole constellation of disturbances, the identification of the state's autistic population has been a slow process.

The state's bright hope for a residential program for the autistic—the Undercliff Mental Health Center—is beset by other problems (see accompanying article). Some of the trouble is financial. Another problem lies in the very use of the word "autism."

Difficulties of Autistic Care

Dr. Harold Mark, director of program development at the Department of Mental Health, puts it this way: "Autism itself is very ambiguous. Giving (the condition) a name also gives it the administrative and clinical imperative to use that name, requiring (state bureaucrats) to make distinctions we're not always comfortable with."

Jack Bell of the Foundation School agrees. "Five autistic kids in the same classroom could be as different as night and day," he points out. From an educator's point of view, it matters little *why* a child can't say the word "I"; what matters is how the child can be helped to overcome his handicap.

Not only does the label "autism" hinder the bureaucracy's response to what it calls the "atypical" child, it can also lead to a certain amount of typecasting among those studying the disorder. Dr. Leo Kanner did the world a great service when he identified autistic youngsters in 1943, but many professionals today wish they could shake off the term, making it more flexible to embrace a wider range of childhood disturbances.

The origins of the disorder are still unknown, and the temptation to deduce a cause according to a prescribed notion is great. In the '40s and '50s, the thinking was that because autistic children often were first-born males of achievement-oriented, demanding parents, there was an emotional, environmental cause. Theorists labeled these people "refrigerator parents"—cold, neurotic adults, whose autistic child somehow represented the extreme of the parents' nature (or, in some versions, the extreme reversal of the parents' nature).

That idea has been dismissed for some time, but many other misconceptions linger, causing tremendous feelings of guilt in many parents. Now, researchers are looking into the possibility of various biochemical causes: there may be a shortage or overabundance of certain chemicals such as dopamine and norepinephrine which transmit messages from the nerve cells to the brain. The brain metabolism of autistic children is also under investigation, but researchers such as Dr. Cohen say there is still much to be learned.

Controls, But No Cures

Treatment, understandably, is also in the experimental stage. While researchers look for a breakthrough in the biological etiology of the disorder, there is no "cure." Autism can, however, be controlled—depending on the severity of the individual case—through behavior modification, drug therapy, and psychotherapy, although some educators feel that the old Freudian approach has little relevance to the autistic youngster. There have been good intentioned teachers, for example, who have tried to understand where a 12-year-old is coming from when he wets his pants continually; but most in the field favor a more basic, mechanical, repetitive training.

The gains in learning about and treating autism thus far have come from private organizations such as Benhaven and from the work that researchers such as Dr. Cohen and Dr. Sally Provence have accomplished at Yale. The Connecticut Society for Autistic Children has moved into the void created by the bureaucracy's inability to streamline its efforts into a single agency responsive to the needs of the autistic.

Each Year an Eternity of Waiting

But, despite the recent advances, there is still no delivery system, no organized way of bringing the various services together so parents don't have to battle for the rights of their children.

"The autistic youngster needs help to develop as a total human being," says Mrs. O'Brien, "not just as a functioning robot."

Counselling and guidance for parents and siblings. Precision education. Respite care. Crisis intervention. Intensive education six days a week. Pre-vocational training. Residential schools. Life Programs.

The agenda is well mapped out. When the goals will be accomplished, however, is the question, one that must be answered sooner rather than later, because for these lost children and their parents, each year that drags by seems an eternity.

Kids in Mental Hospitals

John had a lot going for him—good looks, athletic grace, a fine mind and a wealthy Los Angeles family. But in his mid-teens, he developed a bizarre habit: toying with explosives. He blew off part of his hand with a firecracker and got expelled from boarding school for breaking into the chemistry lab one night to build a bomb. When John failed to respond after months of psychiatric treatment, his parents reluctantly committed him to a private hospital. Nine months later, the 17-year-old called a lawyer,

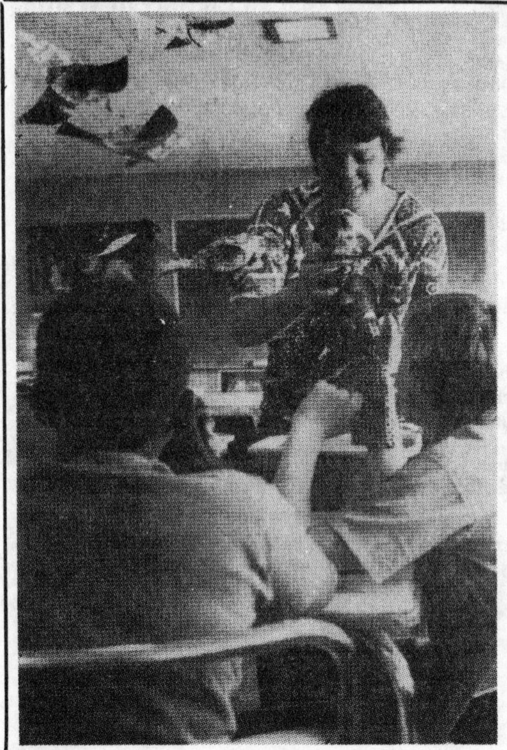

James D. Wilson—Newsweek

Children in custody: A rush to the courts

who filed a petition for habeas corpus. The judge who heard the case sympathized with John's parents, but the teen-ager had been committed without a legal hearing. So the judge ordered John's release, holding that "the rights of parents cannot be said to overrule the constitutional rights of minors."

If John had been an adult, he would have been routinely entitled to a hearing before commitment to a mental institution. But U.S. law has historically granted parents the sole discretion over whether to commit their children. Now, courts and legislatures are being asked increasingly to make Solomonic decisions: under what circumstances should the government intervene in the parent-child relationship? "The majority of situations involve parents who are at the end of their rope; they don't know any alternatives," says David Ferleger, a Philadelphia specialist in mental-health law. "Often, however, kids go to the hospitals not for their benefit, but because of failures in the home or the school. Children are punished for the mistakes of adults."

The process of institutionalizing a child is surrounded with legal ambiguities, often resulting in human tragedies. Although no precise figures exist, a minimum of 10,000 youngsters under 18 are now in mental hospitals because of their parents' actions. Many of them, like John, may be seriously ill, and their parents want to do what they think best for the children. But some children have been committed, without persuasive medical evidence, for astonishing reasons: the parents wanted to go on vacation; the child interfered with "the emotional adjustment" of the parents; the child stayed out too late at night. In reaction, recent court decisions have expanded the children's rights to review of their cases—and some authorities fear the reaction may have gone too far.

Children's Rights: The campaign to provide youngsters a hearing before commitment follows a series of victories by children's advocates in the Supreme Court. In the past decade, the Court for the first time granted juveniles the right to a lawyer when they face imprisonment, gave children the right to due process before they could be suspended from school and allowed girls to have an abortion without their parents' consent. The government may intervene, the Supreme Court held in 1972, when parents' "decisions will jeopardize the health or safety of the child." But last term, after accepting a Pennsylvania case that would have tested commitment standards, the Court ducked a ruling. While the case was pending, the state legislature passed a mental-health statute granting certain due-process rights to children. Ferleger has refiled the suit because he does not think the statute goes far enough.

The issue has already returned to the Supreme Court this term in a similar case from Georgia, where a U.S. district court struck down the state's rules on juvenile commitment. Georgia's appeal, which will be heard this week, flatly opposes granting youngsters a hearing. The lower-court ruling, contends the state's brief, "presupposes that children possess the same right to liberty as adults, a conclusion which is unsupportable in fact or law ... Procedural rights of children cannot be expanded except at the expense of parents' responsibility and authority."

Most states now give parents the right to commit minors up to the age of 12 without a hearing, and usually they allow commitment up to 18. But the rules are changing. Last spring, the New Mexico legislature mandated pre-commitment hearings for children from birth, and last summer, the California Supreme Court held that all youngsters over the age of 14 were entitled to a hearing.

Parents Bristle: When word of the decision reached California's institutionalized teen-agers, they all but rushed the courts. Already, more than half of the 14- to 18-year-olds at the Napa and Camarillo state hospitals have taken steps to qualify for release hearings. "It was fiction that these kids' commitment was voluntary because their parents volunteered them," says David Guthman, who oversees the psychiatric section of the Los Angeles district attorney's office. "The kids had no rights, there were no psychiatric criteria, no nothing."

Parents understandably bristle at what they perceive as state interference. "The court was deciding whether or not we had the right to decide for our child in his best interest," says an outraged California father, who had committed his 15-year-old son after the boy stole from his classmates, beat up his sister and lit fires in the street. The boy was about to win his release, but when his parents said they would not take him back into their home, the frightened youngster meekly agreed to return to the hospital. Mothers and fathers have the right to refuse custody, says Los Angeles lawyer Peter Hoffman, who has represented parents in commitment cases. "But then what happens? The kid sits in juvenile detention hall until someone manages to find a foster home for him."

Who Is Responsible? Doctors are split over the value of hearings. For example, New York psychiatrist Eli Charles Messinger supports the idea because even a few days in an institution can scar a child. "Hospitalization should be used only as a last resort," he says. The American Psychiatric Association is just as eager to protect children, but it views hearings from a different perspective. "The hearing could drive a wedge between parent and child," explains APA counsel Joel Klein. "For younger children especially, it could be traumatic."

"The issue goes to the heart of who is responsible for protecting children," says lawyer Ferleger. Most Americans undoubtedly believe that the responsibility belongs primarily to parents. But clear evidence exists that some children suffer unfairly. As in a dozen other social dilemmas, the courts are saddled with finding a balance—and they won't be relieved of the chore any time soon.

Kids in Mental Hospitals, Jerrold K. Footlick with Susan Agrest, Janet Huck, *Newsweek*, Dec. 12, 1977. ©1977 by Newsweek, Inc.

A New Look at Childhood Autism: School-Parent Collaboration

John B. Kelley, MEd, MS, PhD
Marian Samuels, MSW

John B. Kelley, MEd, MS, PhD, is Director, Brentwood Center for Educational Therapy, 801 Via de la Paz, Pacific Palisades, California 90272 (corresponding author). Marian Samuels, MSW, is Clinical Social Worker-retired, Brentwood Center for Educational Therapy, 801 Via de la Paz, Pacific Palisades, California 90272.

Literature on childhood autism includes an ever increasing number of books and articles pertaining to causation, symptoms, and treatment modalities. Many points of view are presented with emphasis ranging from the psychoanalytic concept of "poor-parenting" to that of subtle central nervous system disorder. Although a great deal about autism continues to be unknown, recent studies[1-8] suggest it is a possible failure of sensorimotor functions, often accompanied by serious disturbances of language, cognition, and human relationships. The syndrome designated as autism occurs on a continuum of intensities and consists of a variety of behavioral disturbances. Frequent difficulties include impairment in establishing emotional contact, retardation with islets of normal or exceptional functioning and delayed, distorted, or nonexistent speech. Study continues with the hope of finding more about etiology and symptoms.

For the autistic child, his parents, and teachers, day-to-day problems require attention, and improved coping methods are needed. The issue is particularly pertinent at this time because many school districts are setting up programs for the autistic children in local schools. Since there are estimated to be about "2.4 autistic children for every 10,000 of the child population,"[9] broad planning is necessary.[10] Since September 1975, the Los Angeles Unified School District has opened 25 classrooms for autistic children. It is evident that parents and professionals in the community must be included in order to provide the most effective assistance for each child.

This article will focus on the parents' part in the helping process and will consider special problems experienced by families of autistic children, methods schools can develop for work with parents, and gains that can be made when parents, school personnel, and other professionals share in home-school evaluation and planning of programs.

Problems of Families

There is need to understand some of the difficulties an autistic child presents to his family. In addition to the frustration and anguish parents face when a child has life-long disabilities such as blindness or cerebral palsy, autism brings many additional pressures. The problem is less understood, the children are frequently unpredictable, and for many years causation was linked to poor handling by parents. Although recent studies[11,12] have emphasized that etiology seems more related to physical dysfunction than to parental relationships, many parents retain the guilty feelings that the former point of view engendered.

The findings that focus on brain dysfunction take the "blame" away from parents and are the basis for educational programs designed to meet the needs of autistic children. This approach not only relieves parents' feelings of guilt, but opens the door to parental involvement in the helping process. Many families have become actively involved with community groups in setting up appropriate educational settings, and have developed increasingly effective methods for assisting their children at home and for working collaboratively with school personnel.

However, many factors influence parents' ability to assist. There are extremely wide differences in the functioning of children classified as autistic and every family must adapt to different problems. In addition to the variations in children's functioning, which are well recognized by authorities in the field, there are equally wide but less frequently considered differences in the strengths and limits of families.

In order to formulate the individualized treatment

A New Look at Childhood Autism: School-Parent Collaboration, John B. Kelley and Marian Samuels, *The Journal of School Health*, Vol. 47, No. 9, Nov. 1977. ©1977 American School Health Association.

5. PARENTING

program necessary for each child, there is need to evaluate the family's ability to help as well as the child's requirements. It has been found that parents of autistic children do not differ basically from other families in their community. However, as is the case in working with any child, the parents' emotional and physical situation as well as their socioeconomic assets and limits need to be considered.

It must be recognized also that family equilibrium is constantly changing and that accumulated stress affects the functioning of even the most adequate individuals. The presence of an autistic child obviously presents a variety of ongoing pressures for all family members. For example, one problem mentioned by parents and siblings is related to the fact that many autistic children are well-developed physically and are "normal looking." While parents of more obviously handicapped children frequently receive understanding and sympathy, families of autistic children are criticized because their children behave badly. Parents are censured so often for "spoiling" these children that they may begin to blame themselves or other family members for the child's problem. They become reluctant to take the children outside the home, and parents may isolate themselves. When tensions of this sort are added to the extra demands of daily coping, it would seem evident that almost all families with autistic children could benefit from support and active assistance in order to maintain satisfying familial relationships and to secure personal satisfaction for family members.

School Relationships With Parents

Schools for autistic children would appear to be a natural setting for this type of assistance. However, frequently school personnel become so engrossed with administrative matters and with the child's school program that contacts with families focus almost totally on ways parents can help the child. Parents are instructed in methods of discipline, techniques for behavior modification, exercises and health care, without considering the families' readiness and ability to carry out these directions. As a result, many parents become increasingly frustrated and ineffective because they cannot meet the school's expectations. Most parents want to cooperate with their child's school, but feelings of being inadequate or overburdened can cause them to withdraw from school contacts or result in their development of incapacitating physical and/or emotional symptoms. In either case, the child loses the help he requires at home, and the school's ability to assist is seriously undermined.

In order to decrease the frequency of these difficulties and in order to secure optimum participation by family members, the school program needs to include ongoing realistic contacts with families. The following ideas have been found helpful:

1. Parent discussion groups in which parents recognize that other people have similar problems and that they are not alone with their feelings of frustration and anger can be very effective. Parents can benefit from sharing ideas regarding their own needs for satisfaction.

2. Recurring social events for the entire family including the autistic child offer parents and siblings an opportunity to interact on a regular basis. Family members become familiar with the school setting and can observe their own and other children. Often another parent will notice evidence of a child's progress that may be too slight for his parent or teacher to observe.

3. Individual conferences should focus on a child's specific needs with discussion of what the family can and cannot provide. Meetings with members of the child's family enable parents and school personnel, including speech and occupational therapists, to share ideas about helping and to rearrange situations before families give up altogether.

4. Group sessions consisting of various families and focusing on the children's problems can minimize parents' embarrassment if they feel unable to carry out the school's recommendations. Sometimes other parents can suggest ways of modifying plans that make them more acceptable.

5. School personnel should offer assistance in referring parents to community agencies when family problems require more intensive help than the school can provide. The school's understanding of the family situation and of community resources makes it possible to arrange for appropriate or ongoing help when indicated.

PROGRAM DESCRIPTION

At the Brentwood Center for Educational Therapy the focus is on parental as well as professional involvement in every aspect of diagnosis and treatment. This center serves autistic individuals ranging in age from 3 to 26 years, who are referred from local school districts, university treatment centers, hospitals, and referral agencies that serve the autistic in the community.

The center's philosphy is based on the concept that human growth follows a developmental sequence in acquisition of skills beginning with basic sensory-motor skills, progressing to perceptual-cognitive skills, language and emotional-social skills. Individuals with developmental delays show an initial delay in some of these basic sequential levels. Following appropriate evaluation by professional staff members to determine the child's developmental level, an appropriate educational and therapeutic program is established to remediate specific areas of developmental delay.

The center believes that the individual's handicaps originate from organic and neurologically based problems. Since medical treatment is in the exploratory stage at this time, the center believes that therapy, special education, and environmental influence can best help to modify some of the autistic child's handicaps.

For this to occur, everyone involved with the child or young adult must be unified in the goals and techniques of treatment.

Individual therapy and educational programs for each student are developed at parent-staff conferences. At this conference, parents, teachers, therapists (educational, speech, and occupational), social workers, teacher's aides, and professionals from other agencies involved with the individual meet to give observations, present evaluations, pinpoint problems, and establish goals and treatment procedures. These programs are revised frequently according to the needs and progress of each child. Continued parental input is encouraged through follow-up formal conferences, parent observation at school and informal daily contact between staff and parents. Monthly parent-child-staff luncheons are held at the center in an informal social atmosphere. This gives the staff and parents an opportunity to know each other as individuals and to observe alternative ways of handling the children. Parents also have the chance to communicate with other parents and to share experiences. Spontaneous discussion groups frequently follow these luncheons.

Residential Placement

There is also a need for residential placement with the community to insure continuity for the autistic child at times when a parent's illness or other family crisis prevents his family from providing care. This idea requires a great deal of cooperative planning by school and community resources. However, the need is urgent because of the lack of potential caretakers for these children. Relatives, friends, and most foster parents feel unable to cope with them. Thus, autistic children, for whom familiar surroundings are particularly important, face the terrifying experience of being placed in settings such as state hospitals where they are often placed with disturbed, aggressive patients. Years of work can be undone in a brief placement. It takes an exceedingly long time to develop trust with these children, and it can be lost in only a few days. If placement is needed, every effort should be made to keep the child in his own school. The goal should be provision for residential settings within the child's home community. This type of placement also makes it possible for family members to have needed respites.

Parents' Role

When help is provided that enables parents to recognize that family needs are genuinely accepted, family members can become increasingly effective partners with school personnel. There are many ways in which families contribute to planning and treatment:

1. Information from parents and siblings provide the detailed material regarding early development that is necessary for assessment of the child.

2. Material concerning day-to-day behavior at home gives an ongoing picture of problems and progress. Frequently, family members have developed ways of assisting at home that can be included at school.

3. Carry-over of the school program into the home setting is vital, and family members can become efficient in using methods that school personnel develop for working with the child. For example, they can continue the school programs in the areas of speech development and self-help skills.

CONCLUSION

The combined work of families, schools, and other community resources is opening new possibilities for understanding and for providing assistance to autistic children. A variety of professionals including social workers, occupational therapists, speech therapists, and recreational workers are adding their expertise in the growing number of programs for these children. The community school (public or private) is a natural base for integrating the contributions of professionals in individualized planning for each child. Until recently, parents had little direction or support, and many families spent years in their search for help. They went to numerous settings and frequently received contradictory suggestions. School-parent planning can minimize the random searching and can maximize the effectiveness of everyone involved in helping. Despite all efforts, progress is slow. Many autistic children, however, are beginning to benefit from a coordinated approach. With the continued collaboration of parents, schools, and other professionals, new insights are being obtained, and increasingly effective services for autistic children and their families can be anticipated.

REFERENCES

1. Ritvo ER: *Autism Diagnosis, Current Research and Management.* New York, Spectrum Publ Inc, 1976.
2. Wing L: *Autistic Children - A Guide for Parents and Professionals.* New York, Brunner/Mazel, 1972.
3. Ornitz EM: Childhood autism - A disorder of sensorimotor integration, in Rutter M (ed): *Infantile Autism: Concepts, Characteristics and Treatment.* London, Churchill Livingstone, 1971.
4. Rutter M (ed): *Infantile Autism: Concepts, Characteristics and Treatment.* London, Churchill Livingstone, 1971.
5. Martin JAM: Sensory disorders in the autistic child and implications for treatment, in Rutter M (ed): *Infantile Autism: Concepts, Characteristics and Treatment.* London, Churchill Livingstone, 1971.
6. Des Lauries AM, Carlson CF: *Your Child Is Asleep - Early Infantile Autism Etiology, Treatment, Parental Influences.* Homwood, Ill, Dorsey Press, 1969.
7. Creak M: Childhood psychosis. *Br J Psychiatry* 109:84-89, 1963.
8. Rimland B: *Infantile Autism, The Syndrome and Its Implications for a Neural Theory of Behavior.* New York, Appleton-Century-Crofts Inc, 1964.
9. Wing L: *Children Apart.* National Society for Autistic Children, 1974.
10. Cohen D: Congressional Record, 120, 1974.
11. Mahler MS: On early infantile psychosis, the symbiotic and autistic syndromes. *J Am Acad Child Psychiatry* 4:554-568, 1965.
12. Bettelheim B: *The Empty Fortress - Infantile Autism and the Birth of the Self.* New York, New York Free Press, 1967.

Adolescence and Early Adulthood

Adolescence is the stage of development where children desire to become independent of their parents. The behavior disorders seen in some adolescents are abnormal or deviant extensions of normal desires.

The rejection of parental values and a desire to formulate one's own moral code is a normal part of the process of seeking independence. The deviant extension of this is extreme anti-social behavior: sexual promiscuity, stealing, aggression and violent behavior.

Alcoholism, drug addiction and suicide are other abnormal extensions of the process of gaining independence. Adolescence is also a time of evaluating one's self and developing a complete personality - along with being independent. The incongruity of this period is that though independence is the goal, peer pressure and peer acceptance, therefore, conformity with the peer group is the first step. This desire to be like and unlike, to be dependent and independent causes tremendous cognitive dissonance. This dissonance leads some adolescents to the abnormal coping mechanisms of booze, pills, dope and suicide. The desire for independence creates a need for the adolescent to handle his/her problems by one's self. Their immaturity sometimes prevents them from solving those problems. Peer pressure disallows seeking parental advice, therefore, the only alternatives some adolescents see open to them are alcoholism, drugs or, with acute depression, suicide.

Research has identified another problem area -- the hyperactive young adult. The hyperactive preschooler continues through school and may, or may not, outgrow his/her disability. The hyperactive adolescent is seen by his/her high school teacher as uncooperative and a poor worker. In an article presented here, when these same teenagers become young adults, their employers rate them as good, dependable, cooperative workers. The situation, where a choice is available, rather than the individual makes a difference.

Juvenile Delinquency and Antisocial Behavior

By FRANK T. RAFFERTY, M.D.

Dr. Rafferty is director of the institute for Juvenile Research, Illinois Department of Health, and Professor of Psychiatry, University of Illinois College of Medicine.

Delinquency is not to be understood as a single or even multiple event, such as an accident or an infectious illness, but must be perceived, investigated, and treated as a cumulative series of transactional events involving individuals and their various social systems. This is difficult to do, since in our language and in our basic mental processes action appears to be initiated and carried out by individuals. So we speak of "the delinquent," bring the individual delinquent before our courts, treat him in our clinics, and confine him in our institutions. The problem of differentiating, defining, and responding to persons who disturb and threaten others has presumably been a part of the human scene ever since this sentient group emerged. Ethology demonstrates similar behavior in animals, which lack the language and cognitive competence of human beings.

As far back as we know, a distinction has been made between those who are sick and those who disturb and cause distress to society. Such behavior is mentioned in the Greek and Roman literature. Modern institutions, however, first began developing and relating to the distinction between the sick and the bad sometime around the 15th century. This distinction was well developed by the late 1800s, with institutions for correction and for mental illness. At that time, no distinction was made between adults and children.

In 1900 a distinction was formalized in the establishment of a juvenile court in Chicago, beginning the process of dividing the bad into those who were adult and those who were children. Closely related to this was the inception of the child guidance clinic. The Institute for Juvenile Research, of which I have the privilege to be director, was established in connection with the Chicago Juvenile Court in 1909. It began its study of delinquency almost immediately with the publication of Dr. William Healy's *The Individual Delinquent*, a series of case studies presenting the life histories of delinquents. Dr. Healy initiated a theory that remains with us to the present — namely, that the essential cause of delinquency is rooted in the family relations of the delinquent.[1] The clinic applied this theory in its treatment of delinquents. It was not long, however, before questions were raised about the concept of the individual delinquent. In the late 1920s, Clifford Shaw and Henry McKay began research on the sociologic aspect of delinquency and developed what came to be known as the Chicago school of sociology. During the 1930s they became very much aware of the differential distribution of delinquency in the city.[2] Characteristically, areas of the city that become disorganized would have higher rates of delinquency.

The distinction between the child and the adult, the child delinquent and the adult criminal, held through the 1940s. The original concept of the juvenile court was that it was to administer a welfare process rather than a legal proceeding; the dominant value was to be the welfare of the child. But as time went on and the number of children in our clinics and our correctional facilities grew, it became apparent that at least two kinds of children were seen by the court. So in the mid-1960s came another differentiating concept, to distinguish between children who actually committed an act that would be a crime if committed by an adult and

Juvenile Delinquency and Antisocial Behavior, Frank T. Rafferty, *Psychiatric Annals*, Vol. 6, No. 7, July 1976. ©1976 by Psychiatric Annals.

those who were minors in need of supervision — i.e., children who were unruly, truant, runaway, or neglected. About the same time, it became apparent that children were not receiving the usual rights of any criminal in the United States to due process under the law. In 1966 the Gault decision[3] required that every delinquent have access to legal counsel, be informed of the charges against him, and have privileges against self-incrimination.

In addition, a continuing attempt has been made to define the delinquent. A massive field of criminal sociology and statistical data concerning the delinquent has developed. However, those working in the field became more and more suspicious of the official statistics. These would report 2, 3, or 4 per cent of our adolescents as being delinquent. Working professionals in the field believed that the real numbers were much higher. We knew that statistics varied from town to town; we knew that police departments varied from station to station and from officer to officer. These variations had much to do with determining how a child would be managed and who would be referred because of delinquency. Those of us in psychiatry became aware that children of more affluent parents came to see us in our private hospitals and offices, while children without the same financial resources were managed in the public courts and correctional facilities.

Thus another area of research developed as investigators asked, "What are the reliable and valid statistics on delinquency? How many delinquents are there?" Various studies attempted to estimate the magnitude of unreported delinquency. We are all limited by our particular perspective on the human scene. The psychiatrist is overwhelmed by the number and the distress of patients who enter his office, and he is seldom able to look up to see who does not come in, much less be concerned about the sampling problem. Likewise, the juvenile court judge, the probation officer, the correction officer, the parent, and the teacher are all limited by their particular views and functions. Studies discovered the problems of interpreting statistics — e.g., the numbers were small, or the sample included only boys, only one social class, or a limited range of proscribed behavior.

Finally, in 1971, the Social Research Laboratory of the Institute for Juvenile Research initiated a sociologic and anthropologic study designed to be the ultimate of such studies.[4] This will not be the final answer, but it will be a long time before the financial and human resources for such a study are again available. The project was planned to address the issues of delinquency and, more broadly, the total quality of life for adolescents between the ages of 14 and 18, using both anthropologic and sociologic methods. The sample was drawn from the entire state of Illinois, with its great racial, cultural, and financial diversity, comparable with that of the United States as a whole.

Graduate students in anthropology lived in 12 areas of the state for approximately 18 months, working from a field guide developed to address the same issues as a questionnaire. On the sociologic side, a sample of 19,000 households was chosen to represent race, culture, financial status, and population density. Questionnaires were given to 3,200 adolescents between the ages of 14 and 18, 1,500 of their parents, and 500 other people, such as police chiefs, clergymen, and school principals. Although major methodologic problems exist with the type of questionnaire used, this technique does appear to be the best way of collecting data on delinquency, antisocial behavior, drug abuse, etc. In areas in which we have checked our data, we have found them to be quite accurate.

Let me remind you of the official stereotypical delinquent: he is a black male from a low socioeconomic stratum in the inner city. This study found an entirely different picture.

The respondents were asked if they had ever performed any of 36 kinds of delinquent, antisocial acts and, if so, how often. They were also asked a series of questions to delineate the way in which they related to their families, schools, religions, peer groups, and police. They were asked such questions as whether they had ever cheated on an exam at school or turned in work that was not their own; drunk alcoholic beverages with or without parents' consent; had fist fights; been drunk; driven a car without license or permit; driven a car recklessly; deliberately damaged private or public property; had sexual intercourse; carried a weapon of any kind, such as a knife, razor, or gun; run away from home; taken part in a gang fight; used or attempted to use force to take money away from another person; ridden in a stolen car; placed a bet; stripped a car; or used marijuana or other drugs, such as LSD, mescaline, "downers," "speed," or heroin. The answers were subjected to analysis and were found to break down into the five major classes of delinquency that, with the exception of one, form Guttman scales. This means that the child who has performed the less severe antisocial acts does not necessarily go on to the more severe delinquency, but the adolescent who engages in the seriously delinquent acts has usually engaged in the lesser activities.

These five classes include one called general deviancy, which is not on the scale. It includes cheating at school, drinking without permission, and getting drunk. The other categories relate to crimes against property, crimes of violence, automobile violations, and drug use.

Some of the statistics are that 73 per cent of all the youngsters had cheated at school at least once, 61 per cent drank alcoholic beverages without permission, 47 per cent had been drunk, and 23 per cent had bought liquor. The percentages are impressive. If these are projected into actual numbers, 23 per cent represents 200,000 children in Illinois. On the scale including crimes against property, 56 per cent of the youngsters admit to petty theft (stealing something worth less than $20) and 13 per cent have engaged in serious crimes, such as breaking and entering. On the violence scale, 50 per cent have had fights and 13 per cent have engaged in strong-arming — i.e., threatening another child with violent harm in order to obtain money or possessions. Regarding automobile violations, 43 per cent admitted to driving without a license, 10 per cent had gone joy-riding (a euphemism for stealing a car, though presumably with no great amount of criminal intent), and 8 per cent had engaged in stripping cars.

In the matter of drug use, 22 per cent of the youths between 14 and 18 had used marijuana; at age 18, slightly under half had used it. Use of other drugs was much lower, with 3 per cent having used heroin at least once. It must be recognized that of all substances abused, alcohol is still by far the favorite, with over 61 per cent consuming alcohol without parental permission and 47 per cent consuming enough to be drunk at least once.

The primary finding of this study was that, aside from some minor differences, the rates of delinquency for girls were equal to those for boys; the rates for the rich were the same as for the poor; the rates in the country were the same as those in the city; and the rates for blacks were the same as those for whites. Black delinquency did have a slight tendency to be somewhat more violent, while white delinquency was higher in automobile violations. It is important to emphasize that although delinquency is widespread and is certainly undesirable behavior, it does not lead inevitably to a delinquent career. Unfortunately, the adolescent who goes on to a delinquent career is the one who comes before the court, the probation office, and the correctional institutions. Thus we encounter the fascinating phenomenon that the ways in which we try to help may be the very ways in which we fix the delinquent in a delinquent career.

Data such as those gathered in our survey can be used to evaluate and test the major theories of delinquency that have been developed over the past 50 years. Only in a very simplistic way can this task be approached here. In the late 1930s, Edwin H. Sutherland developed a theory

> *"The child who has performed less severe antisocial acts does not necessarily go on to more severe delinquency"*

of differential association that stressed the importance of the socializing process of primary groups. Exposure to norms conducive to crime causes a person to internalize these attitudes and skills rather than those of the normal society.[5] Subsequently, Albert Cohen applied Sutherland's theory to the gangs formed by youths, especially boys in lower-class neighborhoods.[6] Study of such gangs suggests that boys in a neighborhood join gangs and form subcultures that have codes of conduct, beliefs, attitudes, and values different from those of the middle class. These gangs frequently engage in vandalism and violence for nonutilitarian reasons, such activities providing opportunities for establishing and symbolizing status, self-esteem, and masculinity.

Later, Ohlin and Cloward suggested a different interpretation of subcultural delinquency. They proposed that the lower-class delinquent had the same values as those of the dominant culture but lacked the opportunity to realize his aspirations. Crime, then, represented the use of illegitimate channels to reach the same goals.[7]

More familiar to psychiatrists, of course, are the personality abnormalities attributed to delinquents. In fact, relatively few of the youngsters examined in juvenile court clinics are either psychotic or neurotic in the classic sense. The predominant diagnosis is that of personality disorder — which presents some logical problems, since the major information leading to the diagnosis is the history of the disturbing behavior.

As the interpretation of the data progresses, more detailed testing of the above theories will be possible. At this point, only modest support for all the theories seems possible, while clearly no single theory explains all the phenomena of delinquency. Analysis may reveal the interaction of many variables. To indicate the direction of this analysis, let me simply relate the following: The influence of the peer group over the adolescent has been substantiated, and family data seem to have little effect on the distribution of delinquency, whereas peer-group participation consistently has a substantial impact. The use of alcohol by white males demonstrates this. White boys who demonstrate a high use of alcohol also have a very high level of peer activity. With strong peer affiliation there is an associated frequency of trouble, extensive dating, low participation in school, and high peer alienation from school. No family factors approach significance, except perhaps the finding that 50 per cent of the youngsters to whom religion was important never committed an alcohol violation, in contrast to 20 per cent who did. Religious involvement is positively correlated with family closeness.

In summary, our study of delinquency and antisocial behavior in the United States suggests that such behavior is widespread, almost ubiquitous in its minor forms, and quite substantial in serious degrees. This behavior sometimes elicits the reaction that it is dangerous to the security of others and even threatening to the national systems of justice and government. By this reaction, a stereotyped career delinquent is selected to be the target of labeling, control, containment, treatment, etc., by thousands of well-meaning police, judges, probation officers, welfare workers, and psychiatrists. Unfortunately, there is little real scientific understanding of the process. In the United States, these efforts at social control are rendered more impotent by the fact that our culture worships the individual freedom to be wrong and therefore cannot find the lever of public intervention to alter the membership of the adolescent in our social system.

BIBLIOGRAPHY

1. Healy, W. *The Individual Delinquent*. Boston: Little, Brown and Company, 1929.

2. Shaw, C., and McKay, H. *Social Factors in Juvenile Delinquency: A Study of the Community, the Family and the Gang in Relation to the Delinquent*. Washington, D.C.: U.S. Government Printing Office, 1931.

3. U.S. Supreme Court. *In re Application of Gault*, 387 U.S. 1, 87 S. Ct. 1428, 1967.

4. Rivera, R., et al. *Juvenile Delinquency in Illinois*. Chicago: Institute for Juvenile Research, 1972.

5. Sutherland, E. H., and Cressy, D. R. *Principles of Criminology*, Fifth Edition. Philadelphia: J. B. Lippincott Company, 1955.

6. Cohen, A. K. *Delinquent Boys: The Culture of the Gang*. New York: The Free Press, 1955.

7. Cloward, R. A., and Ohlin, L. E. *Delinquency and Opportunity: A Theory of Delinquent Gangs*. New York: The Free Press, 1963.

SYMPOSIUM: SEX EDUCATION AND RESIDENTIAL CHILD CARE

Paul M. Gitelson, Editor
School of Social Welfare
State Univ. of N.Y. at Stony Brook

Sex Education and the Behavior Problem Child

Lois Partak and Gregory P. Berner
Herman M. Adler Mental Health Center

Background

The Herman M. Adler Mental Health Center is a residential treatment center serving the needs of emotionally disturbed and developmentally disabled children. Students live in a cottage setting with a maximum of 15 students per cottage. Students are considered to be children with severe behavior problems. Specifically, these problems include noncompliance; throwing tantrums; aggressive behaviors toward peers, adults, and self; and a lack of social skills necessary in order to function at home, in school, and in the community. Each child is assigned a team of counselors who develop an individualized treatment program designed to teach appropriate behaviors. The students involved in the sex education classes were 11 males and 3 females aged 10 to 14 years, in the average range of intelligence. These students all attend school in special classrooms on the Adler grounds.

The Problem

For several years, sex education programs at the institution had been taught in the traditional textbook manner. Students memorized anatomical diagrams of the reproductive systems, viewed a film on birth, and took a test on medical terminology.

Shortly after last year's sex education instruction was completed, a counselor overheard a discussion by several students. They were attempting to match up their "everyday" words (fuck, dyke, blow job) with the more technical terms (intercourse, lesbian, fellatio) used by

Sex Education and the Behavior Problem Child, Lois Partak and Gregory P. Berner, *Child Care Quarterly*, Vol. 6, No. 3, Fall 1977. ©1977 by Child Care Quarterly.

the instructors. The results were uncertainty and confusion. The students had been unable to internalize the textbook information. It then became apparent to the counselor that a new approach would be necessary.

A review of the literature indicated that few programs have been developed to teach sex education in similar residential treatment centers (Farley, 1970; Maddock, 1974; Wexner, 1969).

A core group of teachers and cottage counselors joined in an effort to set up methods and objectives for a program that would meet the needs of these children. The results were:

METHODS	*OBJECTIVES*
1. Instructors allow the use of street terms.	1. Students able to give the medical term that corresponds with the street term.
2. Instructors present actual examples of personal hygiene and birth control articles.	2. Students able to identify each article and understand its function.
3. Instructors model appropriate social attitudes.	3. Students have basis for setting up personal guidelines.

The Program

This same group of staff members devised a list of 10 specific topics to be covered that would serve as the means toward meeting these objectives. The topics were:

    a. the difference between love and sex
    b. a comparison of everyday or street terms with medical terms
    c. female reproductive system
    d. male reproductive system
    e. dating
    f. conception, development, birth, and aftercare
    g. pregnancy—including premarital and teenage
    h. contraception
    i. venereal disease
    j. effects, attitudes, consequences, and responsibilities of sexual relationships

The topics were divided up for instruction among those staff members who felt most comfortable with a given area. (It might also be noted at this point that the areas of homosexuality and bisexuality were mentioned as alternative sexual roles. Questions on these subjects were answered as they arose, but they were not discussed in depth as there were no staff members who felt comfortable with these areas.)

The sessions were taught daily by the same team of teachers and counselors during regular school hours for a period of two weeks. Students were encouraged to ask questions. Questions that students felt uncomfortable asking aloud were placed in a "Question Box" to be answered later for the entire group. More informal discussion groups covered the day's material each evening on the cottage. The repetition of new facts was welcomed by the students as was the opportunity to ask any additional questions that had arisen in their minds since the initial instruction had taken place.

Two changes from previous presentations proved especially effective. These were (a) a unified effort on the part of the school and the cottage and (b) having everyday staff, rather than outside sources, teach most of the sessions. Discussing sex with the classroom teacher and students' own counselors aided in the realization that human sexuality is an awareness of self to be lived and not a dirty word to be whispered behind closed doors.

Session I—Getting the Terms Straight

Session I began with instructors and students discussing the differences between love and sex. Instructors presented the following areas for discussion: love for friends, family, pets, members of the opposite sex; sex as a role; and sex as a physical relationship.

The second part of the session was a comparison of street and medical terms (Gordon, 1967). Instructors presented pictures of male and female anatomy (Goldstein, 1972) to the students, who gave the street terms they used. These terms, along with the corresponding medical terms, were written on the board. Sexual functions were presented similarly, with instructors explaining functions and students associating street terms with the correct medical terms.

All of the students had street terms for the anatomy and sexual functions, but few of them knew the corresponding medical terms. By doing this comparison, the students had a better understanding of the material presented in later sessions when medical terms were used. This session also provided an outlet for embarrassment and silliness. Since the "dirty" words were out in the open, there was no need to be whispering them to a friend.

Session II—Female Reproductive System

This session began with a discussion of terms that would come up that day and that had not been covered in Session I. Instructors and students viewed the second half of the filmstrip *Understanding Human Reproduction I* (Guidance Associates, n.d.). The material presented was discussed afterward.

Instructors then showed and explained the use and function of the following articles: sanitary napkin; sanitary belt; tampon; vaginal hygiene spray; douche liquid and powder; and a douche bag. The session included the showing of the film *Girl to Woman* (Churchill-Wexler, 1965). This was followed by a sample test on the female reproductive system. This test was for the student's use and was not graded but retained for future reference.

Session III—Male Reproductive System

This session followed the same format as Session II. The class viewed the first half of the filmstrip *Understanding Human Reproduction I* (Guidance Associates, n.d.). This material was discussed and compared with the female reproductive system. During this session, students' questions resulted in a discussion of the actual mental and physical changes that take place during sexual intercourse.

Instructors showed the students an athletic supporter with cup and explained its use and function. The students watched the movie *Boy to Man* (Churchill-Wexler, 1962). Instructors again passed out a sample test to be used as a basis for evening discussion.

Session IV—Conception, Development, Birth, and Aftercare

At this point, it proved profitable to involve a staff nurse to cover the areas of fertilization, development of the fetus, and the stages of birth. Following the filmstrip *Understanding Human Reproduction II* (Guidance Associates, n.d.), discussion turned to such areas as miscarriage, stillbirth, twins, labor, and the various methods of childbirth.

After tracing the growth of the embryo to the birth of the baby, instruction covered the care of the infant. This included a demonstration of changing diapers, handling a child, and breast-feeding by a volunteer mother and child.

Session V—Pregnancy

The sex education team included two pregnant women; one was in the four month of her second pregnancy, and the other was only two weeks away from delivery. In this way, students gained knowledge of the emotions and physical sensations of the pregnant woman. The highlight of the session came when one of the unborn babies began to kick and students were permitted to feel the movements of the new life by pressing a hand on the mother's stomach.

Also important in the discussion of pregnancy was the role of the father—how he can be of help during pregnancy and his role during labor, especially should a couple wish to consider natural childbirth.

Another aspect of pregnancy covered was the unmarried pregnant teenager. Students considered: (1) Whom should she tell? (2) What are her options? (3) How does the father fit into the picture? (4) The economics and reality of another life. (5) A baby has rights too!

Session VI—Contraception

For expert information, we turned to a volunteer from the local chapter of Planned Parenthood. Her presentation emphasized the ideal that both husband and wife be settled with their own lives before consideration of having a baby. She discussed all common methods of contraception, pointing out which methods were effective and which were considered ineffective. Along with an explanation of each method (Fischer & Snyder, 1974), the contraceptive devices were shown. The use of the IUD, diaphragm, foam, cream, and jelly was demonstrated by means of a plastic model of the female reproductive system.

Session VII—Venereal Disease

Instructors began this session by passing out the pamphlets "What You Should Know About Gonorrhea" (Illinois Department of Mental Health, Circular No. 5405) and "What You Should Know About Syphilis" (Illinois Department of Mental Health, Circular No. 5405). These pamphlets were used as the basis for a discussion on how V.D. is spread, its symptoms, the effects on the body, and the treatment and where to get it.

Session VIII—Effects, Attitudes, Consequences, and Responsibilities

In this session, the instructors and students discussed the realities of love and sex. This began with a review of the differences between the two. Discussion continued to the responsibilities involved in love, in parenting a child, and toward a sexual partner. The group discussed the rights of each individual to his or her own value system concerning sexual involvement and the possible consequences of a sexual relationship, such as illegitimate children, illegal abortion, V.D., and divorce (Gordon, 1971).

Session IX—Dating

Students were asked to list the characteristics they wanted in a dating partner. The boys made one list and the girls another. A comparison of the two lists showed virtually no difference in ideals. "Respect" was the characteristic that was most important to both groups.

Conclusions and Discussion

In all sessions, instructors maintained a nonmoralizing attitude, being careful not to subject students to their many and varied value systems. Instead, they concentrated on helping the students set up realistic guidelines, but never absolute rights and wrongs.

In the final wrap-up session in the cottage, it was obvious that our realistic methods of using pictures, showing actual examples of personal hygiene and birth control articles, and allowing street terms for comparison had worked! The students were carrying on a healthy, detailed conversation about the material and how it related to themselves—using the medical terms.

As successful as the program proved to be, it was not without problems. The initial difficulty was finding staff who felt comfortable with the open manner in which the material was presented. Single staff had concerns about personal questions and how their answers might influence the children. This type of question was asked by the children. Staff answered only those questions that they felt had educational value.

In our final evaluation of the overall program, it was determined that in future sessions we would increase the degree of realism of instruction by addition of the father-to-be and a more recent film on birth. The only area we seem to be unequipped to change was one of the last questions asked by a student: "Why don't more parents tell their kids about sex?"

References

Churchill-Wexler Productions. *Boy to man.* 16 min., color, sound, 1962. Distributed by Churchill Films.

Churchill-Wexler Productions. *Girl to woman.* 16 min., color, sound, 1965. Distributed by Churchill Films.

Farley, G., & Goddard L. Sex education for emotionally disturbed children with learning disorders. *Journal of Special Education,* 1970, 4, 445-450.

Fischer, N., & Snyder, M. J. (Eds.). *The inside story.* Chicago: Planned Parenthood Association (Rev. Ed.), 1974.

Goldstein, M., & Haeberle, E. J. *The sex book, a modern pictorial encyclopedia.* New York: Seabury Press, 1972.

Gordon, S. *Facts about sex for exceptional children.* East Orange, N.J.: New Jersey Association for Brain-Injured Children, 1967.

Gordon, S. Ten heavy facts about sex. Syracuse: Family Planning and Population Information Center, 1971.

Guidance Associates. *Understanding human reproduction* (Parts I and II, filmstrip with records). Pleasantville, N.Y.: Harcourt, Brace & World, 1968.

Illinois Department of Public Health. What you should know about gonorrhea. Division of Preventive Medicine, Circular No. 5405.

Illinois Department of Public Health. What you should know about syphilis. Division of Preventive Medicine, Circular No. 5405.

Maddock, J. Sex education for the exceptional person: A rationale. *Exceptional Children,* 1974, **40**, 273-278.

Wexner, I. H., & Anderson, L. Sex education for exceptional children: A discussion. *Academic Therapy,* 1969, 4, 221-223.

Learning Disabilities and Juvenile Delinquency

Failure to Recognize the Impact of Academic Underachievement on Family and Peer Relationships and on the Developing Self-Concept of the Individual May Result Ultimately as Disturbed Adolescent Behaviors and Juvenile Delinquency

Peter W. Zinkus, Ph.D., Marvin I. Gottlieb, M.D., Ph.D.

JUVENILE delinquency represents a form of adolescent maladaptive behavior, arising out of a complex of socioeconomic, psychologic, neurologic and emotional disturbances. Academic underachievement has been implicated as a significant factor contributing to juvenile delinquency during the past decade.[1-3] Earlier it had been believed that the delinquent child failed to develop adequate academic skills because of his rebellion against school and other social institutions. More recently it has been suggested that perhaps the lack of academic success and the resulting frustrations were contributing factors to the development of juvenile delinquency.[4,5] The poor educational development of the youthful offender is usually not the result of impaired intellectual ability[6,7] though recent evidence does suggest that developmental dyslexia, dysgraphia, auditory and visual perceptual disturbances and impaired language development are frequently found in delinquent populations.[8-10]

Subtle neurologic abnormalities are often observed in children with learning disabilities.[11,12] Similarly, many children with antisocial behavior have electroencephalographic abnormalities, neurologic "soft signs" and perceptual deficits.[13,14] Although the neurologic deficits are not grossly apparent, they do seem to have a profound effect on learning and social adaptation.[15] In addition to learning deficits, the characteristic behavioral disturbances associated with "Minimal Brain Dysfunction" also appear to interfere with the social adaptation of the learning-disabled child, placing him at high risk for conflict with society.[16] Furthermore, in the learning-disabled child, difficulties with self-concept frequently develop as a consequence of the academic underachievement.

The studies here described were designed to survey the prevalence, characteristics and significance of learning disabilities in a population of adolescent delinquents. Comprehensive psychologic, educational and personality evaluations were carried out with a group of institutionalized youthful offenders in order to assess their intellectual functioning, perceptual skills, and academic achievement in reading, spelling and arithmetic. Their self-concept and self-esteem were evaluated by personality inventories. Epidemiologic statistics identify the prevalence of perceptual disorders in the normal population at approximately 10 per cent.[17,18]

The Population Studied

The subjects were 44 male delinquents

between the ages of 13 to 18 years (mean age: 15.9 years), who were committed by Juvenile Court to a residential treatment program. Placement in this program was based on the subject's rehabilitation potential as assessed by Juvenile Court staff, independent of considerations of the present study. The presence of learning disabilities was *not* part of the admission criteria to the residential treatment program. Assignment of youthful offenders to the study series was done randomly.

Twenty four of the subjects (54 per cent) were white; twenty (46 per cent) were black. All had histories of multiple legal offenses, ranging from habitual disobedience and vandalism to more serious felony convictions. The average number of appearances in Juvenile Court for the group was 7.8. Analysis of social data indicated that most of these young men had come from a lower middle income background. Based upon previous screenings, all subjects were judged to have normal vision and hearing. From the original pool of forty-six subjects, two subjects were later removed from the study series, since they failed to demonstrate adequate motivation or full co-operation during the examinations. The final population for the survey then consisted of forty-four subjects.

Methods and Procedures

General intelligence in subjects under 17 years of age was measured with the Wechsler Intelligence Scale for Children-Revised (WISC-R); in those over 17 years of age, with the Wechsler Adult Intelligence Scale (WAIS).

Auditory and visual perceptual skills were assessed by analyzing the pattern of verbal and nonverbal subtest performances on the WISC-R and WAIS. Particular emphasis was focused on auditory sequential memory, visual-spatial orientation and visual-motor coordination, as these are common deficit areas in perceptually handicapped children.[19,20] The Rhodes Scatter Profile procedure[21] was utilized to further assess those perceptual deficits which were statistically significant at the .05 level. The Bender-Gestalt Visual-Motor Test was employed to evaluate visual-perceptual and visual-motor deficits. Scoring of this test, by the Koppitz method,[22] enabled the assignment of a test age to the subject's performance. Deficits in visual perception result in a test age lower than a subject's chronologic age.

Reading, spelling and arithmetic skill levels were determined with the Wide Range Achievement Test.[23] The grade levels obtained for each of these academic skills were compared with the subject's actual grade placement and also an expected achievement level (EAL) which is derived from the subject's age and I.Q. The expected achievement level was obtained from normative data on the general population.[23] The normative group for expected achievement levels included all socioeconomic levels; this makes its usage appropriate for comparison purposes in this survey.

A lateral dominance examination to determine hand, foot and eye preference employed standard test procedures familiar to most clinicians.[24]

Measures of self-concept were obtained from the Tennessee Self-Concept Scale[25] which was routinely administered by the staff at the residential center. Additional impressions of self-esteem and self-confidence were obtained by clinical interviews.

Observations Made

The initial data analysis defined the intellectual ability of the juvenile delinquent group as a whole. As indicated in Table 1, the mean I.Q. scores were within the average range (90–109) for overall intelligence (Full Scale I.Q.). Verbal (Verbal I.Q.) and nonverbal (Performance I.Q.) intelligence scores were also within the average range. Individual scores

TABLE 1. *Results of Intelligence Testing on Forty-four Delinquent Subjects (Mean I.Q. Values for the Normal Population = 100, S.D. = 15)*

	Mean	S.D.*	Range of Scores
Full Scale I.Q.	91.8	14.6	127 to 73
Verbal I.Q.	91.6	13.9	123 to 70
Performance I.Q.	92.9	14.8	130 to 77

* Standard Deviation.

ranged widely in all three areas of intellectual competence. Due to the variability of the scores, a cut-off point of minus one standard deviation (I.Q. = 85) below the mean for the normal population was chosen to define the lower limits of average intelligence. Seventy-five per cent (N = 33) of the subjects obtained Full Scale I.Q.'s at or above this cut-off point. Furthermore, of the 25 per cent (N = 11) of the subjects with Full Scale I.Q.'s below the cut-off point, 54 per cent (N = 6) had either a Verbal I.Q. or Performance I.Q. above 85. Therefore, of the delinquent subjects, 88 per cent had evidence of intellectual ability or potential at or above the average range.

The past academic performance for each member of the delinquent group was reviewed. Of the subjects, 43 per cent had not been required to repeat grades in school; 36 per cent had repeated *one* grade and 21 per cent had repeated *two* grades. Of those who repeated grades, 35 per cent repeated during the first three grades, 20 per cent during the 4th through 6th, and 45 per cent from the 7th through 12th. Whereas 57 per cent of the subjects repeated one or more grades, only 18 per cent had access to special education programs in elementary school. Thus, even though most of these delinquent individuals evidenced average or above average intelligence, deficient overall academic performance was common.

Achievement levels in reading, spelling and arithmetic were evaluated. Examinations in each of these academic areas were given and the obtained grade level scores subtracted from the subject's actual grade placement. As a group, these individuals were significantly below grade level in all three academic areas (Table 2). The scores ranged widely, but only a few of the delinquents performed above their actual grade level placement.

TABLE 2. *Achievement Testing Discrepancies from Grade Level (GL) on the Wide Range Achievement Test*

| | | | Percentage of Subjects | |
	Mean	Range	Above Grade Level	Below Grade Level
Reading	−3.40	+1.6 to −7.7	11%	89%
Spelling	−4.39	+1.1 to −8.8	2%	98%
Arithmetic	−4.61	+1.6 to −8.0	2%	98%

Deviations from grade placement can be misleading due to variations in intellectual ability. Therefore, reading, spelling and arithmetic test performances were compared with expected achievement levels (EAL) based upon age and intellectual ability calculated for each subject. The results (Table 3) indicate that academic skills were performed at or above their expected level in only a few.

The relationships between reading level on the WRAT and Full Scale I.Q. were analyzed. The correlation coefficient for the two variables was −.063, indicating no significant relationships between reading level and general intelligence.

Perceptual skills were evaluated from per-

formances in the WISC-R subtests (Table 4). Only 21 per cent had intact visual and auditory perceptual abilities. 60 per cent had significant deficits in auditory sequential memory and 55 per cent had significant difficulty with visual-motor coordination. Almost half (46 per cent) of those with perceptual disturbances were categorized as having mixed auditory and visual processing disturbances involving auditory sequential memory and visual-motor coordination.

Performances with the Bender-Gestalt

TABLE 3. *Achievement Testing Discrepancies from Expected Achievement Level (EAL) on the Wide Range Achievement Test*

| | | | Percentage of Subjects | |
	Mean	Range	Above EAL	Below EAL
Reading	−2.84	+2.5 to −7.7	4%	96%
Spelling	−3.82	−0.3 to −8.0	0%	100%
Arithmetic	−4.49	+0.7 to −8.4	2%	98%

Visual-Motor Test further established the degree of deficit in visual perceptual skills. Utilizing the Koppitz scoring method,[22] 37 per cent of the subjects were judged to have visual-motor and visual-perceptual skills which were age equivalent. Another 27 per cent had mild visual-motor and visual-perceptual deficits (less than 2 years below chronologic age), and 36 per cent were judged to be moderately to severly abnormal in these areas (greater than 2 years below chronologic age).

The influence of visual and auditory processing deficits on reading, spelling and arithmetic skills was analyzed. Delinquent subjects with intact perceptual skills were compared with three deficit groups: (1) pure visual-perceptual (2) pure auditory-perceptual and (3) multiple auditory and visual perceptual deficits. As indicated in Table 5, the

TABLE 4. *Percentages of 44 Juvenile Offenders with Specific Deficit Patterns*

	Total Group (N = 44)	Deficit Group (N = 35)
No Deficit	21%	—
Auditory Sequential Memory	60%	76%
Visual-Motor Coordination	55%	70%
Visual-Spatial Orientation	18%	23%
Auditory SEQ Memory + Visual-Motor Coordination	35%	46%

visual-perceptual deficit group did not differ significantly from subjects with intact perceptual skills on any of the measures utilized (p > .05). The auditory-perceptual deficit group was significantly deficient (p < .05) in reading and arithmetic. The most significant (p < .05) deficiencies in reading, spelling and arithmetic were observed in subjects with multiple auditory and visual-perceptual deficits. The significance of these findings lies in the fact that the severity of perceptual dysfunction, rather than delinquency *per se*, appeared to be the primary factor in the observed academic deficiencies.

While the significance of mixed cerebral dominance is widely debated, this phenomenon has been associated with perceptual deficits[26,27] and has also been reported to occur with increased frequency in delinquent populations.[28] Each of the subjects in this study was tested for eye, hand and foot dominance. 64 per cent (N = 28) had mixed cerebral dominance and 36 per cent had (N = 16) unilateral dominance. Of those with mixed dominance, 89.2 per cent (N = 25) had mixed eye-hand dominance, and 10.8 per cent (N = 3) consistently showed unilateral eye-hand dominance but contralateral foot preference.

Self-concept (self-esteem, self-confidence, feelings of worth) was evaluated from personality tests. As a group, juvenile delinquents scored at the 8th percentile with measures of overall self-concept, as compared with distribution of values for children of the same age and intelligence. The results indicate that those in the delinquent group were significantly deficient in self-confidence and generally saw themselves as undesirable.

Discussion

These observations suggest several important considerations for pediatricians and other health care professionals. If the associations between impaired learning, academic underachievement and subsequent behavioral and emotional complications are valid, early detection becomes critical. As the first professional to deal with a child during early development, the pediatrician is in a unique position to recognize a learning disability and to initiate treatment. Such early detection and therapeutic intervention may help to forestall the later development of behavior disorders such as juvenile delinquency. Yet nearly all of the reports on the long term sequelae of learning disorders appear in educational and psycho-

logic journals, not in the pediatric literature. The relatively high incidence of severe aca-

Table 5. *Deviations from Expected Achievement Levels in Various Deficit Groups*

	Reading	Spelling	Arithmetic
No Deficit Group (N = 9)	−1.23	−1.64	−2.21
Pure Visual-Perceptual (N = 7)	−1.28	−2.38	−2.13
Pure Auditory Perceptual (N = 8)	−2.75*	−2.10	−2.92*
Multiple Visual and Auditory Perceptual (N = 20)	−4.40*	−5.46*	−5.63*

* Significantly different from no deficit group at .05 level of significance.

demic underachievement, auditory and visual-perceptual disturbances and associated damage to self-image appear to carry a significant potential for antisocial behavior. Understanding these effects of learning disabilities on subsequent social adaptation may be an extremely important key in helping to prevent juvenile delinquency.

The youthful offenders in this series, despite average intellectual capacity, presented profiles in the various tests which are characteristic of many learning-disabled children. Most had significant visual and auditory perceptual deficits, so often associated with academic failure. Poor performance with the Bender-Gestalt by many of the subjects further supported the presence of visual-perceptual or visual-motor deficits.

The significance of the high incidence of mixed eye-hand dominance in the test subjects is somewhat puzzling but seems to support the need for investigation of the neurologic integrity of delinquent subjects. Mixed dominance has been correlated with reading deficits, such as dyslexia[28] but the mixed cerebral dominance, as it relates to abnormal brain function, still remains an enigma. Additional neurologic studies with delinquent populations may provide needed answers.

The implications are readily apparent. Perceptual disturbances, academic underachievement and poor self-esteem may represent a vicious cycle which, in combination with other psychosocial and organic factors, can contribute to the behavioral maladaptation of the juvenile delinquent. The child does not leave his learning disability behind when he leaves the classroom. Social learning of values and norms may also be impaired, as evidenced by the delinquent's difficulty in profiting from past experiences.

During the past decade, the traditional scope of the pediatrician's intervention in health care delivery has been modified dramatically. Major successes in preventing and controlling infections, competencies in managing acute problems and advances in neonatology have altered roles and responsibilities. Chronic handicapping disorders, problems of exceptionality, family psychodynamics and other issues of psychoeducational and social significance are the new challenges for pediatricians. Possibly the single most challenging problem is the appreciation of learning disabilities and their effects on psychosocial maturation. As the first professional to assess development and behavior, the early detection of these disorders is particularly a unique responsibility for the physician.

Professionals serving the total health needs of children are obligated to consider new entities: visual and auditory perceptual deficits, dyslexia, minimal brain dysfunction and other less specific learning disabilities. If problems of this nature are to be suspected, the physician must expand the "routine" examination to include developmental and behavioral evaluations. Inventories such as the Denver Developmental Screening Test for preschoolers, and achievement tests and evaluation of perceptual skills for school-age children can be performed by other professionals and incorporated into the pediatrician's assessment. The norms of development extend beyond growth grids and the traditional gross motor, fine motor and language skills. Evaluations of perceptual development, receptive and expressive language, reading skills and more sophisticated cognitive levels are to be considered. Recognition of a deviant development, regardless of a child's age, should prompt a referral to professionals with specialized skills such as a psychologist, speech pathologist or special educator.

Recapitulation

Child health care professionals must be alert to the early recognition of academic and behavior problems. Learning-disabled children with perceptual deficits are at high risk for incurring educational and social disabilities.[29,30] When such disability is undiagnosed and untreated, the risk and complications may become exaggerated during adolescence.[31] The combination of learning difficulties, perceptual disturbances, poor self-concept and behavioral reactions represent a challenge to pediatricians, teachers, parents and all other child health care professionals. Failure to recognize the impact of academic underachievement on family and peer relationships and on the developing self-concept of the individual may result ultimately as disturbed adolescent behaviors and juvenile delinquency. The dictum of "the earlier the diagnosis, the better the prognosis" is particularly applicable here.

References

1. Kratoville, B. L., Ed.: Youth in Trouble. San Rafael, Calif., Academic Therapy Publications, 1974.
2. Monroe, M.: Children Who Cannot Read. Chicago, University of Chicago Press, 1932.
3. Fendrick, P., and Bond, G. L.: Delinquency and reading. J. Genet. Psychol. **48**: 236, 1936.
4. Kvaraceus, W.: Delinquency: A by-product of the schools? School and Soc. **59**: 350, 1944.
5. Jacobson, F.: Learning disabilities and juvenile delinquency: A demonstrated relationship. *In*: Handbook of Learning Disabilities: A Prognosis for the Child, the Adolescent, the Adult, New Jersey Association for Children with Learning Disabilities, R. Weber, Ed. Englewood, N.J., Prentice-Hall, 1973.
6. Kessler, J.: The Psychopathology of Childhood. Englewood, N.J. Prentice-Hall, 1966.
7. Woodward, M.: The role of low intelligence in delinquency. Br. J. Delinquency **5**: 281, 1955.
8. Weinschenk, C.: The significance of diagnosis and treatment of congenital dyslexia and dysgraphia in the prevention of juvenile delinquency. World Med. J. **14**: 54, 1967.
9. Tarnapol, L.: Delinquency in minimal brain dysfunction. J. Learn. Disabil. **3**: 200, 1970.
10. Critchley, E. M. R.: Reading retardation, dyslexia and delinquency. Br. J. Psychiatry **115**: 1537, 1968.
11. Clements, S.: Minimal Brain Dysfunction in Children. NINDB Monograph No. 3, Washington, D.C.: U.S. Government Printing Office, 1966.
12. Myklebust, H., Ed.: Progress in Learning Disabilities, vol. 2. New York, Grune and Stratton, 1971.
13. Wikler, A., Dixon, J., and Parker, J.: Brain function in problem children and controls: Psychometric, neurological and electroencephalographic comparisons. Am. J. Psychiatry **127**: 94, 1970.
14. Denhoff, E.: Bridges to burn and build. Develop. Med. Child. Neurol. **7**: 3, 1965.
15. Keldgord, R.: Brain damage and delinquency: A question and a challenge. Acad. Ther. Q. **4**: 93, 1968.
16. Williams, J.: Learning disabilities: A multifaceted health problem. J. School Health **46**: 515, 1976.
17. Walzer, S., and Richmond, B. R.: The epidemiology of learning disorders. Pediatr. Clin. North Am. **20**: 549, 1973.
18. Lerner, J., Ed.: Children with Learning Disabilities. New York, Houghton Mifflin Co., 1971.
19. Rampp, D. L., and Plummer, B. A.: Auditory Processing Dysfunctions and Impaired Learning, Learning Disabilities: An Audio Journal for Continuing Education, Vol. 1, No. 7., New York, Grune and Stratton, Inc. July 1977.
20. Chalfant, J. D., and Scheffelin, M. A.: Central Processing Dysfunctions in Children: A Review of Research. National Institute of Neurological Diseases and Blindness, Monograph no. 9, Bethesda, Maryland, US Dept. HEW, 1969.

21. Rhodes, F.: Rhodes WISC Scatter Profile. San Diego, Educational and Industrial Testing Service, 1969.
22. Koppitz, E. M.: The Bender-Gestalt Test for Young Children. New York, Grune and Stratton, 1964.
23. Jastak, J., and Jastak, S.: The Wide Range Achievement Test. Wilmington, Guidance Associates, 1965.
24. Eames, T. H.: Frequency of cerebral lateral dominance variations among school children of premature and full-term birth. J. Pediatr. 51: 300, 1957.
25. Fitts, W. H.: Manual for the Tennessee Self-Concept Scale. Nashville, Counselor Recordings and Tests, 1964.
26. Orton, S. T.: Reading, Writing and Speech Problems in Children. New York, W. W. Norton Co., 1937.
27. Satz, P.: Cerebral dominance and reading disability: An old problem revisited. In: The Neuropsychology of Learning Disorders, R. Knights and D. Bakker, Eds. Baltimore, University Park Press, 1976.
28. Critchley, M.: Developmental Dyslexia. Springfield, Charles C Thomas, 1964.
29. Wender, P. H.: Minimal Brain Dysfunction in Children. New York, Wiley, 1971.
30. Olson, M. E.: Minimal cerebral dysfunction: The child referred for school-related problems. Pediatric Ann. 4: 69, 1975.
31. Mauser, A. J.: Learning disabilities and delinquent youth. In: Youth in Trouble, E. E. Kratoville, Ed. San Rafael, Calif. Academic Therapy Publications, 1975, pp. 91–102.

Two Contemporary Tragedies:

Adolescent Suicide/Adolescent Alcoholism

Edwin Caine, M.D.

The death of a teenager from any cause is tragic; but, suicide, the purposeful taking of one's own life, seems to me a greater tragedy. Since twenty percent of teenage suicides are alcohol-related and alcoholism itself may be considered a form of chronic suicide, both problems—adolescent suicide and alcoholism—will be examined in this article. The first section of this article will explore adolescent suicide, its etiology and treatment; the latter section will examine adolescent alcoholism.

What motivates the teenager to take his life? How prevalent is the problem? What can be done to recognize and, if possible, prevent this problem?

Statistics on Suicide

Approximately 25,000 suicides take place in the United States per year; there are nine times as many suicide attempts per year. Twelve percent of the suicide attempts are made by adolescents. Seventy-five percent of the suicide attempts are made by adolescent girls. For completed suicides, the ratio is three males to two females. This ratio, however, is substantially higher for females than in the past and at this time, an increasing number of girls commit suicide. Approximately ten percent of all people who commit suicide are under twenty years old and this percentage has been rising over the last ten years.

Suicide is presently the second leading cause of death for people aged ten to twenty-four. Accidents are the first leading cause of death. Many people feel that accidents frequently can be suicidal equivalents and, therefore, the suicide rate might be substantially higher. In successful suicides, boys usually choose guns, girls poison. Ten percent of people who attempt suicide, later go on to commit suicide. This is an extremely important statistic, implying that a suicide attempt should not be taken lightly at any time.

Etiology

The etiology of adolescent suicide in this article will concern some of the individual, social, and cultural determinants that affect the adolescent. The following are individual determinants in the etiology of adolescent suicide:

- *Genetic Tendencies* There is no evidence that self-destructive tendencies can be transmitted genetically. Multiple studies, including twin studies, have produced no evidence of a genetic transmission.

- *Puberty* At puberty suicide attempts substantially increase. At this point in time, there is an increase in sexual and aggressive drives and a reactivation of old problems that have not been resolved. Suicide may at times seem to the child to be the resolution of overwhelming feelings and conflicts.

- *Mental Disorders* Depressive states and schizophrenia are the most frequent mental disorders linked to suicide. In young people, there is often loss of a love object through death or separation; in fifty percent of the cases of suicide, there is definite depression related to loss. Other studies suggest that up to fifty percent of children who attempt suicide do so as a response to hallucinatory commands that tell them to kill themselves. At least ten percent of these children can be diagnosed as schizophrenic. Other statistics show the percentage to be higher.

- *Identification, Imitation, and Suggestion* Frequently identification with a dead parent and a wish to rejoin the parent are precipitants. At times, the teenager will imitate a family member who has attempted suicide as a method of coping. If a parent harbors suicidal thoughts or suicidal preoccupations, their children frequently may attempt suicide. They identify with the parent, actually seem to pick up the parent's depression, and act out the parent's suicidal preoccupations.

Children who are rejected by a parent or who have extremely hostile parents may respond to what they perceive as death wishes that their parents have for them and attempt suicide. I have seen many cases where a death wish actively seems to be present on the part of the parents toward the child; and, the children do respond to it.

- *Aggression* Frequently the child is unable to directly express rage provoked by disappointment or loss and it is turned inward as revenge or spite. The child feels, "if I kill myself, this will hurt you (parent)," or "you will be sorry when I am dead," or he experiences the fantasy of watching his own funeral procession with the parents crying as a means of hurting the parent. Frequently there also is guilt over hostility felt about the parents; it is turned toward the

> "If a parent harbors suicidal thoughts or suicidal preoccupations, their children frequently may attempt suicide. They identify with the parent, actually seem to pick up the parent's depression, and act out the parent's suicidal preoccupations."

self with a subsequent suicide attempt.

- *Impulsivity* There are many studies stating that suicide attempts frequently are impulsive, especially with teenage girls. This is in contradistinction to Dr. Joseph D. Teicher's theories, which in my experience with suicidal teenagers seem to be of great importance. He feels that suicide attempts are planned, are a last choice, and must be understood longitudinally in relation to the full life history of the child. He breaks the pathogenesis of suicide into three stages: a history of long-standing problems before adolescence; a period of escalation of these problems after the onset of adolescence; the culminating stage that ends with suicide attempt.

- *Drugs or Alcohol* This is an extremely important individual determinant. Twenty percent of teenage suicides are alcohol-related. The suicide rate among alcoholics is fifty-eight times higher than nonalcoholics. Seven to twenty-one percent—a very startling figure—of all alcoholics will die by means of suicide. Many people feel that alcoholism itself is chronic suicide, making these statistics more meaningful.

At this point, the developmental sequence in children about the understanding of death will be mentioned. Children do not perceive death as adults do; a suicide attempt at one age may have a different meaning from a suicide attempt at another age. The first stage concerns children under five years of age. Death seems temporary and is equated with separation because little children do not perceive the finality of death.

The second stage involves children aged five to nine.

> "The family life of suicidal children is frequently very disruptive and chaotic. There are frequent moves and changes of schools, frequent family quarrels, financial difficulties, and broken homes. Eighty-eight percent of children who attempt suicide are from families with either divorce, death of a parent or stepparent, alcoholic parents, or suicide attempts by parents."

Death is very concrete and seen as a person, such as the "grim reaper." The reality of death is not clearly perceived by the child at this stage. If there is a suicide attempt in a seven- or eight-year-old, the eight-year-old does not perceive it as the final termination and this should definitely be understood. In the third stage, involving children nine years of age and older, death is seen as permanent, as an end.

Social Determinants and Family Relationships

The second part of the etiology of adolescent suicide involves some of the social and family relationship determinants:

■ *Family Life* Family relationships are extremely important in the etiology of adolescent suicides. There have been many studies stating that this is the most important element in teenage suicide; whereas in adult suicide, this is not necessarily the case. The family life of suicidal children is frequently very disruptive and chaotic. There are frequent moves and changes of schools, frequent family quarrels, financial difficulties, and broken homes. Eighty-eight percent of children who attempt suicide are from families with either divorce, death of a parent or step-parent, alcoholic parents, or suicide attempts by parents. Frequently there is illness in one of the parents of a child who attempts suicide.

■ *Social Isolation* The most important dynamic factor in teenage suicide is social isolation. The child frequently has no close friends to share confidences, he is chronically isolated, and he seems to have loneliness with no other alternatives.

■ *Communication* The patient frequently has difficulty communicating with others. Frequently the suicide attempt is seen as a cry for help, as a communication of grave distress that never should be ignored. Most suicide attempts are by and large ambivalent. There are clues before the suicide. The person frequently feels it is the last resort he has, but usually there is a part of him that wants to live; and, this is why suicide prevention is so important. Frequently, if one can get through the acute suicidal crisis, the wish to live remains and can be worked with successfully. Frequently suicide is seen as a means of solving chronic problems of living. The child feels he has no other ways of coping.

■ *Socio-Economic Status* There is no evidence that suicide is more frequent among the rich or the poor. It seems to be more directly related to the home and family life.

There are different behavioral, verbal, and situational clues for children who are going to attempt suicide. Verbally, ninety percent of children who attempt suicide talk to at least one person before the attempt. Behaviorally, the child can be withdrawn, have poor grades, be preoccupied in school, have dreams of death, have weight loss, and begin to give away favorite objects.

Situationally, the loss of a significant person frequently occurs before the suicide attempt. Three-

> "Three-quarters of the teenagers who attempt suicide see a physician within four months of their suicide attempt. This is extremely important for physicians to recognize, yet frequently, it is unrecognized. . . .and, at this time it is extremely important for the doctor to recognize that the child may be breaking down and that this may be a reflection of severe depression."

quarters of the teenagers who attempt suicide see a physician within four months of their suicide attempt. This is extremely important for physicians to recognize, yet frequently, it is unrecognized. The child will come in complaining of depression, of stomach pains, sleeplessness, or general malaise; and, at this time it is extremely important for the doctor to recognize that the child may be breaking down and that this may be a reflection of severe depression. At this point in time, the child can be helped. Nevertheless, this is frequently missed.

Cultural Determinants

In different cultures, there are different rates of suicide. Frequently, these differences are related to the early childhood training in the particular culture. In Sweden, for example, with very high expectations for achievement, there is a high suicide rate related to the fact that people get very depressed when they cannot live up to the expectations within the culture. In Denmark, there is a high suicide rate and there seem to be many conflicts over dependency and separation.

In Norway, in contradistinction, there is a very low suicide rate. Mothers seem to be more accepting of aggression and striving for independence in their children. In certain cultures, an acceptability of suicide exists, for example hara-kari and the kamikaze pilots of Japan. These are actually examples of a culturally induced acceptance of suicide. The present suicide rate in Japan, especially with teenagers, is extremely high.

Treatment

The first treatment is primary prevention: identification of the presuicidal individual. This is an area needing much work. In part, we can try to recognize the verbal and behavioral clues that have been mentioned in this article. Again, some of the behavioral clues are anorexia, psychosomatic complaints, rebellious behavior, neglect of school work, use of alcohol or drugs, neglect of personal appearance, loss of weight, difficulty concentrating, personality changes.

6. ADOLESCENCE

Some of the related emotional factors that are clues are depression, loneliness, isolation, self-destruction, schizophrenia, extremely morbid dreams and fantasies, hallucinations and extreme hypersensitivity. Some of the other related characteristics are previous suicide attempts, withdrawal from people, broken homes, sleep disturbances, a long history of parent-child conflicts, and recent losses of a love object.

All suicidal behavior has to be taken seriously and the patient has to be protected. I recently evaluated a thirteen-year-old girl at a local hospital who had attempted suicide. This was a very serious suicide attempt. She had a family history of two successful suicides in her immediate family; her parents, however, stated that she "just wanted attention," and would not accept that this was a serious suicide attempt. It was the recommendation of the pediatrician and myself that she be hospitalized. When I mentioned hospitalization to the child, she jumped up and hugged me. Her parents never followed through and she was subsequently lost to follow-up. The odds of this child attempting suicide again are very high and she is in a high risk category.

Secondary prevention occurs during the acute phase of crisis intervention. Such prevention relates to hospitalization, outpatient care, and suicide prevention centers where a helpful person can be a lifeline for the depressed person. With teenagers, the families must be involved in treatment. There is no treatment of the suicidal teenager without the treatment of the family; otherwise, it is not workable. Other treatment modalities are hospitalization, medication, psychotherapy, environmental intervention.

With early recognition and assistance of public and/or private personnel, the prognosis for successful intervention with the suicidal teenager is very good. Many suicides can be avoided and we can do our part in helping disturbed teenagers learn to live and learn means of coping with severe problems of living other than suicidal behavior.

As previously stated, twenty percent of teenage suicides are alcohol-related; alcohol is now the drug of choice for teenagers and its use is increasing. The following sections of this article will give a general overview of the problem of teenage alcoholism.

Alcohol and What It Does

Alcohol—ethyl alcohol—is a mind-altering drug and is used in wine, beer, spirits. The alcohol industry produces one billion gallons a year and consumers pay 24 billion dollars a year for alcohol in the United States. Ethyl alcohol is a central nervous system depressant; it depresses higher functions like judgment, orientation, intellectual faculties. It diminishes controls and inhibitions. It can lead, with enough alcohol, to paralysis of respiration, heartbeat, coma, and death.

Alcohol is an addicting drug involving increasing tolerance as well as withdrawal symptoms. In a definition of a true addiction both tolerance and withdrawal symptoms must exist, for example delirium, convul-

---

> "With teenagers, the families must be involved in treatment. There is no treatment of the suicidal teenager without the treatment of the family; otherwise, it is not workable."

---

sions, collapses. Full-blown delirium tremens (DTs) occur after three to five years of heavy usage of alcohol. For adolescents such cases of DTs are becoming more frequent and are occurring at earlier ages.

The body metabolizes three-quarters of an ounce of whiskey an hour. Therefore, the faster one drinks, the higher the blood level is. Two shots will produce a blood alcohol level of .05 percent, which is sedation and tranquility. Four shots will produce 0.1 percent, which is lack of coordination, and approximately twenty shots or thirty ounces will produce a blood alcohol level of 0.5 percent and death.

The medical effects of alcohol abuse include: esophagitis, gastritis with GI bleeding, cirrhosis of the liver leading to hepatic failure. In 1970, cirrhosis of the liver was the ninth cause of death in the United States and in 1973, it was the first cause of death in the U.S. Pancreatitis, anemias with low white counts, and increased sensitivity to infection can exist. At times there can be heart disease, although this is very rare, with weakening of the myocardium. There can be neurological symptoms such as peripheral neuritis, abnormal EEGs and progressive deliria and dimentia with chronic brain damage.

What Is an Alcoholic?

Alcoholism is now thought of as an illness not moral depravity, and is America's major health problem. The definition in the Diagnostic and Statistical Manual II of the APA, "a patient whose alcohol intake is great enough to damage their physical health or their personal or social

---

> "Alcohol is the drug of choice for teenagers today and its use is increasing. We see this in the hospital, we see it in the community . . . . Figures from the National Institute of Alcoholism and Alcohol Abuse state that five percent of teenagers have a drinking problem and at this time there are something like 1.3 million severe problem drinkers who are teenagers."

---

functioning, or when it has become a prerequisite to normal functioning," is a very broad definition of an alcoholic. "Problem drinkers" will fit into this category. Another workable definition of an alcoholic is someone whose drinking causes a continuing and growing problem in his life.

Statistics on Alcoholism

There are nine million alcoholics in the United States. Only three to five percent of them are the "skid row" types. Most live with normal families. They work, they function, and they are represented by all areas and all socio-economic classes. Forty million spouses and children are affected by alcoholism. There are 25,000 traffic fatalities that are caused by alcohol-associated diseases, and approximately half of the five million arrests per year are alcohol-related. The cost to the economy is something like fifteen billion dollars per year.

Adolescents and Alcohol

Alcohol is the drug of choice for teenagers today and its use is increasing. We see this in the hospital, we see it in the community. In a 1970 study in San Mateo County, south of San Francisco, eleven percent of ninth grade boys had had alcoholic beverages fifty or more times within the year. In 1970, twenty-seven percent of twelfth grade boys had had alcoholic beverages fifty or more times a year and in 1973, it was up to forty percent.

In Los Angeles, studies show that in 1974, ninety-two percent of high school seniors were using alcohol intermittently. In 1969, seventy percent did. These are general figures that show an increasing usage in teenagers. Figures from the National Insitute of Alcoholism and Alcohol Abuse state that five percent of teenagers have a drinking problem and at this time there are something like 1.3 million severe problem drinkers who are teenagers.

Another study, the Yale Study—one of the most famous on alcoholism—started in 1947 and got more results twenty years later. Researchers took approximately 17,000 students from twenty-seven colleges and studied them on their use and abuse of alcohol; twenty years later they traced down as many as they could to see what the problems with alcohol were at that time. Findings revealed that fifty percent of men and women who exhibited signs of problem drinking in college were having severe alcohol problems twenty years later.

This is a very important statistic: the habits that one develops in the teenage years most decidedly, at least fifty percent, can carry into adulthood. I have had many patients who were adult alcoholics whose drinking actually started in their teenage years. It didn't stop and it was not a "phase" they were going through. The patterns of drinking that one learns in the teenage years, in a large proportion of patients, continue throughout adult life.

Etiology

There is no one known cause. It is felt that there are

> "There is no one known cause. It is felt that there are multiple determinants that lead to a final common pathway of alcoholism. There is no single personality configuration, there is no particular socio-economic class. It is ubiquitous throughout society."

multiple determinants that lead to a final common pathway of alcoholism. There is no single personality configuration, there is no particular socio-economic class. It is ubiquitous throughout society. Therefore each case has to be studied on its own merit. Some of the factors that can be considered involve the individual, social, and cultural determinants affecting the adolescent.

Individual Determinants

The following are some of the individual causes for alcoholism:

- *Genetics* Although there have been many studies, some of which have pointed to genetic transmittal, such possibilities have not been proven one way or another at this time.

- *Alcohol As An Attempt at Self-Treatment That Fails* There are multiple stresses on teenagers: struggles of identity, sexual conflicts, dependency-independency conflicts; for certain kids, alcohol seemingly offers a solution for handling some of the anxiety and stress. For example, for the very shy, withdrawn child who has difficulty with relationships, alcohol gives the appearance of making the child more social. In a 1974 study on Scandinavian boys who were arrested for alcoholism, approximately eighty percent of them were described as very shy, withdrawn kids who had severe problems with peer relationships and the alcohol was a way to help them with their inhibitions.

Social and Family Determinants

Some of the social determinants and family relationship factors involved in adolescent alcoholism are:

- *Peer Pressures* There is tremendous pressure on peers to drink. It is hard to abstain and a definite desire for acceptance recognition and peer identity exists. This is one of the problems with our patients—on discharge, where do they go? If they go back to the normal peer group, drinking is very much accepted and there are pressures on kids to drink. And, it is increasing.

- *Family Life* Drinking parents produce drinking kids. The children of parents who perhaps are not alcoholics, but nevertheless are substance abusers, have a greater tendency to abuse substances also. Simply through identification with one's parents a greater proportion of kids are drinking.

Adolescents who see in the family that the parents utilize alcohol as an escape from their problems and as a way of dealing with their anxiety, also tend to do so. In addition, within the family are dynamics that reenforce and create alcoholism. This is one of the issues that Al-Anon deals with. The family has to be involved to help the alcoholic because the alcoholic is not in a milieu all by himself. There are multiple forces within his family that also lead toward his abuse of alcohol.

Cultural Determinants

■ *Societal Symbol* Alcohol is a symbol in our society of hospitality, fun, sexuality, and manliness. Within our society, alcohol is a very acceptable part of the culture. One of the problems in our culture is that responsible drinking is not taught. There are cocktail parties and there is toleration of someone who drinks to the point of getting drunk. In our culture the patterns of drinking are not taught as responsible drinking.

For example, in a study of first generation Italians wine was a part of the meal at a very early age, and was served where there were warmth, companionship, and the family together. Alcohol is part of the culture and there is very little alcoholism; in this way responsible drinking is taught. It is within the cultural pattern. In a study of second generation Italians, a much higher percentage of alcoholism was present.

Treatment

How do we handle the problem? First, it is a public health problem. The issue is primary prevention to prevent the expression of the disease. Thus, to lower the rate of onset of teenage alcoholism, much effort should center on education.

What do parents say to their teenagers who drink? What are you supposed to say? This is partially primary prevention that starts in the home, but it also should involve the school.

"Drinking parents produce drinking kids. The children of parents who perhaps are not alcoholics, but nevertheless are substance abusers, have a greater tendency to abuse substances also. Simply through identification with one's parents a greater proportion of kids are drinking."

"If the teenager is to be a tee-totaler, I think that this should be very much reinforced; but, to think that if we simply tell teenagers they should not drink and they are not going to drink is absolutely bizarre and foolish. One thing we can do is to teach responsible drinking, which will diminish some of the consequences that we see."

Secondary prevention involves treating the active disease of alcoholism to avoid further complications. Tertiary prevention deals with the end stage complications of the disease. In a very large proportion of chronic patients who are in mental institutions, alcohol-related illness is the cause for them being in the institutions.

The big issue now for the treatment of teenage alcoholics is responsible drinking, which is always a very questionable idea. The reality is that we would like to say teenagers should not drink, it is bad, illegal, immoral, unethical, you can get into trouble with the law, you really should not drink—just the same way you say you should not take marijuana, you should not take pills and so on. Prohibition was an excellent solution to the problem of alcoholism. What it stated was that it was illegal to serve alcohol in the United States and no one should drink. Prohibition, in my opinion, created more alcoholics than any other time in the history of the United States. It did not work just to prohibit it.

If the teenager is to be a tee-totaler, I think that this should be very much reenforced; but, to think that if we simply tell teenagers they should not drink and they are not going to drink is absolutely bizarre and foolish. One thing we can do is to teach responsible drinking, which will diminish some of the consequences that we see. Some of the issues of responsible drinking include: avoid seclusion while drinking, avoid drinking to relieve tensions and anxiety, avoid drinking to excess, avoid drinking to drunkenness, avoid drinking while driving, avoid drinking when not eating, avoid the big parties where there is machismo involving who is going to drink the most.

Conclusion

Alcohol is an attempt at an external means to ward off depression and to achieve control over feelings of fear, helplessness, and deprivation. It is an external means of asserting control over an internal problem. There are all sorts of theories about why kids drink. We have to study each child in his own right. We have to understand what the internal problem is and the child has to understand as well. With teenagers who have a difficult time tolerating their anxiety, alcohol temporarily relieves it and fills a need. Other ways of coping must be learned.

Our task in the hospital with children who are substance abusers and alcoholics, is to give them a certain degree of external control. We must cut them off from alcohol and help them get more in touch with who they are, what their feelings are, and what the motivating factors are that have created the substance abuse. We must help them in their growth so they can begin dealing in different ways with their anxiety, other than trying to find a magical external cure for something that is truly an internal problem □

Selected Bibliography
(Suicide)

1. Ackerly, W. C., M.D. 1967. Latency-age children who threaten or attempt to kill themselves. *J. of Child Psychiat.* 6:242-61.
2. Arieti, S. 1974. Depression and suicide. *Amer. Handbook of Psychiat. VII.* New York: Basic Books.
3. Beck, A. T., M.D.; Weissman, A.; and Kovack, M. 1976. Alcoholism, hopelessness and suicidal behavior. *J. of Studies on Alcohol.* 37(1):66-7.
4. Bibring, E., M.D. 1951. The mechanism of depression. Revised version of a paper read in May 1951 at the annual meeting of the American Psychoanalytic Association as part of the panel on depressive and manic states. pp. 13-48.
5. *Family Weekly.* 1976. Five dangerous ideas our children have about life. pp. 22-5. September 19.
6. Frederick, C. J., and Lague, L. 1972. *Dealing with the crisis of suicide.* Public Affairs Pamphlet No. 405A. Washington, D.C.:U.S. Government Printing Office.
7. Glaser, K., M.D. 1968. Masked depression in children and adolescents. *Annual Progress in Child Psychiatry and Child Development 1968*, eds., Chess, S., M.D., and Thomas, A., M.D. pp. 345-55.
8. Gallagher, N. 1976. Why people kill themselves. *Today's Health.* pp. 46-50.
9. Havens, L. L., M.D. 1965. The anatomy of suicide. *N. Eng. J. Med.* 272:401.
10. Havens, L. L., M.D. 1967. Recognition of suicidal risks through the psychologic examination. *N. Eng. J. Med.* 276(4):210-15.
11. Kraft, D. P., M.D., and Babigian, H. M., M.D. 1976. Suicide by persons with and without psychiatric contact. Arch. Gen. Psychiat. 33:209-15.
12. Moore, P. 1975. Danger of depression—what ails the troubled teen? *Chicago Daily News.* Dec. 26.
13. Neil, K. 1965. Self-poisoning. This chapter is a condensation of the Milroy Lectures delivered at the Royal College of Physicians of London in February 1965, and printed with the permission of the British Medical Journal, wherein these lectures appeared under the title "Self-poisoning, 5473:1265-70 and 5474:1336-48. pp. 345-66.
14. *Newsweek.* 1973. Coping with depression. Jan. 8.
15. Poznanski, E., M.D., and Zrull, J. P., M.D. 1970. Childhood depression. *Arch. Gen. Psychiat.* v. 23.
16. Scheidman, E. S., and Swendon, D. D., M.D., eds. 1969. *Suicide among youth.* A review of the literature, 1900-1967. National Clearinghouse for Mental Health. Washington, D.C.:U.S. Government Printing Office.
17. Schneidman, E. S., and Mandelkorn, P. 1967. *How to prevent suicide.* New York: Public Affairs Committee, Inc.
18. Schneidman, E., and Farberow, N. 1961. *Some facts about suicide.* PHS Pub. No. 852. Washington, D.C.: U.S. Government Printing Office.
19. Smith, D. 1976. Adolescent suicide: a problem for teachers? *Phi Delta Kappan.* pp. 539-42.
20. Teicher, J. D., M.D., and Jacobs, J. 1966. Adolescents who commit suicide: preliminary findings. *Amer. J. Psychiat.* 122:1248-57.
21. Teicher, J. D., M.D. 1975. Children who choose death. *Emergency Med.* Aug. pp. 136-42.
22. Weiss, J. 1966. The suicidal patient. *Amer. Handbook of Psychiat. III*, ed. Arieti, S. New York: Basic Books.

Selected Bibliography
(Alcoholism)

1. Alexander, C. N., Jr. 1967. Alcohol and adolescent rebellion. *Social Forces.* 45(4):542-50.
2. American Academy of Pediatrics. 1975. Alcohol consumption: an adolescent problem. *Pediatrics.* 55(4):557-59.
3. Chafetz, M. E., M.D. 1976. Alcoholism. *Psychiat. Ann.* 6(3):9-93.
4. Cohen, S., M.D., ed. 1975. Teenage drinking: the bottle babies. *Drug Abuse and Alcoholism Newsletter.* 4(5).
5. Dosti, R. 1975. Teenage drinking on rise. *Los Angeles Times.* May 29.
6. Maddox, G. L., and McCall, B. C. 1964. *Drinking among teenagers.* Copyright 1964 by Journal of Studies on Alcohol, Inc., New Brunswick, New Jersey. New Haven: College and University Press.
7. Nylander, I., and Rydelius, P. A. 1973. The relapse of drunkenness in non-asocial teenage boys. *ACTA Psychiat. Scandinavia.* 49:435-43.
8. Pollack, J. H. 1966. Teenage drinking and drug addiction. *NEA J.* May 8-12.
9. Ryback, R. S., M.D. 1975. Teenage alcoholism, medicine and the law. *N. Eng. J. Med.* 293(14):719-21.
10. Smart, R. G., and Schmidt, W. 1975. Drinking and problems from drinking after a reduction in the minimum drinking age. *Br. J. on Addiction.* 70:347-58.
11. Straus, R. 1973. Alcohol and society. *Psychiat. Ann.* 3(10):9-103.
12. Zucker, R. A. 1975. Problem drinking in adolescence. *AFP.* 12(1):103-6.

Dr. Caine is in private practice of child, adolescent, and adult psychiatry. He is assistant clinical professor of psychiatry at UCLA and is an attending staff member at Harbor General Hospital, Torrance, California and Del Amo Hospital, Torrance, California.

HYPERACTIVES AS YOUNG ADULTS:

School, Employer, and Self-Rating Scales Obtained During Ten-Year Follow-Up Evaluation

Gabrielle Weiss, M.D., Lily Hechtman, M.D., Terrye Perlman, M.Ed.

The Montreal Children's Hospital, Montreal, Quebec

A ten-year prospective follow-up of hyperactive adolescents and young adults indicates that they are rated as markedly inferior to normal controls by teachers but not by employers. On self-rating scales, they view themselves as inferior to controls on a personality test, but no different than controls on a psychopathology scale.

Follow-up studies have shown that the prognosis of hyperactive children as they enter adolescence is relatively poor. A significant minority (approximately 25%) show antisocial behavior, and they have a history of poor school performance.[6, 8, 9] School records indicate that they fail more grades, have lower ratings in all subjects on report cards, and are scored by teachers as doing worse on a behavior checklist than are normal controls in the same classroom.[7] In addition, on clinical evaluation they were found to have impaired self-esteem.[9]

The school situation is a very difficult one for hyperactive children and adolescents. Their poor concentration, impulsive cognitive style, difficult behavior, and, occasionally, specific learning disabilities all interact to produce academic failure and unpopularity with teachers and peers. The experience of school failure (which keeps increasing over the school years) contributes towards poor self-esteem and decreased motivation in many hyperactive children, thus enhancing their primary problems of learning.

Given the preceding background, the adult prognosis for this group of children does not look optimistic. However, many professionals who have worked with hyperactives have wondered how they fare in adult life in a work situation. It has been hypothesized that some of the typical behavior of hyperactives, such as their high activity level, might actually be an asset in some type of work situations, although a detriment in the sedentary school setting. To investigate this hypothesis further, rating scales of behavioral items relevant to work and school success were sent to

Hyperactives as Young Adults: School, Employer, and Self-Rating Scales Obtained During Ten-Year Follow-Up Evaluation, Gabrielle Weiss, Lily Hectman, Terrye Perlman, *American Journal of Orthopsychiatry*, Vol. 48, No. 3, July 1978. ©1978 by the American Orthopsychiatric Association, Inc.

employers and to high schools. The scales contained seven identical questions regarding the performance of a group of adult hyperactive subjects and a group of matched normal controls.

Because of the clinical finding of low self-esteem in adolescence [9] and the chronic experience of failure, we also wanted to assess how hyperactives as young adults view their functioning. For this purpose, we chose two self-rating scales that tap quite different areas of functioning. One of the scales, the California Personality Inventory [2, 5] was designed to measure folkloric ideals of social living and interaction. This inventory measures positive aspects of the personality rather than the morbid or pathological. The second scale chosen was designed to measure self-ratings of classical psychopathology (SCL 90),[1] with its questions focusing on common psychopathological symptoms.

On all scales used the responses of the hyperactive adults were compared to those of normal matched control subjects.

METHOD

Seventy-five hyperactive subjects and 44 normal matched controls were the

---

Table I

BACKGROUND VARIABLES OF CONTROL (N=44) AND HYPERACTIVE (N=75) SUBJECTS

VARIABLE	CONTROLS	HYPERACTIVES
Age	19.0 (17–24) [a]	19.5 (17–24)
Socioeconomic class [b]	3.4 (1–5)	3.4 (1–5)
WAIS IQ	108.1 (87–129)	105.0 (89–136)

[a] Mean figures are given, with range in parentheses.
[b] Hollingshead scale.

---

subjects of a comprehensive ten-to-thirteen-year follow-up study, of which this study forms one part. The two groups were matched with respect to age (17 to 24 years), socioeconomic class, and sex. However, as indicated in TABLE 1, hyperactive subjects tended to have slightly lower scores on the Wechsler Adult Intelligence Scale.

The hyperactive subjects had previously participated in acute drug studies at the age of six to twelve years [3, 4] and in five-year follow-up studies at the age of eleven to sixteen years.[7, 8, 9] Of an initial 106 children, 91 were traced for the five-year follow-up and 76 of the latter were traced for the ten- to- thirteen year follow-up evaluation. One subject was excluded from the study for the purpose of matching. Children were originally admitted into the study if they met the following criteria: 1) restlessness and poor concentration were the chief complaints, and had been present since the earliest years; 2) the complaints were a major source of worry both at home and at school; 3) all children had IQ scores (WISC) above 85; 4) none of the children was psychotic, borderline psychotic, epileptic, or had cerebral palsy; and 5) all children were living at home with at least one parent.

Ten of the hyperactive subjects had received 25 or more sessions of individual psychotherapy or family therapy. The remainder of the group had received ten to 25 interviews over five years for crisis intervention, general follow-up, management or regulation of medication. The hyperactive subjects had received various lengths and types of drug treatment including no drugs (32 subjects), chlorpromazine (27 subjects), dextroamphetamine (6 subjects) and a mixture of drugs (9 subjects). None had received methylphenidate.

The majority of the control subjects were selected in 1968 at the time of the five-year follow-up study. Notices were posted on three high school bulletin boards asking for male volunteers who were willing to do some pencil and paper tasks and talk with a psychiatrist. Payment was offered for each visit. Criteria for selection of normal controls included: 1) no grades failed, and 2) both parents and teachers reporting that their child had no significant behavioral or emotional problems. Subjects were included in the study if they met the above criteria and matched with the hyperactive group on age, sex, IQ and economic class. The three high schools were selected to represent a cross-section of socioeconomic class. At the time of the 10-year follow-up study, in order to enlarge the control group, ten additional control subjects were chosen (by asking controls if they knew people at work or at school) using the same inclusion criteria as before. One control subject was excluded from the study for the purpose of matching.

Rating Scales
Sent to Schools and Employers

Two hyperactive subjects did not give permission for us to send questionnaires to their school. A few schools, even after several telephone calls, failed to return the questionnaires. Altogether, 38 out of 44 controls and 39 out of 64 hyperactives living in Montreal had school questionnaires returned. (The lower percentage of returned forms from the hyperactive group represents the wider range of schools attended by this group, several of which did not return the form. The controls all came from three high schools whose principals knew about the study and were very cooperative.

Teachers were asked to base the questionnaire on the last grade completed by the subjects. The questionnaires sent to high schools and to employers contained the same seven questions: 1) "Is he punctual?", 2) "Does he fulfill his assigned work adequately?", 3) Does he get along well with his teacher or supervisor?", 4) Does he get along well with peers (or coworkers)?", 5) "Can he work independently?", 6) "Can he complete tasks?", and 7) "Would you hire him again (or, Would his teacher enjoy having him in class again)?" The school questionnaire contained two additional questions ("How does he compare to others his age with respect to mathematical ability?" and "How does he compare in language and literature ability?"). Each question was rated on a five-point scale.

Rating scales were sent to employers of subjects who had worked long enough to be well known to them. This ruled out several subjects in each group who were attending school and had only had summer jobs. However, summer jobs were included if the subject felt his employer knew him and his work well, and if he had held the same job over two summers. Forms from employers were returned more faithfully than were those from the schools; completed forms were received for 31 out of 37 hyper-

active subjects and 24 out of 26 control subjects. Five hyperactive subjects did not give us consent to send questionnaires to their employers. They felt that it might "label them" as abnormal even though the letter to the employer indicated that this was "a study on normal young adults." None of the controls refused consent.

For all comparisons between the two groups on employer and school questionnaires, the groups were matched on age, socioeconomic class, and sex. There was a trend for the IQ of the hyperactive group to be lower (the same trend noted previously for the total subject groups).

A separate analysis was performed for 21 control subjects and nineteen hyperactive subjects who had both school and employer questionnaires returned. Analyses were also carried out as to whether hyperactive subjects were scored better on employers' than on teachers' questionnaires, and the same analyses were done for the control subjects. Data were analyzed via analysis of variance.

Self-Rating Scales

California Personality Inventory.[2, 5] This scale is made up of 481 questions to be completed by each subject. The questions are grouped into eighteen standard scales, such as self-control, sense of well being, and so on. The inventory took between 45 and 90 minutes for subjects to complete. Forty-three control and 51 hyperactive subjects completed the inventory. The lower percentage of hyperactives completing the forms reflected the difficulty some hyperactives had in completing what they felt was a tedious task. Several gave up in the middle and a few were willing to complete the inventory only if the psychiatrist helped the subject by asking the questions and recording their answers. One hyperactive subject returned the completed form to us two years later, too late for the analysis!

SCL 90.[1] Nearly all subjects from both groups completed this self-rating scale, originally designed to measure type and degree of psychopathology of psychiatric adult outpatients. The scale was standardized on a normal population, but in our study we used our own matched control groups, since the age group was a young one. Items on this scale include somatization, obsessive behavior, compulsive behavior, interpersonal relationships, sensitivity, depression, anxiety, hostility, phobic anxiety, paranoid ideation, and psychoticism.

RESULTS

School and employer questionnaires. When all of the questionnaires returned were analyzed, hyperactive subjects scored significantly lower than normal controls on all nine questions and on total score on the school questionnaire. On the employer questionnaire, there were no significant differences in scores on any of the seven questions or on the total score.

When the scores of the nineteen hyperactive subjects and 21 controls for whom *both* forms were returned were analyzed separately, the hyperactive group scored significantly lower than the control group on six of the seven behavioral questions (getting along with classmates was the lone exception). On the employer questionnaire, none of the items differentiated significantly between the hyperactive and control groups.

scored significantly higher by the control group than by the hyperactive group. None of the items on the SCL 90 scale of psychopathology differentiated significantly between hyperactive and control subjects.

DISCUSSION

The marked discrepancy between the teacher and the employer questionnaires, which tapped seven identical items, is of great interest. Hyperactive adults were seen by employers to function as competently at work as normal matched controls. In contrast, teachers saw the hyperactives (during their last year of high school) as being significantly inferior to normal matched controls. This suggests that, for hyperactive subjects, the setting in which they are working or learning may determine the extent to which they are viewed as competent. Obviously, hyperactive subjects can do well in one setting and badly in another. The finding that hyperactive subjects are rated differently in different settings was also observed by Langhorne *et al,*[4] who performed factor analytic studies using widely agreed upon measures of the core symptoms of hyper-

Table 2

COMPARISON OF MEAN RATINGS OF HYPERACTIVE SUBJECTS (N=19) BY TEACHERS AND BY EMPLOYERS

QUESTIONNAIRE ITEM	SCHOOL	EMPLOYER	T VALUE	SIGNIFICANCE
Punctuality	3.36	4.12	2.28	p<.04
Fulfills assigned work	2.63	4.32	6.95	p<.01
Gets along with classmates/ coworkers	3.32	4.42	3.88	p<.01
Gets along with teacher/ supervisor	3.16	4.42	3.91	p<.01
Works independently	2.84	4.10	3.71	p<.01
Completes task	2.94	4.10	3.45	p<.01
Would you want him in your class again/hire him again?	2.58	4.05	3.98	p<.01
Total	20.95	29.53	5.35	p<.01

Hyperactive subjects scored significantly higher on the employer rating scale than on the teacher rating scale on all questions (see TABLE 2), while the scores of control subjects were not significantly different on six out of the seven questions asked of employers (see TABLE 3).

Self-rating scales. As indicated in TABLE 4, nine of the eighteen items on the California Personality Inventory were

kinesis in a group of 94 boys. Three stable factors accounted for 64% of the variance and each of the factors was defined mainly by variables from a particular source of information.

Possibly the many choices of types of work (versus lack of choice of schools or of activity within one school) as well as the degree of physical activity permissible (and sometimes even desirable) on the job are factors resulting in com-

Table 3

COMPARISON OF MEAN RATINGS OF CONTROL SUBJECTS (N=21) BY TEACHERS
AND BY EMPLOYERS

QUESTIONNAIRE ITEM	SCHOOL	EMPLOYER	T VALUE	SIGNIFICANCE
Punctuality	3.95	4.00	0.18	NS
Fulfills assigned work	3.57	4.14	2.03	p<.06
Gets along with classmates/ coworkers	3.76	4.14	1.71	NS
Gets along with teacher/ supervisor	4.19	4.42	1.00	NS
Works independently	3.52	3.76	0.79	NS
Completes task	3.57	4.04	1.69	NS
Would you want him in your class again/hire him again?	3.81	4.19	1.22	NS
Total	26.38	28.71	1.60	NS

petence in one situation and not in the other. In the school situation, the demands made of students which result in success tap some of the qualities that are weakest among hyperactives (*e.g.,* concentration, neatness, memorization, prolonged sedentary activity, prolonged listening, reflective cognitive style, and enjoyment of academic pursuits), whereas, on the job, other kinds of qualities (*e.g.,* capacity for hard physical work, general energy level), may be required for success. In addition, if a hyperactive subject does not get along with his employer, he can change his job and keep changing until he finds one that suits him. This is not possible in the school situation.

In an earlier paper,[9] it was noted that the job status (as measured on the Hollingshead Scale) does not differentiate between the hyperactive and control groups, indicating that at least at the age groups of the subjects (17 to 24) the jobs of the hyperactive subjects were not inferior to the jobs of normal matched control subjects.

With respect to the school questionnaires, it is unfortunate that many from the hyperactive group were not returned to us. Naturally the question must be asked whether this produced a bias in the results. School questionnaires were returned for 69% of the hyperactive subjects and 88% of the control subjects. Can we be sure that this is a random sample of the hyperactive group? It is likely that the reason for this differential return rate resulted from the hyperactive subjects attending many different high schools, several of which failed to return the forms even when telephoned several times. The control group, however, came from only three high schools (chosen to represent different economic classes for the purpose of matching). These three schools had already cooperated with us in allowing requests for volunteers to be posted on their bulletin boards. Because they

Table 4

CONTROL (N=43) AND HYPERACTIVE (N=51) SUBJECTS' SELF-RATINGS (MEAN SCORES)
ON CALIFORNIA PERSONALITY INVENTORY

ITEM	CONTROLS	HYPERACTIVES	ITEM	CONTROLS	HYPERACTIVES
Dominance	44.0	42.8	Good impressions	43.2	39.0**
Capacity for status	42.1	33.9	Communality	45.0	39.9*
Social ability	45.0	39.9	Achievement		
Social presence	49.9	52.0	(conformance)	40.2	35.2**
Self acceptance	52.1	51.7	Achievement		
Sense of well being	41.6	32.1†	(independence)	48.3	43.8**
Responsibility	38.2	32.1†	Intellectual efficiency	42.5	36.4***
Socialization	44.5	35.3†	Psychological mindedness	50.9	47.3
Self control	44.2	39.0***	Flexibility	55.6	55.6
Tolerance	40.7	37.0	Femininity/masculinity	50.6	49.1

* p<0.08 (trend); ** p<0.03; *** p<0.02; †<0.01.

knew about our study, they were more conscientious in filling out forms when requested. If an actual bias operated within the hyperactive group affecting the return of questionnaires, it is likely that it would be towards the poorer subjects not having their forms returned, in which case the strength of our findings would have been increased. Hyperactive and control subjects who had school and employer questionnaires returned were not significantly different within their respective total groups in mean age, IQ, sex, or economic class.

Forms were returned by most employers for both groups, and there is no difference between the groups in the percentage of forms returned by employers. We hope our finding that hyperactive adults are rated more competent at work than in high school, and that in the work situation they are rated the same by their employers as are normal control subjects, will be confirmed by others, so that a higher level of confidence can be placed in this finding. Further studies to determine whether hyperactives and controls differ with respect to duration of particular jobs and type of employment chosen are currently being conducted by us.

The discrepancy between the results of the two self-rating scales is relevant to understanding the kind of problems experienced by hyperactives as young adults. They do not score themselves as more pathological in the traditional psychiatric sense than do normal subjects. However, on more subtle questions relating to society's ideals of social interaction, self-esteem, and competence, they see themselves as inferior to normal matched controls. (The California Personality Inventory, designed to measure "folkloric ideals of social living and interaction,"[2] was a most sensitive instrument in distinguishing hyperactive adults from normal controls.) Hyperactive subjects, then, see themselves as socializing and interacting with others less well and feel less positive about their own personality strengths, but do not see themselves as having more psychopathological problems than do normal subjects. To further clarify this finding we are investigating self-esteem and social skills in a subgroup of hyperactives and matched controls.

These findings are supported by the psychiatric evaluation of these same subjects. Hyperactive subjects had more car accidents than normal controls, moved more frequently, and had a higher incidence of impulsive or immature personality traits. However, only a small minority had become chronic offenders of the law or seriously emotionally disturbed.[10]

REFERENCES

1. DEROGATIS, L., LIPMAN, R. AND LOVI, L. 1973. An outpatient psychiatric rating scale: preliminary report. Psychopharmacol. Bull. 9(1).
2. GOUGH, H. 1957. California Personality Inventory. Consulting Psychologists Press, Palo Alto, Calif. (revised 1975)
3. HECHTMAN, L. ET AL. 1976. Hyperactives as young adults: preliminary report. Canad. Med. Assoc. J. 115:625–630.
4. LANGHORNE, J., JR. AND LOVEY, J. 1976. Childhood hyperkinesis: a return to the source. J. Abnorm. Psychol. 85:201–209.
5. MEGARGEE, E. 1972. The California Psychological Inventory Handbook. Josey-Bass, Palo Alto, Calif.
6. MENDELSON, W., JOHNSON, N. AND STEWART, M. 1971. Hyperactive children as teenagers: a follow-up study. J. Nerv. Ment. Dis. 153:273–279.
7. MINDE, K., WEISS, G. AND MENDELSON, N. 1972. A five year follow-up study of 91 hyperactive children. J. Amer. Acad. Child Psychiat. 11:595–610.
8. MINDE, K. ET AL. 1971. The hyperactive child in elementary school: a five-year controlled follow-up. Except. Child. 38:215–221.
9. WEISS, G. ET AL. 1971. Studies on the hyperactive child, VIII: five year follow-up. Arch. Gen. Psychiat. 24:409–414.
10. WEISS, G. ET AL. 1978. Hyperactive children as young adults: a controlled prospective 10 year follow-up of the psychiatric status of 75 hyperactive children. (in press)

Adult

Depression is a major cause of maladaptive behavior in adults. It causes anxiety, tension, delinquent acts, alcoholism and or drug abuse. The changing nature of society has contributed to women suffering from depression and one of its consequences-alcoholism.

When women began to compete in the "man's working world", the man's warning system of excess tension-ulcers-began showing up more and more often in women. Women now not only do a man's job, but also retain the traditional role of mother and housekeeper. These two full time jobs cause many women to turn to alcohol as a relief. It is a socially acceptable crutch for women to turn to. No one condemns the divorced mother of two who is trying to juggle a career, motherhood and a social life for having a "few" drinks to unwind. Unfortunately, more of these women (happily married women whose husbands don't want "my wife" to work are not exempt from alcoholism) are not stopping at a "few", and are becoming alcoholics. They are beset with anxiety and are seeking relief; very likely they will deny their condition and resist efforts to get treatment.

Another coping mechanism, which has been endorsed by doctors and is therefore quite acceptable in adults, is drugs. Psychotropic drugs work in the human brain to alter our moods and change our behaviors. These same drugs can cause increased anxiety and addiction. Recent research reported in this section unveils Dr. Sol Synder's work. He has found and photographed something in our brains that looks and acts like opium.

The use of psychoactive drugs is very common with the elderly. The articles in this section provide other less drastic measures that can help alleviate the mental anguish of the elderly. Research has shown that many times senility is neither psychological nor is it biochemical. Senility can be caused by the minor loss of faculties, - the individual is not really aware that they are not hearing whole conversations - and the slowing down of reflexes, including thinking skills; in these cases senility is appropriate coping.

The Special Problems of Women Alcoholics

*Alcoholism used to be a "man's disease."
Now there are more than two million female
problem drinkers, and their numbers
are rising. Why? And can anything
be done to meet their unique needs?*

JAMES H. WINCHESTER

A HOUSEWIFE AND MOTHER in Mississippi comes out of a mental blackout to realize with horror that she is driving the family car around the countryside with her three small children in the back seat. A middle-aged Kansas City woman sits every day at the shadowy end of the neighborhood bar. A ten-year-old Texas boy arrives home from school to find his mother passed out on the kitchen floor.

These joyless and lamentable women live in the world of the alcoholic, a world increasingly shared with other females. Consider:

• In the last 20 years, the number of women in the United States who drink alcoholic beverages has increased greatly. A 1958 Gallup survey reported that 55 percent of American females drank; a 1976 study indicated that the percentage had risen to 71.

• According to a 1974 survey, women were accounting for one out of every three new members of Alcoholics Anonymous. In 1971, the ratio was only one out of four.

• The National Institute on Alcohol Abuse and Alcoholism (NIAAA) now estimates that one out of every 30 women in the United States—at between two and three million in all, more than the total populations of Idaho, Nevada and Montana—is an active alcoholic.

Why are so many women drinking? Experts cite a number of factors:

Women, more than men, pinpoint a specific, distressing situation as the source of their alcoholism—the death of a loved one, divorce, grown children leaving home, obstetrical and gynecological problems, mastectomy, even the menstrual cycle.

As husbands move forward in life, many women feel left out, and their drinking shifts from social to compulsive. Marianne Brickley, who was once married to the lieutenant governor of Michigan and is the mother of six, told a meeting of the National Council on Alcoholism: "A man calls his wife 'the little woman,' and too often that is exactly the way she feels. While my husband was climbing his political ladder to success, the only changing I did was of diapers. Trying to ease my frustrations, I graduated from beer to martinis. I became an alcoholic."

Other women take up heavy drinking out of a need to make themselves feel more feminine. Says

The Special Problems of Women Alcoholics, James H. Winchester, *Reader's Digest*, Vol. 112, No. 671, March 1978. ©1978 by the Readers Digest Association, Inc.

Sharon Wilsnack, adjunct assistant professor of psychology at the University of Indiana: "Many alcoholic women have a fragile sense of their adequacy as women. They drink to gain heightened feelings of womanliness. The tragedy, of course, is that the typical consequences of heavy drinking—neglect of appearance, reduced ability to meet the demands of home or work, disapproval of friends and family—eventually make her feel less of a woman, causing her to drink even more heavily."

Many other kinds of frustration cause women to turn to alcohol as an outlet: A young wife grieving over her inability to have children; a doctor with her nerves tensed by the life-and-death decisions she has to make; a schoolteacher needing a morning pickup before facing her charges. Nearly 4.8 million families in the United States today are headed by single women who have children to raise, homes to run and, for many, full-time jobs. Says one of these caught-in-a-trap solo parents: "Try being a 27-year-old with no husband, three kids, and a job that doesn't even begin to pay the bills. Maybe you would drink, too!"

As more and more women turn to drink, there is a growing (and long-overdue) recognition that women alcoholics are special people with special needs. Says Sharon Wilsnack: "Women alcoholics differ so significantly from men that their drinking problems might almost be considered a separate illness." For example, studies have indicated that women alcoholics may have a greater vulnerability than men to liver diseases resulting from prolonged alcohol abuse and that they may run a higher risk of pneumonia. Their alcohol consumption compounds the problems of miscarriages and difficulties in conception, and increases the incidence of hysterectomies.

Forty-four percent of the offspring of chronically alcoholic women have serious problems in development, according to well-documented scientific findings reported last year. These include mental retardation, physical deformities, stunted growth, and eye defects. Warns Dr. Joseph R. Cruse, an obstetrician-gynecologist at the University of Southern California: "The only 100-

percent-safe course for a pregnant woman is to abstain."

Alcohol affects women more during the days immediately prior to menstruation than during the remainder of the monthly cycle, and women taking oral contraceptives metabolize alcohol more slowly than those not on the pill. This means that women taking oral contraceptives will probably become intoxicated faster and remain drunk longer.

All these problems are made still worse by the fact that many doctors misdiagnose a woman's alcoholism as "nerves" or depression. Thus treatment may be only a tranquilizer, which complicates an already serious situation. Consider the case of a 36-year-old recovered alcoholic.

"I was having husband problems," she told me. "My nerves were at a breaking point. On a doctor's advice I started having a drink before bedtime every night to help me relax, and it wasn't long before I was also drinking in the daytime. Liquor was my friend. It didn't talk back.

"I was still tense, though, and another doctor prescribed tranquilizers. I started taking two or three at a time and washing them down with beer or whiskey. One night I went into a coma, was taken to a hospital, and didn't regain consciousness for two days. It was a close thing."

The problem of alcoholism for the working woman is compounded to a large degree by employer attitudes. Although most experts agree that the percentage of women alcoholics in the work force is rising, only a few of the larger companies and major unions recognize this trend. Indeed, surveys of occupational alcoholism programs in New York State show that less than ten percent of all employe referrals to company or union-run rehabilitation programs are women.

"It's the old double standard," says Karen Zuckerman, labor liaison for New York State's Division of Alcoholism. "Alcoholism as a problem at work first has to be recognized by a supervisor, most likely a man. He can spot job performance in a woman which is adversely affected by drinking easily enough, but he may feel uneasy about confronting her. Too often, he sweeps it under the rug as 'women's problems.' "

There is today, however, a growing awareness in business and industry that early detection and help are needed as much for women alcoholics as they are for men. Treatment programs designed just for women are opening, and results from previous programs indicate that at least 70 percent of all women getting such help will eventually return to productive work.

Still, on a nationwide basis the lack of understanding of the problems of women alcoholics remains scandalous. For example, the Department of Health, Education and Welfare funds 540 alcoholic rehabilitation programs in the United States, but only 17 of them are specifically for women. And since the great majority of studies on alcoholism are still all-male, most women alcoholics, despite their special problems, are treated the same as men.

As the scope of this problem becomes more apparent, attempts to help *are* increasing. Task forces in 49 states are now working to develop special research, education and treatment programs on alcoholism geared exclusively to women. Private groups are also being formed. One of them is the non-profit Women for Sobriety, with headquarters in Quakertown, Pa., and 100 chapters in 40 states. At Family House, a residential facility in Norristown, Pa., mothers can keep their children with them while they get treatment for their alcoholism.

Many more such treatment centers are needed to meet the unique needs of women alcoholics. Better training of physicians and social workers in recognizing women alcoholics and their unique problems is another priority. Says the NIAAA:

"A woman alcoholic is today most likely to seek help for such difficulties as marital instability, depression, physical ailments or financial troubles. She will make the rounds of marriage counselors, child-guidance clinics, clergymen and doctors, none of whom is likely to identify her real problem, which is the abuse of alcohol. Instead, she is referred from agency to agency, from professional to professional, never getting the kind of help she really needs. It's time this sad situation was changed."

Children's reactions to mental illness in the family

Jane S. Sturges

The idiosyncratic role a child assumes when a mentally
ill family member is hospitalized reflects the family's
interaction and indicates how it deals with stress

Jane S. Sturges, M.S.W., is assistant professor of
social work in psychiatry, Yale University
School of Medicine, New Haven, Connecticut,
and is in private practice. This article
is based on a paper presented at the
Twenty-ninth Annual Meeting of the American
Association of Psychiatric Services for Children,
Washington, D.C., 17 November 1977.

The mental illness and the resulting
hospitalization of a family member is a major
crisis that creates stress for all members of
the family, but children are especially
vulnerable. As in any crisis, every adult and
child experiences and reacts to the stress from
their own perspective and in their own individual way, often producing changes in in-
teractional patterns within the family.
Although general family reactions to the
mental illness of a relative have been widely
covered in the literature,[1] little has been
written about specific reactions of children.[2]

Knowledge of children's varied reactions to
mental illness in the family can lead to a
better understanding of adaptive and
maladaptive ways in which children react to
stress.

The reaction of the family as a whole to the
stress of physical and mental illness has been
described by E. James Anthony and J. P.
Spiegal in terms of role theory.[3] When a
member of the family becomes ill he assumes
a sick role, affecting his capacity to function
in his usual family role. Subsequently, role
expectations for other family members may
become unclear, creating what Anthony
refers to as a disruption in the complemen-
tarity of adult and child roles in the family.[4]
There may be shifts in performance of
traditional family roles and adoption of what
family theorists have termed "idiosyncratic"

[1]Delores E. Kreisman and Virginia D. Joy, "Family
Response to the Mental Illness of a Relative:
A Review of the Literature," *Schizophrenia
Bulletin* 10 (Fall 1974): 34-57; and Margaret E.
Raymond, Andrew E. Slaby, and Julian Lieb,
"Familial Responses to Mental Illness," SOCIAL
CASEWORK 56 (October 1975):492-98.

[2]E. James Anthony, "The Influence of a Manic-
Depressive Environment on the Developing Child,"
in *Depression and Human Existence*, ed. E. James
Anthony and Therese Benedek (Boston: Little,
Brown and Co., 1975), pp. 279-315; E. James
Anthony, "Mourning and Psychic Loss of the

Parent," in *The Child in His Family*, vol. 2, ed.
E. James Anthony and Cyrille Koupernik (New York:
John Wiley and Sons, 1973), pp. 255-64; E. James
Anthony, "The Mutative Impact of Serious Mental
and Physical Illness in a Parent on Family Life,"
Canadian Psychiatric Association Journal 14 (October
1969): 433-53; and Jane S. Sturges, "Talking with
Children about Mental Illness in the Family," *Health
and Social Work* 2 (August 1977): 88-109.

[3]Anthony, "The Mutative Impact," pp. 433-53; J.
P. Spiegal, "The Resolution of Role Conflict
Within the Family," in *The Patient and the Mental
Hospital,* ed. Milton Greenblatt, Daniel J. Levinson,
and Richard H. Williams (Glencoe, Ill.: Free Press,
1957), pp.1-16.

[4]Anthony, "The Mutative Impact," pp. 433-53.

roles in attempts to maintain psychological equilibrium within the family system during the stressful period.[5]

This article discusses children's reactions to mental illness in a family member in terms of effects on and changes in children's role performance within the context of the family. The descriptive material presented represents four years' work in assessing 150 children and families at the time of the psychiatric hospitalization of a family member.

Roles

A clarification of the meaning of roles, both traditional and idiosyncratic, follows. Role is defined as behavior connected to a position in the family or in society.[6] The role a person learns to play in relation to the social world not only determines his evaluation of and behavior toward others but also influences the way in which he evaluates and behaves toward himself.[7] The evaluation of the quality of role performance has been found to be an important measure in the psychiatric and social assessment of an individual and in the social diagnosis of a family.[8]

Generally defined and accepted traditional family roles are those of mother, father, wife, son, daughter, worker, student, and child. The traditional roles of the child include those of son or daughter, brother or sister, grandson or granddaughter, student, and friend. Although these roles are not always clearcut, and vary from family to family in relation to individual family styles and cultural and socioeconomic factors, there is a broad area of agreement regarding them. In general, the child who functions adequately in traditional roles maintains close ties to family members and participates in household duties and family life. As students they attend school regularly with a positive attitude and participate in academic and school activities that approximate their abilities. Acting out behavior at school is limited to occasional pranks. They are generally liked as a friend, have friends and participate in the activities of one or more peer groups with minimal conflict.[9] During adolescence, the child's role is to differentiate himself gradually from his parents through investing more of his energy into peer group and heterosexual relationships and initiating adult role activities, such as driving a car, working, and assuming more responsibility for his lifestyle. How the child functions in traditional roles is influenced by family members and is a determining factor in the process and outcome of his psychosocial development.

Idiosyncratic roles enacted by family members deviate from, although intermesh with, traditional roles, so that each family member functions within a cluster of roles.[10] Idiosyncratic roles are behavioral expressions of patterns of interaction within a family which serve to meet varied psychic needs of individuals and the family as a whole. Examples of terms used by family members and family theorists to describe idiosyncratic roles are good child, binder, spokesperson, peacemaker, and scapegoat.[11]

The enactment of idiosyncratic roles in conjunction with performance of traditional roles represents transactions of family members in the reciprocal processes of conscious and unconscious expectations and behavior reinforcements that all family systems impose on their members.[12] From a psychoanalytic and family systems viewpoint Horace E. Richter sees role performance as complex psychosocial defense formulations analogous to the classical intrapsychic defense mechanisms delineated by Anna Freud: the bestowing and accepting of various roles among family members serving to free them from the tension of their own inner conflicts.[13] As with intrapsychic defense

---

[5] Leopold Chagoya and H. A. Gutterman, "A Guide to Assess Family Functioning," mimeographed (Montreal: Jewish General Hospital, July 1971); Norman B. Epstein, J. J. Sigal, and V. M. Rakoff, "Family Categories Schema," mimeographed (Montreal: Family Research Group of Department of Psychiatry, Jewish General Hospital, 1968); and Sidney Lecker, "Family Therapies," in *The Therapist's Handbook,* ed. Benjamin B. Wolman (New York: Van Nostrand Reinhold, 1976), pp. 184-98.

[6] Herman Borenzweig, "Role Enactment: A Social Work Method for Inducing Behavior Change," *Clinical Social Work Journal* 2 (Spring 1974): 15-28; and Herbert S. Strean, "Role Theory, Role Models, and Casework: Review of the Literature and Practice Applications," *Social Work* 12 (April 1967):77-88.

[7] Kaoru Yamamoto, ed., *The Child and His Image* (Boston: Houghton Mifflin, 1972).

[8] Helen H. Perlman, *Persona* (Chicago: University of Chicago Press, 1968); Robert L. Spitzer, Jean Endicott, Joseph L. Fleiss, and Jacob Cohen, *Psychiatric Status Schedule* (New York: State Department of Mental Hygiene, 1968); Chagoya and Gutterman, *Guide to Assess;* Epstein, Sigal, and Rakoff, "Family Categories Schema"; and Yamamoto, *Child and His Image.*

[9] Ludwig L. Geismar and Beverly Ayres, *Measuring Family Functioning* (St. Paul, Minn.: Family Centered Project, Greater St. Paul Community Chest and Councils, 1960), pp. 99-100.

[10] Lecker, "Family Therapies," pp. 184-98.

[11] Chagoya and Gutterman, *Guide to Assess;* and Epstein, Sigal, and Rakoff, "Family Categories Schema."

[12] Spiegal, "Resolution of Role Conflict," pp. 1-16.

[13] Horace E. Richter, *The Family as Patient* (New York: Farrar, Strauss and Giroux, 1974); and Anna Freud, *The Ego and the Mechanisms of Defense* (New York: International Universities Press, 1946).

mechanisms, roles, viewed as psychosocial forms of defense, can be adaptive or maladaptive in handling anxiety and coping with stress. For example, parents may be supportive of a child's performance in traditional roles or, because of their own conflicts and unmet psychic needs, may project onto the child images and role expectations that interfere with socially desirable role performance. In addition, the imposing of idiosyncratic roles and the subsequent enactment of those roles by children may be in the interest of healthy family functioning and normal child development or may be the result of, or play a part in, the development of psychopathology in the family and in the child.

Study and evaluation of role performance

The following method was used to evaluate the role performance of children during the hospitalization of the child's parent or adolescent sibling in an adult psychiatric inpatient unit.

1. In-depth interviews were conducted with the healthy parent or parents, and sometimes extended family members, in regard to the child's functioning at home, school, work, and in relationship to his family members, teachers, and peers.
2. Children in the family were interviewed individually or in sibling groups, as well as observed in their interactions in individual family therapy and multiple family therapy.
3. Nurses' observations of children's visits with the hospitalized family member were recorded.
4. Schools and agencies involved with the family were contacted.

No attempt was made to quantify the data; the intention was only to obtain descriptive material on role relationships and role changes. Of particular interest were the idiosyncratic roles played by the children at the time of the mental illness and hospitalization of their family member and how these roles fit into the operation of the family as a system.

Children's idiosyncratic role performances

The idiosyncratic roles played by the children studied can be classified under the following descriptive labels: caretaker, baby, patient, mourner, recluse, escapee, good child, and bad child.

Caretaker

It is often the oldest daughter, or the only child in the family, who assumes the caretaker role or has this role imposed on him or her by other members of the family. The child in this role tries to provide nurturing for the hospitalized family member, as well as for family members at home. In hospital visits the child is observed reassuring the patient, offering encouragement to get enough rest and to take their medication. In the case of hospitalization of the mother, the caretaker child may substitute for the absent mother and wife at home in terms of taking over household responsibilities, caring for younger children, and becoming father's confidant. In the case of the hospitalization of a sibling, the caretaker child may attempt to provide nurturance and extra help for the mother at home. The other family members may impose this role on the child out of their need for nurturance and concrete services. On the other hand, assumption and enactment of the caretaker role by the child may, through identification with the mother, provide a feeling of security needed at the time. It may also relieve guilt over his or her part in the illness. The caretaker child's assumption of instrumental tasks may serve, as well, as a defense against feeling helpless, which has been found useful in mastery of other types of threats to families.[14] This role can become pathological in its crossing of generation boundaries within the family and in its interference with peer relations because of the age inappropriateness of the role played.

The following illustrates an adolescent assuming the caretaker role:

Jonathan is an articulate, sensitive, fifteen-year-old boy, who appears several years older than his chronological age. He is the third of five children in his family; the older two of his siblings are schizophrenic. He was nervous during the first interview with the social worker on the unit where his twenty-year-old sister was hospitalized. He smoked continually and hyperventilated at times. Jonathan described a chaotic situation at home, in which his twenty-one-year-old brother had recently made a suicide attempt. His parents' long-standing marital conflict had escalated because of the problems of their two mentally ill children. Jonathan talked of his parents' inability to set limits for any of their children. As a result, he assumed the role of father in the family. He described trying to discipline his younger siblings, to modify the behavior of his psychotic brother and sister, and to make family decisions. A friend had said to him that he seemed "like fifteen years old going on thirty." Jonathan said that that was the way he felt. He talked wistfully of parents of a friend "who acted like parents instead of children." Clearly, Jonathan served the family's need for a caretaker. He appeared conflicted about

[14]Edward H. Futterman, "Studies of Family Adaptational Responses to a Specific Threat," in *Explorations in Child Psychiatry*, ed. E. James Anthony (New York: Plenum Press, 1975), pp. 287-301.

playing the role, finding some satisfaction in helping, while needing to escape from an extremely chaotic family in order to function in the normal roles of an adolescent.

Baby

At the other extreme is the child who assumes the role of the baby. This role is most often taken on by a younger child. In this role the child may regress to a clinging, whining, demanding state. Enuresis or encopresis may occur. The child may become fearful of going to school and of playing with friends. He or she may develop nightmares and terrors and may want to sleep with a parent or a sibling. Infantilization of the child may be imposed by the sick sibling or mother out of guilt, or by other family members in an attempt to take the sick mother's place. In turn, the child's behavior may serve a need for extra attention when the family and child are under stress. If temporary, this regression to the baby role can be in service of the child's ego; if chronic, it can affect school performance, relationship with family members and peers, and psychosocial development.

Mourner

The child in this role demonstrates excessive and prolonged grief over separation from the ill parent or sibling. The child may cry a great deal and refuse to eat. This role appears to be most common in younger children of mentally ill mothers, who may go through stages of protest and despair, with detachment from the mother by the time of her discharge from the hospital.[15] Some degree of open grieving for a sick family member is appropriate and beneficial psychologically. In the presence of chronic disability in the mother, however, the child's mourning may never be completed and lead to chronic depression. In the mourner's role the child may be expressing grief for the entire family, some members of which are suppressing their feelings of abandonment and loss.

Billy, for example, adopted the roles of baby and mourner:

Billy, age four, adopted the role of baby and mourner in the family when his mother was hospitalized for depression. He became fearful at night and insisted on sleeping with his father. He ate very little and lost several pounds in a short period of time. He would no longer go out in the yard to play; he followed his unemployed father from room to room in the house. In early hospital visits Billy clung to his mother and threw a tantrum when it was time to leave. In later visits he

would cry softly. By the time his mother was well enough to take passes home, he ignored her, pushing her away when she tried to be affectionate, in turn seeking out his father.

Patient

The child in this role may develop somatic symptoms, become depressed, act like the sick family member, or actually become psychotic. It may be a temporary identification with the sick sibling or parent or may reach the proportions of a folie à deux. This role may be imposed and adopted out of the child's (and family members') fantasies that incorporation of the symptoms may reduce the illness in the patient or reunite the child with the family member experienced as psychically lost because of the illness.[16] Although this role can be temporarily adaptive for the child, clearly it will be maladaptive if the symptoms are severe and persist for a long period of time. For example,

Susie is a shy, pretty twelve-year-old girl whose mother was hospitalized for psychotic depression. Susie's mother was mute in her presence, but was verbally abusive to Susie's father because she had delusions that he was seeing another woman. Susie's mother also had the delusion that she had cancer, although it was her sister who had actually had a recent mastectomy. During her mother's illness Susie had trouble concentrating at school and stopped seeing her friends. She complained to her father of severe headaches, which was one of her mother's symptoms. Hesitantly, she asked her father some questions about sex and told him that she thought she had a lump in her breast. In the past, Susie had been close to her mother but distant from her father. Her assumption of the patient role at home during her mother's illness, while interfering temporarily with her functioning at school and at home, secured for her the attention she needed from her father. He, in turn, found satisfaction in helping her at a time when he felt helpless to do anything about his wife's illness.

Escapee

It is often the adolescent who adopts the escapist role, attempting through it to handle anxiety with overactivity and involvement in activities away from the family. These children may refuse to visit the patient or to participate in family therapy, may avoid family members as much as possible, and may even move out of the home. Family members often view the child who responds in this way as not upset by the illness. Actually, the escapee may be a prisoner emotionally, trying to get a distance from the psychopathology in the family but finding it

---

[15]Ibid.

[16]Anthony, ''Mourning and Psychic Loss,'' pp. 255-64.

difficult to do so. They may be acting out desires of other family members to deny the illness and to take flight under the stress. This role can be adaptive, in that it helps adolescents differentiate themselves from the illness and family problems, but may be maladaptive if it precipitates a premature separation from the family. For example:

Nancy, a pretty, vivacious high school senior, showed signs of tension and anger during her older sister's hospitalization for an acute schizophrenic episode. When Nancy's mother sought comfort from her as a replacement for her sick sister, with whom the mother seemed emotionally fused, Nancy stayed away from the family as much as possible. She took on two jobs after school, returning from her job as a waitress late at night, and spent spring vacation at a married sister's home in Florida. She withdrew from family therapy sessions when each parent attempted to engage her as an ally. Her temporary role as an escapee appeared to save her from the sick role her parents tried to place her in. Marital therapy for her parents freed her to resume a normal role.

Recluse

Some children withdraw from peers, school, and family. They may spend a good deal of time alone in their rooms when at home. They are embarrassed over how to answer questions about the patient's illness. Again, it is often the adolescent who assumes this role. The family's way of dealing with the illness of the patient and its feelings about the stigma attached influence the child's assumption of this role.

Good child

Some children become extremely well-behaved, no longer fighting with siblings, assuming tasks they complained about before, and making an effort to avoid controversy. Older children may become more religious. Sometimes this role is assumed in an attempt to atone for guilt, the feeling that something the child said or did caused the patient to become ill. This guilt is sometimes reinforced by other members of the family who project their own guilt onto the child, scolding him and telling him to be "good." The assumption of this role by one or more children may serve the family's need to minimize stress at home. However, it may be detrimental in that it can cause the child to suppress the emotions most children experience regarding the mental illness of a family member.[17]

---

[17]Sturges, "Talking with Children," pp. 88-109.

Bad child

Children assuming the role of bad child become openly angry, hostile, and defiant, or show aggression in more covert ways. Younger children may throw temper tantrums or fail to cooperate with work at home and in school. Adolescents may act out through use of drugs or alcohol, sexual promiscuity, or violations of the law. The behavior may serve as an attention-seeking device and is sometimes a mask for depression. The child in this role may be the scapegoat for unresolved tensions of other family members. For example:

Paul, an active nine-year-old, the second of five children, became a behavior problem during the second hospitalization of his father for a psychotic episode which had involved physical abuse to the children and the family pets. Although his older sister cheerfully helped their mother with meals and with the care of the baby, and his two younger brothers voluntarily cleaned the house, Paul was disruptive at school and at home and on two occasions threw a large rock at the car when his mother left to visit his father in the hospital. His siblings were praised for being "good, helpful children," whereas Paul became the focus of much negative attention on the part of his grandparents and mother for his "bad" behavior during his father's illness. It appeared that he was, to some extent, identifying with his father, as well as acting out anger and aggression for other members of the family who were busy taking care of things.

Discussion

Although the description of these idiosyncratic role enactments by children may sound simplistic, the varied roles played represent complex family reactions to stress, the dynamic levels of which are sometimes hard to comprehend. The intrapsychic defense mechanisms of denial, reaction formation, suppression, projection, incorporation, identification, and repression can be seen operating in the more complex psychosocial defenses, the roles enacted by family members. Children usually function in an amalgam of roles, sometimes shifting back and forth between opposite role positions, for example, caretaker and baby, prisoner and escapee. Particular roles imposed upon and enacted by the child in transaction with other family members relate to sex, sibling position in the family, temperament, physical characteristics, personality style, psychosocial phase of development, relation to the patient and other family members, severity and duration of the patient's illness, and the child's and family's previously learned ways of coping with stress.

In the interest of children potentially at risk because of the mental illness of a family member, the mental health professional in an adult psychiatric setting should take the following steps:

1. Assess the child's functioning in the traditional roles of a child.
2. Assess the idiosyncratic roles the child is assuming under stress and how this affects his functioning in traditional roles.
3. Attempt to understand the dovetailing of traditional and idiosyncratic roles within the family system and whether this is pathological or meeting the needs of the family under stress.
4. Help family members understand the child's needs and the meaning of changes in his role functioning in reaction to the illness and in relation to the role functioning of other family members.
5. Clarify for the family role changes that may be needed for healthier coping.
6. Determine which children and families need additional help and provide services as needed or refer them to appropriate agencies.

In summary, the evaluation of a child's role performance in relation to others in his family at the time of the mental illness and hospitalization of a family member can be one measure for assessing the child's capacity to deal with stress. Role flexibility within a family during a period of transition and stress can be a sign of strength,[18] just as temporary changes in the role performance of children may be adaptive in meeting the needs of child and family. However, temporary role changes can become fixed, particularly in cases of severe, chronic mental illness in the mother, and may lead to enduring, perhaps undesirable, changes in the child's personality. More investigation is needed to understand how the enactment of roles within a family system can affect the process of development of the child and of the family.

---

[18]Epstein, Sigal, and Rakoff, "Family Categories Schema," and Herbert A. Otto, "Criteria for Assessing Family Strength," *Family Process* 2 (September 1963):329-38.

Hospital Commitment and Civil Rights

PHILIP R. SULLIVAN

«Philip R. Sullivan, M. D., *is a psychiatrist presently practicing in Boston, Mass.*»

When I was growing up in Boston, we spoke of the community's state psychiatric hospital simply as "Mattapan," after the section of the city in which it was located. If a boy did something out of line, one of us would commonly say: "Send him to Mattapan!" And, in mock agony, he might then say something like: "Don't put me away!"

It was all good fun . . . sort of. But behind the humorous repartee lay a genuine awe mixed with fear of that institution and of the strangers who lived there. Even the technical language of that bygone era emphasized the deep moat between hospital and community. Doctors who examined patients to determine if "institutionalization" was necessary received the official title, "alienists." And, indeed, those persons "put away" did represent aliens in our midst. With little known in the way of effective treatment, when "the man in the white coat" came for them, their enclosure might well be permanent.

Rather quickly, we have journeyed to a different world. Medically speaking, we can now successfully treat many of the schizophrenic illnesses and most of the manic-depressive illnesses. We can prevent the irreparable brain damage of tertiary syphilis and certain other conditions.

When a modern psychiatrist considers hospitalization, he does not think, therefore, of a patient being "put away." He thinks primarily of a time-limited hospitalization with active treatment enabling, in most cases, a rapid return to the community. Commitment laws provide for involuntary hospitalization when this is necessary.

The reason commitment laws exist has to do with the nature of certain psychiatric illnesses. Take, for example, a paranoid delusional illness. A patient may be convinced that every black car with a C. B. antenna is following him to report his activities to some central command. He feels frightened, unable to attend to his daily activities, and considers desperate measures to "protect" himself.

While in this state, a person cannot be expected to admit himself to a hospital for protection and treatment. He does not and cannot see himself as sick. Hospitalization and treatment, if it is to occur, must be arranged against the patient's own judgment. And indeed he will often experience it at the time as just another part of the plot against him.

Severe depression represents another example where commitment provisions for involuntary hospitalization have been provided by law. A person in this condition may have no delusions. Rather, he feels hopeless. He suffers excruciatingly and can see no possibility of relief. Suicidal impulses come as naturally as the dusk, and the patient may see no point to hospitalization and treatment efforts. The law has provided for his protection against himself and for the treatment he feels too blackly pessimistic to pursue.

How do these commitment procedures work? The laws and regulations vary from state to state, though following a certain pattern. In Massachusetts, emergency hospitalization used to be provided on an involuntary basis by the examining doctor's signing a "pink paper." For those judged to be in need of care and treatment by reason of mental illness, this form permitted hospitalization for a period of time not to exceed 10 days. If further hospitalization was required and the patient still refused hospitalization on a voluntary basis, the court was required to make a further formal determination.

This was the situation medically and legally when I entered full-time psychiatric practice in 1961. Since that time, community consciousness has moved far in the direction of improved civil rights for all citizens. A number of issues was combined, including the imposition of hospitalization, the right to treatment *and* the right to refuse treatment. Because of space limitations, I will speak only of the first of these concerns, though all are intertwined.

Within the past several years, in response to these concerns, Massachusetts revamped its commitment pro-

Reprinted with permission of *America Press, Inc.* ©1978 by America Press. All rights reserved.

cedures. The old regulation was recognized as too vague and therefore too subject to the possibility of abuse. Now, the criteria for involuntary hospitalization are more specific. A doctor may still authorize emergency hospitalization for a period not to exceed 10 days. He must certify, however, that the patient represents a serious danger to himself or others or that he is incapable of taking care of himself in the community by virtue of mental illness. It is not sufficient in itself that a patient suffers from a mental illness needing hospital treatment.

That represents the present state of affairs. But where will the pendulum stop? Polemicists like Thomas Szasz would do away with mental illness by defining it out of existence as a myth, ironically just at a point in history when we are beginning to unravel the subtle biochemical abnormalities that underlie severe psychiatric disease.

But the pendulum's swing is not influenced solely by these theoretical extremists. Writing in The New England Journal of Medicine (Feb. 2, 1978), William J. Curran, J. D., reported on the Federal District Court's recent ruling in Hawaii on the issue of emergency commitment.

In the previous statutory standard for emergency commitment, there was a requirement that the person be found dangerous to self, to others or to property. The degree of dangerousness, as with most American statutes in this field, was not further defined. In this new case, Judge Samuel King ruled that personal-injury danger was required and the danger must be *imminent* and *substantial* as evidenced by a recent overt act, attempt or threat. Regarding the degree of dangerousness, he ruled that there must be "extreme likelihood" that the patient would do "immediate harm" before an emergency commitment could be authorized. Also, danger could not be proved by "sufficient evidence" in emergency situations. The standard to be applied was that of the criminal law: "beyond a reasonable doubt."

Now, come down from the bench and put yourself in the place of a practicing psychiatrist guided by such criteria. You see a young married woman for emergency consultation after she has superficially cut her wrist, enough to require sutures but not deeply severing tendons or arteries. Does her action issue from a psychological condition that *substantially* endangers her life and health, or does it represent a dramatic effort to manipulate her family with no real suicidal intent? The patient refuses to cooperate with psychiatric examination, remaining negativistically silent. Does this represent a catatonic reaction of severe mental illness or a stubborn sullenness toward her husband, who has told her she should "go see a psychiatrist"?

The traditional decision of the psychiatrist in such a case might be to arrange hospitalization because sufficient evidence exists to fear serious harm to the patient. Temporary hospitalization will allow for appropriate observation and evaluation in a protected setting.

But has it been shown beyond a reasonable doubt that she represents an immediate and substantial danger to herself? Hardly! By such criteria, the psychiatrist could not arrange involuntary hospitalization in cases of this sort. A number of otherwise preventable fatalities will occur but we will all have the consolation that those patients died with their rights intact.

Another case. A 40-year-old man goes to a stranger's door in the same vicinity where a close relative lives. He leans on the bell and, when the occupant answers irritably, starts a fight. The police arrive and he gives them no explanation beyond a few hollered obscenities. His relative is contacted, who expresses concern because his cousin has not gone to work all week and has a past history of a paranoid psychotic episode. The patient will no more cooperate with the examining psychiatrist than he did with police, but hospitalization is arranged for observation and treatment on the working assumption that he has had a recurrence of his illness.

Again, this assumption hardly represents proof beyond a reasonable doubt. Using that criterion, the immediate outcome would have been jail, without treatment, on charges of assault and battery. For those who believe there is nothing new under the sun, this brings us around full circle to an earlier era in the management of the mentally ill—before concerned reformers caused laws to be enacted that provided hospitalization instead of imprisonment for the acutely mentally ill.

What should the reader make of my concerns? Some reformers appear to see psychiatrists as the enemy and would discount their opinions as self-serving. At times, psychiatrists have been depicted as fretting about the tightening of commitment laws because their "rights" are being restricted, their wings clipped.

Ironically, as the commitment regulations tighten, the psychiatrist's work is made easier. First, it lessens his responsibility to make the difficult decisions about commitment to a progressively smaller number of instances. Second, it decreases an unpleasant aspect of his work, having to care for angry patients against their will.

What parent would not be relieved, in part at least, by not having the duty to insist against his small child's wishes that it is time to turn off the television and get to bed? That represents one of the unpleasant but necessary duties of parenthood. Yet, would not the parent feel a little uneasy about being relieved of this duty/right insofar as he is genuinely concerned with his children's welfare? I would say this analogy fits the practicing psychiatrist fairly well as the pendulum seems to swing to the extreme in the matter of hospital commitment.

We have already achieved a reasonable balance between the need to protect the civil rights of the emotionally ill and the need to protect their health and welfare. We must avoid extreme rulings that will interfere with life more than protect life.

Beyond Valium

By Toby Cohen

"...Brain researchers have found new ways to stop pain, anxiety, and depression without addiction or disturbing side effects..."

"I'd have been better off to have thrown away my pills . . . and gone for a long walk whenever I was hurting. . . . I took pills for pain, I took pills to sleep, I took mild tranquilizers." This is Betty Ford on the complex addiction that was a side effect of what began as a well-meant prescription for a pain-killing drug. For a young law student forced to drop out because of crippling anxiety, the case was much the same: "After years of psychoanalysis my shrink and I agreed it was time to turn to Valium. The first two weeks I was taking it was the first time in ten years that I felt like a normal human being. I liked being with people, I felt happy. I almost cried with joy. After that, the very same drug made me more anxious than I had ever been before. I couldn't think, and I *looked* not only anxious but drugged. Go for a walk, that's about all I can do. I can't function with drugs or without them. Nothing seems to help. I might as well be dying of some awful disease."

Two dramatic testimonies to the bewildering mystery of how certain drugs —call them psychotropic, psychoactive, what you will—work in the human brain to alter our moods and change the contours of our behavior, and how the same drugs go wrong. The sale of tranquilizers in the United States tops the sale of any other prescription drug —over 350 million prescriptions for Valium are filled in a year. But the truth is until now doctors have had only the sketchiest knowledge of where, on what, and precisely how such drugs work. Many people have come to see the "cure" as far worse than the disease, a game of Russian roulette with one's psychic life.

But the mystery is lifting. Last November, three brain researchers were given the prestigious Albert Lasker Basic Medical Research Award for a discovery that sheds new light on the way the brain works and will help drug companies design a drug so specific that it will zap anxiety, pain, schizophrenia, or depression without interfering anywhere else in the brain, or causing any side effects. Solomon H. Snyder, John Hughes, and Hans W. Kosterlitz discovered that protruding from some of our brain cells like antennae are opiate receptors—little molecules that are perfectly shaped to fit an opiate molecule. They also found that the human body itself manufactures opiates that lock into these receptors to produce relaxation, pain relief, and euphoria. It's almost as though ancient Chinese medicine and our early apothecaries just lucked into this system with their poppy extract.

But there is a big and important difference: Opium from a poppy, or any of our manufactured drugs for that matter, is a very rough diamond by comparison with our own endogenous drugs. Externally derived opiates lock into our opiate receptors (see box on page 40), but they also seem to fit into all manner of other brain pathways, creating the kind of havoc and addiction that the law student and Betty Ford had to endure. Our own internal opiates, however, are so exquisitely designed that they fit only one type of receptor and serve only one purpose —relief. Imagine what would happen if our drug companies could match this design. But more of that later.

In 1971, when President Nixon made $1 billion available to "fight addiction,"

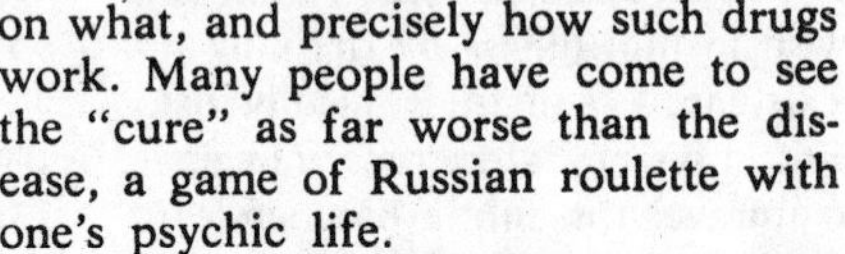

Dr. Feelgood: Once upon a time we relied upon the delicate poppy and its powerful sticky extract —opium—to take away our cares, but Dr. Sol Snyder, with his electron microscope, has found and photographed something in our brains that looks like and acts like opium. Yes, we make our own opiates. The little mouse, with many others, helped him in his work.

he fueled one of the most exciting scientific quests of this century. One million to two million dollars was for research, and Johns Hopkins was declared one of the several drug-abuse centers and would be headed by Sol Snyder.

The path Dr. Snyder pursued was logical enough. It was already thought that psychoactive drugs must work by making some very specific contact with our brain cells. In 1971, in fact, Avram Goldstein, a professor of pharmacology at the Stanford University Medical School and a longtime student of addiction, had tried unsuccessfully to find receptors in the brain for opiates. Undaunted, Snyder, with his student Candace Pert, joined the hunt. Two hours after setting up his first test tube, on October 23, 1972, Snyder knew he had found them.

But having found them, what was Snyder to make of them? Everyone knows that heroin and other opiates "work." Snyder had found *where* they work—at sockets, so to speak, in brain cells. But what on earth were those sockets doing? Obviously we were not designed by nature to ingest pain pills or to take shots of morphine. Or were we? Snyder could only conclude that our bodies themselves manufacture substances which the opiate receptors stand ready to attract and use.

The search for the body's own opiates was on, and in 1975 Drs. John Hughes and Hans W. Kosterlitz of the University of Aberdeen in Scotland discovered them. The two Scottish researchers named the short, small molecules they isolated "enkephalins," from the Greek word *"kephalé,"* meaning "head," because the head was where they found them.

No sooner had Hughes and Kosterlitz published their results, in 1975 in the journal *Nature,* than other scientists noticed that one of the enkephalins discovered by the pair was wholly contained in a protein called beta-lipotropin, which had been isolated from the pituitary gland of sheep in 1964, and then from camels in 1972, by Dr. C. H. Li of the University of California in San Francisco. Would Li's protein molecule have opiate properties too? Li found that when he injected a segment of it into the brains of laboratory animals it proved 48 times stronger than morphine.

How practical is it to treat mental illness with these animal opiates? Dr. Li's camel certainly won't do: Li used up the pituitary glands of 2,000 camels to get one milligram of the powerful substance, and at that, the substance was addictive.

What seems to be needed is a drug with a more calculated "aim" at the brain's receptors. With this we would have the most effective medication available. And it may already be here.

A few months ago at the annual conference of the Society for Neurosciences in St. Louis, Robert Frederickson, a scientist for Eli Lilly and Company, said that by rearranging the molecules of the body's own opiates the Lilly laboratories had managed to synthesize a drug whose slightly different structure fitted the brain's opiate receptors in such a way as to effect the relief of pain with substantially reduced addiction or tolerance, at least in laboratory mice. (When offered a choice of substances, mice who are not in pain will choose morphine over food. But they will pass up the Lilly drug in favor of food.) Currently, Lilly has FDA permission to test its drug in human beings to see if it is safe. If it proves non-addictive it will be marketed as a pill for relief of pain of all kinds, whether from major or minor ailments. And since the opiates are known to modify anxiety, Lilly's new pill promises relief to the millions of Americans who are debilitated or paralyzed by anxiety—relief without havoc or side effects elsewhere in the brain.

Meanwhile, Snyder has been working on another receptor that may be our brain's main anxiety switch.

It has long been known, Snyder explains, that the sympathetic nervous system—that unconscious part of us that among other things commands our "flight or fight" reactions—plays an important part in stress. It is also known that a chemical called norepinephrine is of critical importance to what goes on in our sympathetic nervous system. Briefly, this chemical locks into one or the other of two types of receptors, called alpha and beta receptors, depending on what kind of stress we are under. The beta receptors are thought to respond to emergency situations—the need, say, to flee the assault of a mugger. Alpha receptors come into play when we are under chronic, low-key stress, the kind of stress that is brought on by things like coping daily with a disapproving boss. Might a drug "aimed" at alpha receptors turn off anxiety?

Snyder decided to see whether any of the drugs currently used in psychiatry act directly at alpha receptors in the brain to somehow curb the alarms being set off there, warning of stress. He looked first at the drugs used against schizophrenia and found that some of them not only blocked the receptors involved in schizophrenia but also blocked the alpha, or chronic-stress, receptors. The beta receptors—available for emergency responses—were not affected. "In short," says Snyder, "it became apparent that drugs like Thorazine, which had the greatest calming effect, block the alpha receptors."

Next, Snyder tested the drugs used against depression, with identical results: Drugs such as Elavil, which possessed the greatest calming effect, not only blocked the receptor involved in

The poppy was the source of . . .

Illustrated by Carol Wald

all opiates, but it turns out . . .

"…These pills will usher in a new psychiatry where we think of ourselves as an orchestra of chemical voices in our heads…"

depression but were most effective in blocking the alpha receptors as well; anti-depressant drugs without tranquilizing effects, like Tofranil, blocked only receptors involved in depression.

For purposes of treating neurotic anxiety, then, the trick was to isolate the calming agents, "to manufacture," Snyder says, "a drug that blocks only the alpha receptors in the brain and leaves all other receptors, there or in the sympathetic nervous system, strictly alone. No side effects. That should not be hard."

Snyder's reasoning gains impressive support from research here and abroad on the use of an anti-hypertensive drug called Clonidine, which likewise interacts with alpha receptors to shut off the release of norepinephrine. Professor Torgny Svensson and his colleagues at Sweden's Karolinska Institute gave Clonidine to eleven patients under treatment for extreme neurotic anxiety, many of them hospitalized for years, and witnessed extraordinary recoveries: Patients who had been chronically incapacitated were suddenly capable of work and able to live with their families. At the Yale University School of Medicine, Drs. Eugene Redmond, Mark Gold, and Herbert Kleber gave Clonidine to eleven addicts in the process of withdrawing from methadone maintenance treatment—and found that it blocked their withdrawal symptoms, symptoms not unlike those of neurotic anxiety. At New York Medical College Drs. Richard Resnick and Arnold Washton are currently using Clonidine to help addicts through their withdrawal symptoms, and are so impressed by the results that they are offering free treatment to anyone who is seriously trying to get off heroin or methadone.

All of this powerfully suggests a future for drugs that are designed to lock into only the alpha receptors, thus shutting down the release of norepinephrine in the brain's alarm system, while leaving the rest of the brain alone.

Another hope for the chronically anxious may come out of the work of Richard Squires and Claus Braestrup, who within the past year have reported sites in the brain that act as Valium receptors. At the meeting of the American College of Neuropsychopharmacology in Hawaii this past December, Squires suggested that another segment of that same large molecule from the pituitary that divides to provide the enkephalin may be the brain's own Valium. If this is so, it would be a great step forward, for the natural tranquilizer could be studied, and the new drugs based on it could be better than Valium. While Valium is good at reducing anxiety and relaxing muscles, it is bad in that it also sedates, interfering with one's intellectual and reasoning powers; moreover, people using it can become addicted, requiring larger and larger doses.

Snyder points out that the bad effects of Valium occur because it acts not only at its own receptor site but also at the as yet undiscovered sites for alcohol and barbiturates, as shown by the fact that any of them will relieve the symptoms of withdrawal from each of the others. Presumably the body's own Valium would act only at its own receptor site—since that is what it is there for—and thus would do only Valium's good and none of its harm.

that the brain can do it alone.

That speculation seems to have been confirmed by the work of Squires, Arnold Lippa, Bernard Beer, and other researchers at Lederle, where in recent weeks a second Valium receptor has been isolated with characteristics slightly different from the first. Valium interacts with both receptors. With their knowledge of the molecular shape of both, the Lederle researchers were able to design a drug that locks into the Valium receptors to inhibit and relieve anxiety but does not drag in its wake the sedative and tolerance-producing effects. On the basis of its tests on animals, Lederle has applied to the FDA for permission to begin human trials with the drug.

What to make of all this brain research? For the millions of chronically anxious Americans who are in serious, desperate pain, the arrival of pills that will relieve the suffering without adverse side effects will be invaluable.

But there's more to it than that. These discoveries may eventually give rise to new brain pills so safe, so free of besetting side effects, that they will usher in a new psychiatry. Says Dr. Arnold Mandell, a professor in the department of psychiatry at the University of California at San Diego and himself a psychoanalyst, "Here psychoanalytic observation will be used, if it is used at all, to measure the effects of drugs on the quality of the transference relationship, on the patient's memories, and on dreams and fantasies. All of these will be viewed as data from the brain, testifying to its biological status. Blood tests or spinal-fluid taps will tell just what pills we need. We will learn to think of ourselves, our personalities, as an orchestra of chemical voices in our heads. Psychiatry will become the most scientifically precise of medical specialties, relying not at all upon subjective judgment."

Freud showed extraordinary prescience when he wrote, "In the future we will be allowed to exercise a direct influence by means of particular chemical substances upon the amounts of energy and their distribution in the apparatus of the mind." Drug psychiatry come of age will be the fulfillment of this bold prophecy.

LATE-LIFE PARANOID STATES
Assessment and Treatment

Karen Sommer Berger, M.S.W., M.S.G., and Steven H. Zarit, Ph.D.

Paranoid states are a frequent and often disturbing disorder in the elderly, but treatment potentials are often overlooked. Etiological factors are reviewed, with attention to differential diagnosis. Treatment issues, including the role of a therapeutic relationship, the impact on the person's social network, and prognosis, are discussed.

Paranoid states in later life, though less prevalent than depressive disorders, have a more disturbing impact, prompting immediate and sometimes angry responses from family members and various community agencies. Repeated accusations about someone entering one's house and about items being stolen, or reports of voices conspiring against the person, are likely to lead to the labeling of the individual as mentally ill, with little attempt at active treatment. Correspondingly, there have been few systematic attempts at the differentiation and treatment of paranoid states; the major emphasis of treatment has been custodial. This paper will review existing research on etiological and precipitating factors in paranoid disorders in the elderly, and suggest treatment approaches.

The distinction between paranoid states in older persons and paranoid schizophrenia is not always clear. Some authors see the difference as a matter of degree, while others conceptualize these disorders as separate entities.[12, 22]

In general, however, paranoid schizophrenia is looked upon as involving greater distortion of thought processes, a loss of contact with reality, and more severe personality disorganization. Such first-rank symptoms of schizophrenia are present in only a minority of persons with late-life onset of paranoia.[12] Paranoid states in the elderly are more typically characterized by circumscribed delusions and the absence of other psychotic symptoms.[23] In reviewing the literature on late-life paranoia, Tanna[22] concluded that it is

> . . . distinct from schizophrenia, affective disorders, or organic brain syndromes. Its main features are . . . paranoid symptoms [which] occur for the first time in the 5th or 6th decade or later . . . The clinical picture consists of delusions and hallucinations, but usually without thought disorders, gross affective, volitional or psychomotor symptoms, or characteristic personality deterioration, all considered typical of schizophrenia. . .

Symptoms similar to those of both late-life paranoid states and paranoid schizophrenia can also be manifested by persons with acute or chronic organic brain syndromes, where brain dysfunction appears as the precipitating factor.

PREMORBID AND PRECIPITATING FACTORS

Two etiological factors, social isolation (perhaps as a consequence of poor lifelong social adjustment) and sensory losses, have been found to be associated with late-life paranoid states. Patients are likely to be women, single or widowed, have few close relatives, and typically have lived alone for many years before their illness. Few have children and those with children have limited contact with them. They are commonly in good physical health except for problems with vision and hearing.[16, 23] Kay and Roth [12]

. . . concluded that the setting of social isolation in which a high proportion of the paraphrenics were living was, at least to some extent, due to a self segregation of personalities for whom social contact and communication was difficult.

Along the same line, Post [17] said that shy

. . . and poorly socialized persons may in later life become suspicious, odd, eccentric, seclusive, or even prone to persecutory interpretation.

Persecutory states

. . . arise most commonly in persons who had been quite well adjusted as far as their working lives were concerned. However, they had very often failed in their more intimate relationships, were often single or divorced, and only rarely reached a stage of full and normal sexuality. . .[17]

The person who becomes paranoid may be particularly lonely and insecure, and the interaction between this type of personality and stressful external events can lead to the paranoid psychoses.[12, 16] While Kay and his associates [12] found that stresses such as bereavement, physical illness, or domestic quarrels were reported more frequently in patients with affective psychoses, 50% of persons with paranoid disorders also mentioned these types of incidents. These stressful situations may give the person the feeling of no longer being adequate or in control, or may mean the loss of love and attention.[19, 23]

Sensory losses, particularly in hearing, are also common in those with late-

life paranoid states. Cooper and his associates [4] reported that the incidence of hearing disorders in older persons with paranoid disorders is higher than expected by chance. Deafness was often bilateral and severe, and followed chronic middle-ear infections. Onset of deafness typically was in middle age or earlier.

Other sensory losses may also be a factor in the development of late-life paranoid states. In a recent study, Cooper and Porter [6] found that optimum visual activity was substantially worse in a group of paranoid patients, compared to persons with affective disorders.

It has been suggested that these sensory losses lead to a heightened sense of isolation. Cooper discussed changes that occur in the hard of hearing, such as inattention, lack of sympathy, depressive tendencies, feelings of loss, bitterness, suspicion, persecutory ideas, and anger and rage against one's fate. He suggested that changes lead to social isolation, which impedes communication and social interchange.[3] Hoogerbeets et al [9] similarly suggested that

. . . sensory deprivation, often caused by decreased hearing or visual acuity, may add to the elderly person's preoccupation with his own mental production and decrease his ability for reality testing.

Post [16] has proposed that the manifestation of paranoia differs, depending on whether the principal premorbid characteristic is sensory loss or a long-standing personality style, the latter being associated with greater disturbance of thought and behavior. In comparing deaf and nondeaf patients with paranoid disorders, Cooper et al [5] reported that the deaf had fewer of the predisposing personality factors for psychosis than did the nondeaf, especially when there was earlier onset of the deafness. The literature therefore suggests that, among the nondeaf, paranoid states frequently occur in persons who earlier in life displayed emotional coldness, had difficulty forming intimate relationships, and had problems in their sexuality. On the other hand, persons who became deaf by their middle years or perhaps had other sensory losses did not necessarily exhibit those premorbid characteristics, but the deafness and resulting sensory deprivation decreased their ability for reality testing, increased isolation, and made them prone to paranoid psychoses in old age. In general, a combination of adverse circumstances such as prior social isolation, difficulties in interpersonal relations, deafness, and current stresses that increase feelings of insecurity, inadequacy, and loneliness appear to create a vulnerability for the development of paranoid thinking.[12]

FUNCTIONAL SIGNIFICANCE OF PARANOID SYMPTOMS

It has been proposed that paranoid symptoms in the elderly develop in response to the circumstances of isolation, inadequacy, and loss of control described above. From a psychodynamic perspective, these feelings are dealt with through projection and displacement. The person feels a sense of inadequacy in managing his or her affairs, and may deal with this by saying someone is causing these difficulties. The person who feels rage at an important loss may project this rage onto others. According to Verwoerdt,[23] the

. . . premorbid personality may have counterphobic features and an inclination to use defenses of the "high energy" variety (mastery through attack; projection), with subsequent attempts to move aggressively against the externalized threat.

Some of the literature also suggests the presence of a strong superego. When a person feels great upset and rage and a sense of inadequacy he

. . . may be saved from [self-persecution], shame, or guilt by the formation of paranoid delusions, and real objects within the world become endowed with all the characteristics of intolerance and sadism which the superego might formerly have directed toward the self. Now instead of being a frightened, helpless, and a guilt-ridden failure, the person seems righteously indignant and pugnacious.[2]

Savitsy and Sharkey[21] provided an example of the use of projection. An elderly woman would complain that things were stolen from her by nurses when she did not feel that her daughter was paying enough attention to her. This was seen as both an example of projection of her anger and an attention-getting device. When the staff worked with the daughter to give more attention to her mother, the paranoid symptoms subsided.

As this last example suggests, paranoid behavior may be reinforced by the attention or other consequences that result from it. An isolated, lonely person who gets dramatic effects from family, police, or others by complaining about an intruder may continue to manifest this symptom unless alternative sources of rewards are developed to compete with the dysfunctional behavior. These behaviors may be persistent in part because of intermittent reinforcement; that is, complaints are attended to some of the time and ignored in other instances, or because the person has no other behavioral skills for obtaining similar reinforcements. The consequences of paranoid states need to be carefully explored, both for suggesting appropriate ways in which these reinforcements could be gained and to ensure that treatment is not undermined through continued reinforcement of the paranoid behaviors.

Another facet of paranoid states is that they can function to compensate or "fill in" stimuli that the person does not receive, because of social isolation or deafness.[14] A deaf person may create or complete those words that he cannot hear, and these can take on a conspiratorial tone. Similarly, a lonely person may fabricate voices or a companion, even a malevolent intruder, as a substitute for social interaction. Following recovery from an acute paranoid dis-

---

Table I

DEVELOPMENT OF PARANOID DISORDERS IN LATE LIFE

PREMORBID FACTORS: An individual with either: 1) difficulty with interpersonal relationships, or 2) sensory loss—especially bilateral deafness beginning in the middle years.

PRECIPITANTS: An acute stress, usually a loss, which gives the person the feeling of no longer being adequate and in control, or the feeling of a loss of love and attention, to which the person responds with feelings of rage.

DEFENSES: Use of the strong and high-energy maladaptive defenses of projection or displacement.

SECONDARY GAINS: Positive reinforcements or compensations of symptoms.

turbance, a patient seen by one of the authors (s.z.) stated that she had made up the voices she had reported hearing because she missed the sound of human conversation. This process of compensating can also be seen among persons with chronic brain syndrome manifesting paranoid symptoms, who accuse persons of stealing or hiding objects that they cannot locate because of memory loss.

TABLE 1 summarizes the major characteristics in the development of paranoid states in the elderly.

OTHER POSSIBLE CAUSES

Several somatic factors have been suggested as related to the development of paranoid states, including chronic illness,[15] acute medical problems such as myxodema and pernicious anemia,[27] and acute or chronic organic brain syndrome.[14] Vitamin B12 deficiencies have been reported in a small number of cases.[24] Sleep deprivation, often reported as a consequence of psychosis, may actually precipitate or exacerbate the mental symptoms. In a review of the literature in 1969, Wilkinson[26] noted that, with total sleep deprivation (*e.g.*, five nights without sleep)

. . . frank psychotic symptoms commonly appear. They are often of a paranoid schizoid type with emotional lability and delusions of reference, grandeur, or persecution.

This may be due to a breakdown in biochemical energy transfer systems. Sackner *et al*[20] have also suggested that poor sleeping can lead to personality changes and paranoia.

DIAGNOSIS AND TREATMENT

Evaluations of a person with presenting paranoid symptoms should include, as a first step, assessment of physical and mental status to determine if medical conditions or acute or chronic organic brain disease are precipitants. When symbolic language changes or other signs of an acute organic brain syndrome are present,[10] possible causes include tumors, malnutrition, a toxic drug reaction, somatic illness, a recent fracture, or a reaction to recent stress.[28] Treatment of the precipitating factor will lead to a gradual diminishing of the paranoid symptoms over a period of one to four weeks. With chronic brain syndrome, treatment with phenothiazines has not been found to be effective.[25] Two approaches, however, can be suggested. First, paranoid symptoms appear to cover up the increasing memory difficulties that the person is experiencing. By responding to and emphasizing other areas of competence, family members or a therapist may diminish the need to present oneself as unimpaired in memory. Second, as intellectual impairment increases, the use of paranoid thoughts has been observed to diminish correspondingly. Families or other supporting persons can be encouraged that these symptoms are not likely to persist, and may be directed to reinforce other behaviors that can compete with paranoid expressions. Direct confrontations that the person is actually forgetful have not typically been found to be effective in reducing inappropriate behaviors.

Second, a differential diagnosis between depression and a paranoid state needs to be made. When depression is a significant correlate of the paranoid symptoms, antidepressant medication is often an effective treatment.[27]

Third, assessment should involve a careful family and personal history, identifying the person's typical functioning, possible social resources, and the consequences of the paranoid state. Finally, losses and other immediate precipitating factors need to be taken into account.

In working with a paranoid older person, it is suggested first to develop a trusting relationship by showing care, expressing regret at the difficult time the person is going through, and accepting uncritically any accounts of the paranoid delusions.[16] Establishing the relationship has two goals: encouraging the use of medication when appropriate, and facilitating support and trust that can diminish the presenting symptoms.

Phenothiazines have been reported to result in the elimination or attenuation of paranoid symptoms in older persons.[8, 25] Post[15] indicated, for example, that, of 71 patients treated with phenothiazines, 43 had complete remissions, 22 presented only slight symptoms, and only six were unchanged. In presenting medication to a paranoid patient, he emphasized an uncritical and supportive atmosphere, stating to the patient:

[Your] nerves have been affected by all these experiences, and the tablets which are about to be prescribed will place [you] . . . in a better position of resisting these onslaughts against . . . [your] health.

Phenothiazine therapy, however, needs to be carefully monitored in the aged, because of the possibility of side-effects, some of which can lead to irreversible damage such as tardive dyskinesea.[13]

The development of a supportive therapeutic relationship can complement drug therapy or may help diminish symptoms when medication is contraindicated or if the patient refuses it. Therapy can have several functions. First, the acceptance shown by the therapist may compensate to an extent for the increasing sense of social isolation and vulnerability that many persons with paranoid ideation have experienced. Second, the development of a therapeutic relationship may facilitate exploring prior stresses or losses, their meaning to a client, and alternative ways of expressing these concerns. One should not confront the person directly over the lack of basis in fact for his or her delusions, but rather should respond empathically either to the feelings of loss, anger, or vulnerability that are indicated by the paranoid ideation, or through discussions of the person's life circumstances prior to and apart from the paranoid concerns. Third, where feelings of lack of control or vulnerability appear prominent, it is suggested that the person be helped to develop a greater sense of control both within the therapy relationship and by appropriate involvement of community agencies and possibly family members. Many older persons seeking help from social service agencies express considerable concern about the future and what might happen to them if their current situation worsens. By providing what Kahn[11] has called "potential service," that is, the assurance that services will be available to the person when needed, the feelings of vulnerability may be diminished. Fourth, the development of a thera-peutic relationship may facilitate shaping of more appropriate behaviors. If the consequences of the paranoid symptoms, such as drawing attention of others to the client, can be identified, attention can then be given by the therapist and others contingent on appropriate behaviors. In this manner, social skills can be developed and reinforced. Finally, it has been noted that some paranoid persons prefer a somewhat distant relationship, and that this preference for personal space needs to be respected by the therapist.[7]

The following case examples illustrate the effects of different courses of treatment. In the first, a trusting, supportive relationship was emphasized; in the second, there was a deliberate attempt to shape more positive behaviors. Despite these differences in approach, there was an attenuation of paranoid symptomatology in both, and the persons were able to continue to reside in community settings.

CASE EXAMPLES

Mrs. X

Mrs. X, a 72-year-old Jewish woman living alone, requested help from a family service agency. She complained that her neighbor was putting gas in her cupboards, ripping her curtains, and doing other damage. She wanted a case worker to come out and prove that she was right, since others did not believe her.

Mrs. X had two children. Her husband had left her when she was only 25 years old. She moved to Europe at that time from the Middle East, placed the children in an orphanage, went to work, and visited them on weekends. She came to the U.S.A. as a middle-aged woman to be close to her children, who had arrived here earlier. She never remarried and said she had had no desire to do so. When she came to the U.S.A., she lived with her single son in his little house until two years before this contact, when *he* moved out. She expressed anger that she used to work and be her own boss and now her children were bossing her around. She was remorseful about not having remarried. She apparently had not had any paranoid symptomatology while her son lived with her. Her relationship with her son had been poor since he left the house, and she was not seeing much of him. Her daughter and grandchildren visited her fairly regularly. Mrs. X was able to clean, cook, and care for her dog. (The dog was kind to her, but vicious with strangers and she had to call him off every time the caseworker arrived at her home.) Mrs. X was both friendly and aloof.

She would offer the caseworker tea and food, but would always express relief when only the tea was accepted. On numerous occasions, she would indicate that she preferred not to feed visitors.

Mrs. X did not see herself as sick. She would not have anything to do with her daughter's insistence that she see a psychiatrist. The consultant for the family service agency felt she should be placed in a "nice" locked facility where she would get good treatment and care. The caseworker, however, decided to disregard this advice and attempt instead to develop a trusting relationship and to maintain her in her own home. She listened to Mrs. X's stories, and never told her that she did not believe them. Mrs. X sensed that her stories were not fully believed, but was able to accept the case worker anyway, perhaps because she was such a willing listener.

Mrs. X was visited in her home every two weeks for five or six months. During that time, she continued having her paranoid symptomatology, but became calmer and more willing to go out occasionally. When the caseworker was leaving the family service agency, she proposed that Mrs. X see another worker or a volunteer. Mrs. X declined, stating that she had enjoyed these visits but was aware that the worker did not believe her stories. Though ending prematurely, this supportive therapy appeared to have enhanced Mrs. X's abilities to continue to function in her home.

Miss S

Miss S, an 82-year-old woman, was referred to a senior day care center by a famliy service agency because of her recent complaints about poisoning. Miss S claimed, variously, that the superintendent or the doorman for the apartment-hotel where she lived was spraying "bug spray" into her apartment during the night and waking her. She felt they were trying to drive her out of her apartment, because they wanted to rent to a lower class of tenant.

Miss S had never married and appeared throughout her life to have functioned effectively (holding jobs, supporting herself) but never to have made many close friendships. Her closest contacts were her brothers and sisters, who lived in the suburbs. Apparently corresponding to the onset of symptoms, one of her brothers died, and another, who visited her regularly, became ill and could no longer visit.

The day care staff decided on a program of listening politely to her paranoid complaints and initiating conversation about other, more appropriate activities, including her appearance and dress. Miss S gradually began to converse about other topics, mixing well with other day care participants and making some friends. She also started dressing much better, taking more care with make-up and hair, and took on a striking appearance. In addition, the day care staff made a visit to her building, where there was a faint odor of disinfectant but no apparent attempt to get her to move. The staff told her that they enlisted the manager to watch over her and prevent the spraying from happening again. Over the course of six months, her paranoid complaints diminished considerably, though they were never completely eliminated.

In these two cases, there are similar histories of a degree of lifelong social isolation predating the paranoid symptoms. Both women responded to attention and interest in them. The development of a therapeutic relationship in the first case, and appropriate social outlets in the second, was related to a diminishing of symptoms. In both cases, the clients were capable of self-care activities and the interventions, which reduced somewhat their distress and complaints, allowed them to continue in a community setting rather than be placed in a protective setting.

The issue of hospitalization or placement in a long-term care facility often arises in dealing with paranoid patients, because of the disturbing nature of these symptoms to other people. Despite the bizarre nature of paranoid ideations, however, most older paranoid patients appear capable of functioning in a community setting. Post,[16] for example, recommended outpatient treatment, provided there are no suicidal tendencies and family members can tolerate the person a while longer. He suggested that a socially isolated person may be more difficult to treat as an outpatient, if the person is unreliable in keeping appointments and taking medications. Bratfos *et al*[1] compared outpatient treatment and hospitalization for various categories of mental illness. They found no contraindications for paranoid patients who had outpatient treatment. At the outset, families prefer hospitalization since they see the patient as a burden. However the family's attitude changes when treatment gets under way and they realize the advantages of treatment at home. Home treatment also leads to better collaboration with families. Bratfos *et al* recommended that it may be necessary to pressure patients to cooperate in taking drugs at first, but felt that such outpatient care is a better alternative than hospitalization, since the patient is more likely to establish a therapeutic relationship.

In general, the issues of hospitalization and medication are difficult ones. Even when broached in the context of a supportive relationship, the paranoid client may refuse. At that point, whether the person is doing harm to himself or herself must be carefully assessed. The paranoid symptoms may, in fact, interfere little with the person's functioning. With depressed older persons, fairly severe degrees of impairment are often tolerated in community situations. Correspondingly, it would be inappropriate to institutionalize 'a paranoid client solely because of the bizarre nature of the symptoms, without considering whether the person possesses at least minimal abilities for self care and is not dangerous in other ways. Persons refusing treatment are making a choice that they prefer their current situation, despite the distress involved, and they should only be coerced into treatment when their situations become potentially dangerous.

PROGNOSIS

There are few available studies of the prognosis of older persons with paranoid disorders and few comparisons of different treatment approaches; the reported findings are somewhat equivocal. Retterstol[18] found that people with late onset of a paranoid state have a far better prognosis than do those with paranoid schizophrenia. In his study, those with reactive psychoses had a favorable outcome 81% of the time, as against a 23% favorable outcome among paranoid schizophrenics.[18]

In contrast, Tanna[22] viewed late-life paranoia as chronic, with poor prospect for recovery but without adverse effect on life span or mortality. Post[16] reported that prognosis depends on the maintenance of an effective therapy with phenothiazines. In a series of one to three year follow-ups, he found that there was a reduction or elimination of paranoid symptoms in most patients. Post noted, however, that there was some decline in social adjustment among half the sample, specifically in maintaining a work role and interpersonal relationships. Whether these changes were due to advanced age or to deteriorating effects of the mental disturbance could not be determined in the absence of a control group. While limited, these studies suggest that maintenance and perhaps some improvement is possible in the older paranoid patient.

SUMMARY

Paranoid states that occur late in life are characterized by some distortion in reality testing. In some cases, there can be delusions and hallucinations but no progressive personality deterioration.

The late-life paranoid patient is likely to be female, single or widowed, and living alone; has few children; had failed in her more intimate relationships in earlier life; and only rarely reached a stage of full and normal sexuality. Patients are often in good health except for problems with vision or hearing. Persons who were deaf before age 45 have less deviant personalities than patients who had late onset deafness or were not deaf.

An acute paranoid reaction can be precipitated by a major stress or loss. The individual may feel inadequate and out of control or feel a loss of love or attention. Ego strength fails and the person adopts a strong defense, such as projection or displacement. The symptoms may also be reinforced by attention or other positive consequences.

Before concluding that an older client has an involutional paranoid state, one must carefully evaluate the person in a number of areas, and rule out the presence of an acute or chronic organic brain syndrome and other health factors that can precipitate paranoid symptomatology. Once the diagnosis is made, a relationship should be established with the helping professional that will enable the client to accept needed treatment. Phenothiazines are often helpful, but the side effects can be dangerous and they must be given with caution. A small percentage of individuals do gain insight. Outpatient treatment is usually preferable to hospitalization. The prognosis for late-life paranoia is unclear, depending in part on the development of a successful regime of medication.

7. ADULT

REFERENCES

1. BRATFOS, O. ET AL. 1972. Out-patient treatment of psychoses. Acta Psychiatrica Scandinavica 48(1):30–42.
2. CATH, S. 1973. Comments. J. Geriat. Psychiat. 6(2):227–235.
3. COOPER, A. 1976. Deafness and psychiatric illness. Brit. J. Psychiat. 129:216–226.
4. COOPER, A. ET AL. 1974. Hearing loss in paranoid and affective psychoses of the elderly. Lancet 2(7885):851–854.
5. COOPER, A., GARSIDE, R. AND KAY, D. 1976. A comparison of deaf and non-deaf patients with paranoid and affective psychoses. Brit. J. Psychiat. 129:532–538.
6. COOPER, A. AND PORTER, R. 1976. Visual acuity and ocular pathology in the paranoid psychoses of later life. J. Psychosomat. Res. 20:107–114.
7. FOLSOM, J. 1972. From custody to therapy. Military Med. 134:209–214.
8. FRACCHIA, J., SHEPPARD, C. AND MERLIS, S. 1973. Treament patterns in psychiatry: relationships to system features and aging. J. Amer. Geriat. Soc. 21(3):134–138.
9. HOOGERBEETS, J. AND LA WALL, J. 1975. Changing concepts of psychiatric problems in the aged. Geriatrics 30(8):83–87.
10. KAHN, R. 1976. Psychological aspects of aging. In Clinical Geriatrics, I. Rossman, ed. J.B. Lippincott, Philadelphia.
11. KAHN, R. 1977. The mental health system and the future aged. In Readings in Aging and Death, S. Zarit, ed. Harper and Row, New York.
12. KAY, D. ET AL. 1976. The differentiation of paranoid from affective psychoses by patients' premorbid characteristics. Brit. J. Psychiat. 129:207–215.
13. KENNEDY, P. 1975. Schizophrenia and related paranoid states. Brit. Med. 2:257–260.
14. PFEIFFER, E. AND BUSSE, E. 1973. Mental disorder in later life—affective disorders: paranoid, neurotic and situational reactions. In Mental Illness in Later Life. E. Busse and E. Pfeiffer, eds. American Psychiatric Association, Washington, D.C.
15. POST, F. 1973. Paranoid disorders in the elderly. Postgrad. Med. J. 53(4):52–56.
16. POST, F. 1966. Persistent Persecutory States of the Elderly. Pergamon Press, New York.
17. POST, F. 1968. Psychological aspects of geriatrics. Postgrad. Med. J. 4:307–318.
18. RETTERSTOL, N. 1968. Paranoid psychoses. Brit. J. Psychiat. 114(510):553–562.
19. ROSS, F. 1973. Social work treatment of a paranoid personality in a geriatric institution. J. Geriat. Psychiat. 6(2):204–217.
20. SACKNER, M. ET AL. 1975. Periodic sleep apnea: chronic sleep deprivation related to intermittent upper airway obstruction and central nervous system disturbance. Chest 67(2):164–171.
21. SAVITSKY, E. AND SHARKEY, H. 1972. The geriatric patient and his family: study of family interaction in the aged. J. Geriat. Psychiat. 5(1):3–24.
22. TANNA, V. 1974. Paranoid states: a selected review. Comprehens. Psychiat. 15(6):453–470.
23. VERWOERDT, A. 1976. Clinical Geropsychiatry. Williams and Wilkins, Baltimore.
24. WHITEHEAD, J. AND CHOHAN, M. 1972. Paraphrenia and pernicious anemia. Geriatrics 27(5):148–158.
25. WHITEHEAD, T. 1975. Long-acting phenothiazines. Brit. Med. J. (May 31):502.
26. WILKINSON, R. 1969. Loss of sleep. Royal Soc. Med. Proceedings 62:903–904.
27. YOUNG, J. 1972. Acute psychiatric disturbances in the elderly and their treatment. Clin. Practice 26(11):513–516.
28. ZARIT, S. 1977. Aging. In Psychopathology Through the Life Cycle. L. Allman and D. Jaffe, eds. Harper and Row, New York.

Psychotherapy of the Elderly

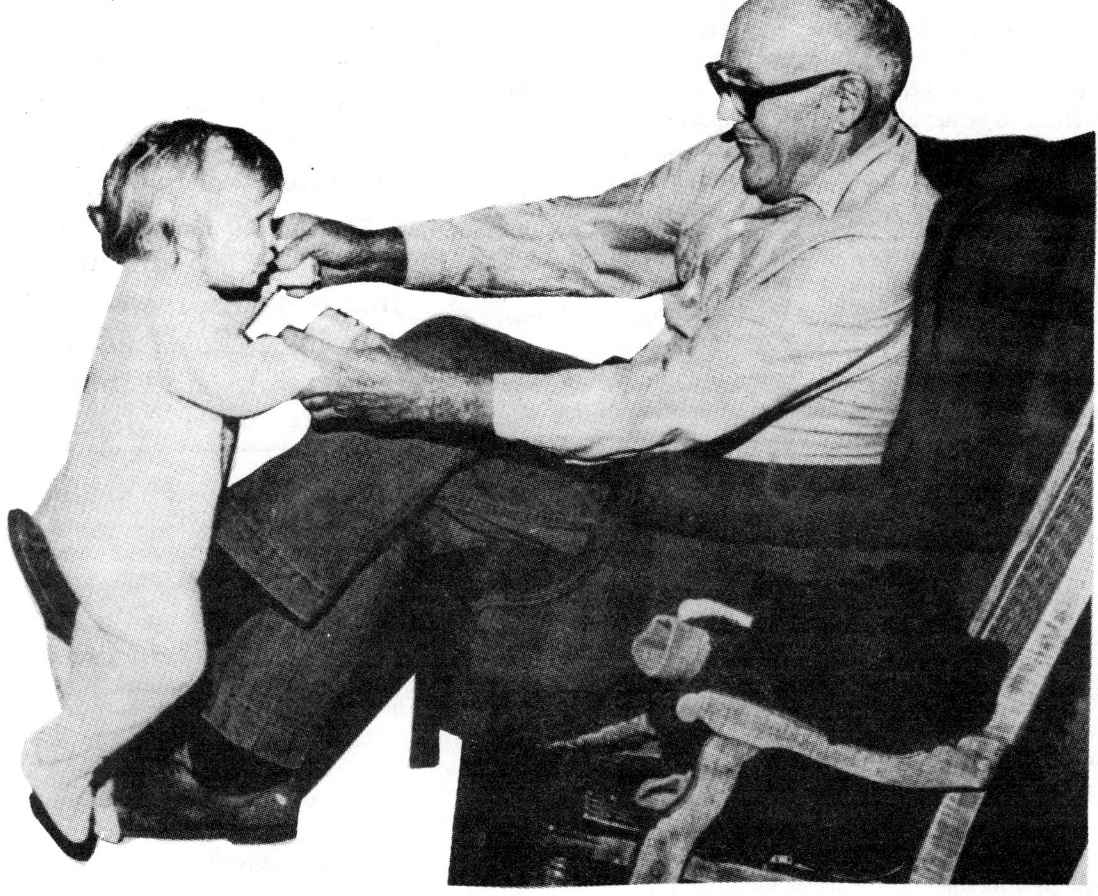

Eric Pfeiffer, M.D.

The purpose of this article is to delineate the role of psychotherapy in the overall treatment approach to elderly psychiatric patients. Defining the topic in this way, two points are quickly made:

- psychotherapy has an important place in the psychiatrist's repertoire for treating older patients;
- goals, skills, and techniques involved in psychotherapy of the old differ from those involved in psychotherapy of the young.

For purposes of this presentation the word old or elderly will refer to persons aged sixty-five years and older.

Although the field of psychotherapy and its literature is vast, it will nevertheless be useful to begin with the author's own definition of the term psychotherapy as it will be used throughout this article. According to this definition, psychotherapy is "a method of bringing about changes in behavior through psychological interaction between a recognized therapist and an identified patient." In this definition the term behavior refers not only to overt motor activity on the part of the patient but also to the sum total of his or her behaviors, including thoughts, feelings, and actions.

There are of course many forms of psychotherapy. The following listing identifies some of these, arranged somewhat hierarchically in decreasing order along the dimension of degree of patient responsibility in therapy:

- psychoanalysis;
- insight-oriented psychotherapy;
- nondirective psychotherapy;
- behavior therapy;
- supportive therapy;
- directive therapy; and,
- environmental manipulation.

This list could obviously be extended, rearranged, or organized along differing dimensions. However, in its present form it gives a clear indication of the range of activities, skills, prerequisites, and procedures that may be involved.

Additionally, each of the preceding therapies can be applied individually or in groups, with the exception of classical

Reprinted from *National Association of Private Psychiatric Hospitals Journal*, Vol. 10, No. 1, 1978. ©1978 by E. Pfeiffer. All rights reserved.

psychoanalysis.

Clinical experience and clinical research have shown that older psychiatric patients differ from younger patients in a number of important respects. These differences are not sharply drawn so as to set off all older individuals from all younger individuals. But they are very noticeable in practice with predominantly older patients. These differences, in part, dictate the somewhat differing psychotherapeutic practices to be detailed. These differences include:

■ **situational factors** These factors (rather than internal conflictual factors) can almost always be identified in the onset of psychiatric problems in older patients;

■ **coping with losses** These situational factors are relatively predictable, with a variety of losses, physical illness, and displacements accounting for a large portion of them;

■ **few syndromes** The range of psychiatric syndromes arising for the first time in old age tends to be somewhat narrow, with depression, anxiety, hypochondriacal concerns, and paranoid reactions predominating, somewhat in that order;

■ **simple defenses** There is a predominance of relatively simple defense mechanisms or coping devices, with withdrawal, somatization, projection, and denial being exceeded only by unmodified (or untransformed) anxiety or outright panic;

■ **multiple system interactions** Social and Economic support factors, mobility, and the quality of the immediate environment (or living arrangements) dramatically influence both the development and the resolution of psychiatric symptomatology;

■ **limited goals** The goal in therapy is much more likely to be a return to a previously attained symptom-free status than an achievement of a never-before attained level of personality integration, although the latter may well result from successful resolution of a situational problem that is actually a generic version of the type of problem with which older persons must learn to cope.

Given these differences, the choice of certain therapeutic strategies follows.

Crisis Resolution

Because situational factors are frequent precipitants of psychiatric disturbance in the elderly (having to move, sudden bad news, unexpected financial stress, losses of various kinds), crisis intervention and crisis resolution techniques play an important role. While techniques of crisis intervention and crisis resolution are well known, it will nevertheless be useful to review the basic steps:

■ empathetic understanding;

■ ventilation of affect;

■ reestablishment of emotional equilibrium; and,

■ exploration of alternative solutions.

Crisis resolution begins with attaining and communicating a thorough and accurate empathetic understanding of the patient's situation. It is not sufficient that the therapist merely understand why the patient feels how

> **"Crisis resolution begins with attaining and communicating a thorough and accurate empathetic understanding of the patient's situation. It is not sufficient that the therapist merely understand why the patient feels how he does; that understanding must also be effectively conveyed to the patient. Experience has shown that a combination of verbal and nonverbal communications, including cognitive understanding, vocal but nonlexical expressions, and touch are particularly effective with older patients."**

he does; that understanding must also be effectively conveyed to the patient. Experience has shown that a combination of verabal and nonverbal communications, including cognitive understanding, vocal but nonlexical expressions, and touch are particularly effective with older patients.

The next step is to facilitate full and adequate ventilation of the patient's feelings about his or her situation. This frequently can take place only after effective understanding of the situation has been communicated. Efforts must be made to put patients "in touch" with both the nature and the depth of their feelings. It is not possible for a patient to undertake constructive or reconstructive action unless they are aware of the full extent of their response to the precipitating circumstances.

While the next logical step in this process is the examining of alternative courses of action that might be taken by the patient, this cannot be undertaken until the patient has regained a modicum of composure.

> **". . . I have called old age 'a season of loss.' Losses are in fact predictable and ubiquitous in this phase of the life cycle. They commonly include loss of spouse; loss of friends (through death, illness or loss of mobility); loss of job identity; loss of work and work-related roles and structured activities; decline in health; economic decrements; a contracting social network. While not each of these losses is experienced by every aging person, a substantial number of such losses predictably occur to the vast majority of elderly."**

In many instances the psychological interventions already described are enough to restore emotional equilibrium; in many others they are not. In these instances the use of the so-called minor tranquilizers and/or sedatives, both for daytime anxiolytic and nighttime hypnotic action, is useful and indicated. However, they are intended for short-term (one to seven days) and not for continuous use. Continuous use is not warranted in situational disturbances, and can lead to a number of adverse reactions including decreased alertness, disorientation, loss of equilibrium and consequent falls, as well as habituation or addiction. The benzodiazopenes have been particularly useful medications in this type of situation. On the other hand the major tranquilizers (antipsychotic agents) are to be avoided here unless frank psychotic behavior exists. In any case, the minor tranquilizers must serve as an adjunct to, not as a substitute for, psychotherapy.

When a reasonable equilibrium has been restored through psychological or pharmacological intervention, then the restitutive work of finding alternative solutions can begin. Here the therapist must draw a sensitive balance between encouraging the patient to devise his own list of alternatives and assisting the patient by assuring him that the list of alternatives is substantial. In short, if the patient cannot come up with any alternatives himself, it is better to suggest at least a few to him to stimulate his thinking rather than leave him suspended as though no solution or only one solution to the problem were possible.

One particularly useful source of alternative suggestions for problem resolutions are other older patients with similar problems. This is particularly effective in group therapy situations. But even in individual therapy, the therapist can obviously draw on his experience with other older patients who have devised successful solutions to their often similar problems.

Following such "brainstorming" about alternative solutions one can then move on to devising a treatment plan. To the extent that such a plan can be broken down into component parts, phases, or stages, it will be less overwhelming to the patient and easier to monitor for both patient and therapist.

Coping With Losses

We have focused on helping elderly patients to adjust to unpredictable or impredicted adverse circumstances; in this section we will deal with the patient's response, including possible proactive response, to a very predictable phenomenon of old age, that of loss in general and especially the loss of important relationships.

Elsewhere in my writings, I have called old age "a season of loss." Losses are in fact predictable and ubiquitous in this phase of the life cycle. They commonly include loss of spouse; loss of friends (through death, illness or loss of mobility); loss of job identity, loss of work and work-related roles and structured activities; decline in health; economic decrements; a contracting social network. While not each of these losses is experienced by every aging person,

a substantial number of such losses predictably occur to the vast majority of elderly.

Taking cognizance of this phenomenon, one must in fact marvel that not all old people become depressed. Most of them do not. Various studies have shown that the prevalence of depressive mood among persons age sixty-five and older may be between ten and twenty-five percent, while the prevalence of a depressive syndrome may be only five to ten percent. A depressive syndrome is here defined as a persistent disturbance of affect suffuciently severe to interfere with the individual's work, social and interpersonal activities. In old age it is most commonly a pathological response to one or more losses, in which pathological is defined as being either more intense or more persistent than a normal grief reaction.

The most important strategy in coping with losses is the development of replacement relationships, or of new relationships or activities to substitute for some of those which have been lost. It is not realistic to seek to replace all lost object relationships or significant activities, nor is it necessary; replacing a fraction of them restores self-esteem and a sense of continued relatedness. An important first step in this regard is the development of the therapeutic relationship, which is in fact a new relationship. This alone can demonstrate to the patient that he/she is capable of forming new relationships. In turn, this relationship can then be used as leverage for the patient to establish additional new relationships "in the real world," as it were. Exploring sources of substitute relationships is certainly one of the focal points of individual counseling or psychotherapy.

Group psychotherapy is of exceptional value for persons with depressive syndromes precipitated by significant ob-

> "Group psychotherapy is of exceptional value for persons with depressive syndromes precipitated by significant object loss. A single therapist can treat more than one patient in a given amount of time (between six to ten patients are ideal for group therapy with older patients); more importantly, however, other patients often provide excellent models of coping behaviors and replacement strategies. Furthermore, the fact of belonging to a group is of itself an important therapeutic tool. Relationships to groups, not only to individuals, have often been lost, and the capacity to reestablish me.nbership in a group is itself of therapeutic value."

ject loss. A single therapist can treat more than one patient in a given amount of time (between six to ten patients are ideal for group therapy with older patients); more importantly, however, other patients often provide excellent models of coping behaviors and replacement strategies. Furthermore, the fact of belonging to a group is of itself an important therapeutic tool. Relationships to groups, not only to individuals, have often been lost, and the capacity to reestablish membership in a group is itself of therapeutic value.

In such groups, and in psychotherapy with elderly patients in general, patient and therapist each can be allowed to develop much more of a "real" or social relationship with each other. There is little need for therapeutic distance with most older patients, and the sharing of personal interest, and social and family information frequently enhances the strength of the therapeutic relationship.

Emphasis on a Few Psychiatric Syndromes

Depression, hypochondriasis, paranoid reactions, situational disturbances, and alcoholism are the principal psychiatric syndromes seen to arise in old age. Depression and situational reactions have been dealt with to some extent in the preceding sections. In this section we will focus primarily on therapeutic activities best suited for patients with hypochondriacal, paranoid, and alcoholic features.

Hypochondriasis is an intense preoccupation with bodily functioning or malfunctioning in which there are multiple somatic complaints but sparse physical findings. This is coupled with a strong aversion on the part of the patient to see himself/herself as psychologically disturbed or emotionally distressed, rejecting all suggestion from family, friends, or physicians that "there is actually nothing wrong." This is in fact a well-defined psychiatric disorder, with somatic symptoms. The patient is in fact sick and in need of care.

It is a syndrome that arises in response to the patient's perception that the surrounding environment is increasingly ungiving and interaction with it increasingly unrewarding; he/she therefore seeks refuge in the patient role, which is defined as "being taken care of." Unfortunately, instead of finding this role satisfying and rewarding, family, friends, and physician alike "see through" this coping device and respond with anger, rejection, and derision, thereby intensifying the patient's perception of the environment as hostile and unrewarding.

While a correct understanding of the dynamics of the patient's needs and responses is important for the therapist, these cannot simply be shared or explained to the patient. Instead, this dynamic understanding should primarily influence the structure of the therapeutic relationship, which will be the principal tool of the behavioral change. The elements of successful therapy with hypochondriacal patients include, therefore, these items:

- a thorough examination;
- acceptance of the patient as sick and in need of care;
- a regular schedule of appointments;
- supportive psychotherapy measures; and,
- placebo medication.

Unless hypochondriacal patients are correctly understood and handled, they tend to be frustrating to health care personnel. Such frustration is reflected in a number of counterproductive techniques that have been tried without success with hypochondriacal patients. While they are not effective, the following counterproductive approaches to hypochondriacal patients do illuminate the nature of this syndrome further:

- extensive, expensive, or esoteric tests;
- psychological explanations;
- "reassuring" the patient that "there is nothing wrong";
- p.r.n. schedule of appointments; and,
- referral to yet another physician.

With an accepting, highly structured, supportive approach, one may expect a lessening of somatic complaints and, after a period of time, even the volunteering of some situational or psychological problems. Once the patient gets to this point, a more standard psychologically minded approach may be employed, so long as such an approach does not threaten the patient's definition of himself as someone "sick and in need of care."

Paranoid reactions require quite a different approach. They originate from a different set of circumstances, and it should be quickly stated that in this article we are not referring to paranoid schizophrenia (which in my opinion rarely if ever arises in old age) but the simple syndrome of paranoid reactions, which actually have many positive or

---

"It is becoming clear that alcoholism, arising in old age, is an increasing problem. Contributing to this occurrence are: social isolation, lack of a strong formal or informal social support system, paucity of meaningful activities or productivities, presence of depression and/or anxiety, easy availability, and the pharmacological effects of alcohol, including both initial CNS-depression and tolerance and dependency effects. Such alcoholism is occurring at all socioeconomic levels, in stable residential communities—especially planned retirement communities—as well as retirement ghettos."

---

adaptive elements. Paranoid symptoms arise from a perceived threat from the environment and an incomplete cognitive understanding of that threat. On the basis of what has been previously stated about the aging experience, such threats from the surrounding environment are frequent and one must again wonder why all older patients do not become paranoid. The additional element that is needed is some kind of cognitive distortion or gap caused by hearing loss, decreased vision, impaired memory, or insuffient cognitive input from the environment.

The patient perceives the threat, cannot interpret it correctly, and responds with "paranoid" explanations, which in reality are little more than incorrect explanations. In other words, the delusions of the older patient are not the complex, esoteric, far-fetched delusions of young paranoid schizophrenics, but are more regularly the "down-home" variety; for example, "the nurse is trying to steal my glasses"; "the postman is stealing my mail from me"; "the neighbors are putting lint in my laundry"; "my daughter is trying to poison me." Each of these "delusions" is based on a combination of some real observed event, and an inadequate understanding of that event. Therapeutic approaches with elderly paranoid patients should, therefore, include:

- clarifying the environmental circumstances;
- correcting sensory deficits;
- assuring stable and friendly environment; and,
- reducing anxiety, including use of low doses of antipsychotic agents (in liquid form).

It is becoming clear that *alcoholism*, arising in old age, is an increasing problem. Contributing to this occurrence are: social isolation, lack of a strong formal or informal social support system, paucity of meaningful activities or productivities, presence of depression and/or anxiety, easy avail-

ability, and the pharmacological effects of alcohol, including both initial CNS-depression and tolerance and dependency effects. Such alcoholism is occurring at all socio-economic levels, in stable residential communities—especially planned retirement communities—as well as in retirement ghettos.

Therapeutic approaches must be related to the underlying causes of excessive alcohol use. To the extent that drinking is used to overcome depression and anxiety, the symptoms must be treated by other means. To the extent that social isolation and lack of meaningful activity are casually related, therapeutic approaches must emphasize re-socialization, strengthening of the informal social support system, and channeling of the patient into individually tailored programs of meaningful and productive activity. Peer group support is particularly desirable for older patients drifting into alcoholism.

Enlarging the Repertoire of Coping Devices

There is a preponderant use of relatively simple defense mechanisms in psychiatrically disturbed elderly patients: depression-withdrawal, somatization, projection, and very prominently, denial. These mechanisms provide more of a passive protection for the individual rather than an active coping mechanism aimed at changing adverse life circumstances. It is first of all important to realize how frequently these mechanisms are used, especially denial. Older patients will often simply say that nothing is wrong and they don't need any help. This should not necessarily by taken at face value when there are other indications that the patient is indeed in trouble and needs help. Denial is a very useful mechanism for dealing with circumstances that cannot be changed. Where it is used vis-a-vis circumstances that could be changed, it is maladaptive.

In this regard we have come to regard assertiveness training for older people to be a particularly effective approach. It puts a sense of control and of being in charge of one's own destiny back into the patient's hands and powerfully improves self-esteem. While one has to be careful not to present assertiveness training to older patients as advice simply to become more aggressive and demanding, successfully accomplished assertiveness training can equip the older individual with techniques for dealing with many potentially adverse situations. Assertiveness training can best be accomplished in groups; and, in addition to the specific benefits of increased skills in assertiveness, the benefits of belonging to a defined group also accrue.

Systematic Multidimensional Functional Evaluation

It has been pointed out that health, social, and economic factors powerfully influence the mental state of well-being of older persons. In addition, the degree to which the above dimensions cause functional incapacity is important. For this reason, psychotherapists, in order to be successful, must begin with a comprehensive multidimensional assessment of the functional status of each individual as well as

---

"We have come to regard assertiveness training for older people to be a particularly effective approach. It puts a sense of control and of being in charge of one's own destiny back into the patient's hands and powerfully improves self-esteem. While one has to be careful not to present assertiveness training to older patients as advice simply to become more aggressive and demanding, successfully accomplished assertiveness training can equip the older individual with techniques for dealing with many potentially adverse situations."

---

an assessment of how these areas of functioning interact with one another.

This author has been working actively for the past seven years in developing standardized quantative reliable and valid methodologies for this purpose. The Older Americans Resources and Services (OARS) multidimensional functional assessment methodology, developed by a team of clinicians and researchers under the author's leadership at Duke University, has now received widespread attention as one systematic way of accomplishing this goal. Apart from providing a clinician with a solid foundation for clinical decision-making for the patient, this instrument has also been extremely useful as a device for teaching the nature of multidimensional and multidisciplinary interactions in older patients.

Emphasis on Establishing Clear-Cut Goals

To assist both patient and therapist in monitoring progress in psychotherapy, establishing a set of clearly-defined, hopefully stepwise goals to be attained in therapy is very useful. These should reflect both the patient's desires and

the therapist's understanding of the patient's real situation. Successful accomplishment of even modest goals fuels enthusiasm for patient as well as therapist for accomplishing more ambitious goals. Goals established should be measurable rather than intangible. They can readily be modified as circumstances and improvements warrant, and they should be reevaluated at regular intervals.

Other Unique Aspects of Psychotherapy With Older Patients

Transference phenomena obviously occur in psychotherapy with older patients. The therapist must be particularly aware of the frequent projection by the patient onto the therapist of expectations that he not only had of his parents but also has of his offspring. Thus, hopes, aspirations, fears, and disappointments in regard to marriage, occupation, and status are frequently projected onto the therapist. This is a new phenomenon for the beginning ther-

> **"Transference phenomena obviously occur in psychotherapy with older patients. The therapist must be particularly aware of the frequent projection by the patient onto the therapist of expectations that he not only had of his parents but also has of his offspring. Thus, hopes, aspirations, fears, and disappointments in regard to marriage, occupation, and status are frequently projected onto the therapist."**

apist, and can best be dealt with in psychotherapy supervision.

Countertransference phenomena also occur in psychotherapy with older patients and again differ somewhat from psychotherapy with younger patients. Thus, most psychotherapists expect that some of their younger patients may have sexual transference or even countertransference dealings. Disapproval on the part of a beginning therapist of a patient's expressed sexual feelings often leads to powerful countertransference feelings and anxiety on the part of the therapist. Many young therapists do not expect older patients to have sexual feelings at all and certainly not for the therapist. Again, this can be handled adequately in psychotherapy supervision.

Conclusion

I want to end on a more personal note. This author, in working psychotherapeutically with many older patients, professionally and emotionally has found this work to be extremely rewarding. He has learned a great deal from many of the older patients who came under his care. He has also been impressed with the remarkable responsiveness to psychotherapeutic input on the part of older patients and the extent to which they could resolve crisis, overcome obstacles, and forge new solutions to extremely difficult situations. Thus, the author has become convinced that not only are older patients responsive to psychotherapeutic intervention, but also that such intervention can be uniquely pleasurable and stimulating to both therapist and patient. Given the fact that the number of elderly persons in our population is increasing, we in psychiatry would do well to systematically gear up for psychotherapy with elderly patients

Bibliography

Bellak, L., and Karasu, T. 1976. *Geriatric psychiatry.* New York: Grune & Stratton.

Birren, J. E., and Schaie, K. W. 1977. *Handbook of the psychology of aging.* New York: Van Nostrand Reinhold Co.

Busse, E. W., and Pfeiffer, E. 1977. *Behavior and adaptation in late life.* Second Edition. Boston: Little, Brown and Company.

Busse, E. W., and Pfeiffer, E. *Mental illness in later life.* Washington, D.C.: American Psychiatric Association.

Butler, N., and Lewis, M. I. 1977. *Aging and mental health.* Second Edition. St. Louis: Mosby.

Davis, R. H., ed. *Drugs and the elderly.* Los Angeles: Andrus Gerontology Center, University of Southern California.

Eisdorfer, C., and Fann, W. E. 1973. *Psychopharmacology and aging.* New York: Plenum.

Fann, W. E., and Maddox, G. L. 1974. *Drug issues in geropsychiatry.* Baltimore: Williams and Wilkins.

Nandy, K., ed. 1978. *Senile dementia: a biomedical approach.* New York: Elsevier/North-Holland Biomedical Press.

Palmore, E., ed. 1970. *Normal aging.* Durham: Duke University Press.

Palmore, E., ed. 1974. *Normal aging II.* Durham: Duke University Press.

Pfeiffer, E. 1971. Psychotherapy with elderly patients. *Postgrad. Med.* 50:254-58.

Pfeiffer, E. 1975. A short portable mental status questionnaire for the assessment of organic brain deficit in elderly patients. *J. Amer. Geriat. Soc.* 23:433-41.

Pfeiffer, E. 1976. *Multidimensional functional assessment: the OARS methodology. A manual.* Durham: Duke University Center for the Study of Aging.

Pfeiffer, E. 1974. Sexuality in the aging individual. *J. Amer. Geriat. Soc.* 22:481-84.

Verwoerdt, 1976. *Clinical geropsychiatry.* Baltimore: Williams and Wilkins.

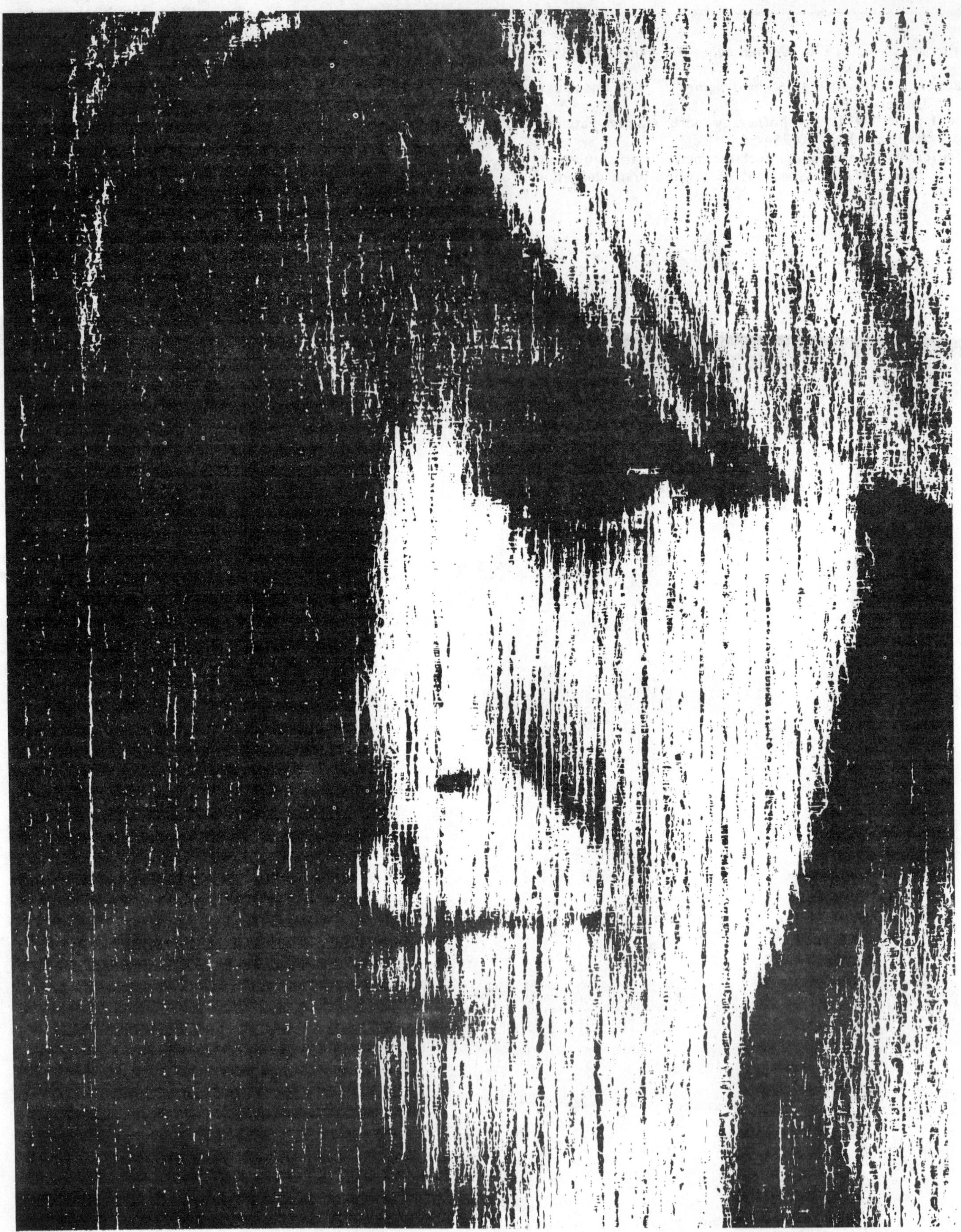

Death and Dying

The final section of this book deals with death and dying; its effects on children, parents and trained professionals. The inevitable conclusion of life can be lamentable, as in the suicide of adults, heartbreaking, as in the suicide of teen-agers, grievous, as in the death of an infant, pitiable, as in the death of parents, and distressing, if dealt with on a daily basis. The new field of thanatology is teaching people how to cope with death.

The schools have an obligation to children whose parent, or parents, died. Ignoring the death is heartless and causes emotional distress for the child. The child has suffered a profound loss and the comfort of teachers, administrators and friends helps to assure the child that he/she is being neither ostrasized because of the loss, nor abandoned.

The second loss dealt with in this section is the death of a newborn. Too often still-born babies are hurriedly carried away and buried. The parents never get a chance to see the "baby" they waited nine months for. The grieving parents often feel that the doctors are hiding something, and that either their babies were born alive and spirited away, or that the doctors "threw away" the "evidence" (the baby) of malpractice. One solution for this inappropriate grieving is to allow the parents to view the dead baby and when the parents are desirous of holding their baby to allow them to do so. This gives the family (parents and baby) a chance to separate.

Suicide at any age is a tragedy, but when the victims are teen-agers it is more horrible. The trend in society is for younger children to consciously take their own lives. Depression in childhood is becoming less uncommon.

The final article deals with the professionals who deal with death on a daily basis. These people are in need of therapy to help them keep a perspective on life. On falls prey to depression when one deals with grief on a personal level every day.

Helping Children Cope with Death

Perhaps there are some among you who find the topic of death particularly trying because you have recently lost a loved one or because you suffer from old bereavement wounds that are still sore and painful. To those who are hurting and struggling to cope, I extend my sympathies and also my apologies lest this article contain thoughts that might inadvertently make things harder for you.

Erna Furman

Erna Furman, B.A., is a faculty member of the Cleveland Center for Research in Child Development and Assistant Clinical Professor, Department of Psychiatry, Case Western Reserve University Medical School, Cleveland, Ohio.

Many of us go through life for long periods without thinking about death. When it suddenly strikes very close to us, it comes as a shock, not only because it always represents a loss but also because we get the horrible feeling that "this could be me; this could happen to me, to my family, to my children and friends." We have a tendency to deal with this fear by adopting one of two extreme attitudes. We may feel the impact as though the tragedy had really happened to us. We put ourselves in the shoes of the bereaved or of the dying and feel so overwhelmed and anxious that we are unable to extend ourselves appropriately to those who need our help. At the other extreme, we shield ourselves and behave as if "this is not real; this did not happen to me; I don't want to hear, read, or talk about it." This reaction too prevents us from extending a helping hand because it keeps us from coming to terms with our own feelings. Often we waver from one extreme to the other until, hopefully, we reach a kind of middle ground where we are able to feel, "There but for the grace of God go I; it is not me but it could be." When we arrive at this hard-to-reach point we begin to be able to think and feel with others and to help them as well as ourselves.

Many years ago at the Hanna Perkins (therapeutic) Nursery School, we were working without thinking about death. Then within one year, two mothers of young children died, leaving their families as well as therapists, teachers, peers, and friends stunned. We had to cope with the immediate reality and struggle to come to terms with what had happened. But this was only the beginning. In the course of the next few years, we found that, without having sought cases of bereavement, we had in intensive treatment 23 children of all ages who had lost a parent through death. Each analyst who treated a bereaved child and worked with the family found it so difficult and painful that we turned to each other to share and learn together. We hoped that in this way we would be better able to understand and help our patients and, perhaps, formulate some thoughts that might be of general interest and serve to assist others (Furman 1974). I would like to share with you some of the things we learned, trying to pick out what might be particularly helpful to teachers of young children.

As you know, it does not take the death of a parent to bring children to an encounter with death. Many grandparents, siblings, relatives, and pets die. There are also many daily events which bring children face to face with death, be it a passing funeral procession or a dead worm in the backyard. The worst bereavement is the death of a parent. It is a unique experience distinct from all other losses, such as divorce or separation, and distinct from other experiences with death. Many nursery school teachers may be fortunate enough never to have a pupil whose parent dies, but they are surely called upon to help with some less tragic bereavements and the many daily encounters with death—the ants a child steps on or the dead mouse

Helping Children Cope with Death, Erna Furman, *Young Children*, Vol. 33, No. 4, May 1978. ©1978 by The National Association for the Education of Young Children.

someone brings for show-and-tell (Hoffman 1974).

The danger of parental bereavement does not lie in the formation of isolated symptoms or difficulties. The main danger is that it may arrest or distort a child's development toward becoming a fully functioning adult.

Our bereaved children came to treatment with many different symptoms. Parental death is unique; it happens to unique people who respond in unique ways. Our patients most often responded in a disturbed, unhealthy fashion, sometimes at the time of the bereavements, sometimes not until many years later. But we were deeply impressed that some children only about two years of age, because of very optimal circumstances, could master their tragic loss. By contrast, we had much older patients who could not master it at all. I do not mean to imply that the two-year-olds master this stress more easily; on the contrary, it is harder. Nor is it short-lived for them; it lasts longer. I am not speaking of the degree of pain and anguish, but the ability to master ultimately. To me that means that these children were upset, struggled and suffered, but were able to mourn their parents and to progress in their development. The danger of parental bereavement does not lie in the formation of isolated symptoms or difficulties. The main danger is that it may arrest or distort a child's development toward becoming a fully functioning adult. Many of the factors involved touch upon the role of the teacher and offer an opportunity to develop in children those qualities which will enable them to master a future bereavement or to help them and their peers to cope with a current loss or minor encounter with death.

Helping Children Understand Death

The first crucial factor is children's ability to understand death in its concrete manifestations, *i.e.*, to understand that death means no life, no eating, no sleeping, no pain, no movement. Those children who at the time of bereavement already had a rather good grasp of the concrete facts of death had a much easier time. We found that children from toddler age on show interest in dead things. They find dead insects or birds. When they can tell that a sibling is different from a teddy bear, that one is animate and the other not, they can also begin to understand what *dead* means. For example, when the toddler plays with a dead fly and notes that it does not move, it helps to confirm the child's observation by using the word *dead* and explaining that the fly will never move again because it is dead. Most young children have not yet been helped to acquire this kind of basic concrete understanding of what *dead* means, how things die, and what we do with the corpse. It is much easier to acquire concrete understanding of death from insects or small animals, since they do not have great emotional significance for the child; this knowledge paves the way for later understanding of death in people.

McDonald (1963) studied the responses of the peers of our two bereaved Hanna Perkins Nursery School pupils. She found that children's first interest focused on what death is. They could not direct themselves to the aspects of loss, empathy, or sympathy for a peer's loss until they could understand concretely what death means. McDonald also noted that each of the children's questions required a special effort of thoughtful awareness and listening by the teachers. Initially, and without knowing it, teachers closed their eyes and ears and implied, without words, that death was not a welcome topic. Once their attitude changed, the children's questions just poured out. It is very difficult for all of us to talk about death, even dead insects. Most of us were not helped in this respect when we were children so we tend not to help children or do not know how to help. With special effort and by struggling to come to terms with questions about death ourselves, it is possible to overcome our difficulty to some extent.

Support for Parents

Parents usually do not mind when teachers talk at school about death as it relates to insects, worms, or even animals. Some teachers have found it helpful to meet with parents to discuss how such incidents are handled. Parents, perhaps even more than teachers, find it very difficult to talk with children about death, fearing that sooner or later the child will say, "Will I die?" "Will

8. DEATH

you die?" We are frightened of the answers that we would rather not give. However, the eventual next step in children's understanding death is that of relating it to themselves and to those they love and need. A meeting with parents on this subject does sometimes help to bring such questions into the open and offers the teacher an opportunity to help the parents. Whether a teacher wishes to arrange such meetings depends on the teacher's relationship with the parent group and the extent to which both sides are ready to grapple with the subject of death.

When a child asks, "Can this happen to me or to my mommy?" the answer should take into account the child's sense of time. A parent is hesitant to say, "No, I won't die," because he or she eventually will die. Yet should the parent say, "Yes, I will die," the child understands this to mean tomorrow or next week. We find that a young child can best understand when the parent says, "No, I do not expect to die for a long, long time," stressing the *no*, and adding that he or she expects to enjoy the child as a grown-up and have many years of being a grandparent.

Children before age five or six are incapable of abstract thinking and therefore unable to grasp religious or philosophical explanations. They usually distort them into concrete and often frightening concepts that have little to do with religion.

Parents usually also raise the question of spiritual answers to the question of death. Children before age five or six are incapable of abstract thinking and therefore unable to grasp religious or philosophical explanations. They usually distort them into concrete and often frightening concepts that have little to do with religion. I know some very religious parents who chose not to introduce religious explanations to their children under the age of five precisely because they knew these concepts would be distorted and might later interfere with the children's attitudes about religion. By contrast, doubting or unbelieving parents quite often use explanations that involve *heaven* and *God*. This happens because they have not thought matters through themselves and want to shield the child from something frightening. In shielding the

James Baritot

child they only shield themselves and create confusion in the child. Something that is not really believed by the adult cannot come across as true or reassuring to the child.

In our experience the most understanding parents have given concrete explanations of death and burial. When, in response to what they had heard from others, the children asked, "What about heaven?" or "Does God take people away?" the parents replied, "Many people believe that. Many people believe other things too and as you get older you will learn about them and will understand them better. Right now it is important that you understand how we all know when someone is dead."

The concrete facts of death are usually much less frightening to children than to adults. An anecdote about one of Barnes' (1964) patients illustrates this point. A father had struggled very hard to help his young children understand what *dead* meant and what being in a coffin meant because their mother had died. Some months later their grandfather died. As the father tried to tell his little girl that they would choose a nice box with a soft blanket inside so that grandfather would be very comfortable, the little girl interrupted him and said, "But daddy, if he is really dead then it doesn't matter about his being comfortable in the coffin." For that moment the child certainly had a better grasp than the father.

Bearing Unpleasant Feelings

Another factor which facilitates a child's mastery of bereavement is the ability to bear unpleasant feelings, particularly sadness and anger. Obviously, there is no way to anticipate the kind of feelings that come with a bereavement. Separations are very different from a loss through death, but there are some similarities. Separations, to a small extent, involve the same feelings of longing, sadness, and anger that we find in much greater intensity at a time of bereavement. Young children are able to bear these feelings to an incredible extent if they have been given appropriate help in developing this strength.

How does one help a child achieve such mastery? Basically there are two ways. One is to expose children only to bearable separations. When separations are too long they become unbearable and therefore not conducive to experiencing feelings. A very few hours of separation are bearable for a baby, perhaps half a day for a toddler, and at most a couple of days for a nursery school child. But it takes more than adjusting the lengths of separation. The second important step is the adults' willingness to help children recognize their feelings, express them appropriately, and cope with them. Before and after the separation this is the parents' task; during the separation the caregiving person can help.

The goal of assisting bereaved persons is not to foreshorten their or our own pain and anguish but to strive toward inner mastery.

It is often thought that children who do not react, do not make a fuss, or even enjoy the parents' absence, are well-adjusted, good children. To me, these children have not built appropriate mental muscles to bear unpleasant feelings. They shut themselves off from such feelings and therefore have no control of them. For nursery school teachers an excellent time to practice with children in building up the mental muscles for knowing and bearing unpleasant feelings is, of course, during entry to nursery school. At that time one can help parents understand that children who have no feelings, who react as though nothing has happened, or who immediately "love" the school, are children who are shut off from their feelings and in danger of stunting their emotional growth. Many mothers who do not welcome the child's unhappy

or angry response to separation at the start of school would be very concerned if the child did not react feelingly to the loss of a loved person or readily preferred someone else in that person's stead. Yet how could a child acknowledge very intense feelings without previous help to cope with them in less threatening situations?

Coping with Bereavement

So far we have considered how difficult it is to talk about death even in terms of animals and insects, and how hard to bear loneliness, sadness, and anger in terms of brief separations. We know, of course, how much greater the hardship is when we have to think about and feel fully the total loss of a loved person. There is no easy way to cope with bereavement. There is no shortcut, either for the bereaved or for those who help them. The goal of assisting bereaved persons is not to foreshorten their or our own pain and anguish but to strive toward inner mastery. Even if we achieve it, it does not mean that we have come to terms with death once and for all. In order to be able to help we too have to empathize anew with each bereavement and struggle through it again.

I would like to turn now to what teachers can do, and often have done, when a child in the nursery school suffers the death of a parent, sibling, or close relative. I do not have any easy remedies to offer, and my suggestions are much more easily said than done because pain and anxiety are an essential part of the task.

The teacher's first question often is, "Should I mention the loss to the child?" I have heard time and again about the fear of causing a child hardship by referring to his or her loss. Some years ago I met a boy whose father had died. His teacher had reported that the boy had no feelings about, or reaction to, the death of the father. When I saw this boy, said "Hello" and expressed my natural sympathy, he broke into tears at once. He cried for an hour and I had to see him a second time before he could begin to talk. I asked him later why he had never shown his feelings at school. The boy replied, "You know, that teacher was so mean! He never even bothered to come to me and say 'I am sorry your father died.' I would never show my feel-

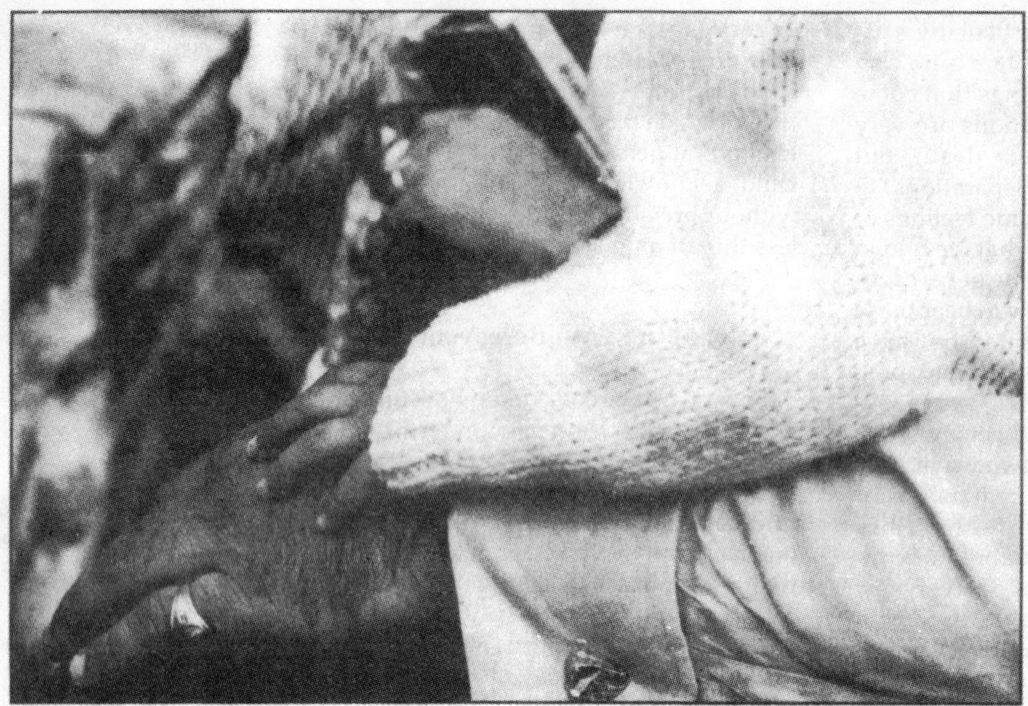

ings to that kind of guy." I suspect that this was not a mean teacher but that his reaction of silence built a barrier between the child and himself.

This and similar experiences have convinced me that the teacher has to take the first step by mentioning the loss and expressing sympathy in a way that implies, "This will be with us a long time. I hope you will feel free to come to me, talk with me, or feel with me about it." In practice, some children will come to the teacher much more than others. However often they do or do not come, the teacher needs to empathize with each and every feeling that may arise and help children tolerate them. This means not to falsify feelings, not to hold them back, not even to pour them out in order to be rid of them, but to recognize and contain them.

It is most important that the children understand not only that the parent or sibling is dead, but also what the cause of death was.

At opportune times the teacher can also help by talking with the child about the factual aspects of the bereavement—how the loved one died, where he or she is buried, and changes in the family setting and routine. I think it is equally important for the teacher to report to the parent what the child shows, thinks, or feels about this experience so that the parent can further help the child and perhaps be alerted to some aspect which has not yet been expressed at home.

In addition to work with the child, a second area in which the teacher can be helpful is with the parents or surviving parent. Hopefully, before a loss occurs, the teacher will have built the kind of relationship with the parent which will make it possible for him or her to inform the teacher as a friend, a special professional friend who has the parent's and child's welfare at heart. The parent will welcome talking with this teacher and perhaps accept some suggestions—how to tell the child about the death, how to talk it over with the child, whether to take the child to the funeral, what plans to make for the immediate future.

Assisting Parents

Let me now share with you some of the things we have found helpful to parents at such a time. Adults with young children do not die uncomplicated deaths; the deaths are always untimely. This is also true about the death of siblings. It is most important that the child understand not only that the parent or sibling is dead, but also what the cause of death was. When these two things are not understood, when they are distorted or denied, it is impossible for the child even to begin mourning. I do not mean overwhelming the child with frightening details. Hopefully a teacher can help a parent to tell the child enough and in such a manner that the child can achieve a considerable amount of understanding.

Parents always want to know whether they should take the child to the funeral, and what they should say about it. We can only give an answer after we learn more about the specific situation. The child's attendance at the funeral will depend on the type of service, how the parent feels about it, how comfortable the parent is with the rites the family observes, and how able the parent is to extend himself or herself emotionally to the child during the funeral.

Many families are willing to adapt the services to the needs of all the family. Children often find an open casket difficult. They find long services difficult. If the funeral rites are not suitable for a young child or if the parent is unable to care effectively for the child during the services, it is better that the child remain at home with a familiar person and with the full verbal knowledge of what is happening during that time. I had a patient who was sent to the zoo on the day of her father's funeral in the hope that she would not have to be sad. This hope was not fulfilled, and the arrangement produced an almost insurmountable barrier within the child and between child and surviving parent. Mourning has to happen together. Pain and anguish have to be shared. It is not fair to shut out the child.

When it comes to immediate plans for the future, the teacher can sometimes impress upon parents how very important it is for the child to keep the home and remaining family together. Adults often find it much easier to leave the place of distress, to throw away the things that remind them of the deceased. For children the opposite holds true. They need the concrete continuation and help of their surroundings in order to come to terms with what is missing. Sometimes people have asked how parents and children can ever be of support to one another when they have such different needs. When parents understand that their children's greatest need is continued physical and emotional care by the surviving parent, they usually compromise for the sake of the child and find that they

benefit as well. Being a good parent brings a measure of self-esteem that cannot be gained in any other way and is especially helpful at a time of bereavement when so many other things seem not worthwhile.

Helping Others in the Group

Along with assisting the bereaved child and parent, the teacher has to extend help to the other children in the nursery school. This usually starts by discussing with the bereaved parent what to tell the other children and their families. Hopefully the bereaved parent is able to share the truth in simple realistic terms with his or her own child and is willing to have this information passed on. Then the teacher needs to take a few painful hours to call every parent in the nursery group. Each call is long and difficult and should, if possible, include several items: a brief account of what happened to their child's peer, which terms or phrases will be used in the nursery school to discuss the sad event, how the parents can tell their own child and how helpful it would be if the child learned the news first from them, and how to cope with some of the child's questions.

If a bereaved parent is initially unable to allow discussion of the cause of death, the teacher may have to say, for example, "Chris's father died. It is still too hard for Chris's mommy to talk about it, but she will tell us what happened later and I will share it with you." Hopefully, the teacher's relationship with the parent will help to make this delay brief.

Mourning . . . is a process that is not always visible from the outside. . . . Sometimes there are no overt signs of upset and yet the feelings may be there.

The next morning all children will have been told of the death, even if not its cause, by their parents, and the teacher can sit down with them and initiate the first discussion of facts and feelings. The most important point to cover is, "This talk is only a beginning. We will talk about it and feel about it often and for a long time. It will be with us because it is a sad and scary thing."

There are usually three main questions that arise sooner or later: "What is dead?" "Can it happen to me?" and "Can it happen to you?" Until these questions are accepted and coped with, it is generally not possible for the peers or for their parents to extend genuine sympathy to the bereaved. When we are able to assist children in gaining gradual mastery, many months of painful struggle seem indeed worthwhile.

The Mourning Process

If the death is understood, if its cause is understood and the disposal of the body is understood, and if the bereaved child is reasonably sure of his or her own survival and of having bodily and emotional needs met to a sufficient extent, mourning will start of itself. It is a process that is not always visible from the outside because, contrary to what many people think, mourning does not consist of wailing, rages, crying, or complaining. Sometimes there are no overt signs of upset and yet the feelings may be there.

I worked with a mother and child. The little boy lost his father two years previously and experienced some difficulty in the aftermath. The mother told me that she had never cried in front of the child, since she only cries when she is alone in bed. The boy, who supposedly had not reacted at all to his father's death and had certainly never cried or raged, told me in his separate interview that he was not a person who ever cried in front of people. He only cried when he was alone in bed and nobody knew that he cried. He cried night after night but his mother never cried. Although mother and child expressed feelings in the same form, they did not know that the other even had feelings. It was sad to see how hard they had made it for themselves and for each other. However, even if they had not cried at all they might have been able to mourn because mourning is a mental process that consists primarily of two parts: on one hand, a very gradual and painful detachment from the memories of the deceased, and on the other hand almost the opposite, a taking into oneself some traits or qualities of the deceased. How much there is of each part and whether the proportion leads to a healthy adaptive outcome depend on many factors, including the age of the bereaved person, the nature of the bereavement, the preceding relationship, the personality of the deceased. With young children it is particularly important that they take into themselves the healthy rather than the sick attributes of the dead parent and that they detach themselves sufficiently, so that, in time, they will be free to form a parental bond with a new person.

Sometimes parents intuitively understand the ways in which their child's long inner mourning proceeds and sense when the child encounters difficulties. Sometimes it is much harder. It certainly is not a mark of failure to seek professional assistance at such a time. That is yet another area where the teacher can support the surviving parent. The sooner help is given, the better the chances of preventing possible damage to the child's growing personality.

This article is adapted from a talk given in May 1975 at the Seventh Annual Workshop of the Cleveland Center for Research in Child Development for Preschool Educators of North Eastern Ohio.

References

Barnes, M. J. "Reactions to the Death of a Mother." *The Psychoanalytic Study of the Child* 19 (1964): 334-357.

Furman, E. *A Child's Parent Dies*. New Haven, Conn.: Yale University Press, 1974.

Hoffman, Y. "Learning about Death in Preschool." *Review, Spring 1974*. Cleveland: Cleveland Association for the Education of Young Children, 1974, pp. 15-17.

McDonald, M. "Helping Children to Understand Death: An Experience with Death in a Nursery School." *Journal of Nursery Education* 19, no. 1 (1963): 19-25.

PERINATAL AND INFANT DEATHS:
FOCI OF MOURNING

Lewis M. Cohen, M.D., Assistant Professor of Psychiatry, Boston University School of Medicine, Boston, Massachusetts; Associate Director of Emergency Psychiatric Services, Boston City Hospital, Boston, Massachusetts Department of Psychiatry, Massachusetts General Hospital. *Elizabeth McAnulty, R.N., M.P.H.,* Coordinator, Massachusetts Center for Sudden Death Syndrome, Boston City Hospital, Boston, Massachusetts.

The dramatic reduction of childhood infections and nutritional disorders has provided us with a relatively new confidence that our children will live long and productive lives. In the United States alone, however, approximately 70,000 babies die each year during the perinatal period and there are an additional, 6,500 deaths among infants from the Sudden Infant Death Syndrome (SIDS).[1] While there are similarities in the manner in which families cope with perinatal mortality and SIDS, there are also differences in the mourning reactions to these two forms of bereavement.

Parents who experience a perinatal mortality need to direct a significant portion of their energy to affirming, in the face of societal and other pressures, that they have indeed been pregnant and delivered a child and that the child has died. Since there are rarely private funerals, the question "what happens to the body" is often a central, even if unvoiced, concern of parents and medical staff. In this article we will reiterate some of our findings regarding "viewing", "autopsy", and "public burial"[2,3] Knowledge of these three processes is essential for health professionals and families in facilitating adaptation through affirmation.

The quite different issue in SIDS centers around families' attempts to apportion responsibility for a tragedy which modern medicine is still unable to explain. Efforts should be aimed at educating parents, and on a broader scale influencing public opinion, by widely dispersing current information about this phenomenon.

Comparatively little emphasis has been hitherto focused on siblings' reactions to perinatal mortality and sudden infant death. We will conclude with a brief description of some of our recent efforts in this direction.

PERINATAL MORTALITY:

Perinatal mortality refers to stillbirths and babies who die within the first 28 days of life. These differ from miscarriages, where the fetus has not achieved a viable weight or gestational age, and sudden infant deaths, which occur usually at 2 to 6 months. One of us, (LC), participated in 1974 in instituting at the Downstate-Kings County Hospital Medical Center, a Perinatal Mortality Clinci. The multidisciplinary clinic is one of the few such services in the country and is composed of volunteers from the hospital who provide counseling and review obstetrical and pediatric records and autopsy reports.

Viewing

After a baby dies in the medical center an official nursing and nurse-midwifery policy has evolved in which parents or other family members are given the option to "view" the body. Viewing does not appear to cause additional trauma even in cases involving congenital anomalies and prolonged fetal demise. Parents comment favorably on this aspect of their hospitalization and some of our data suggests that non-viewers and those couples not asked to view make up a disproportionately large percentage of the small group of individuals who require additional psychiatric intervention.[2]

Autopsy

Pathological examinations are now routinely

"Perinatal and Infant Deaths: Foci of Mourning." ©1979 by Lewis M. Cohen M.D. and Elizabeth Mcanulty, R.N., M.P.H. Reprinted with permission.

performed at the medical center. Although autopsies are rarely valuable in establishing diagnoses, they serve the inestimable function of allaying parental fears by ruling out the possibility of covert congenital abnormalities.

Burial

Contrary to parents' and staffs' fantasies, all babies are buried and in 96% of our sample this took place in Potter's Field. The term probably first occurs in English in the King James version of the Bible (Matt. 27:7): "and they took counsel, and bought Potter's Field to bury strangers in." New York City's Potter's Field is on Hart Island in Long Island Sound and in its 105 year history over 650,000 people haved been interred there. In 1973 there were 2,182 babies buried in small pine coffins by prisoners and correctional officers.[4]

> A first grade teacher, whose pregnancy and delivery had necessitated her taking a leave of absence from school, returned on the last day of class. She explained to her students that her prematurely born son had died the day after his birth and both the class and teacher cried together. Later she showed her colleagues snap-shots of the baby taken at the funeral parlor.

In the classic view of Freud, effective mourning permits the libido, which was invested in the dead person, to be freed up and become available to the survivor to invest again in new love objects.[5] There is a restoration of damaged self-esteem and renewal of the capacity to establish and develop relationships. Mourning consists of the evocation and assimilation of the multiplicity of experiences which bound one to the deceased. Understandably, this is extremely difficult for families who have perinatal deaths, where the loss is almost more of an unfulfilled wish than the death of a "real" person.[6] What we have chosen to call "affirmation" is the effort that many of these parents make to establish and express to others the full, even if time-limited circumstances of their pregnancy, delivery and bereavements. In addition, since there are few established societal and religious rituals for mourning the death of babies, families especially need to "view" the body and require detailed knowledge of the autopsy and burial.

SUDDEN INFANT DEATH SYNDROME

Sudden Infant Death Syndrome (SIDS) is a medical entity which is at least as old as biblical times, but only in the past decade has become the focus of federally funded research and public education. SIDS is the most prominent cause of death of infants between one month and one year of life.[7] It occurs most frequently during sleep and characteristically is quiet and without evidence of a struggle. Despite vigorous research, it is not yet possible to predict the infant at risk and hence to prevent the death of a seemingly healthy infant. Clinical investigation of SIDS has escalated since the passage of the Sudden Infant Death Syndrome Act of 1974[8] and includes studies directed at cardiopulmonary function; respiratory physiology; immunology; genetic susceptibility and neurophysiology. Efforts of the National Sudden Infant Death Syndrome Foundations, which largely represents bereaved families, and the SIDS Centers, funded through H.E.W., have effected a marked increase in public awareness and sensitive response to affected families.[9]

SIDS typically occurs at a time when parenting roles have been established. Unlike perinatal mortality, the infant has a name and has been integrated into the family. After the second month of life infants begin to give some "return" to parents and establish stable and affectionate relationships which are distinguishable from the earlier process of attachment. (10) Parents at this stage derive much of their own self-esteem from the interaction and the promise it holds. When SIDS occurs at this point is *sudden, unexpected* and *unexplained.* The circumstances of the baby's death and the appearance of the baby when found evoke parental fears and community concerns that they allowed their infant to suffocate, choke, aspirate a feeding or succumb to an illness. The task of the health professional in aiding families is to alleviate the inevitable guilt and self-blame, by acting as a two-way conduit for all data concerning the individual circumstances and through the provision of currently available information about SIDS. A non-delayed autopsy is a necessary first step in establishing the diagnosis.

> One family did not receive an accurate report of their infant son's autopsy until several months after the death. During that time the 34 year old father evidenced a tight control of emotional expression which he described as typical of his response at the time of catastrophic losses during childhood and battle in Vietnam. Two months after the infant's death

the father experienced seizure-like episodes which strikingly resembled his own desciption of his son's death. These attacks elicited responses of exquisite anxiety and helplessness in his wife. A complete medical and neurological work-up failed to reveal an organic basis.

CHILDREN'S REACTIONS TO PERINATAL MORTALITY AND SIDS

Parents, prior to either perinatal mortality or SIDS, often feel relatively insulated from danger. These nightmarish events may foster a tremendous sense of vulnerability. Many parents have never experienced a loss before and the somatic distress and psychological pain of grief are extremely frightening to them. It is now well recognized that anticipatory guidance and support in the mourning process can be a significant intervention. We have come to see that parents may also specifically need guidance in helping their other children to deal with the death. We are increasingly concerned that children who are sheltered from the honest expression of parental grief, or exposed to pathological parental grief, or deprived of accurate information about the baby's death, are at psychological risk. They need the opportunity to assimilate information and express in play or language their own conceptualizations.

Parents need to be educated as to the age-dependent phases of the death concept. Children five years old or younger regard death as a reversible, sleep-like process and later may personify death in the form of a boogeyman who takes one away. Only around age 8 or 9 is death's irreversibility and universality recognized.[5] Siblings must be allowed to participate in their own fashion in the family's mourning, and we are investigating different ways to involve them in our interactions. This may include sensitizing parents to the means in which their children utilize play as communication and also composing a story book for family readings.

A 30 year old Ph.D. candidate seen in analytically oriented psychotherapy was able to reconstruct some of the impact that his brother's death 25 years before had made on the entire family. "He was a real person, he had a name, Frankie, and each year we celebrate his birthday!....and yet there were also the secret aspects...How did he die? I've been led to believe there were congenital abnormalities and he didn't survive...but I wonder whether the doctor's hastened his demise with my parents' consent...Most important, why didn't they mourn his death...I never saw they cry...they just would keep bringing his name up...casual-like...If they loved their kids you would think they would mourn him, bury him, have a ceremony or something, get upset...but I remember nothing like that occuring..."

A 42 year old mother was seen six months after experiencing a neonatal death. Asked to describe the reactions of her five children, she focused on the youngest, her 7 year old son, who had spoken little during the initial few weeks of the bereavement. One morning, however, he presented her with one of his T-shirts and a pair of shorts into which he had stuffed a towel, declaring "Momma, here's a baby for you,...I'm going out ot play."

REFERENCES

1. Vital statistics of the United States, 1973. 1975. Vol. 2, Mortality, Part B. National Center for Health Statistics, Rockville, Maryland.

2. Cohen, L. et al. "Perinatal Mortality: Assisting Parental Affirmation," **Amer. J. Orthopsychiatry,** 48(4), 1978.

3. Cohen, L. et al. "Perinatal Mortality: Obstetrical Nightmare," Presented to the American Psychiatry Association, 1977.

4. Sellers J., Last Stop for the Unclaimed Poor, **New York Sunday News,** June 2, 1974: 16:36.

5. Cassem, N., Treating the Person Confronting Death in **The Harvard Guide to Modern Psychiatry** ed. by A. Nichols, Belknap Press of Harvard University Press, Cambridge, Massachusetts, 1978.

6. Deutsch, H., **The Psychology of Women,** Vol. II, Grune and Stratton, New York, 1945.

7. Beckwith, J.B. "The Sudden Infant Death Syndrome," DHEW Publication No. HSA 75-5137, U.S. Government Printing Office, 1977.

8. Sudden Infant Death Syndrome Act of 1974, P.L. 93-270, Enacted April 22, 1974, Title XI, Part C, Section 1121 (a) and 1121 (b) of the Public Health Service Act.

9. Sudden Infant Death, Syndrome Information and Councilling Projects, DHEW Publication No. HSA 76-5144, U.S. Government Printing Office, 1976.

10. Klause, M.H., Kennel, J.H., Human-Maternal and Paternal Behavior in Klaus, M.H., Kennel, J.H. **Maternal Infant Bonding,** St. Louis, C.V. Mosby Co., 1976, pp. 38-98.

Teen-Age Suicide

Harry, 17, arrived at the University of Missouri last fall to begin his freshman year. His parents dropped him off on a Saturday and left on vacation—and Harry promptly asked his new roommates about an easy way to commit suicide. They jokingly suggested that he throw himself in front of a train or get himself a gun. Four days later, Harry left a handwritten note in his chemistry notebook saying he was having "a hard time adjusting" and just wanted to "rest in peace." Then he went out and placed his head on the railroad tracks in front of a freight train. Neither his family nor his roommates had any idea that Harry was disturbed or depressed.

Harry is one of 5,000 young Americans a year who commit suicide—a near-epidemic average of thirteen a day. Suicide is now the third leading cause of death for 15-to-24-year-olds, after accidents and homicides. Though the country's over-all suicide rate has not varied much in the past half-century, the rate for young people has nearly tripled between 1955 and 1975, from four suicides per 100,000 people to 11.8 (chart). Some, like Harry, are middle-class college students away from home for the first time. But for the most part, they are a startling cross-section of youth from all social, economic and racial backgrounds. "There is little doubt that this is a monumental increase," says Dr. Calvin J. Frederick, chief of emergency mental health and disaster assistance at the National Institute of Mental Health. "It is an alarming problem."

There are nearly as many reasons for the increase as there are experts offering them. The special anxiety of adolescence is one of them. "It is full of emotional fluxes, self-doubts, searches for identity and the need for peer acceptance," says Washington psychologist Alan Berman. "Often, kids don't know how to deal with it"—especially if they lack strong support from family or friends. Also, young people generally take setbacks harder than adults and act out their frustrations more dramatically. "With teen-agers, suicide is often an impulsive thing," says Thomas Hanratty, an investigator for the Milwaukee County medical examiner's office. "A guy's girlfriend tells him to go to hell and that will do it."

Young suicides may be even more common than the numbers show because of suicidal "accidents," often involving alcohol, drugs or automobiles. Not long ago, for example, a young man in Washington took LSD and tried to walk across a branch of the Potomac River. He drowned. In Massachusetts officials called it an accident when a young woman drove on the wrong side of a highway with her headlights off and was killed.

Saving a 19-year-old on a Georgia water tower

Frederick attributes the suicides, obvious or disguised, to depression brought on by "haplessness, helplessness and hopelessness" in young people. "When they run into hard luck, they feel they just can't pull themselves together."

NO SENSE OF BELONGING

Perhaps more than anything else, the shifting state of the American family is a major cause of the growing suicide problem. "There's no real sense kids have that they belong anywhere or to anyone as they did ten or fifteen years ago," says Reina Gross, chief psychiatric social worker at Illinois Medical Center in Chicago. Many parents, busy pursuing their own lives and careers, often stir feelings of isolation, alienation and rejection in youngsters—emotions that can trigger thoughts of suicide. And when parents, for whatever reason, fail to provide rules and restraints for their children, it is often seen as a lack of caring. "Parents have loosened the reins and kids are kind of floundering," says Dr. Michael Kalogerakis of the New York State Department of Mental Hygiene. Soaring divorce rates can also have an unsettling effect on children, who may feel responsible for the parents' breakup or simply lost in a new family situation. A study at New York's Bellevue Hospital of 102 teen-agers who attempted suicide showed that only one-third of them lived with both parents—and it was usually the father who was absent.

Carolyn was 12 when her parents were divorced, and she suddenly began to feel that her mother didn't love her. She overdosed on pills several times, once so severely that she had to be hospitalized for six months. She threatened to jump off bridges and once actually had to be talked down from one. She drank a bottle of vodka in ten minutes and then walked out in front of cars on a highway. Her mother, with whom she had gotten along well before the divorce, finally threw her out of the house. Now 15, she has her own apartment and has been seeing a psychiatrist. "There's been a real disruption in the mother-child relationship," says the doctor. "I think there's a good chance she'll try again to kill herself."

Even if their family life is relatively secure, many young people suffer severe anxieties stemming from the competitive pressure of getting high grades or a good job. Dr. Seymour Perlin, professor of psychiatry at the George Washington University Medical School, believes that American society is becoming more like Japan's—where career competition is fierce and the suicide rate high among young people. "There, the student who doesn't get onto the ladder at a certain point won't," Perlin explains. "What the suicide increase among 15-to-24-year-olds says is either 'There's no way on' or 'I'm falling off'." Dr. Pamela Cantor, a clinical psychologist at Boston University, suggests that "kids are more willing to give up. Many feel it's not worth living, that jobs won't be there after they graduate. Society can't absorb them, and they know that most of them simply won't make it."

Heightened competition for school

Photos by Ed C. Thompson

'A cry for help': Atlanta policeman approaches a girl threatening to jump . . .

. . . and talks her out of it

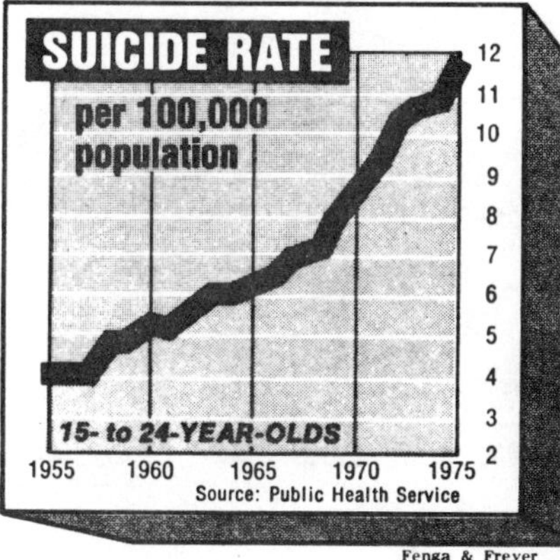

Fenga & Freyer

Epidemic: Thirteen deaths a day

and jobs seems to have boosted the suicide rate for young blacks, which in the past ran one-third to one-half the rate of young whites. Now, as one distinctly unwelcome sign of black progress, the rates for black and white teen-agers are about the same. "As opportunities for education and employment increase, there's more opportunity for things to go wrong," suggests Dr. Richard Seiden of the University of California at Berkeley School of Public Health. "If you have your hopes raised and then they are dashed, your sense of frustration and failure may increase."

THE SUICIDAL GESTURE

The male suicide rate is about four times as high as the female rate. But women attempt suicide nearly three times as often as men: they succeed less often because they use less lethal methods, such as taking pills, while men tend to favor guns. Dr. Frederick of the NIMH explains the difference this way: "A suicide attempt is a cry for help, a cry for someone to care. But men don't feel free to cry for help. Women do." Consequently, he says, women use slower, less final methods—but the underlying stress on both men and women is about the same.

Younger people are particularly prone to the suicidal gesture to try to win attention or to punish authority figures—a

sometimes fatal version of holding one's breath until turning blue. Dr. James M.A. Weiss of the University of Missouri Medical Center has recently completed a study indicating that a large number of young people who attempt suicide have a "relatively low psychological intent" to go through with it. And many experts theorize that the number of attempted suicides among younger people is as much as 100 times the number of actual suicides—suggesting a great amount of indecision. "Threatening suicide becomes a way of getting some power, some control," says Reina Gross. "It's not so much that the person wants to die; he just doesn't see any alternative." The suicidal gesture becomes especially dangerous with even younger children—who may not realize that death is permanent. Some experts, in fact, are increasingly concerned about the suicide rate among 10- to 14-year-old children, which has risen nearly as fast as the rate for 15- to 24-year-olds.

What can be done? Experts stress that family and friends must not ignore certain warning signs: fatigue and loss of sleep, sudden loss of appetite, mood changes, a significant decline in school work, heavy smoking, writing lots of letters to friends, an increase in drug or alcohol use, giving away prized possessions. Such signs often come in bunches,

and while the underlying problems may seem trivial to an adult, they can be very serious to the child. If the child threatens suicide, it may be helpful to assign small tasks in order to keep him busy. In any event, says Frederick, "It is important to take every threat seriously."

At 14, Mark was an impulsive, hostile kid with an explosive temper. When he was angry or frustrated, he would take his older brother's motorcycle and tear dangerously across the desert or zoom down steep hills on his skateboard at 30 to 40 mph. When things got really bad, he knotted a tie around his neck and pulled it tight to scare people into caring for him. He was fidgety and disruptive in school because he was a terrible reader. His parents and teachers dismissed his rambunctious behavior as childishness. Last summer, Mark lost a card game to his older brother—and he ran into his room and hanged himself with a belt from the closet door.

Increasingly, troubled kids like Mark are being treated in institutions. There are about 200 independent, locally-funded suicide-prevention centers in the U.S. in addition to 675 federally-funded community health centers that have crisis-intervention services. Many colleges, with a rising student suicide rate, have set up walk-in counseling services, and nonprofessional help—usually emergency telephone hotlines—also is becoming more common.

The Teenage Resource Center in Fullerton, Calif., for example, provides counseling for troubled youngsters, nearly a quarter of whom are suicidal. The TRC helps about 4,000 people a year, one-third of them teen-agers and the rest members of their families. TRC staffers routinely ask if those who come for help have considered suicide. "If there is a present danger, they'll tell you," says TRC worker Wayne Daniels. "It's rare when they say no and then go out and kill themselves. They don't want death. They want life."

TALKING IT OVER

One of Daniels's current cases is an introverted, slightly plump girl of 17 who found herself unable to compete with her more successful siblings and satisfy her demanding parents. Last summer, after a typical blowup over nothing, she left home. In her travels she was raped and later seduced by an older woman. As a last resort, she went to the TRC. "She said her parents would never change and she would never change, so why go on?" Daniels recalls. "But she came to be talked out of it." Daniels persuaded her to go back home and now she comes in frequently to talk out her troubles.

When people who have attempted suicide seek help, the first step is to determine just how serious they are about killing themselves. If their situation appears to be grave, they may be

Susan T. McElhinney—Newsweek

Counseling: Opening up alternatives

hospitalized—voluntarily or by court order—for at least a month, where they are usually treated with antidepressant drugs. Whether the patients are hospitalized or not, the most crucial part of the treatment is psychiatric therapy.

PSYCHOLOGICAL FIRST AID

"If they see life as bad and can't see shades in between, then the alternative, death, is not negative to them," says Washington psychologist Dan Lettieri. "In therapy, it's most important to try to open alternatives, to show the shades in between." Marcia, a Missouri graduate student who twice tried to kill herself, testifies to the validity of that approach. "It's especially important to impress upon a young person that things can change for him." She remembers the first time someone told her she was a valuable person. "I never wanted to kill myself after that," she says.

Dr. Frederick of the NIMH is optimistic that the juvenile-suicide rate can be reduced, primarily by training nonprofessionals such as teachers, counselors and teen-agers themselves in "psychological first aid"—recognizing suicidal danger signals. With such training, those closest to young people are the best-equipped to help someone in trouble—by talking to them, listening to their problems and, if necessary, steering them to proper professional help. To that end, the National Institute of Mental Health has proposed a five- to eight-year program that concentrates on preventive education. That is likely to be a long, slow process, and the unhappy fact is that the suicide rate is likely to go up still more.

Suicide in Psychiatric Patients

By D.H. Myers and C.D. Neal

SUMMARY The study relates to suicides occurring in Shropshire during 1965 to 1973 inclusive. Psychiatric patients who had committed suicide were compared with others, matched by sex and age who had not done so. The suicide group included a higher proportion of members who had behaved violently, experienced a broken marriage (through death, separation or divorce) or earlier had deliberately harmed themselves, often by dangerous means. Of the psychiatric patients who committed suicide 63 per cent had seen a doctor within a month beforehand, yet very few were receiving adequate physical treatment for depressive illness at the time of their death. Immigrants from eastern Europe were found to be particularly prone to suicide.

Introduction

The study had two main purposes. The first was to find simple ways of deciding which psychiatric patients are likely eventually to commit suicide. To do this patients who had committed suicide were compared, on some of the factors known to be associated with suicide (Stengel, 1964), with a control group of patients matched for age and for sex who had not done so. The second purpose was to find out if those who committed suicide and who had a previous diagnosis of depressive illness had been having adequate physical treatment at the time of their death.

The study was conducted in Shropshire, a largely rural county. Its 337,100 inhabitants (1971 census) live in small towns and villages at a mean population density of 0.4 persons per acre. The population, so far, is a settled one and many of the people who live in the county were born there. However, this is less true of the new town of Telford. This town in the east of the county has been formed by welding together a collection of small towns and hamlets—places like Wellington and Ironbridge—in which the Industrial Revolution had some of its early beginnings. Telford's population had grown by 1971 to 79,450 mainly through an influx of people from the industrial West Midlands.

The estimated mean annual suicide rate per 100,000 population in Shropshire for the period of the study (1965–73 inclusive) was very similar to the corresponding rate for England and Wales: for Shropshire, 10.8 for men and 7.01 for women; for England and Wales, 10.75 for men and 7.40 for women.

Method

The available depositions were read on all persons whose deaths in Shropshire during 1965 to 1973 inclusive had been given a verdict of suicide. From these, and from hospital records, a list was made of those who had seen a psychiatrist (the 'referred' group).

We wished to compare the referred group of suicides with sex-matched psychiatric controls in respect of psychiatric history and circumstances at the time of suicide. Matching for age at suicide and date of suicide was also undertaken. It was therefore necessary to designate some event in the lives of the controls as the reference point for matching. Their last hospital admission was chosen as this reference point, because it was equivalent to suicide at least in marking an episode of mental disorder of comparable severity (those who had committed suicide would almost certainly have been admitted had the risk been recognized). This method of matching, while avoiding any need for following up controls, is certainly not ideal. The act of suicide, or for the controls the last admission, is referred to here as the 'key episode'.

Since the controls' last admission was not treated as an admission but as a suicide-equivalent, the matching was done as follows: suicides who had never been admitted were matched with controls with only one admission; suicides who had been admitted in the past were matched with controls who had more than one admission. In order to ensure as far as possible equivalence of data source, the last admission of the controls was not used for any type of information (mainly clinical) which could not be culled from the coroners' records. There was only one exception. If the one-admission controls had had no prior out-patient attendance, the admission notes were used for clinical information. Matching for date of suicide was undertaken because the nine-year period of the study had seen big changes in psychiatric policy over admissions, discharges and community care.

Age was matched in five-year intervals, date in two-year intervals (relaxed for the last 15 patients to five-year intervals). An alphabetical register of patients, giving dates of birth and of admissions, was used as the source of the controls. A letter of the alphabet was chosen at random by taking one bean from a jar of beans labelled with the letters of the alphabet. The number of beans labelled with any one letter of the alphabet was the same as the number of pages of the register listing patients whose names began with that letter. All patients whose names began with the selected letter were scrutinized, and a short-list was drawn up of those who satisfied the matching criteria. A final choice was made from the short-list, using random numbers.

The matched pairs data were analyzed by McNemar's test. The significance of the binomial proportions yielded by this test, and the significance of the differences between the proportions in the unmatched data, were determined by the χ^2 test approximation based on one degree of freedom and with Yates' correction.

Results

The coroner's records of 256 of the 260 deaths with a suicide verdict occurring in Shropshire during 1965 to 1973 inclusive were examined. One hundred of these suicides had seen a psychiatrist: 49 men and 51 women with mean ages respectively of 54.4 and 53.8 years.

Method of committing suicide

At the beginning of the study an arbitrary distinction between town-dwellers (in communities of 5,000 or more) and country-dwellers (in communities of less than 5,000) was made. Lethal overdose was favoured more by town than by country-dwellers: 61 out of 161 town-dwelling but only 23 out of 95 country-dwelling suicides used this method ($\chi^2 = 4.4$, P < 0.05). Two methods, hanging and shooting (almost always with a shotgun), alone accounted for 55 per cent of the male country-dwellers' suicides.

Physical illness

Seventy-six (30 per cent) of the whole suicide sample were physically ill at the time of their death. Sixteen (6.2 per cent) had definite organic cerebral disease diagnosed during life. A further ten, not diagnosed during life were found to have cerebral atrophy when examined post-mortem.

Suicide in a small immigrant community

There is a population in Shropshire of Eastern Europeans, mainly Poles and Ukrainians. Although it is small, numbering 690 in 1961 and 700 in 1971 (1961 and 1971 census) it contributed seven suicides, giving a much higher suicide rate than for the rest of the Shropshire population during the period studied ($\chi^2 = 63$, P < 0.001).

Civil state

From Table I it can be seen that in 25 pairs the suicide member was not leading a married life at the time of death but the control member was: in only 11 pairs was the situation reversed ($\chi^2 = 4.7$, P < 0.05).

If the comparison is narrowed to those whose marriages have ended (through death, divorce, or separation) a significant difference is still apparent: in 13 pairs the suicide member had experienced the end of a marriage, while the control member had not, but in only four pairs was the position reversed (P = 0.049 exact test).

Diagnosis

To keep categories manageably small, only the main diagnoses were recorded. For mixed diagnoses, precedence was given to one, and the other dropped. The order of precedence was: organic (other than epilepsy), schizophrenia, affective disorder, personality disorder. The distinction between depressive (D) and manidepressive illness (MD) depended on whether

TABLE I

Civil state of suicide and control pairs at key episode

n = 100 pairs		Civil state of suicide members of pairs			
		Married	Widowed	Divorced or Separated	Single
	Married	42	7	6	12
Civil state of control members of pairs	Widowed	2	6	1	2
	Divorced or Separated	2	0	1	0
	Single	7	4	2	6

Please note that in this Table and in Tables II and III: (1) the entries refer to pairs, not to individuals. The composition of the pairs is given by the marginal legends. Thus the '12' in row 1 column 4 refers to the 12 pairs in which the suicide member was single but the control member was married.

(2) the total number of pairs in a table may be less than 100 because the necessary information was not always available on each member of a pair.

TABLE II

Diagnosis

n = 83 pairs		Diagnosis of suicide members of pairs				
		D	MD	S	O	Ot
	Depressive illness (D)	36	1	6	1	2
	Manic-depressive illness (MD)	7	1	1	0	0
Diagnosis of control members of pairs	Schizophrenia (S)	11	0	2	1	2
	Organic syndrome (O)	9	0	1	0	0
	Other diagnosis (Ot)	1	0	1	0	0

TABLE III

Clinical features which distinguished between suicides and controls

		Suicide members of pairs			
		Non-psychotic violence n = 94 pairs		Earlier deliberate self-harm n = 87 pairs	
		Present	Absent	Present	Absent
Control members of pairs	Present	0	5	8	13
	Absent	17	72	37	29
P values		$\chi^2 = 5.5, P < 0.025$		$\chi^2 = 10.6, P < 0.01$	

there was a history of mania or hypomania; if there was, the patient was classified as having a manic-depressive illness whether or not there was also a history of depression. In respect of diagnoses there was only one statistically significant difference between suicides and controls. In the twelve pairs in which one partner had an organic psycho-syndrome, that partner was the control member in ten pairs, but the suicide member in only two pairs ($\chi^2 = 4.1, P < 0.05$). The diagnosis in all the ten controls was senile dementia.

Epileptics are classified in Table II according to the associated psychiatric disorder. Six of the suicides, but only one of the controls, had epilepsy ($P = 0.12$).

8. DEATH

Distinctive clinical features

The choice of items was determined by the information available in the notes. A history of violence was studied because it was well documented in nurses' and social workers' notes. The term 'violence' is used here to mean attacking others or damaging possessions but not to mean self-violence. A special category was made for violence done when the patient was psychotic, that is having or experiencing one or more of the following: hallucinations, delusions, passivity experiences, incoherent thinking and disorientation. This is referred to as 'psychotic violence' in contrast to violence without such accompaniments, which is referred to as 'non-psychotic violence'.

Twenty of the 45 suicide patients who had already deliberately harmed themselves had used dangerous methods in doing so: suffocation, strangulation, jumping from a height, carbon monoxide poisoning, carbolic acid poisoning and self-inflicted injury with a hammer.

The following features were non-significant: chronic physical illness, adversity in preceding year, living alone at key episode, deluded before key episode, or violence while psychotic.

Effective treatment at time of suicide

There were 64 suicides with a previous diagnosis of depressive illness, but twenty had been discharged from psychiatric care so long ago that their treatment at the time of death could not be established. In order to summarize the antidepressant medication prescribed to the other 44 at the time of their death, the manufacturer's recommended full dose was taken as the unit of dose. If more than one antidepressant had been prescribed, each was translated into this unit and then summed. The dose ranges and the number of patients (quoted in brackets) falling within each range was as follows: 1 to > 0.75 (five); 0.75 to > 0.5 (one); 0.5 to > 0.25 (seven); 0.25 to > 0 (five) and 0 (twenty-six).

Only one patient was having ECT at the time of suicide. This patient was also receiving more than 0.75 of a full dose of oral antidepressant and is therefore included in the figures above. In all instances but one the antidepressant prescribed was a tricyclic, the exception being one patient on tranylcypromine in full dose. Nineteen of the patients not receiving any antidepressant medication at the time of their death were nevertheless receiving sedatives or tranquillisers, usually a barbiturate or a benzodiazepine, but a few patients were taking a phenothiazine, and one was taking meprobamate.

Time between last consultation with a doctor and suicide

This was established for 90 of the patients. The ten on whom no information was available were almost certainly not representative of the group as a whole, and probably had longer than average periods between seeing a doctor and killing themselves. Of the 90, 32 (36 per cent) had killed themselves within a week, 50 (56 per cent) within a fortnight and 57 (63 per cent) within a month of seeing a doctor.

Discussion

This study was retrospective, and thus confined to easily accessible, limited and rather crude data. We justified this on the grounds that we were looking for predictors, not causes of suicide, and a predictor must be easily available and likely to remain so. At the same time we wished our predictors to be, as far as possible, causes. For this reason we matched for age and sex. We could then at least be sure that any differences between suicides and controls were not just an indirect result of the fact that suicides tend, say, to be elderly men. In matching, however, we gave those direct causes of suicide which are associated with being old and male less opportunity to show themselves. Our findings have to be seen against these rather contrived circumstances.

Given these circumstances, it is of interest that diagnosis did not give any really worthwhile clues as to which patients might kill themselves. The only significant finding was rather trivial: senile dementia was associated with a lesser suicide risk than were other diagnoses. This is possibly because senile dementia, being largely if not entirely endogenous, develops in people who are no more prone to the social and personality factors likely to lead to suicide than are members of the general population of comparable age. It may also be because the illness in the advanced stage which brings about admission to a mental hospital deprives patients of the will or ability to kill themselves. The only other bearing that diagnosis had on suicide risk was the trend (P = 0.12) towards a greater risk in epileptics. One of the six epileptics who committed suicide had a schizophrenic psychosis; it is possible that people with this double handicap are particularly suicide-prone. Falconer (1973) found that 16 per cent of a small sample of such patients on whom he had performed temporal lobectomy subsequently committed suicide.

Social factors were more helpful in predicting the suicide-prone. Significantly more suicides than controls were 'not married'. Being born in Eastern Europe was another risk factor (but revealed in the whole suicidal sample, not in the comparison between suicide patients and controls). This applies to England and Wales generally: Adelstein and Mardon (1975) found the standardized suicide mortality ratios for 1970–2 for immigrants born in Poland to be 227 per cent for males and 251 per cent for females. Sainsbury and Barraclough (1968) found that the suicide rate of immigrant communities within a single host country mirrored the rates in the countries of birth. The 1969 suicide rate (per 100,000) in Poland was 18.6 for men but only 4.2 for women (WHO, 1974). Thus although country of birth may be an important determinant of suicide rate in Polish men living in England and Wales it seems to be less important for Polish women. There may be special factors which put the Eastern European community at risk. Its early nucleus was formed, not by any planned or orderly immigration, but through political upheaval. This probably accounts for the abnormal constitution of the Shropshire population of Eastern Europeans, with males out-numbering females 3.5 to 1 and the ratio of divorced to married members higher than for Shropshire as a whole (NS for its women, but P < 0.025 for its men: 1971 census). Linguistic difficulties with consequent inability to communicate the subtle symptoms of mental illness to their doctors may also have contributed to the higher suicide rate. The scale of immigration may also be important. The Eastern European community appears to be large enough not to make integration of its individual members with the host population an absolute necessity; but not so large that it can sustain any invigorating and broadly-based culture of its own. Without this self-sufficiency its members may always have the sense of estrangement from society which Durkheim (1897) regarded as an important contribution to suicide.

The association we found between suicide and non-psychotic violence (Table III) was seen only in patients diagnosed as having a depressive illness. It is possible that the episodes of violence occurred in previous, but not always diagnosed, bouts of depressive illness. Strictly, therefore, we cannot assume that it is a premorbid personality trait; it may merely be a trait brought to light by the stress of illness. Nevertheless, it is clear that those who are violent during a depressive illness are particularly prone eventually to harm themselves. There may be other links: violence over the years may have alienated family and friends and in this way made suicide more likely, and in some violence and suicide may both be the outcome of alcohol abuse. Bagley *et al* (1976) found that violence was a feature of a distinctive type of suicide which they called 'sociopathic suicide'. Psychotic violence points the other way, showing a tendency (P = 0.064) to be linked with the control group.

There are probably several reasons for this difference between psychotic and non-psychotic violence. Psychotic violence does not always spring from anger but as often from fear and bewilderment, emotions which are less likely to lead to calculated destruction. It is possible that psychotic violence, occurring as it often does in eruptions when the patient is evidently ill, is less damaging to social relationships than is violence rooted in the personality. The findings in the present study agree with those of other workers (Robin *et al*, 1968; Barraclough and Pallis, 1975), that an earlier episode of self-harm is an important predictor of suicide.

It is a striking finding that so few patients earlier diagnosed as having a depressive illness were having drug treatment for this illness in an adequate dose at the time of their death. This is further confirmation of an observation made by several authors, and most recently by Barraclough *et al* (1974). Our findings almost certainly overestimate what patients were actually taking, because so many fail to take the prescribed dose (Blackwell, 1976). Like Barraclough *et al* (1974) and Jacobson *et al* (1972), we found that many of our suicides had visited a doctor within a month of death. Failure to get medical attention can therefore take only part of the blame for the lack of adequate physical treatment.

The belief, which may be mistaken (Wittenborn, 1962), that neurotic depression does not respond to antidepressant medication, probably contributed to the low incidence of prescription. This belief must save some lives by keeping potentially poisonous drugs from those for whom the likely benefit is small and the risk of deliberate overdose is high but it will also deny effective treatment to some who would benefit. Difficulties in diagnosis (Raskin and Crook, 1976) also contribute to uncertainty about correct prescribing.

Nineteen of the suicide patients were receiving tranquilliser instead of an antidepressant. There are undoubtedly several reasons for this; one may be that in some patients an earlier diagnosis of depressive illness had been supplanted by one of anxiety state. The acceptance of anxiety state as a diagnosis on a par with other psychiatric diagnoses has drawbacks. It might be safer to regard anxiety as a universal, fairly easily aroused, and not very specific response to a wide range of disorders, physical and mental, amongst which depressive illness is particularly important.

The best opportunities for suicide prevention in psychiatric patients are probably still to be found in those with depressive illness. For this reason the findings of Coppen *et al* (1971) and of Mindham *et al* (1973) are particularly important: they showed, respectively, that lithium and the tricyclic antidepressants reduce the relapse rate in depressive illness. A considerable difficulty in preventing suicide is to know when, in

8. DEATH

what may be a long illness, the danger periods occur. Copas *et al* (1971) found that suicides tend to occur soon after referral to a psychiatric service, though this effect was not very pronounced. Patients who could report the danger periods, often do not do so. For them the main attraction of suicide may not be death but relief from intolerable distress without having to break the ice in seeking help from others. It would be interesting to know from psychiatric patients who have made suicide attempts whether they considered seeking help instead; and if they did what dissuaded them.

References

ADELSTEIN, A. & MARDON, C. (1975) *Suicides 1961–1974.* Population Trends No. 2, 13–17. Office of Population Censuses and Surveys. London: H.M.S.O.

BAGLEY, C., JACOBSON, S. & REHIN, A. (1976) Completed suicide: a taxonomic analysis of clinical and social data. *Psychological Medicine,* **6,** 429–38.

BARRACLOUGH, B. M., BUNCH, J., NELSON, B. & SAINSBURY, P. (1974) A hundred cases of suicide: clinical aspects. *British Journal of Psychiatry,* **125,** 355–73.

—— & PALLIS, D. J. (1975) Depression followed by suicide: a comparison of depressed suicides with living depressives. *Psychological Medicine,* **5,** 55–61.

BLACKWELL, B. (1976) Treatment adherence. *British Journal of Psychiatry,* **129,** 513–31.

CENSUS (1961) England and Wales. County report, Shropshire. General Register Office. London: H.M.S.O. 1964.

—— (1971) England and Wales. Report for the County of Salop, as constituted on 1st April, 1974. Office of Population Censuses and Surveys. London: H.M.S.O. 1975.

COPAS, J. B., FREEMAN-BROWNE, D. L. & ROBIN, A. A. (1971) Danger periods for suicide in patients under treatment. *Psychological Medicine,* **1,** 400–4.

COPPEN, A., NOGUERA, R., BAILEY, J., BURNS, B. H., SWANI, M. S., HARE, E. H., GARDNER, R. & MAGGS, R. (1971) Prophylactic lithium in affective disorders. *Lancet, ii,* 275–9.

DURKHEIM, E. (1897) *Le Suicide.* Paris. Translated 1952 as *Suicide: A Study in Sociology,* by J. A. Spaulding and C. Simpson, pp 191–206. London: Routledge and Kegan Paul.

FALCONER, M. A. (1973) Reversibility by temporal-lobe resection of the behavioural abnormalities of temporal-lobe epilepsy. *New England Journal of Medicine,* **289,** 451–5.

JACOBSON, S. & JACOBSON, D. M. (1972) Suicide in Brighton. *British Journal of Psychiatry,* **121,** 369–77.

MINDHAM, R. H. S., HOWLAND, C. & SHEPHERD, M. (1973) An evaluation of continuation therapy with tricyclic antidepressants in depressive illness. *Psychological Medicine,* **3,** 5–17.

RASKIN, A. & CROOK, T. H. (1976) The endogenous-neurotic distinction as a predictor of response to antidepressant drugs. *Psychological Medicine,* **6,** 59–70.

ROBIN, A. A., BROOKE, E. M. & FREEMAN-BROWNE, D. L. (1968) Some aspects of suicide in psychiatric patients in Southend. *British Journal of Psychiatry,* **114,** 739–47.

SAINSBURY, P. & BARRACLOUGH, B. M. (1968) Differences between suicide rates. *Nature,* **220,** 1252.

STENGEL, E. (1964) *Suicide and Attempted Suicide.* Harmondsworth: Penguin Books.

WITTENBORN, J. R., PLANTE, M., BURGESS, F. & MAURER, H. (1962) A comparison of imipramine, electro-convulsive therapy and placebo in the treatment of depression. *Journal of Nervous and Mental Disease,* **135,** 131–7.

WORLD HEALTH ORGANISATION (1974) *Suicide and Attempted Suicide.* Public Health Paper 58. W.H.O. Geneva.

Death on Every Weekend

Robert F. Kopel, BA
University of California at Los Angeles

ABSTRACT: This essay is a personal account of situations experienced by a medical technician in a large emergency room. It includes examples of stressful situations that daily confront medical personnel and the inability of medical institutions to aid them in understanding and coping with death and dying. Stemming from these stressful situations, the paper illustrates the importance of the need for medical institutions to pay direct attention to the stressful topic of death itself if the medical personnel are to work efficiently in an environment where death and dying are everyday occurrences. Although some institutions do offer in-service sessions to nurses, these services are far and few between. But the stress for all medical personnel remains high, and there remains an unfulfilled need to teach effective thanatological techniques to all medical personnel.

There was a deafening silence as the doctors and nurse waited for the reply over the paramedic transmitter. After what seemed an eternity a voice cracked the reply, "Yes doctor this is Central City paramedics and we're at the scene of a cardiac full arrest. The patient is a 12-year-old male with no previous history of heart failure. At this time there are no visible vital signs." Then there is silence. The doctors look at each other in dismay as they decide what the next steps will be in trying to save the patient's life. At the end of a nerve-wracking hour on the transmitter, the paramedics are ready to transport the patient, who has been given all of the care possible in the field. The signal is given, and the ambulance begins on its way with lights and siren to the hospital emergency room. Meanwhile technicians, nurses, and doctors prepare the necessary equipment for the incoming patient. An entire room, full of sophisticated machinery, has been set aside for this specific emergency. The loudspeaker breaks into the hum of activity as the desk clerk announces the arrival of the patient. The paramedics roll down the hall with the stretcher and into the second operating room. Immediately medical personnel begin to work on the patient in a struggle against death. Doctors and specialists are "stat paged" (urgently) from all parts of the hospital to help in the life-saving effort. The technician administering heart massage looks at the cardiac monitor in dismay, and then up at the clock, noting that the team has been working on the patient for more than an hour with no response. Finally, the resident in charge looks up at the clock and shakes his head.

Looking at the body of the child and then the assembled staff one by one, almost as if he were asking for both approval and forgiveness, he says, "Let's call it." There is a profound silence as each of the staff glances at the small body and then leaves the room in order to assist other patients who are waiting for help. The anaesthesiologist carefully shuts the eyelids and brushes a wisp of hair from the tiny forehead and then takes leave of the room, slowly dragging his feet. The head nurse and the technician now remain. While the head nurse goes to bring the family in, the technician prepares the body so the family may view it. The resident has already told them what has taken place and the end result of all of the efforts. As the technician waits silently for the family to come out of the second O.R., he hears a small moan and then some crying. A moment later the door opens, and the head nurse escorts the parents to the conference room where they may gather their thoughts. The technician then wraps the body and takes it to the morgue located two floors above. He then returns to the emergency room to find the head nurse working on a terminal cancer patient who is going to be admitted to the hospital ward. They each glance at each other out of the corner of their eyes and the technician returns to his duties.

There is a piercing noise up and down the corridors of the twelfth floor. Doctors, nurses, and medical personnel come running from all parts of the floor to assist. The hospital page system beings to blare the signal that a life-and-death situation is taking place in a specific place on the ward. A terminal cancer patient has ruptured his carotid artery leading to the brain. The amount of blood draining on the floor is incredible. But all of the medical staff is standing around the now-unconscious patient not lifting a finger. After several minutes the resident checks for any vital signs and looks up with a sad face to indicate that the suffering is over. The doctors and nurses slowly return to their stations. Housekeeping staff is called to clean up the blood stains. An orderly removes the body and takes it to the morgue. The head nurse dials the patient's relatives and explains what has occurred, telling them that there is no use in coming to the hospital tonight. She hangs up the phone feeling emotionally drained and returns to her work. All is quiet again on the Ward 12-East.

Several hours later the technician walks into the emergency staff room to get some equipment and sees across the room one of the nurses who participated in the cardiac arrest crying silently to herself as she draws some medication into a syringe for a patient. Later that night the technician leaves work on his bicycle and arrives at his apartment. He lies down on his bed and begins to cry uncontrollably for several minutes and then falls off into a deep sleep.

A nurse who has served on 12-East for several years sits down at the end of her shift to write out her notes on every patient. Finally she comes to the last chart and opens it to see the words written in big red letters, "DO NOT RESUSCITATE!" She writes the date, and on one line the words "Patient terminated at 9:36 p.m." Thumbing through the pages, she thinks back over the 3 months that she has known the patient.

It is all written in the notes. Two weeks before the patient was told that his 16-year-old daughter was killed in a car accident. The next few lines told of his reaction to the incident. The nurse read no further and put the folder into its correct space. She slowly walked down the corridor, which seemed longer than usual tonight, and tears came to her eyes no matter how much she tried to squelch them. Another night had ended for the nurses and doctors in the emergency room and on Ward 12-East.

Incidents such as these take place in medical facilities all over the world every day. Death becomes a common occurrence on both emergency and dire-patient wards. The emotional stress experienced by the families and relatives of these patients is often very great. Thanks to modern clinical thanatology there are ways in which the survivors may learn to accept and live with the events that take place. But have we not forgotten one aspect of this entire process? To what and to whom are the medical staff able to refer for their emotional needs in coping with death and the stress it causes each and every day? I looked for the answer in nursing and medical school curricula, in-service lectures, and books written on both the subject of death and hospital practices. The following will be a breakdown on each of these categories and their service to the medical personnel involved.

Few medical schools include in their curricula a course on death or the dying person. The training in regard to death and dying is left to the student's own personal experiences. The new physician is put into a position where he becomes the apex of all that is happening to a dying patient. The relatives, community, and patient all look to the doctor for support, understanding, and, many times, miracles. Therefore, it is not sufficient that the physician dedicate himself only to preserving life, for he is also responsible for the general climate of feelings and thoughts within the sphere of the dying patient. With this in mind, it is apparent that the pressures put upon him are extremely great and that some type of outlet is needed to vent emotional strain.

Feifel and his colleagues (1967) conducted a survey of 81 physicians and medical students in an attempt to explore their feelings about death. They interpreted the data as indicating that physicians (and medical students) tend to have an above-average fear of death. The authors believe that a number of physicians enter the medical profession, through which the individual secures prominent mastery over disease, in order to help control personal concerns about death. They also found that physicians tended to respond in an introversive way to the death of another person. The physician was inclined to reflect on his own mortality.

How then does the physician cope with death in his everyday dealings with people and patients? August M. Kasper believes that the medical training frequently encourages an attitude of "counterphobic bravado," or a desensitization toward death (Kasper, 1965). There is so much emphasis on the strictly scientific aspect of medicine that a doctor many times does not fully come to terms with death and its full emotional meaning. At present there are few courses offered on the subject of coping with death and dying for the new or old physician. Each doctor must learn to live with death in his own way. The push toward scientific curriculum in our medical schools has substituted itself for the more humanistic aspects of medicine. The graduating physician is left out in the "cold" with respect to understanding his own feelings and the feelings of others in regard to the dying patient and his ultimate death. He learns to keep his feelings inside and eventually becomes desensitized to the pain and suffering around him, although many times he may wish to express himself and his emotions. The attitude becomes one of ignoring the situation in terms of death and concentrating on the strictly medical aspect of the patient's affliction. There is a great need for the physician to be able to vent the emotional strains that he must bear. Each physician must learn to understand his feelings and not run away from them. An expression of care may be shown in many ways and may also become an outlet for the doctor.

The doctor and nurse rose to leave the room. It wasn't much, in fact it could have gone unnoticed, but the nurse saw the doctor lay his hands on the shoulders of the boy's parents for a brief moment, and she knew—this living and dying had managed to become at least a small part of him.

The physician has only himself to look to in times of stress. He must learn from experience how to understand and live with a battle that can never be won.

At one of the most advanced and prestigious nursing schools in the United States an assistant clinical professor who is teaching a course on "The Concept of Grief and Loss" told me that the objectives of the course are twofold: first, to deal with the concepts of grief and loss and then to consider the care to be given to the person and/or family involved in a life-threatening situation. The professor gives each student a bibliography containing 70 books and periodicals written on the topic of death, dying, and suicide, covering all related subjects except one: to whom are the nursing staff able to refer in times of emotional stress related to death and dying. That is left for the nursing student to learn from personal experiences in regard to her feelings about death and dying and how to manage them.

Most often it is the nurse's hand that touches the terminal patient most. She has the hour-to-hour responsibility in caring for the patient, and the death will many times affect her the hardest of all, although she may appear aloof to the situation. This outward appearance is a mask for the internal conflicts and emotions that face many nurses. The nursing professor says: "While some nurses, as some physicians, manage to insulate themselves from the emotional implications of their work, it is more typical for the nurse to care about what her patients are going through. Yet it is also typical for the nurse to believe that she should not give in to her feelings, even to the extent of letting them show to others."

The medical model of efficient but essentially impersonal care exerts its influence not only over the physician, but also over the nurse and, increasingly, over the patient himself. We find the nurse is placed in a dilemma. She begins with strong feelings toward the dying patient, which continues and grows as time and interaction go on. As the downhill process of dying continues, her feelings grow even stronger—yet she remains impelled to keep a stiff upper lip and hide what she really feels.

The nurse's difficulties in dealing with the emotional needs of the terminal patient are increased due to the lack of training in this area. She must fall back upon whatever guidelines are available to her from other sources. Pressure from fellow workers to conform to their standards of what makes a good nurse or the socioeconomic background in which the nurse was brought up and its orientation to life and death situations play an important role in what influences a nurse toward her care for the terminal patient. All of these influences would take on a minor role if the nurse had received training and supervision in this area.

Jeanne C. Quint (1967), one of the foremost advocates for improving training for terminal care, believes that educational programs in nursing have not generally provided environments through which nursing students develop the capacity to function effectively in situations that are either personally or professionally threatening. Neither have nursing instructors always recognized the emotional impact carried by certain types of patient assignments. This educational heritage is not surprising when one considers that nursing in the United States is by tradition somewhat authoritarian, with a premium attached to self-control and dedication. Quint finds that terminal care is one of the most demanding and stressful situations encountered by many nurses. Keeping the patient clean, fed, and comfortable, until he dies is neither pleasant or easy. In addition, the nurse is under the added strain of working with the family of the dying patient, of which she might have more than one. We can, therefore, arrive at a general overview of the nurse as a person who must deal with the daily challenges and demands of the death situation, yet lacking the authoritative balance of the physician, the relevant job training from her own profession, and the on-the-job environment that would support her in times of personal distress or in her more innovative and involved efforts. It is no wonder that she falls back heavily upon those unseen background values or the standards that have been set for her by her peers. We really have no right to ask her to give up the self-protective rituals that enable her to function within the vicinity of the terminal patient. Since today's system does not provide the teaching with which to fall back upon in times of emotional stress, the nurse needs every possible emotional outlet she can provide if she is to continue caring for the terminally ill patient and his family.

This evening the visiting time was different. A boy's parents questioned for any change in their son's condition, silently gazing at him as they absorbed the negative reply. Then they began telling of special memories they had of him: the new bicycle he had longed for but never received, the squabbles he and his sister were always having, the paper route he ran, and his love of sports, especially baseball, in which his ability as a pitcher was widely known. As they spoke, the nurse found the form in the bed taking on a new shape—that of an active, spirited, normal boy, much like her younger brother. Her involvement was deepening. Too often it was easy to forget that those present at the bedside weren't the only ones who grieved.

After speaking with the nursing supervisor of an emergency room, I found that some hospitals do provide in-service lectures and discussions on the topic of coping with death and dying. At this supervisor's institution these meetings are generally held every other week and are attended by nurses working in the emergency room. Discussions involve how to handle death, the family, and ways in which the nurse might vent her emotions as well as the quality of medical assistance being offered and ways to improve it. Almost all of the nurses agreed that merely discussing the way they felt made them feel more at ease with their co-workers and less guilty about the death of patients. The question is always raised in a nurse's head whether or not she could have done something more for the patient. Guilt is a big part of death, particularly of the survivor-victim, and must be dealt with on a level that will help ease the emotional burden. Postvention is as important to the family as it is for the medical staff.

There is a wide gap between the type of nursing care required in an emergency ward and a dire-patient ward. In the emergency room the patient-staff relationship is a short one where there is no time to develop any type of relationship. Here the patient is looked at more in terms of his physiological functioning. Death on such a service is not mourned as deep personal loss. It is a happening, distressing but seldom totally unexpected. On the dire-patient ward, however, interactions between patient and staff are most intense.

On this type of ward the patients have terminal diagnoses and remain in the hospital for extended periods of time. There is plenty of time for personal relationships to form between staff and patient, whose passing is mourned as a "real" human being. It is especially important that the medical staff involved with these patients interact among themselves in an attempt to vent their emotional stresses. All hospitals should provide some type of working organization, so the staff can work together in a comfortable and constructive way.

Most of the literature dealing with hospital practices are mainly concerned with disease and their management. The newest material deals with emergency situations but still holds to the old guidelines of management and care. In the material that does deal specifically with death and dying there are frequent references to the physical and mental care of the patient and the survivor-victims, and several of the more recent works do deal with the new procedures in caring for the terminally ill patient from a medical standpoint. There is no mention, however, of the subject of maintenance of the medical staff. There are examples, such as those cited above, of the stress that is placed on both the nurse and physician in dealing with the dying patient. Much of this new literature does begin to touch upon the subject of the medical staff, but only in limited amounts. There are several psychiatric analyses explaining from a medical standpoint why nurses and doctors react the way they do. These analyses merely serve as an explanation rather than an outlet.

An instructor of nursing explained to me that this field of research dealing with death and dying is so new that there is currently a group involved with the medical profession who are meeting now to open discussion on the topic. Death research has blossomed so much in the past 20 years that few subjects relating to it have not been touched upon. Yet death and dying and the medical staff has been pushed aside until very recently. This could be an indication that the professionals working in this field realize their own need for help in coping with and understanding their emotions. It is not surprising that this did not occur sooner because of the aura that society places around the physician and nurse of today's institutions. It requires of them a specific behavior in which there is no room for deviation. The professional must be stoic in his work although underneath he may be extremely troubled. It should not be a shock to find that the second highest suicide rate in all of the professions is that of the physician. The system must adjust itself to include the medical staff among those of the survivor-victims.

When we stop and think for a moment, birth and death are the most common happenings in everyday life. Yet how many of us actually *experience* either of these things in an entire lifetime? For the most part they take place within a hospital, and they are handled by "strangers"—medical professionals. Those who must work with birth and death do so constantly. In the future teaching institutions and hospital administrations must provide services for their personnel to help in coping with life and death in order to maintain a healthy and constructive system in which to work.

We must all come to realize that the medical professional cannot always provide the miracles that are asked of him and that the pressures dealing with our loved ones are as great for him as they are for us. Guilt, sorrow, hurt, fear, and love are all human emotions that are not exclusive to any one section of the population. The first step in giving the medical staff somewhere or someone to go to is to give them our understanding for the situation we many times put them in. Then we might look upon the physician and nurse as one who assists a terminally ill patient in achieving an "appropriate death" for both the victim and all of those that survive him.

The biocom gave off a loud piercing noise as the electrocardiogram was sent by radio over the several miles that divided the emergency room from the scene of the heart attack. There was a brief pause as the doctor studied the tape trying to understand exactly what had happened to the heart. Everyone waited on both ends of the radio for his answer. He broke the silence as he gave instructions to the paramedics to start an intravenous drip with an additional battery of drugs, which would hopefullly start the heart beating in a normal rhythm. Meanwhile the impending arrival of the life-and-death case set the staff in motion as they set up the necessary equipment that would be needed to save the patient. Small talk crossed back and forth across the room in an attempt to piece together what exactly was coming in. At the conclusion of this almost robotlike step-by-step setting-up procedure, it was known by all that whom they were receiving was an 82-year-old male cardiac arrest patient with no previous history of heart trouble.

A volunteer who had never been involved in such a situation before stood idly by, desperately trying to absorb all that was happening. Finally he walked out of the operating room and into the doctor's office that contained the paramedic transmitter. The doctor stood up with a jubilant look on his face and several other doctors and a nurse congratulated him on a job well done. The patient had been stabilized in the field and was on his way into the emergency room. The 15 minutes needed to transport the patient seemed to fly by in no time, for when the volunteer finally looked up from his clean-up duties, he saw the paramedic stretcher glide smoothly into the prepared room. He quickly finished what he was doing and walked into the busy room.

People were running everywhere, each doing a specific job. The volunteer moved into the corner trying to comprehend all that was happening. The monitor across the room showed a line that went up and down in a steady rhythm. One doctor kept his eye constantly on the monitor, while the other gave orders to the nurses, asking them to speed this up or to slow that down, to get a pulse and blood pressure, and, finally, to call the cardiac care unit (CCU) to inform them that they had a patient to send upstairs to their team of doctors. The nurse walked in several minutes later to relay the message that the team was on its way down and that the unit had prepared a bed for the patient. Finally, after what seemed an eternity, two doctors opened the door and pushed a monitor on wheels ahead of them. The emergency room doctors seemed as if they had been relieved of their burden. The doctors exchanged data explaining the patient's condition as the nurse and technicians prepared to move the patient upstairs on the stretcher.

The old man was unhooked from the large monitor in the emergency room and hooked up to the portable one that the CCU doctors had provided. Slowly at first and then picking up speed the entourage of doctors, technicians, and equipment moved toward the elevator which would whisk them several floors above to the coronary care unit. Just as the elevator door started to close, the volunteer squeezed his way in, wedging himself into the corner. The doctor kept a close watch on the monitor, and as the elevator door opened, he said in an almost muffled voice, "We'd better hurry. The patient has arrested again." All of this time the volunteer had been watching the patient's face closely trying to understand why he felt the way he did. He shook his head once in an attempt to get his mind back on the situation. The team moved quickly down the corridor yelling ahead to open the door to the procedure room located right outside the cardiac care unit. A group of medical personnel met them as they entered the room. The volunteer quickly placed himself in the most inconspicuous corner he could find and looked about him. All types of complicated equipment were located around the room. The staff had manned their stations and were working on the patient. A young doctor was giving the orders from the end of the bed where the monitor was located. Another doctor was doing heart massage while nurses were buzzing around the patient in an attempt to keep up with the doctor's orders. The volunteer looked up at the clock and saw that they had already been here for more than an hour. It seemed to him that time had simply ceased to exist.

A moment later the young resident looked up at the clock and slowly shook his head. He looked around the room at the busily working crew and said aloud, "Does anybody have any suggestions?" Everyone looked up at that instant and realized that they had lost the battle. For some reason unknown to him the volunteer felt tears come to his eyes, but it was all right because he assured himself that nobody had noticed. Finally, the doctor looked up and said in a low voice, "Let's call it." As the nurses began to disconnect the life-saving equipment, the patient gave out a last sigh and his hand moved as if to clutch the side of the table. Then all was still. This was too much for the volunteer, and he could no longer hold back his tears as they slowly dripped from the corner of his eyes. This time the young resident saw the tears and looked down as he said to the volunteer in a sad voice, "I'm sorry; I did all I could." The volunteer looked up and said to the doctor, "I guess this is where the medical books end." The doctor seemed to acknowledge what the volunteer said and slowly walked out of the room to look for the old man's wife who was waiting for any news on her husband.

The volunteer walked slowly from the room and down the corridor toward the elevator. The halls had never seemed so long to him as they did now. Finally, he arrived at a window, next to the elevator, that overlooked the dark and electrically lit city. He cupped his face in his hands and began to cry softly to himself, for he now knew what had bothered him before in the elevator. The patient had resembled his grandfather whom he loved dearly. The volunteer finally looked up again and out at the glimmering city in front of him.

He shook his head once and pushed the button for the elevator. The door opened in front of him, and he stepped in. He glanced at his watch as the elevator sped back toward the emergency room and realized that 2 hours had gone by. For the first time in his life the volunteer realized how much those he loved meant to him, but in addition he realized that both the old man's wife and the young doctor had had their lives changed in that room upstairs.

References

Feifel, H., Hanson, S., Jones, R., & Edwards, L. Physicians consider death. *Proceedings 75th Annual Convention of the American Psychological Association.* Washington, D.C.: American Psychological Association, 1967.

Kasper, A. M. The doctor and death. In H. Feifel (Ed.), *The meaning of death.* New York: McGraw-Hill, 1965.

Quint, J. C. *The nurse and the dying patient.* New York: Macmillan, 1967.

STAFF

Publisher	John Quirk
Editor	
Permissions Editor	
Director of Production	Donald Burns
Director of Design	Carol Carr
Typesetting	
Cover Design	Donald Burns
Cover Photo	

SPECIAL LEARNING CORPORATION
COMMENTS PLEASE:

Does this book fit your course of study?

Why?   (Why not?)

Is this book useable for other courses of study? Please list.

What other areas would you like us to publish in using this format?

What type of exceptional child are you interested in learning more about?

Would you use this as a basic text?

How many students are enrolled in these course areas?

______Special Education ______ Mental Retardation ______ Psychology ______ Emotional Disorders

______ Exceptional Children ______Learning Disabilities   Other ________________

Do you want to be sent a copy of our elementary student materials catalog?

Do you want a copy of our college catalog?

Would you like a copy of our next edition?   ☐ yes ☐ no

Are you a ☐ student or an ☐ instructor?

Your name ________________________________ school ________________

Term used ________________________________ Date ________________

address ____

city ________________________ state ________________ zip ______

telephone number ________________________________

CUT HERE ● SEAL AND MAIL

COMMENTS PLEASE:

Readings in Early Childhood Education

Readings in ABNORMAL PSYCHOLOGY: The Problems of Disordered Emotional and Behavioral Development

Readings in DEVELOPMENTAL PSYCHOLOGY: The Problems of Disordered Mental Development

Readings in Child Abuse

Readings in Child Psychology

Readings in Special Olympics

Readings in Trainable Mentally Handicapped

Readings in Hyperactivity

SPECIAL LEARNING CORPORATION

42 Boston Post Rd.

Guilford, Conn. 06437